Lodestone and Evening Star

By the same author

THE MIDNIGHT SEA
RED DUSTER, WHITE ENSIGN
WINGS OF THE MORNING

LODESTONE AND EVENING STAR

The saga of exploration by sea

by

IAN CAMERON

HODDER AND STOUGHTON

The light begins to twinkle from the rocks,
The long day wanes; the slow moon climbs; the deep
Moans round with many voices. Come, my friends,
'Tis not too late to seek a newer world.
Push off, and sitting well in order smite
The sounding furrows; for my purpose holds
To sail beyond the sunset and the baths
Of all the western stars, until I die . . .

—ULYSSES

PRINTED IN GREAT BRITAIN FOR
HODDER AND STOUGHTON LTD., ST. PAUL'S HOUSE, WARWICK LANE, LONDON, E.C.4, BY
HAZELL WATSON AND VINEY LTD., AYLESBURY, BUCKS

Contents

Line Drawings and Maps

List of Plates

Acknowledgements

THE writing of *Lodestone and Evening Star* involved a good deal of research, and I should like to thank the many societies, organizations and individuals whose friendly co-operation turned what could have been drudgery into a pleasure. In particular I should like to express special gratitude to the Royal Geographical Society and the National Maritime Museum.

I am indebted to the following authors and publishers for permission to quote from their works. W. H. Schoof and Longmans, Green & Co. Ltd., for extracts from *The Periplus of the Erythraean Sea*: Geoffrey Ashe and Collins, Publishers, for extracts from *Land to The West*: M. Cary and E. H. Warmington and Methuen & Co. Ltd. for an extract from *The Ancient Explorers*: Ernle Bradford and Hutchinson & Co. (Publishers) Ltd. for extracts from *Southward The Caravels*: Gilbert Renault and George Allen & Unwin Ltd. for extracts from *The Caravels of Christ*, and C. M. Parr and Robert Hale Ltd. for an extract from *So Noble a Captain*. Extracts from *The Three Voyages of William Barents* by Gerrit de Veer, and *The Voyages of De Quiros* by Sir Clements Markham are reproduced by kind permission of The Council of the Hakluyt Society. I am also indebted to J. R. Muir and Blackie & Son for an extract from *Life of Captain Cook*: W. E. Parry and John Murray (Publishers) Ltd. for extracts from *Journal of a Voyage of Discovery of a North-West Passage*: James Clark Ross and John Murray (Publishers) Ltd. for extracts from *A Voyage in The Southern and Antarctic Regions*: Deputy Inspector General R. McCormick and Sampson, Low, Marston & Co. Ltd. for extracts from *Voyages of Discovery in the Antarctic and Arctic*: Emma De Long and Routledge and Kegan Paul Ltd. for extracts from *The Voyage of the Jeanette*; and Fridtjof Nansen and Constable Publishers for extracts from *Farthest North*.

The line drawings and maps have been assembled from a wide variety of sources. No. 2 is reproduced by permission of Uni-Dia-Verlag, Stuttgart: Nos. 3, 9, 16 and 20 are reproduced from Gordon Grant's original drawings in *Unrolling The Map* by permission of Leonard Outhwaite and Constable Publishers. Nos. 4 and 7 are reproduced from *Conquest by Man* by permission of Paul Herrmann and Hamish Hamilton Ltd. Nos. 11, 18 (c), 18 (d), 18 (e), 18 (f) and 28 are reproduced from *The Ship* by permission of Bjorn Landstrom and George Allen & Unwin Ltd. No. 13 is reproduced from *Land to the West* by permission of Geoffrey Ashe and Collins Publishers. Nos. 14 and 30 are reproduced from *The Story of Sail* by permission of G. S. L. Clowes and C. Trew, and Eyre & Spottiswoode Ltd. Nos. 18 (a) and 18 (b) are reproduced from *The Caravels of Christ* by permission of Gilbert Renault and George Allen & Unwin Ltd. No. 22 is reproduced from *Ships — A Picture History in Colour:* Paul Hamlyn, London. Nos. 23 and 25 are reproduced from *Worlds Beyond the Horizon* by permission of Joachim Leithauser and George Allen & Unwin Ltd. No. 26 is reproduced by permission of The Council of the Hakluyt Society. Nos. 32, 34 and 36 are reproduced by permission of the trustees of the National Maritime Museum, Greenwich. No. 31 is reproduced by permission of The Royal Geographical Society. No. 38 is reproduced from *The Voyage of The Jeanette* by permission of Emma De Long and Routledge and Kegan Paul Ltd. No. 40 is reproduced from *Farthest North* by permission of Fridtjof Nansen and Constable Publishers.

It proved none too easy to find photographs which combined artistic merit with an accurate portrayal of the various coastlines as seen by the first explorers; and here again my very best thanks are offered to the great number of people from all over the world who provided the thousands of photographs from which a final selection was made. I am especially indebted to the following: For photographs Nos. 1, 8 and 15 Paul Popper Ltd: No. 2 Camera Press: Nos. 3 (a) and 3 (b) Royal Geographical Society: No. 4 W. Lüthy, Berne, Switzerland: and No. 5 Eric Shipton Esq.: Nos. 6 (a), 6 (b) and 6 (c) are reproduced from *Nine Against The Unknown* by permission of J. L. Mitchell and L. G. Gibbon and Hutchinson & Co. (Publishers) Ltd. No. 7 is acknowledged to Tom Weir/Barnabys: Nos. 9 and 12 are reproduced from the photobook *The Sea* by Hein Wenzel, published by Kummerly and Frey, Berne: No. 10 is published by courtesy of The High Commissioner for New Zealand. No. 11 (a) is reproduced by permission of The National Portrait Gallery, and No. 11 (b) by permission of the Scott Polar Research Institute. No. 13 is reproduced by courtesy of Peter Otway Esq. Nos. 14 (a) and 14 (b) are reproduced by permission of John Murray Ltd., and No. 16 by permission of Jack Calvert (Photo Researchers).

The jacket design is taken from an engraving by W. Westall based on a sketch made on the spot by Lieutenant Beechy.

ONE

"Through a Glass, Darkly"

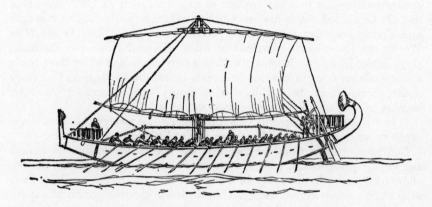

Introduction to Part One

THE secrets of the world we live in — the outline of its continents and oceans — have been unveiled slowly over a span of more than three thousand years. The once accepted belief that our world was "discovered" during a sudden burst of voyaging in the fifteenth, sixteenth and seventeenth centuries is now recognized as false. For it is generally appreciated to-day that the voyages of explorers such as Columbus, Dias and Da Gama led not to discovery but to rediscovery — both Irish curraghs and Viking longships, for example, preceded the *Santa Maria* to the New World; the Phoenicians rounded the Cape of Good Hope two thousand years before Dias; and Roman merchants were running a white slave trade to the Malabar coast fifteen hundred years before the Portuguese. Our story opens, therefore, in the half-light of antiquity. And it opens tentatively, because of the lack of contemporary documents.

It is this lack of documents which has made the voyages of the ancient explorers so controversial to historians and so little-known to laymen.

Controversy stems from the fact that the documents relating to almost any voyage prior to A.D. 1000 are so scarce and are open to such a variety of interpretation, that it is easy for a writer to arrange the few available facts so as to fit a preconceived theory. This has led to the publication of a spate of erudite sophistry, the classic example of which is the article which sets out to prove from cargo ledgers that the fabulous land of Punt which the Egyptians visited *circa* 1500 B.C. was situated in Peru — notwithstanding the fact that ancient Egyptian vessels are known to have never ventured out of sight of land! It is articles like this which made me feel that a knowledge of seamanship might be as useful in reconstructing the ancient voyages as a knowledge of history; and in *Lodestone and Evening Star* I have paid special attention to the practical and physical aspect of the expeditions: i.e. how their ships were constructed and navigated, and what hazards of current, wind and tide they had to face *en route*. I hope that this new approach will divert controversy into channels that are less academic and more practical.

I hope, too, that it will interest the large public to whom the voyages of the ancients have hitherto been something in a dull and hence unopened book.

Because we have no diary or log of these early expeditions, the personality of their leaders has not come through to us, nor are their exploits illuminated by the sort of detail that brings them to life. The achievements of the early explorers have therefore remained largely unknown — how many people to-day have heard of Pytheas, the discoverer of the Arctic, or of Leif Eriksson, the first fully authenticated European to set foot in the New World? Yet these men made voyages at least as remarkable as those of Columbus and Nansen; their praise is worth the singing; and by devoting nearly a third of *Lodestone and Evening Star* to their exploits I hope to have rescued them from an ill-deserved obscurity and at the same time given the story of exploration a proper balance.

Some historians argue that although it is interesting to speculate on these early voyages, it is not possible to prove that they took place. This is a tenable belief—though I do not hold it myself; and in describing the ancient voyages as it seems to me they occurred, I have no wish to be dogmatic or to denigrate other interpretations; what I have done in each instance is simply to plead a special case with what I hope is justifiable conviction.

I

A VOYAGE TO THE LAND OF GOD

(Queen Hatshepsut's expedition of 1493 B.C. *to the golden land of Punt)*

THE first man ever to put to sea was probably a river-dweller and his "voyage" involuntary. We can picture him clinging to log or drift-wood, too frightened or perhaps too badly injured to swim, being carried downsteam, out through the river mouth and away into an alien world of salt water, currents and waves. If he survived, it would have been by luck rather than judgement. This kind of thing must have happened many times in the days of prehistory; but such voyagers were guinea-pigs rather than explorers. For the word explore has a connotation of purpose.

The first people known to put to sea of their own free will and for the purpose of exploration were the Babylonians. Their voyages at first must have been purely river runs, up and down the Tigris and Euphrates; but archaeologists tell us that by 4,000 B.C. the delta ports of Ur and Eridu were engaged in tentative seaborne trade with India. Unfortunately we know very little about this trade. We know it took place; but the type of vessel employed and the cargoes carried are largely conjecture. Not till we come to another millennium and another country have we evidence of voyages which can be reconstructed accurately and in detail.

The dawn of recorded exploration was in Egypt round about 3,000 B.C.

The Egyptian Nile flows from south to north, and the prevailing winds blow up it from north to south; it is therefore an ideal river for waterborne trade. The race who built the pyramids were not likely to be defeated for long by the problem of building ships able to utilize these conditions. And in the third millennium B.C. we have evidence of long, low, square-rigged sailing-cum-rowing boats, with collapsible masts, plying between delta and cataracts. These vessels were long and low and had collapsible masts so that they could be easily rowed downriver with the current; and they were square-rigged, with wide oblong sails, so that they could be easily sailed up-river with the prevailing wind. (You can see identical vessels to-day on the Irrawaddy, where conditions of wind and current are similar.) There is plenty of evidence that such ships existed: temple reliefs, engraved vases and scale models left in Egyptian tombs so that the souls of the departed could voyage safely over the waters of the underworld. They were ideal, these early vessels, for river traffic. But they were not so good in the open sea — partly because they were unable to beat to windward and partly because their short planks could not stand up to the strain of waves. Not-withstanding this, we are told that *circa* 3,000 B.C., in the dynasty of Sahu-Rê,

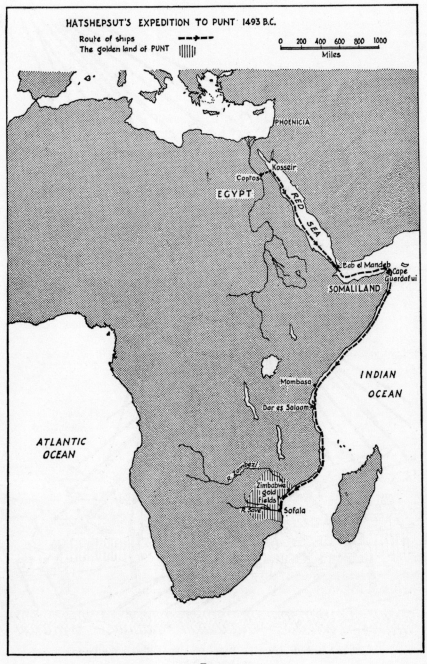

FIG I.

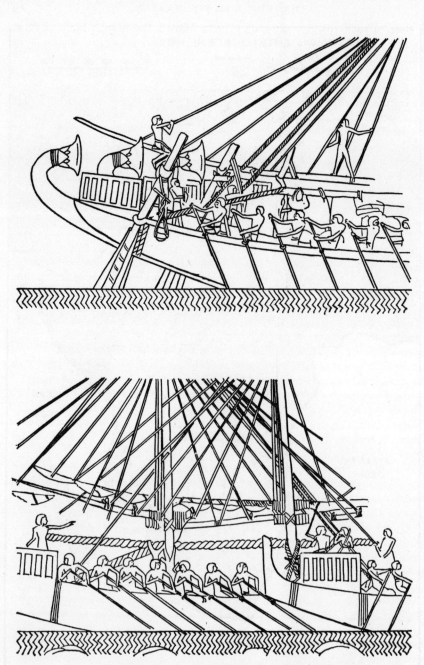

FIG 2. Vessels departing for Punt—from Bas-Reliefs in the Temple
at Dehr El Bahri

a fleet of such rowing-cum-sailing boats visited the distant land of Punt and brought back a fabulous cargo of "myrrh, silver, costly woods, gold and dwarfs".

This is the first great voyage in history of which we have indisputable evidence. But here again the evidence is not full enough for us to reconstruct the course of the expedition in detail. All we know is that its leader was named Hannu, that it was away for four years, that it travelled partly by land and partly by sea, was successful, highly dangerous and was repeated several times in the next few centuries.

Then, abruptly and for nearly a millennium, Egyptian seafaring died: there were no more expeditions to Punt, no more venturing, even, into the Mediterranean.

There would seem to be two reasons for this. In the first place, the expeditions to Punt had been extremely hazardous—it was rare for a man to survive more than one voyage; those who survived two made special votive offerings to the gods—and we can therefore infer that the Nile shipwrights lacked either the material or the know-how to build safe seagoing vessels. In the second place—and this is a far weightier reason—the Egyptians did not like the sea and had little inducement to risk their lives on it. "To sail from Egypt," wrote a second-millennium priest, "is an unholy deed." Unholy, because ungrateful. For the Egyptians were a self-sufficient agricultural community whose lives revolved round the great river flowing constantly through their midst, "the mother of all (their) wants". Why leave such a land of plenty for the perils of desert or sea? Which brings us to a basic fact about exploration: it has not been the highly civilized people —the Egyptians, Chinese, Greeks, Romans or Habsburgs—who have explored the world; it has been the small, initially backward races living in barren lands—the Phoenicians, for example, and the Vikings and the fifteenth-century Portuguese. A bleak littoral tends to breed hardier stock than a lush meadow—and there is more incentive to leave it!

For these reasons there was no resurgence of Egyptian seafaring until the fifteenth century B.C. Then three circumstances combined to bring about the first great voyage in history which can be reconstructed with accuracy: Queen Hatshepsut's voyage to Punt.

Queen Hatshepsut came to power in 1501 B.C. She was beautiful, able and ambitious—"the first great lady in history"—and she was anxious to cement her position as Pharaoh by making some popular coup. When, therefore, her chancellor Senmut suggested an expedition to Punt, "the golden land of god" whose whereabouts for centuries had been a secret of the priests, his suggestion fell on receptive ears. One motive of the voyage, in other words, was personal ambition.

Another motive was economic necessity. For Hatshepsut's father had extracted the last ounce of gold from his mines in upper Egypt, thereby drying up a source of revenue two thousand years old and leaving his successor short of currency. If Egypt had been completely self-supporting, this shortage of currency would not have mattered. But there was one vital commodity in the second millennium which the Egyptians had to import in increasing quantities: incense: the lifeblood of the ancient world. Because of the votive and propitiatory nature of Egyptian religion, incense was consumed the length of the Nile, in both temples and homes, in the most fantastic quantity — the Temple of Amon at Thebes, for example, burnt over 304,000 bushels a year! From time immemorial this incense had been bought from southern Arabia, a miserable wilderness metamorphosised by its resinous trees into the *Arabia Felix* of the Romans and the fabulous dreamland of The Thousand and One Nights. But incense was expensive. We can therefore imagine Queen Hatshepsut's delight when Senmut told her that the distant land of Punt was rich not only in gold but also in incense trees. Here, then, was a chance for her both to replenish her coffers and to break a monopoly both irksome and costly.

It was Hatshepsut's good furtune that her desire to reach Punt coincided with a renascence in Egyptian shipbuilding.

For centuries the Nile shipwrights had been plagued by a shortage of timber: for about the only tree abundant in Egypt is the palm, and palm-wood is unsuitable for ship construction since it splits easily and can only be sawn into short lengths. So up to about 1750 B.C. Egyptian vessels were, of necessity, built out of small two-to-three-foot planks. This method of construction was all right for river work; but in the open sea, waves strained the joints beyond endurance so that the ships tended, quite literally, to fall apart at the seams. This tendency was partly counterbalanced by running a heavy truss — thick as a man's arm and with a breaking strain of three hundred tons — from bow to mast and then from mast to stern; but a ship held together with rope cannot have given its crew much confidence when they ran into heavy seas! As soon as Egyptian influence extended to the mountainous region of Sinai, a certain amount of fair-quality timber found its way to the Nile; but not until trade developed with Phoenicia did the Egyptian shipwrights get a plentiful supply of first-class wood. This trade was initiated round about 1700 B.C., and it was the *rapport* between Egyptians and Phoenicians which made possible the great second-millennium voyages such as the expedition to Punt.

At first the Egyptians spoke slightingly of their uncivilized neighbours in the north — "(they are) miserable Asiatics; evil in the place in which they dwell, inaccessible because of the many trees and with bad water." But it was these "many trees" which were to prove the Phoenicians' passport to immortality. For here on the Israeli seaboard grew the cedars of Lebanon: vast close-grained giants, old and durable as time, whose oil, the Egyptians soon discovered, was first-class for embalming, and whose timber was unsurpassed for the building of ships.

Later, the "miserable Asiatics" were far to surpass their neighbours in all aspects of seamanship; but at the time of Queen Hatshepsut, the Phoenicians' love-affair with the sea was only in embryo, and their contribution to the voyage to Punt was probably limited to supplying timber for the ships, a few seamen for the crew, and a few innovations in design and rig. Yet this timber and these innovations (the broadening of the Egyptian hulls, the abolition of their A-shaped masts and the reduction of their standing rigging) may have made all the difference between failure and success. For the Phoenicians had a maritime flair. They were the first race in history who were genuine seafarers rather than river-dwellers who had taken to the sea by necessity; and Queen Hatshepsut was fortunate to have the benefit of their advice.

Just how much advice the Phoenicians gave in planning the voyage to Punt, we cannot say with certainty. For the records are tantalisingly incomplete. So incomplete in fact that even the whereabouts of Punt is conjecture, and there is little hope of following the voyage step by step (as will be done with later expeditions). Instead we are faced with a fascinating historical jigsaw: how to fit the few pieces of evidence we have into a coherent whole. And our first and most important piece of evidence is the ships themselves.

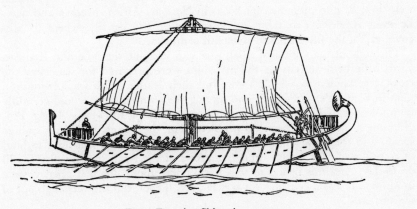

Fig 3. Egyptian Ship: *circa* 1493 B.C.

We know a good deal about them. For Hatshepsut commemorated the triumphs of her voyage in the temples of Dehr el Bahri and Hierakonpolis, and there in magnificent bas-reliefs and frescoes we can see the five great ships of her expedition, first setting out empty from Coptos, then loading up at the incense terraces of Punt, and finally discharging their fabulous cargo on the banks of the Nile. Figure 3 is based on these frescoes. Looking at it, we can see that the vessels had a crew of some twenty-six, that twenty-two of them could row at the same time, and that the rowers sat facing the stern and used oars supported by leather thongs—a technical advance on the days of Hannu when rowers faced the bow and used paddles. Experts who have studied the frescoes calculate the length of the ships as 100 feet, their beam as 22 feet, their draught as 4½ feet and their displacement 85 to 90 tons. They were built of cedarwood, and steered by a pair of massive paddle-like rudders which were mounted on a pillar and slung either side of the stern. One of the frescoes shows a ship manoeuvring to come alongside, and since no fewer than four helmsmen are struggling with the rudder we can assume it was no mean weight. The truss to counteract hogging (splitting apart at the seams) is still in evidence, but significantly it has disappeared from frescoes of the following century, by which time the resilience of Lebanon cedar had evidently been proved. The rig is interesting: simple and with a small area of sail. Hundred-ton river boats of Hatshepsut's reign usually carried a sail area of 400 square yards, supported by a veritable spider's web of standing rigging; yet the Punt ships carry only 200 square yards and their rigging is simple, so that their sails could be easily raised and lowered and used in winds other than those from dead astern. In this we see the influence of the Phoenicians.

The vessels, in other words, were hybrids: an Egyptian hull and a Phoenician rig. And they have a special place in maritime history. For they were forerunners of the most functional and seaworthy vessels ever to grace the oceans: the Tyre and Sidon traders of the first millennium B.C: ships which were to nose into unknown harbours in Norway, Africa, Malaya and maybe even America two thousand years before the usually accepted "discoveries" of the fifteenth and sixteenth centuries.

Throughout the winter of 1494/3 we can imagine the Nile and Red Sea yards astir with activity as the five ships were prepared for sea. How the crew were chosen, we don't know; but their leader Nehsi was obviously a man in Senmut's confidence, and among the seamen there would certainly be a number of Phoenicians accustomed to working the new-style rig. Provisioning would have been no problem. For the vessels had little storage space, and the crew would expect to catch their food *en route* and to land at coastal wells for water—much as crews of the Arab trading dhows still do to-day. And this brings us to a basic point about this first great voyage in history. It was a coasting voyage. Rarely, if ever, did the vessels go out of sight of land.

Notwithstanding this, it was very much a venture into the unknown. And the 130-odd men who in June 1493 pulled out from Coptos cannot have rated their chances of survival as very high.

Three years were to pass and ten thousand miles to slide under their cedarwood keels before they returned in triumph to the Nile.

This much we can unravel from the bas-reliefs of Dehr el Bahri. But when it comes to the actual voyage our sources of information dry up. For Nehsi kept no log; he wrote no memoirs; between the day his ships left Coptos and the day they returned there is nothing but silence, and even the whereabouts of Punt is an enigma only recently solved. So we are back to fitting together the pieces of our jigsaw.

We know from commemorative tablets that Nehsi's ships set out from the Nile emporium of Coptos; we know that Punt was somewhere south of the Red Sea; and we know too that in Hatshepsut's time there was a canal connecting the Nile to the Red Sea—probably between Coptos and Kosseir—and it would be through this canal that the vessels were first rowed. We can almost pinpoint the date: about July 1st, 1493. For the Egyptians were *au fait* with sailing conditions in the Red Sea; they knew that in mid-June the northerly winds set in bringing several months of fair weather, and they would have timed their departure accordingly. We can imagine the crew's satisfaction as they cleared the canal, banked their oars and with a following wind stood south down the Hijaz shore. It would have taken them less than five weeks to reach Bab el Mandeb, "the gate of tears", where in the narrow strait linking the Red Sea and the Gulf of Aden, their seamanship would have been tested for the first time.

"The gate of tears" is an awkward passage. Even modern steamships have been known to get into difficulty among its reefs and tide rips; for the multitude of sandbars off either shore forces vessels into a central channel where wind and current meet head-on, knocking up ugly cross-seas and eddies, which shift hourly through all the points of the compass. Added hazards are the frequent sandstorms, an overpowering humidity, and curious tricks of refraction which throw mirages on to the already troubled waters. Nehsi's ships may well have avoided this central route, and picked a course among the inshore reefs. This needs a skilled pilot with a lifetime of local knowledge. But it can be done—even to-day Arab and Somali dhows slip through the Bab el Mandeb reefs by night, running cargoes of arms and Nubian slaves—and we can picture Nehsi's five cumbersome vessels nosing anxiously among the cays, making slow progress by day and beaching on the sandbars by night. It must have been the better part of a fortnight before they fought clear to the open waters of the Gulf of Aden. Then, with the wind on their port quarter, they should have enjoyed a good run as far as Cape Guardafui, the ancient horn of Africa, which they probably reached towards the end of August. They were on the threshold now of the unknown.

What course did they set on leaving Cape Guardafui: north to the Aden Protectorate, east to India, or south down the African shore? Where, in other words, *was* this fabulous land of Punt?

For years the location of Punt has been hotly disputed among archaeologists and historians who have sometimes displayed in their researches more erudition than common sense. For a long time, for example, it was argued that Punt "must be found somewhere on the Red Sea coast of Somaliland". Yet the Somali coast is only a few hundred miles from Egypt and is on the annual incense route to Arabia; it wouldn't have taken Hannu four years to get there and Nehsi three; also if Punt was so easily accessible why didn't the Egyptians seek out its treasures more often? We can therefore rule Somaliland out, since all our evidence indicates that Punt was somewhere *inaccessible* and that the voyage to it was long, arduous and fraught with danger. Considering the more distant locations that have been suggested—such as Malaysia, India, South Africa, the Persian Gulf, the Celebes and Peru—the obvious thing would seem to be to consult the temple inventories, make a list of the treasures brought back, and see which of the suggested places would be most likely to provide them.

The cargo brought back from Punt can be tabulated as follows:—

Gold.

Incense—"*very much sweet-smelling resin, frankincense, ahem incense, holy resin and trees of myrrh.*"

Ebony and other *"hard and most valuable woods"*.

Jewels (emeralds, turquoises, lapis lazuli, sapphires and pearls).

Ivory.

"Leopard skins, a southern panther alive and several long-tailed apes."

"Natives of the country and their children."

Antimony (which a German scientist found, on analysis of the contents of second-millennium make-up-boxes, to be an essential ingredient of Egyptian rouge).

It is the last of these treasures which gives us the vital clue. For antimony is found in a strictly limited number of areas, and geologists have proved that of all the world's deposits only one could have been mined at the time of the voyages to Punt — the lamellar veins of Mozambique in the lower reaches of the Zambezi.

Given this clue, the bits of our jigsaw click into place. Gold would be mined in the Mozambique hinterland, in the Zimbabwe fields of Southern Rhodesia, where conical defence towers of Egypto-Phoenician origin can still be seen to-day and where Egyptian statues and papyrus have been recently unearthed. Incense, hardwood and ivory would come from the terraces and forests of Sofala and Zambezia. All the animals listed can be found to-day in the Zambezi valley. Only the jewels are not indigenous; and they could have come from Ceylon, brought by the fragile looking but deceptively seaworthy dhows which were sailing the Indian Ocean three thousand years ago with the same fatalistic skill as they sail it to-day. There is no need to search farther for Punt. It was surely for Mozambique, the "Land of the Beautiful Shore", that Nehsi's vessels were bound.

And this conclusion is strengthened by one further piece of evidence: a piece of evidence so simple and obvious that for a long time nobody noticed it. Figure 4 is a reproduction of one of the frescoes of Dehr el Bahri. It shows the Egyptian ambassador (right) receiving the Prince and Princess of

FIG 4. The Prince and Princess of Punt and their retinue
receive the Egyptian Ambassador

Punt, who are followed by slaves carrying tribute and one of the "long-tailed apes" mentioned in the inventories. And one doesn't need to be an anthropologist to see which part of the world the princess came from. Only one race have buttocks like that: the Hottentots. Which surely proves beyond all reasonable doubt that Punt was in South-East Africa.

So on leaving Cape Guardafui Nehsi's vessels stood south.

We can picture them heading, close inshore, down the Somali coast. The fair-weather north-east monsoon would be blowing from almost dead astern; the North Equatorial Current would be in their favour, and even without oars they must have averaged a steady fifty miles a day. At night they would beach; or, if there was no suitable landing place, anchor offshore; and the crew would climb up to the coastal wells to replenish their skins, or maybe fish in waters crystal clear under stars as bright as anywhere on earth. This part of the voyage must have been near-idyllic.

Nor as they approached the equator would conditions have greatly altered. The North Equatorial Current would have been replaced by the Mozambique Drift; but the latter flows south with equal velocity. The monsoons would become a shade less reliable perhaps, and the oarsmen would have had more work. But the Kenya and Tanganyika shores are as balmy and full of good harbours as the Somali; their coastal waters, too, are alive with fish; and neither food, water, weather nor navigation should have presented too difficult a problem.

As his ships stood deeper into the unknown, Nehsi very likely took aboard a succession of local pilots, men who knew the hazards of their own particular stretch of coast and who probably piloted the strangers through some hundred miles of shallows before being dropped ashore. These men would have been proficient navigators. For dhows had been trading along this East African shore from time immemorial, and contemporary records tell of their pilots' skill. "*They study the stars. They study too the portents of good and bad weather. They can distinguish the regions of the ocean by the fish, by the colour of the water and the nature of the bottom; also by the birds and the landmarks.*" This is the first recorded hint of an art which was later to become the cornerstone of sea travel: astronomy. It is confirmation, too, that the voyage to Punt was coastal; one cannot steer by "birds and landmarks" if one is far offshore.

By early November Nehsi would have passed the equator, and his crew would be gazing in wonder at the riotous colours of the incense shore, one of the loveliest and lushest coasts in the world. One by one the harbours with the fairy-tale names would drop astern—Lamu, Malindi and Mombasa: Chake Chake, Zanzibar and Dar es Salaam—it must have seemed a far cry to the bare hills and gentle colours of the Nile. About this time Nehsi would very likely have put ashore to "repay" the ships' keels from the ravages of the teredo worm, against which even the cedars of Lebanon would not have been entirely proof. Then they would head south again, in humid less-settled weather, but helped on their way, still, by the friendly Mozambique drift.

And that winter, after a voyage of over four thousand five hundred miles, they came to Mozambique: threshold to the fabulous land of Punt. Some historians have belittled this achievement of Nehsi's, dubbing it "a mere coasting jaunt". But such a view is surely unrealistic. Nehsi's ships were primitive; his crew were traversing waters which none of his countrymen had seen for a thousand years; and the distance he covered was fantastic—as far as across the Atlantic and half-way back again. Judged by any standard, this was an epic of seamanship.

Having followed Nehsi almost to his destination, we are now faced with a number of problems. Where exactly did he land? How long did he stay

in Punt? How did he persuade the natives to part with their treasures?
Did he stay offshore or penetrate the hinterland? We cannot be dogmatic
on these issues. We can only make inferences.

His most likely landing place would, I think, seem to be Sofala, at the
mouth of the Save, about a hundred and fifty miles south of the Zambezi
delta. When the Portuguese captured Sofala in 1505 they found that its
history as a gold emporium went back over three thousand years; for from
time immemorial gold mined in the rich Rhodesian fields had been floated
down-Save to the mouth of the river, where, in the second millennium, a
great port grew up which some historians have identified (I think wrongly)
as the Biblical Ophir. And it was most probably here, almost exactly five
thousand miles from the Nile, that the Egyptian ships finally dropped
anchor.

They may well have stayed in and around the mouth of the Save for
roughly six months, establishing contact with the natives, repairing their
ships, trading and doing a certain amount of exploring. They cannot have
stayed substantially longer. For the return journey, in laden ships and
with wind and current against them, must have taken all of two years.

It is hard to calculate the value of the goods they took aboard at Sofala,
but an estimate of £30,000,000 according to present-day values would
probably be conservative; and the question at once arises, what, if anything, did the Egyptians give in return? We can dispose of one theory.
They didn't subjugate Punt and spoliate its treasures by force. For they
were not strong enough. And this brings us to an interesting fact about
ancient exploration. The weapons of the explorers were usually so similar
to the weapons of the people whose land they discovered, that force was
out of the question. It was different later, when a well-armed swineherd
like Pizarro and his thirteen "teddy boys" could topple an empire, butcher-
ing in the process some ten thousand defenceless natives; but in ancient
times discoverer and discovered met on more or less equal terms; the former,
of course, were numerically inferior; so trade had to be by consent. We
must therefore assume that the Egyptians took some sort of *quid pro quo* to
Punt: probably a store of barterable trinkets (mostly pottery and glass) —
the equivalent of the nineteenth-century trappers' beads, sharp knives and
fire-water. These would probably have been enough to satisfy the bushmen-
Hottentots who were the original inhabitants of Punt—especially since the
Hottentots as a race have an inbred generosity and a tradition of hospitality to strangers. Indeed, it is not impossible that the prince and princess
simply handed over large quantities of their gold and incense as a gift, for
such an act would have been quite in keeping with what Laurens van der
Post describes as their people's "natural aristocracy of spirit". It is, at any
rate, pleasant to record that there was no bloodshed in Punt, no burning
of homes, no looting and none of the savagery which in years to come was
to brutalize exploration and make it so often synonymous with exploitation.
In all the tablets and frescoes of Dehr el Bahri there is no hint of a weapon
raised in anger. The Egyptians were a civilized people.

Did they leave Sofala and venture inland? Assuming they were on good

terms with the natives, they would almost certainly have visited the gold-
fields of Rhodesia, both to satisfy their own curiosity and to furnish Queen
Hatshepsut with a report. As evidence of this, the vast defence works of
the Zimbabwe gold reefs are believed to be, in part, of Egypto-Phoenician
origin—*vide* the *South and East African Year Book*: "amongst the ruins, a
number of relics have been discovered, including statuettes of Asarte in the
hawk form, Phallic symbols of various dimensions, and bowls and trinkets,
etc." Asarte was the moon-goddess of the Phoenicians.

On Nehsi's return to the coast, his five ships would be loaded for the
voyage back.

The temple reliefs of Dehr el Bahri give us a vivid picture of this part
of the expedition. Some frescoes show the treasures of Punt being weighed
out—the silver, the ivory, the jewels and the 750 cwt of gold (present-day
value some £10,000,000); others show the ships lying off Sofala, a town of
reed huts built on stilts (for the Save delta is marshland); others show the
goods being taken aboard—slaves carrying the thirty-one myrrh saplings,
each in its special tub; while others give us delightful little vignettes of the
problems of loading—the apes, for example, being chased up the standing
rigging, and the "southern panther alive" glowering out of its cage.

And so to the long haul home.

This must have been a very different affair from the voyage out. For the
ships were heavily laden now; currents, all the way to the Red Sea, were
against them; so was the fair-weather monsoon; and for most of the voyage
the sails would have been useless and the oarsmen must have had to row
day after day, week after week, and month after month, into head-wind
and head-sea under a tropic sun. They would have been lucky to average
ten miles a day. How many of the crew, in that terrible journey, died of
exhaustion, sunstroke, fever or dysentery, we shall never know. But we *do*
know that all five ships, somehow, struggled back to the Nile. For the
frescoes show them pulling-in in triumph to Thebes in the summer of 1490.

Their return sparked off a great upsurge of enthusiasm which echoes down
to us through the millennia.

Hatshepsut proclaimed a two days' public holiday; there were processions, banquets, speeches, fêtes and sacrificial offerings; while the triumphs
of Nehsi and his crew were immortalized in fresco, tablet and papyrus. We
can see and read of their voyage to-day, and time cannot dim the feeling
that something great and important had been achieved. "*The ships came back
laden full with the fabulous products of the Land of Punt: with many valuable woods,
with very much sweet-smelling resin, ahem incense, holy resin, fresh frankincense, and
quantities of ebony and ivory set in pure gold from the land of Aamu; with silver and
gold and antimony; with long-tailed apes, a southern panther alive, and natives of
the country and their children. . . . Never was the like brought back to any monarch
since the world began.*" And in the temple of Amon in Thebes, Hatshepsut
paid her father—and the land of Punt—the greatest compliment she could
think of. She planted the thirty-one myrrh trees round her father's tomb.
"And behold," she cried in delight, "I have made him a Punt in his garden;
it is big enough for him to walk abroad in!"

Thus was a little corner of the golden land of god transplanted to the banks of the Nile: a perpetual reminder to a stay-at-home people of the wonders to be found by those with sufficient courage to "go down to the sea in ships, and occupy their business in great waters".

*   *   *

But in the long run it was not the Egyptians who profited most from Nehsi's voyage to Punt; it was those "miserable Asiatics", the Phoenicians.

For on Hatshepsut's death, Egypt was plunged into a series of internecine wars; it was several centuries before her pharaohs had a chance to think of such things as exploration; and by then it was too late. For the Phoenicians had quietly made themselves masters of both the Red and the Mediterranean Seas. They were great adapters, the Phoenicians, of other people's ideas. They took Egyptian hieroglyphics and turned them into an alphabet; they copied Egyptian methods of dyeing and weaving and built up their great cloth emporiums of Sidon and Tyre, and they took the basic design of the Egyptian ship and from it evolved a sailing-cum-rowing vessel of unprecedented efficiency. With these vessels they cornered the seaborne trade of the ancient world.

What was the secret of their monopoly? Partly, I think, the fact that seafaring is an essentially practical art, and the more one works at it the better one becomes; partly the fact that the Phoenicians were first in the field and had few competitors; and partly the excellent design of their ships. Which brings us to the real significance of Hatshepsut's voyage to Punt; it was the Phoenicians' first venture into the Indian Ocean, their first contact with the deep-water dhows of the Arabs.

The Egyptians brought back gold and incense from Punt; and the gold was soon spent and the incense burned. The Phoenicians brought back something less tangible but more enduring: a first-hand knowledge of Arab dhows, those most beautiful and versatile of sailing ships whose triangular lateen rig enabled them both to run with the wind *and beat against it*. How Nehsi's crew, especially on their long haul home, must have envied the dhows this ability to beat upwind; how they must have wished their own clumsy sails had a like versatility, and how, back in the Mediterranean, they must have experimented to improve them! Now it is true that neither the Phoenicians nor their heirs the Carthaginians ever changed over to a wholly lateen rig. But with their flair for adaptation, they did before long evolve a rig which was a cross between an Egyptian riverboat's and an Indian Ocean dhow's: a single square-sail, free of standing rigging, which could be quickly reefed or brailed, and which could be used in winds other than those from dead astern.

With this simple, easily-worked sail, and with their oars, the Phoenicians and Carthaginians were able to anticipate by a couple of millennia the boast of the Elizabethan seamen that there was, to them, "No sea unnavigable, no land unattainable."

II

"AND THEY BEHELD THE SUN
ON THEIR RIGHT HAND"

(*The Phoenicians, in* 600 B.C., *circumnavigate Africa*)

TUGGED at by northerly winds, the vessels swung uneasily against
their anchors of stone. The place was Kosseir, on the Gulf of Suez;
the time 600 B.C.

They were very different, these vessels, from the converted river-boats of
Hatshepsut's expedition to Punt. To start with they were larger; experts
have put their length at 120 feet, their beam at 30 feet, their draught at
7 feet and their displacement at 350 tons. Their single sail had an area of
four hundred square yards and they were manned by a crew of thirty. But
their biggest improvement was that they were decked-in behind a high
freeboard; in other words they were designed not for coasting but for work
in the open sea. Such vessels, traders from Tyre, must have been a commonplace sight off sixth-century Kosseir. But it was no commonplace voyage
that these ships were waiting to embark on. For they were about to sail on
one of the most remarkable voyages in the history of exploration: the first
circumnavigation of Africa.

What evidence have we that this fantastic voyage took place: a voyage
which antedates by two thousand years the usually accepted first rounding
of the Cape by Bartholomew Dias?

First, we have the evidence of contemporary maps.

Looking at these, we can see that in the centuries *before* the birth of Christ
—the Phoenicians' heyday—Africa was known to be surrounded by sea,
except at the isthmus of Suez. Of the maps of this period, that of Eratosthenes of Cyrene is a good example. Eratosthenes' map (*vide* page 32)
shows Africa as a virtual island, with the Atlantic and Indian Oceans
meeting off its southern tip. All maps of this period are similarly accurate.
And if we ask ourselves why, the most likely answer is surely that it was
known in those days that Africa was surrounded by sea because the continent had, in fact, been sailed round. As confirmation of this, we need only
look at the inaccurate maps of the centuries *after* the birth of Christ. By
this time, Phoenician and Carthaginian empires had crumbled, their
records had been destroyed, the deeds of their seamen had been systemati-
cally discredited by the Romans and their knowledge lost. The result was
that landlubber cartographers of the first and second centuries A.D. tried
to turn Africa into a vast southern continent to "balance" Eurasia; this
they did by running the coastline of Kenya and Tanganyika south by east,
to join a non-existent "*terra incognita*" (whose shores turned the Indian Ocean

into a landlocked sea and were to plague cartographers' charts for the next fifteen hundred years). Of these later maps, that of Claudius Ptolemy (*circa* A.D. 150) is typical (*vide* page 32) and we need only compare it with Eratosthenes' map to see how cartography retrogressed after the golden era of the traders of Tyre and Sidon. The fact that the Phoenicians' maps of Africa were much more accurate than their successors' is surely evidence that they had first-hand knowledge of the extent of the Dark Continent: knowledge which was later lost in the flames of Sidon, Tyre and the rest of their trading ports.

The evidence of maps is confirmed by the evidence of contemporary literature, which contains several hints of a circumnavigation. Most important of these are the stories of Eudoxus and Sataspes.

Eudoxus was a merchant. One year, while trading in the Indian Ocean, he was driven by a series of storms far down the east coast of Africa. Somewhere beyond Sofala he came across a wrecked ship, which, the natives told him, had "belonged to traders from the west". Eudoxus regarded this as a tall story at first; then he noticed that the ship's prow was carved into the shape of a horse. This stirred his memory. He cut off the prow, took it back with him to Egypt, and showed it to the shipwrights of Alexandria who told him that such prows were made only in Cadiz. This gave Eudoxus food for thought; for although Cadiz ships often traded down the *west* coast of Africa, they were never known to have ventured through the Red or Arabian Seas; in other words, the wrecked vessel must have sailed down the Saharan coast, rounded the Cape of Good Hope and finally been lost off the east coast. This, at any rate, was Eudoxus's interpretation; and he fitted out an expedition to try to follow the course of the wrecked vessel around Africa—in this he succeeded all too well, sailing from Cadiz in about 105 B.C. and never being heard of again.

The story of Sataspes is equally intriguing—if equally inconclusive. Sataspes was a young Persian nobleman who, as punishment for "a shameful deed", had been condemned to death by impaling. On his mother's intervention, his sentence was commuted to "sailing around Libya (Africa) from the Pillars of Hercules to the Arabian Gulf". The interesting thing about this sentence is its inference that such a voyage, though known to be difficult, was thought to be possible. In the event, the miserable Sataspes failed; he came back to Persia saying his ship had "been stopped" (possibly by the Guinea Counter-Current), and was promptly impaled.

These stories and their implications point, I think, to an earlier and successful voyage of circumnavigation. And it is Herodotus who gives us an actual account of such a voyage.

Unfortunately Herodotus's account is tantalisingly brief; also it is the only one extant. A great many people have therefore discredited it. Yet Herodotus was the most painstaking and accurate of historians; tall stories have no place in his *History*, and it is clear that he himself—writing only some 150 years after the voyage took place—accepted the circumnavigation as an undoubted fact. If he believed it and his contemporaries believed it, why shouldn't we?

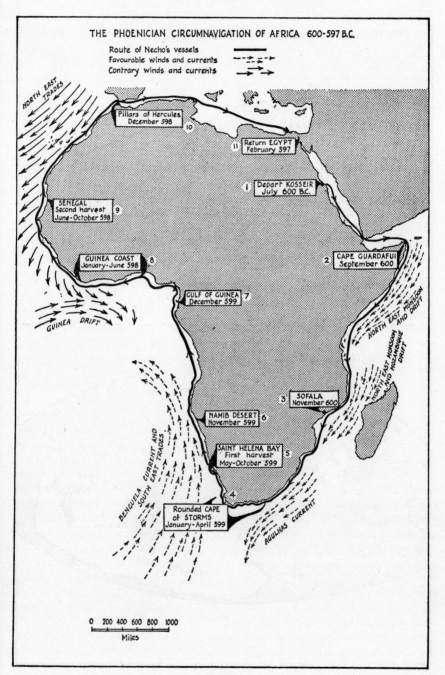

THE PHOENICIAN CIRCUMNAVIGATION OF AFRICA 600-597 B.C.

Route of Necho's vessels
Favourable winds and currents
Contrary winds and currents

NORTH EAST TRADES

Pillars of Hercules
December 598   10

Return EGYPT
February 597   11

Depart KOSSEIR
July 600 B.C.   1

SENEGAL
Second harvest   9
June-October 598

GUINEA COAST   8
January-June 598

CAPE GUARDAFUI   2
September 600

GULF OF GUINEA   7
December 599

GUINEA DRIFT

NORTH EAST MONSOON AND DRIFT

NORTH EAST MONSOON AND MOZAMBIQUE DRIFT

SOFALA   3
November 600

NAMIB DESERT   6
November 599

SAINT HELENA BAY   5
First harvest
May-October 599

BENGUELA CURRENT AND SOUTH EAST TRADES

Rounded CAPE
of STORMS   4
January-April 599

AGULHAS CURRENT

0 200 400 600 800 1000
Miles

FIG 5.

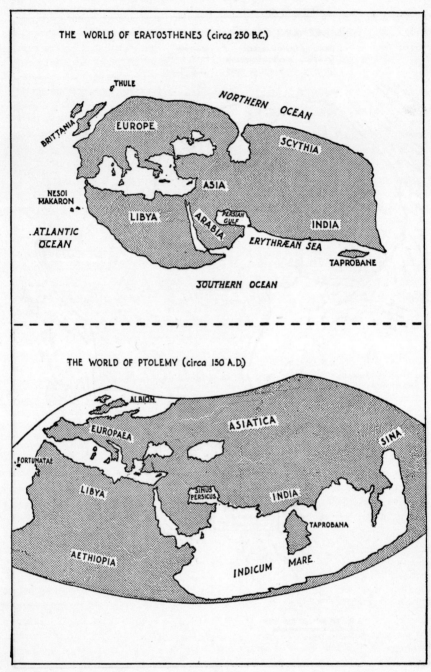

THE WORLD OF ERATOSTHENES (circa 250 B.C.)

THULE

NORTHERN OCEAN

BRITTANIA

EUROPE

SCYTHIA

NESOI
MAKARON

ASIA

LIBYA

ARABIA

PERSIAN
GULF

INDIA

ATLANTIC
OCEAN

ERYTHRÆAN SEA

TAPROBANE

SOUTHERN OCEAN

THE WORLD OF PTOLEMY (circa 150 A.D.)

ALBION

EUROPAEA

ASIATICA

SINA

FORTUNATAE

LIBYA

SINUS
PERSICUS

INDIA

TAPROBANA

AETHIOPIA

INDICUM MARE

FIG 6.

His account is as follows: *"Libya (Africa) is known to be surrounded by sea on all sides, save for that part of it which borders on Asia. The first man to prove this, as far as I know, was Pharaoh Necho II of Egypt. When Necho had stopped building his canal, which was to have linked the Nile to the Red Sea, he equipped an expedition of Phoenician ships and commanded them to sail into the Southern Sea, to round Libya and to return to Egypt through the Pillars of Hercules* (the Straits of Gibraltar). *So the Phoenicians left port and sailed via the Indian Ocean into the Southern Sea. In autumn they landed, tilled the fields, and waited for the harvest, in whatever part of Libya they happened to be. When they had harvested the corn they sailed on, until after two years they came to the Pillars of Hercules, and so returned to Egypt again in the third year. When they got back they related a story which I cannot believe—though perhaps others may—namely that as they rounded Libya they beheld the sun on their right hand."*

Several factors point to the authenticity of this account.

First, the journey is described as being made from east to west; this is by far the easier way, for as we shall see when the voyage is reconstructed in detail, if Africa is rounded in this direction the prevailing currents and winds are favourable for four-fifths of the journey. Second the fact that the ships were said to be away for two and a half years ties up with the distance they would have had to cover and the speed at which they would have been most likely to travel. Third, there is the passage about the sun. And here the very part of the Phoenicians' story which Herodotus found hard to credit points to it being true. For it was unthinkable to a civilized man of Herodotus's era that if a ship sailed west, the sun should be on its right— that just did not happen in the northern hemisphere; and yet as Necho's ships stood west round the Cape of Good Hope they would indeed, being south of the equator, have seen the sun on their right hand. Thus the very passage which made the voyage incredible to the ancients makes it credible to us.

In fact, the only thing now needed to establish that a circumnavigation almost certainly took place is to find a motive.

Necho's motive was simple. He was an able, ambitious ruler who was keen to stimulate his country's trade. In the early years of his reign he started to dig a canal from Bubastis to Suez (Hatshepsut's had silted up by this time); but after 120,000 slaves had died, the work was discontinued—not for humanitarian reasons, but because Necho was warned by an oracle that his canal would serve only to help the Persians. When this scheme fell through, Necho hit on the alternative of offering political asylum to displaced Phoenician traders. Now the Phoenicians at this time had just suffered a series of disastrous wars with Assyria; Tyre had been sacked four times in as many generations, their fleet had been seriously weakened, and trade in the Mediterranean had come to a virtual standstill. A fair number of seamen and merchants were therefore glad to accept Necho's offer and came to settle in the ports of the Nile and the Red Sea, especially in Kosseir. It was to a group of these merchants that Necho put forward his scheme: a dramatic and spectacular scheme which, he must have imagined, would enhance both his own reputation and that of his country.

And what did the Phoenicians hope to gain by sailing round Africa? We can rule out one idea. They did not do it for love of exploration. For the Phoenicians were not interested in voyages of discovery *per se*; they were interested only in trade. They must, therefore, have had some specific economic objective for their voyage. What this objective was we cannot say for certain; but chemists and numismatists can help us to hazard a pretty accurate guess.

In the seventh and eighth centuries B.C., the making of purple dye was the cornerstone of Phoenician industry. For purple, in the ancient world, was the insignia of power; the togas of senators, the cloth of kings, the burial shrouds of pharaohs, all were dyed different shades of purple—the more important the wearer, the deeper, generally, the shade. At first, a select group of Greek and Phoenician families shared the secret of this dye's manufacture—they used to collect *murex* shellfish, squeeze out their fluid, condense it in steam and finally leave it exposed to the sun in a series of vats. Then, about 750 B.C., the Phoenicians leapt suddenly ahead of their competitors and cornered the dye market. For they had discovered a new method of manufacture. And this is where the chemists and numismatists can help us. Chemical analysis has proved that about the middle of the eighth century B.C. a new type of dye was introduced to the Mediterranean: a dye based not on *murex* at all but on *roccella tinctoria*, a lichen peculiar to the Canary Islands. This at first sight seems incredible. For the Canary Islands are nearly a thousand miles out in the Atlantic; they were unknown throughout the Dark and Middle Ages, and their discovery has long been attributed to the fifteenth-century Portuguese. But chemical evidence has now been backed by numismatical; for large numbers of Phoenician coins have recently been found in the Azores (which are even deeper in the Atlantic than the Canaries), coins which, the experts say, are undoubtedly genuine. In other words, Phoenician vessels, *circa* 750 B.C., were voyaging far into the Western Ocean: a fantastic feat which no other ships were to emulate for nearly two thousand years. Having discovered these islands — the Nêsoi Makáron (Islands of The Bless'd) of Greek mythology, which they named after Makar, their city-god of Tyre—the Phoenicians went to incredible lengths to keep their whereabouts a secret. They established a blockade on the Straits of Gibraltar, so that only their own vessels could penetrate the Atlantic; and they spread tall and horrific stories about the perils of the Outer Sea, where, they said, serpents lay in wait to devour whole ships, where the waters boiled, and where rushing winds drove the unwary off the edge of the world. And for a time blockade and tall stories were enough to discourage competitors. Then came the Assyrian wars and the weakening of the Phoenician fleet. Before long, her blockade of the Straits was broken, and Greek, Roman and Persian vessels began to follow her traders into the Atlantic. Now trade was Phoenicia's lifeblood. Her seamen knew this; and they were prepared to go to *any* lengths to thwart competitors. (Evidence of this is the well-known story of the Phoenician merchant who, on his way to the tin islands, was followed day after day by a Roman galley; at last, unable to shake his pursuer off, he deliberately ran into the shallows off Ushant; both ships were wrecked—but the Phoenician, who survived, was indemnified by his city for his self-inflicted loss!) What the Phoenicians could not monopolize, they would not share. They stopped their Atlantic sailings.

So Necho's offer to protect traders and to finance the circumnavigation of Africa came at an opportune moment. We can imagine the Phoenician merchants of Kosseir weighing up the pros and cons. And we can follow their line of thought. Here, they must have argued, was a chance to find an alternative and secret trade route to their Islands of the Bless'd: why shouldn't they try sailing to the Canaries round the bottom of Africa?*

*   *   *

The ships lay anchored off Kosseir. How many of them there were we do not know—but probably at least three and not more than six. We do not know, either, who was in command of them—but events were to prove him a fine and determined seaman. We do, however, know something of the ships themselves. They were largish all-purpose, all-weather traders, with sweet lines and simple rig; they had a shallow draught for coastal work, they could make progress even against a combination of adverse currents and winds by means of their oars, they had storage space for provisions and cargo, and they could ride out bad weather in the open sea. Xenophon has left us a vivid pen-picture of such a ship and her crew.

"*I once went aboard a Phoenician trader,*" he wrote, "*where I observed the best example of good order that I ever met with. I was especially surprised at the vast number of implements which were needed to manage the vessel. What numbers of oars, stretchers, boathooks, marlines and cleats for bringing the ship in and out of harbour! What numbers of shrouds, cables, hawsers, ropes and tackle for sailing her! And what a vast quantity of provisions! And all these were stowed so neatly together, that a far larger place would not have contained them if they had been moved. Yet I noticed that the disposition of everything was so strictly observed, that notwithstanding the great variety of materials, there was not anything on board which the seamen couldn't find in an instant; nor was their captain less acquainted with these particulars than his crew. In addition the captain had to put his mind to many problems: what gear most needed repair, how long his provisions would last etc: for, as he said to me, 'it is no time when a storm comes upon us to start looking for things or to find our tackle is in need of repair. For the gods are never favourable to those who are negligent or lazy; indeed it is only through their goodness that they don't destroy us even when we are diligent.'*"

In this last sentence is all the wisdom of those who know the sea.

Such were the ships and the men who sailed that July from Kosseir; and we can picture them running down the Red Sea before the northerly midsummer breeze, averaging perhaps fifty miles a day and heaving-to at nights off the Hijaz shore.

* Eratosthenes' map proves that this idea would not have seemed as far-fetched to the Phoenicians as it now seems to us. For it was thought in those days that Africa curved round in a shallow arc at the level of the equator; thus the distance round its southern tip was much underestimated.

There have been several attempts to reconstruct the Phoenicians' route in detail, that of Muller being to my mind the most erudite and exhaustive. But none of these attempts strikes me as being wholly convincing; and the reason, I think, is that they have been written by historians rather than seamen, and the historians have tended to indulge in hindsight: i.e., they have started off with the premise that the voyage took two-and-a-half years and then plotted the Phoenicians' timetable on this basis. This seems to me to be putting the cart before the horse, and I cannot accept the usually-

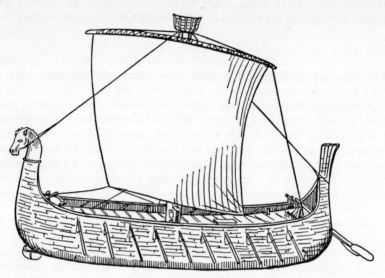

FIG 7. Phoenician Ship

advanced theory that the ships left Kosseir in November. Such a date may fit in with subsequent landings to plant and harvest corn, but when the Phoenicians set sail they cannot possibly have known how long their voyage was going to take nor how many harvests they would be likely to reap *en route;* and I think they must surely have set out at the time which would enable them to gain most benefit from favourable winds during the first part of their voyage: i.e., late summer. In this they would be following a trading tradition which went back to the time of Hatshepsut—down the Red Sea in August and September, helped by the northerlies, then down the African shore in October, November and December, helped by the balmy north-east monsoon. At any rate, let us start with this assumption.

It would have taken them roughly six weeks to run the length of the Red Sea. At first they would have had the northerlies behind them, but later they probably had to row through wayward winds and an awkward current. This southern stretch of the Red Sea has always been unpopular with mariners: "The winds are humid and random," writes a twentieth-century yachtsman, "the currents contrary and the shore uninviting and without water." Still, the hazards of the Red Sea can have presented few insuperable problems to the seamen of a nation who had been trading here for the best part of a thousand years. The same would be true of Bab el Mandeb, "The Gate of Tears"—although the Phoenician vessels, this time, would probably be drawing too much water to keep to the shallows, and would be forced into the central channel. By mid-October of 600 B.C. they would have rounded Cape Guardafui, and be waiting for the onset of the monsoons to carry them effortlessly down the Somali shore.

The monsoon sets in towards the end of October, and soon the vessels would be running freely to the south, helped by both wind and current. They would be in familiar waters still, and this part of their voyage must have seemed—as it had seemed to Hatshepsut's seamen some thousand years before—near-idyllic. For food, there was plenty of sea-fish, mixed perhaps with a little rice and goat's butter; for drink, Persian tea and fresh water, taken aboard nightly in skins from the coastal wells. I doubt if they sailed much by night: although Phoenician skippers by this time were quite capable of steering by the stars if they had to—*vide* Homer's description of Odysseus: "*When leaving Calypso's Island he spread his sail to catch the wind and sat there and never closed his eyes in sleep, but kept them on the Pleides, or watched the late-setting Boötes and the Great Bear, which constellation the wise goddess had told him to keep on his left hand . . . and so for seventeen days he kept to his course.*" When it came to seafaring, anything a Greek could do a Phoenician could do better; and so if Necho's ships had been blown one night away from the coast, they were quite capable of steering back to it by the stars. Normally, though, they can have felt no call to sail by night; for in the hours of daylight alone they must have covered a good fifty to sixty miles.

Some time in November they would have come to Sofala, the last outpost of the known world. Here, undoubtedly, they put ashore for two or three weeks to careen and re-provision their ships, before standing south, in the last days of 600 B.C., into uncharted waters.

This, as they drew away from the Land of Punt, was their moment of decision. Here, as they ran down the narrow Mozambique Channel, was their point of no return.

For in those days ships that ventured through the Mozambique Channel never came back. Currents and winds were too strong and too continuous for a ship to beat up against them to the north; and once past Madagascar there was only one thing for it. If a ship's company were to survive, they *had* to circumnavigate Africa.

Necho's crews must have known this. And we can imagine their feelings as the north-easterly monsoon and the Mozambique Drift bore them swiftly and irretrievably south. And the operative word is swiftly. For the currents in this part of the world are fantastic. One of my friends was forced by engine trouble to crash-land his aircraft in this part of the ocean during the Second World War; he crash-landed it less than thirty yards from an island, and he and his observer scrambled into their dinghy and began to paddle for land; they paddled for their lives, but they hadn't a hope; the current swirled them away far faster than they could paddle, and the island was soon out of sight; at nightfall they were lucky enough to be drifted on to another island, having been carried 150 miles in less than twelve hours! So the Phoenicians, on this part of their voyage, would have needed neither oars nor sail; they would have simply sat tight and prayed to whatever gods they believed in as they were swept through the narrow channel between Madagascar and Mozambique.

On debouching out of the channel, they would have been picked up by the south-flowing Agulhas Current. They were in virgin waters now; farther south, probably, than men from the Mediterranean had ever ventured before – and lived.

To start with, the shores of Natal should have presented them with no great difficulty. But south of Durban the coastline steepens and becomes increasingly rugged and open. Soon, five-hundred-foot cliffs of sand-stone and granite would be frowning down on the vessels, squalls would become increasingly frequent, seas increasingly choppy, and the ships' seaworthiness would be tested to the full. For they were now nearing the Cape of Good Hope, originally and with good reason known as the Cape of Storms.

This would be the most hazardous, though not the most arduous, part of their voyage.

For although they were rounding the Cape at the best possible time (midsummer), the passage is a dangerous one at all seasons, since current and wind are frequently in opposition; also there is an ever-present risk of vessels being blown out to sea and swept away in the "roaring forties", that great belt of frenetic westerly winds which blow non-stop clean round the world. We can therefore picture the Phoenicians edging cautiously along this beautiful but treacherous shore, sometimes avoiding the storms by beaching, sometimes riding them out in the lee of cliffs more majestic than any they had seen in the Mediterranean. They were seamen enough to know instinctively that they were in dangerous waters, and it probably took them the best part of three months to cover the thousand miles from Port Elizabeth to Cape Town. And how thankful they must have been, on rounding Cape Agulhas, to find the coastline running at last not south but north!

One peril at least they would have been spared. They would not have had to round Table Mountain. For the sea, 2,500 years ago, flowed over the present site of Cape Town – from False Bay to Table Bay – leaving Constantiaberg and Table Mountain as twin islands rising steeply out of the water.

And soon after this they put ashore.

Just where they landed we don't know: for they left no convenient tablets, carvings or coins. But almost certainly they would have gone far enough past the Cape to reassure themselves that the coastline had definitely set in to the north, and yet not so far that they came to the arid littoral north of the Olifants River. Saint Helena Bay has been suggested as a possible landing-place; and this, I think, is as good a guess as any. For here, some 150 miles up the west coast, was a site with a sheltered anchorage, a good supply of water, and a hinterland where they could plant their corn.

It would probably be May 599 by this time, which ties up with Herodotus's remarks that the Phoenicians landed "in autumn". And we can picture the crews, in cool pleasant weather, drawing up their vessels on to the sandy beaches east of Great Paternoster Point, and sowing their corn on the slopes of the Berg River—one of the best crop-growing areas in the Republic It would be early November before the corn was ready for harvesting; but the Phoenicians doubtless found plenty to keep them occupied: repaying their keels, repairing rigging, and laying in provisions for the next stage of their journey. Five months ashore in a temperate climate probably did wonders for their health; and they must have been in good heart as late that November they again headed north: for home.

And now once more current and wind were their allies. For the cold-water Benguela flows up this part of the African shore at a steady two-to-three knots; while the south-east trades swing southerly here, slewed off course by the sun-heated mass of the continent. Soon the vessels would again be averaging a steady fifty to sixty miles a day, borne by wind and current along a sea lane which later became the classic route of the home-ward bound East Indiamen. On this part of their voyage the Phoenicians would have had only one anxiety. Water.

For soon they were running parallel to the Namib Desert, one of the bleakest and driest coastlines in the world. The average rainfall of the Namib is under an inch a year; and there are no rivers and few wells—indeed, a nineteenth-century survey report went so far as to state categorically that "along this desolate shore there is no fresh water of any description between the parallels of 16° South and 31° South: i.e., for a distance of over 900 miles." If this were really so it is difficult to see how the Phoenicians could have survived. Yet water *can* be found in the Namib by those who know where to seek it. And here the Phoenicians would have had the edge on a team of nineteenth-century surveyors; for they had learned their trade off a similar shore to the Namib—the shore of the Red Sea—and they would have known where to dig for water by such signs as the colour of the rocks, the bunching of cacti and the tell-tale depressions sunk saucer-like into the sand. I think they must have found the hidden wells of South West Africa—wells which are only just being "discovered" to-day and used as the basis of local irrigation—but they probably had their anxious moments as they beached their vessels through the long Atlantic rollers on a littoral shrouded in near-perpetual fog, and with the threat of death by thirst never far from their minds. They had every incentive to keep moving; and given good weather, they should have covered the thousand-odd miles of the Namib in roughly three weeks.

Then, with wind and current still in their favour, they would have enjoyed a quick and easy passage for the next thousand miles, up the coasts of Angola and French Equatorial Africa. As they crossed the equator and entered the Gulf of Guinea soon after Christmas 599, they probably imagined their troubles were nearly over. In fact they were just about to begin.

For now, for the first time since leaving Kosseir, both wind and current were against them.

The Gulf of Guinea is not an easy place to sail in. For here, where the coast of Africa swings suddenly through ninety degrees, two currents—the Equatorial Counter and the Guinea—and two winds—the north-east and south-east trades—intermingle in a hiatus of baffling calms, sudden squalls and unexpected drifts. And it is the winds and currents from the north-west which prove the stronger; so that throughout the year, between the Canaries and the Cameroons, vessels are swept inexorably south by east.

The Phoenicians could cope with these conditions—just—because they had oars; but when the last of the Phoenician and Carthaginian traders was driven off the seas, no other ships were to venture down this littoral for over two thousand years. For no other ships had their ability to make headway against a prolonged combination of adverse currents and winds, so that once caught in the Counter-Current and north-east trades all subsequent vessels were swept swiftly south down the African coast without a hope of return.

Necho's vessels only escaped a similar fate because they could row. And how they must have rowed! Day after day: week after week: month after month. Literally for their lives.

We can picture the oarsmen sweating under a tropic sun, plagued by mosquitoes and fever, weakened by endemic dysentery, toiling painfully past the lush-green traitorous shore. They probably gazed in awe at "the chariot of the gods" (the volcanic Mount Camerun) as their descendants were to gaze in awe at it a hundred years later during Hanno's attempt to colonize West Africa; they too must have marvelled at "the great rivers full of barbarous elephants and hippopotami", and been "exceeding terrified at night by the sound of cimbals and drummes", and maybe some of them died—as the Portuguese were to die two thousand years later—under the "poisonous darts of the little men of the rivers". All in all, it must have been a long, hard and hazardous haul from the equator to Cape Verde: a haul of some two thousand miles against continuously adverse currents and winds. They would have been lucky if they averaged ten miles a day; which means it must have taken them between five and six months to round the "bulge" of Africa.

They would have been thankful to come to a halt, some time in June, in Senegal.

Senegal, I think, is the most likely place for them to have made their second landing. Some historians have plumped for Morocco—a choice which seems to me a little improbable, since the littoral here is unsuited to crop growing; also, once the Phoenicians had got as far as Morocco they would surely have pulled the extra two or three hundred miles to their emporium at Cadiz. Senegal, on the other hand, was on the fringe of the unknown, and has fertile soil which can grow excellent crops in four months; if the Phoenicians landed here in June and sowed right away, they could have harvested and put to sea again before the end of October.

And soon after leaving Senegal, after two-and-a-half years in virgin waters, they came at last to a familiar shore: the desert littoral of the Sahara: a coastline known to the seamen of Cadiz.

Their joy and relief at coming back to the outposts of the civilized world must have been past describing. For I doubt if any explorers, before or since, have ever taken such a long, hazardous and irrevocable leap into the dark—and survived.

The rest of their voyage home, through the Pillars of Hercules and along the North African shore, must have been anticlimax. Their homecoming must have been anticlimatic, too. For they brought back none of the gold and incense which had led, a thousand years before, to Hatshepsut's seamen being fêted and honoured the length of the Nile; also they returned at a bad moment—Necho had just embarked on a war with Persia, and the war was not going well. So the ships berthed at Kosseir with neither fuss nor celebration, and the Phoenician seamen went quietly to their homes and were soon forgotten. They had made history, but not their fortunes. In fact, their voyage financially must have been a total loss: no fabulous treasures in their hold, no second Punt discovered *en route*, and even their hope of finding a back-door route to the Canaries having failed to materialize—for the passage round the Cape had proved too long and hazardous even to be thought of for trade.

All of which helps to explain, I think, why their voyage was never repeated, was quickly forgotten, and even came in time to be disbelieved. The Greeks would have kept record of so magnificent a feat out of scientific interest: the Romans would have commemorated it in stone for posterity; but the Phoenicians, being interested only in trade, regarded it as a failure and let even the memory of it slide into obscurity.

And this attitude helps us to assess the Phoenicians' and Carthaginians' stature in the galaxy of explorers. They were magnificent practical seamen, working in wonderfully seaworthy ships; and they voyaged farther and more frequently and more skilfully than men were to voyage for over a thousand years. Yet there was something lacking. They were parochial-minded and secretive, and they had none of that love-of-knowledge-for-its-own-sake which is the hallmark of the very greatest explorers. And at the bar of history their shortcomings have told against them. For, because of their obsession with secrecy, we have, to-day, no detailed record of their voyages; we cannot therefore see their exploits in their full and proper glory; we can see them only as through a glass darkly, or as in a faded photograph which we can never look at without experiencing an uneasy qualm that it may be somehow distorted or even faked. History has few better examples of nemesis.

III

"THE WORLD REACHES THIS FAR
AND NO FARTHER"

(Pytheas discovers Great Britain and Ultima Thule: 310 B.C.)

'CHARLATAN", "arch-falsifier", "weaver of fables", "a man whose statements on any subject are not to be trusted": such were the epithets heaped by ancient historians on the explorer Pytheas of Marseilles. But in recent years Pytheas's reputation has been re-assessed, and we are now told that he was "a great man wearing the sober habit of courage and truth". Whom are we to believe?

The difficulty, once again, is our lack of original documents. We have little first-hand information about Pytheas and his travels. We know he was a member of the Greek colony of Massalia (Marseilles); we know he was a contemporary of Alexander the Great; and we know that round about 310 B.C. he embarked on a great voyage into the haunted and unknown waters of north-west Europe. We know too that he came back six years later with reports of many islands—Ierne, Britannia, Orcas and Thule—which he claimed to have visited. He also came back with what obviously seemed to his Mediterranean contemporaries to be a series of "fo'c'sle yarns": stories of tide-ebbs of fifty feet, of waves eighty feet high, and of the ocean congealing into a sort of "sealung" or "jellyfish" which could be traversed neither by boat nor on foot. He wrote two books on his travels: *The Ocean* and *A Description of the Earth.* Unfortunately, not a single copy of either has survived, and all that remains of Pytheas's works are a few short quotations made by subsequent and usually critical historians; so that, as Fridtjof Nansen puts it, "his writings have come down to us only as fragments on the stream of time, as chance wreckage, distorted and perverted by hostile forces." In other words, reconstructing his voyage is like trying to piece together a coherent picture out of a series of brief vignettes. But before we look at the evidence relating to his travels, let us see what we know of the man himself.

Pytheas was born about 350 B.C.; we can judge the date by the fact that Aristotle, who died in 322, makes no mention of him, but Aristotle's pupil Dicaearches knew him well and wrote of him as a contemporary. As a boy he enjoyed a good education, studying astronomy and geography under Eudoxus of Knidos. As a young man he worked in the Massalian library. And this, I think, gives us the clue to both his character and his career. Pytheas was first and foremost a scholar. We do not know the exact nature of his work, but it was clearly some type of astronomical research; for we are told that he became the first man accurately to fix the position of the celestial pole, also that he originated an extremely accurate method of latitude-finding by means of a calibrated *gnomon* or sundial. It was probably during his researches in the library that he came across the sixth-century Carthaginian *Periplus* which sparked off his famous voyage. This *Periplus* must have been a unique document, for the Carthaginians, like their fore-bears the Phoenicians, usually kept their trade routes a secret. It appears to have been a pilots' guide to the coastlines of Spain and France, and to have contained references to the "Tin Islands" and to several "new stars", visible only in the extreme north. It is easy to understand how such a docu-ment must have intrigued the astronomer Pytheas, and how he must have longed to probe more deeply into mysteries at which the *Periplus* only hinted. What is not so obvious is how his dream became reality, and how he, a comparative landlubber, came to assume command of one of the greatest voyages in history. To understand this we must take a brief look at fourth-century Massalia.

Massalia was a colony of those famous explorers and colonizers, the Phocaeans. It was founded in about 600 B.C. Her people were seafaring traders, and had a good deal in common with their rivals in Carthage, Sidon and Tyre. But they were also Greeks, inheritors of the civilization of Pericles and Plato; and as such they had a respect for learning and a catholic love of knowledge for its own sake. Now it is impossible to imagine Tyre or Sidon fitting out an expedition which did not have trade as its be-all and end-all; but it is quite possible to imagine a purely scientific expedition being fitted out from Massalia, whose people were well aware that the world can offer greater wonders than a well-balanced cargo-ledger. Nor is it hard to imagine the Massalians choosing as the commander of their expedition a man who was neither trader nor seaman, but a pure scientist: a man who was pre-eminent in his own sphere, and who was most likely to advance knowledge as a result of his voyage.

To advance knowledge... This, then, was the motive of Pytheas's leap into the unknown: a motive which gives his expedition an up-to-date air and justifies our regarding him as the world's first scientific explorer. This is not to say that affairs of trade played no part at all in his expedition — indeed, it is probable that Pytheas was financed by well-to-do Massalian merchants. But I part company with those historians who think his main purpose was to establish a trade route for his city's imports of amber and tin. All the evidence refutes this: the type of purely scientific information he brought back, the fact that he was away for as long as six years, and above all the fact that on his return he wrote a detailed account of his travels which was freely circulated throughout the civilized world. For the essence of trade is secrecy.

We can therefore picture Pytheas's ship lying openly at anchor in the beautiful Marseilles Road, while the astronomer busied himself with preparations. And these preparations are further evidence of the type of voyage with which we are dealing. For we are told that Pytheas's first step on taking over his command was accurately to fix his point of departure. For this he used his calibrated *gnomon*, working out that on the day of the

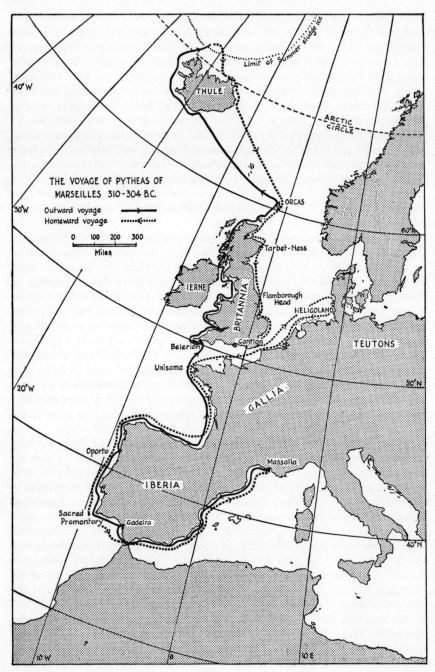

THE VOYAGE OF PYTHEAS OF
MARSEILLES 310-304 B.C.

Outward voyage ⟶
Homeward voyage ·······⟵·······

0   100 200 300
Miles

Limit of Summer sludge ice

THULE

ARCTIC
CIRCLE

40°W

30°W

20°W

ORCAS

Tarbet-Ness

IERNE

BRITANNIA

Flamborough
Head

HELIGOLAND

Belerion

Cantion

TEUTONS

Uxisama

GALLIA

60°N

50°N

Oporto

Massalia

IBERIA

Sacred
Promontory

Gadeira

40°N

10 W   0   10 E

FIG 8.

solstice the altitude of the sun from the Massalian dockyard was 70° 47′ 50″, and that the latitude of Marseilles was therefore 43° 3′ 25″ plus the sun's semi-diameter — a calculation exact to within forty seconds and not bettered for accuracy for five hundred years. His second step was to fix a guide-star by which his ship would be steered. And here again Pytheas was far ahead of his times. For while most of his contemporaries steered by either the Great or the Little Bear, Pytheas discovered that there is in fact no star at the celestial pole, but that true north lies in the middle of a triangle formed by the constellations Ursae Major and Minoris and Draconis. Of these preliminaries, Sir Clements Markham (when President of The Royal Geographical Society) wrote: "Probably there was no other man, in the days of Alexander the Great, who could have prepared for a voyage of discovery by fixing the exact latitude of his point of departure and by selecting correctly the point in the heavens by which he should shape his course."

Under a leader so technically skilled, the expedition would have got off to an auspicious start. Nevertheless, Pytheas must have had qualms as, in the spring of 310 B.C., he stood his vessel north into unknown waters. For to the ancients a voyage beyond the Pillars of Hercules was as much a leap in the dark as a space flight is to us. For in those days the world *was* the Mediterranean; beyond its confines lay darkness and all the nameless terrors of the unknown, terrors magnified by geographers' ignorance and the horrific stories of Phoenician seamen. It is true that by the end of the fourth century B.C. a handful of traders voyaging down Africa had unrolled the map a few degrees to the south. But the north remained unknown: a wilderness of storm and mist and darkness: another world.

It was Pytheas who rolled back the map in the north, unveiling in one great voyage the coasts of Spain, France, Great Britain, Denmark and the Netherlands, and becoming the first man in recorded history to venture beyond the Arctic Circle.

Yet ironically, he voyaged so far and saw such strange phenomena that on his return his reports were not believed! In his lifetime, it is true, his reputation appears to have been held in esteem; but when he died lesser men with lesser gifts were quick to cast doubts on his veracity: "charlatan", "arch-falsifier", "weaver of fables" they came to call him, discrediting him because they failed to understand that truth can often be so much stranger than fiction.

If by reconstructing the evidence we can follow Pytheas's journey north, we shall then be able to decide for ourselves whether he was a charlatan or the first of a long line of explorers who have been disbelieved simply because they told the truth.

Our first fragment of evidence is Strabo's comment that it took Pytheas *"five days to sail from Gadeira to the Sacred Promontory"*. Now there are two interesting things about this. It disproves, I think, the theory — advanced, among others, by Paul Herrmann — that Pytheas initially travelled overland from Massalia to the west coast of France so as to avoid the Phoenician vessels blockading the Straits. Also, five days is a surprisingly long time for covering the distance between Gadeira (Cadiz) and the Sacred Promontory

(Cape Saint Vincent); for we should certainly expect Pytheas's vessel to average more than the knot and a quarter at which he could have traversed the 150 miles in question in five days. And I suggest the explanation of Pytheas's snail-like progress is that along the Gulf of Cadiz he kept close inshore and sailed only by night, thus avoiding the Phoenician warships on patrol in the Straits.

Having rounded Cape Saint Vincent he was in waters which had been traversed before by only a handful of traders. From this moment the peril of Phoenician warships would be superseded by the peril of the unknown.

Our next clue to his route is an aside by the Greek philosopher Diodorus, who tells us: "*Pytheas observed at this place that the longest day was exactly fifteen hours.*" Now the longest day is fifteen hours at latitude 40° 59′ N. That is to say, a shade north of the mouth of the Douro. And here is more evidence that Pytheas voyaged up the west coast of Spain, probably keeping close to land and using his oars to avoid being driven on to a lee shore.

Fig 9. Greek Bireme

This part of the voyage must have tested the seaworthiness of his ship. For the Beira littoral is a death-trap to sailing vessels, with choppy seas being knocked up by the continental shelf and heavy weather blowing continually in from the west against a rocky shore. Pytheas's ship must have been well-built to have survived (*vide* Figure 9). She was probably a typical Massalian trader, a bireme, about 150 feet in length, 25 feet in beam and 10 feet in draught; she would have had between fifty and sixty oarsmen and perhaps a third that number of seamen to work rudders and sails. She would have been fully-decked, swan-necked at stem and stern, and three-masted, with a large square sail on the mainmast and smaller lateen sails fore and aft. This increase in the number of masts and sails must have led to a corresponding increase in standing rigging; but although Pytheas's vessel could in theory have used her lateen sails to pay off or put up into wind, I doubt if in fact she was any more seaworthy or manoeuvrable than a sixth-century Phoenician. Complexity breeds flaws. All the same, she must have been both larger and better built than the cockleshell *Santa Maria* in which Columbus, eighteen hundred years later, sailed to the New World. And we can picture her that summer edging north up the treacherous Beira shore, inching her way cautiously into the unknown.

Our next clue to Pytheas's progress is the not very satisfactory remark by Strabo that *"the Massalian seemed to have acquired a practical knowledge of sailing conditions off the north coast of Spain"*. This remark is probably the origin of the oft-repeated statement that "Pytheas furnished information touching the best way of passing from Iberia to Gallia, and made valuable observations *en route* on the rivers and tides". All this indicates, I think, that he kept close-in-to and charted the Biscay shore. And he seems to have charted it well, being the first man to realize that the Breton promontory extended west into the Atlantic.

And this delineation of Brittany is an example of how Pytheas's reputation was to suffer at the hands of his critics. For Pytheas reported the promontory correctly, and for several years after his voyage it appears on every map of northern Europe. Then came the doubts and sneers of historians such as Polybius and Strabo; Pytheas's reputation was blackened; his reports were no longer believed; and Brittany was removed from the map. The same thing, incidentally, was to happen to Ireland, which Pytheas placed quite accurately to the west of England and Wales but which Strabo saw fit to shift to the north. All of which proves that it is safer to trust a practical seaman than an armchair critic!

We next hear of Pytheas off the Island of Uxisama, where, we are told, he observed that the longest day was exactly sixteen hours. The longest day has sixteen hours along the 49th parallel; and this enables us to identify Uxisama as Ushant, off the Peninsula of Brest. These are dangerous waters, and Pytheas must have made only a brief stay here before shaping course for Land's End. (Some historians have suggested that he first went to Kent, landed there, and then made the journey back to Land's End on foot. But this, I think, is unlikely. Why should Pytheas have left his ship and walked three hundred miles through unknown and virgin forest, when he could have sailed to his destination direct in a fiftieth of the time *via* an already established trade route?)

At Land's End Pytheas found himself in the last outpost of the known world; for never in history had a man from the Mediterranean penetrated farther north than this. He probably stayed here for several months, repaying and re-provisioning in the sheltered reaches of the Helford River and studying the intricacies of the tin trade; and he has left us an account of this trade which is interesting enough to make us lament all the more bitterly that his books are lost to us. *"The natives of Britain,"* he tells us, *"by their headland of Belerium (Land's End) are unusually hospitable, and thanks to their intercourse with foreign traders have grown gentle in manner. They extract the tin from its bed by a cunning process. The bed itself is of rock, but it contains earthy strata along which they cut a gallery. Then, having mined and smelted the tin and refined it, they hammer it into knucklebone shapes and cart it to the adjacent island of Ictis* (Saint Michael's Mount). *They wait until the tide-ebb has drained the intervening firth, and then transport whole loads of tin across the sand on wagons. Merchants then buy the metal, and ship it direct from Ictis to Gallia.*" This description has all the hallmarks of first-hand observation, and it surely disproves the theory that Pytheas's books were no more than a hotch-potch of tall stories retold at second hand.

It is when we leave Land's End that our difficulty in reconstructing his route begins.

Pytheas circumnavigated Great Britain: all but the most adamant sceptics allow him this. But did he go clock-wise or anti-clockwise? Did he venture inland? And where was the island of Thule which he describes as "*six days' sail to the north of Britannia*"?

The fact that he did indeed sail round the British Isles is established by a number of incontrovertible facts. First, he gives a very accurate description of the islands: "*Britannia is triangular in shape like Sicily, with three unequal sides, and extends obliquely along Europe. The promontory called Cantium* (Kent) *is eleven miles from the continent, at which point the sea forms a current; the promontory called Belerium is four days' sail from the mainland, and the third promontory, Orca, juts out into the open sea. The shortest of the sides is the one lying off Europe, which is reckoned at 7,500 stades; the second side from Cantium to the apex is 15,000 stades, and the longest one is 20,000 stades.*" All this is rather too precise to be based on hearsay. Admittedly, Pytheas's distances are overestimated—a failing which his detractors have seized on with relish. But the truth is, I think, that his method of measuring distance was by days' sailings, so that the figures given would include all the ins and outs of a coastline which his vessel doubtless followed closely; if this is accepted, the distances are not unreasonable.

More evidence is provided by the fact that he gives us observations which he took *en route*. "*Here the longest day is exactly nineteen hours,*" (which puts him in the Shetlands); "*here the longest day was eighteen hours,*" (which puts him off Tarbett Ness in Ross-shire); and "*here the longest day was exactly seventeen hours,*" (off Flamborough Head, Yorkshire). And the order in which these observations were taken, indicates that his voyage was probably clockwise.

But by far the strongest proof of a circumnavigation is the mass of factual data which Pytheas brought back about the country and its inhabitants. Some of this data is merely interesting: "*The people of Britannia are simple in their habits and far removed from the cunning and knavishness of modern man . . . Their island has many kings, who live for the most part in peace.*" Some of it has the obvious ring of first-hand observation: "*In consequence of the rain and the absence of sun, the natives do not use open threshing floors, but thresh their corn in large barns. They then store the ears of corn in underground pits, bringing out daily and preparing for food the ears which have been in longest . . . They do not drink wine, but a fermented liquor made from barley which they call curmi*"—the first reference in history to beer; and again, "*As one progresses north, the cultivated grains and fruits gradually disappear, likewise the domestic animals, until the inhabitants are reduced to living on millet and roots.*" From these descriptions I think we can safely assume that Pytheas spent a certain amount of time ashore.

ARAB DHOW IN ZANZIBAR HARBOUR

Vessels such as this were crossing the Indian Ocean 2,000 years ago at the time of Omar Hotel to the at the 2

SAILING CANOE OFF BORA BORA

But a few of the observations he made must have seemed so fantastic to his Mediterranean contemporaries that they were never taken seriously. For who in the calm and tideless Mediterranean could credit *"tide-ebbs of fifty feet"*, or *"waves and spume running eighty foot high"?* "Fo'c'sle yarns!" the stay-at-home historians cried; and their cry was repeated blindly for over two thousand years. Yet it is common knowledge to-day that the sea ebbs more than fifty feet in the Bristol Channel; and that when storm and tide are in opposition, waves ninety feet high surge through the Pentland Firth. And the point about these observations is surely this. Two thousand years ago no man from the Mediterranean could have conjured up such wonders out of his imagination, nor would a man who was a serious scholar have had the nerve to record them as fact unless he had actually seen them himself.

So we can picture Pytheas groping north up a progressively colder, bleaker and more sparsely populated littoral: wondering and recording as lands and seas undreamed of in the civilized south opened up before him. The soft mists and muted colours of the Hebrides, for example, must have seemed like another world to a crew accustomed to the vivid sunlight of the Mediterranean; but if they murmured against their leader, no hint of it has come down to us through the ages. And at last their vessel dropped anchor off Unst, the most northerly of the Shetlands, which Pytheas christened Orcas, a name later transferred to The Orcades or Orkney Islands.

And it was here that he first heard of Thule, an island six days' sail to the north: an island on the very edge of the world, surrounded by mist and a mysterious, breathing and half-frozen sea, the resting-place, he was told, of the sun.

This island, the *Ultima Thule* of the poets, has gripped man's imagination down through the years. Even to-day it survives as a figure of speech for something remote and mysterious on the frontier of the unknown.

Where was *Ultima Thule?*

Even the name is wrapped in mystery. Some scholars think it derives from the Arabic *Tule* (afar off), others from the Phoenician *Thyle* (a shadow or darkness), while others assert with equal eloquence that the word has a Celtic origin. As for *where* Thule is, some historians declare it a mere figment of Pytheas's imagination, others place it in the Orkneys or Shetlands, others identify it as Iceland, and others as part of Norway. Let us look at the evidence.

We can, I think, dismiss the idea that Pytheas invented Thule; for such a theory is contrary to all we know of him. We can dismiss, too, the suggestion that Thule was in the Orkneys or Shetlands. For all reports agree that Pytheas wrote, *"Thule is, by ship, six days' sail from Britannia, towards the north"*; and we know that he considered Orcas (the most northerly of the Shetlands) as part of Britannia.

Which leaves us with Iceland or Norway.

It is possible to make a perfectly convincing case for either. Prehistory is like that; the evidence is often so tenuous that a writer is able to select and interpret it so as to prove a preconceived theory. But if I were asked to make a choice I should cast my vote for Iceland.

If we look at the various references to the whereabouts of Thule that have been made down through the ages, we find that some of them could apply equally well to either Iceland *or* Norway. Under this heading are the following: —

> "*Pytheas says that Thule is, by ship, six days' sail from Britannia, towards the north.*" (Strabo)
>
> "*Pytheas of Massalia tells us that the island of Thule is six days' sail to the north of Britannia.*" (Pliny)
>
> "*In reference to Thule, it is said that here the entire circle described by the sun at the summer solstice is above the horizon.*" (Cleomedes)
>
> "*There are other islands around Britannia, of which Thule is the farthest north; on this island there is no night during the summer solstice, likewise during the winter solstice no day.*" (Solinus)

The point is, of course, that neither Iceland nor Norway is exactly north of the British Isles — the one is north-west, the other north-east — and both are roughly six days' sail away; so Strabo's and Pliny's statements are equally applicable to either. Also, there is no darkness at the summer solstice both off the north coast of Iceland, and also where the Arctic Circle crosses Norway. Nor do the references to Thule being an island rule out Norway, since the latter was not known to be joined to Europe until long after the birth of Christ. These references are therefore inconclusive.

There are, however, other references which seem to point to Thule being in Norway.

> "*For lack of the crops and cattle which exist in more genial lands, the inhabitants of Thule subsist on wild berries and millet.*" (Pliny)
>
> "*From the plentiful honey of their bees, the inhabitants of Thule prepare a drink known as mead.*" (Geminus)

The operative words here are "inhabitants", "millet" and "bees"; and the champions of a Norwegian Thule point out that Iceland was uninhabited in the Dark Ages, that millet cannot be grown there, and that bees are never found as far north as this. These are cogent points; but it does seem to me that they are not altogether conclusive. On the question of whether Iceland would have been inhabited when Pytheas went there, it is wisest not to be over-dogmatic. For both Iceland and Greenland have been inhabited for quite long periods in history and have then relapsed into vacuity — for reasons both climatic and economic — and it is not at all unlikely that the island was sparsely peopled in 313 B.C. and empty again by the time it was rediscovered by Irish monks some five hundred years later. The millet can be explained if we remember that Pliny was writing long after Pytheas's voyage took place, and that the different species of north-growing crops must have been hard for a Mediterranean historian to identify; it is therefore not impossible that Pytheas reported some such crop as oats, and that this became metamorphosized over the years into millet, a crop more familiar to Mediterranean readers. The bees are inexplicable. But if they rule out Iceland, they also rule out Norway. For from all accounts Thule was close to the Arctic Circle, and even in the most sheltered of Norwegian fjords bees are not found in large numbers at this latitude. We must therefore assume either that temperatures on the Atlantic seaboard were higher in those days (which is not impossible) or that the mead and honey were incorporated into Pytheas's travels by later writers. In other words, there is no watertight proof that Thule must have been Norway.

Finally, we come to the references which seem to indicate that Thule was Iceland. By far the most weighty of these are the ones which refer to the frozen ocean and to Pytheas's much-ridiculed sea-lung. They are as follows:

"A little beyond Thule we meet the sluggish and congealed sea." (Solinus)

"After one day's sail from Thule we come to the frozen sea." (Pliny)

"Pytheas tells us that Thule is one day's sail from the congealed sea. In these regions he says there is no longer any distinction between land and sea and air, but a mixture of the three like a sea-lung* which binds all together and can be traversed neither on foot nor by boat; and this Pytheas saw with his own eyes — or so he would have us believe!" (Strabo)

Now Strabo clearly did not believe a word that Pytheas wrote. He poured scorn on the Massalian's "sea-lung". And for two thousand years other writers have followed suit. But early this century, explorers who knew the Arctic began to have second thoughts. Of these explorers, Fridtjof Nansen was the best informed and the most eloquent; and this is what he says. "What Pytheas saw may well have been the sludge which is formed along the edge of drift ice when the latter has been ground to pulp by the waves. The expression 'can be traversed neither on foot nor by boat' is exactly applicable to this sludge. And if we add that thick fog is often found near drift ice, then Pytheas's comment that the air is also involved in the mixture and that land and sea and air are merged into one, appears not absurd but very graphic indeed." And the point is this. Pytheas was far more likely to have encountered sludge off Iceland rather than Norway. If we assume that he made his voyage to Thule in the summer — which is surely a common-sense premise — then he would have run into sludge within a hundred miles of the Icelandic shore (i.e., within "a day's sail"). But off the Norwegian shore, because of the warming action of the Gulf Stream, there is no sludge within eight hundred miles of the Arctic Circle (*vide* map on page 52). And it is, to say the least, highly unlikely that Pytheas voyaged eight hundred miles into the frozen sea lanes beyond North Cape.

So Thule was almost certainly Iceland. And Pytheas the prototype of a long line of Arctic explorers: the first civilized man to savour the beauty of the iceblink, to nose his vessel into the breathing "sea-lung" of floes, and to gaze in wonder at the sun at midnight floating on a horizon of ice.

---

* An alternative translation of Strabo's text substitutes "jelly fish" for "sea-lung". If this is accepted, the passage in question becomes even easier to explain. For when young ice is formed at sea it first appears as a scum of white crystals; these float to the surface, where they are broken up by the waves into small circular pieces about six inches across; these pieces are semi-flexible and semi-transparent, i.e., are exactly like jelly-fish. And they, too, can be traversed neither on foot nor by boat: *vide* Professor Debenham's experiences in the Antarctic: "I steamed through miles of this 'jelly-fish' ice, which gradually thickened and coalesced until we were held fast, unable to move by boat or on foot."

And this last part of his voyage, from the Shetlands to Thule, must be classed as one of the most daring exploits in the history of seafaring.

A thousand years later, the Irish and the Vikings were to push west across the Atlantic to Iceland, Greenland and the shores of the United States. These voyages have long been recognized as magnificent feats of seamanship; yet they were less remarkable than the voyage of Pytheas. For Pytheas not only preceded the Irish and the Vikings by nearly a thousand years, but as a Mediterranean astronomer born to the still waters and academic atmosphere of a Greek city state he had none of their inbred knowledge of northern waters. How he made the passage we can only guess; but he was probably guided to Thule by supernumeraries — Shetland fishermen who were experienced in Atlantic sailing and had visited the island before. Even so, his voyage must have been hazardous in the extreme. For Pytheas was striking deep into an unknown ocean, away from land. And on this count, his voyage has a special niche in history. Up to this time, most sailing

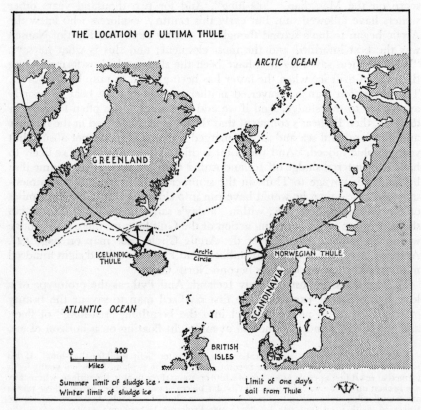

FIG 10.

had been coastal sailing; and on the few occasions when men had ventured away from land it had been either by accident or for some specific purpose of trade. To Pytheas goes the honour of being the first explorer to venture far into the open sea on a voyage of pure discovery.

More than two millennia later, Mallory was to try to climb Everest simply "Because it was there". This same spirit drove Pytheas over the wastes of the Atlantic on his voyage to *Ultima Thule*.

When he got there, he thought he had come to the edge of the world. And the reports he brought back, even though they were only half believed, were to influence geographers, scientists, cartographers and astronomers for over a thousand years. A quotation from Tacitus sums up the attitude of the ancient world to Pytheas's discoveries. *"It is said that beyond Thule lies another type of sea, a sluggish mass, almost motionless. By this sea is the terrestial disc enclosed and encircled—which is proved by the fact that the last gleam of the setting sun endures until the following morning with such brightness that it causes the stars to pale. Rumour has it (and rumour in this case speaks the truth) that the world reaches this far and no farther."*

How long Pytheas spent in Thule we cannot say. Nor can we trace his route back to Massalia with any certainty. We do, however, know that he sailed down the east coast of Great Britain, crossed over to the continent and explored the coastline of the Low Countries and Denmark. Here, he became the first man from the Mediterranean to make contact with the Teutons—"a tall blond people, dressed in the skins of animals". Here, too, he discovered the source of *elektron*, the warm sweet-smelling amber much prized by the ancients for the manufacture of *objets d'art*. This amber Pytheas saw, two thousand years ago, being washed up on the shore of the Heligoland Bight, very much as it is to-day.

Not until 304 B.C., after a voyage of over six years, did he slip back through the Straits and drop anchor in the Marseilles Roads.

He seems to have spent the rest of his life compiling his two great books and defending his discoveries against a rising tide of scepticism.

For Pytheas paid the penalty of being too far ahead of his times. His Mediterranean contemporaries were not foolish, but there were definite limits beyond which their imagination was unable to stretch. Frozen seas! A sun that never set! It was too much for civilized men to believe! So Pytheas's reputation was tarnished; he became the Münchhausen of the classical world: the butt of stay-at-home writers who poured scorn on his discoveries. It has taken more than two thousand years for his reputation to be vindicated.

For only quite recently has the truth begun to emerge: the surprising truth that the more we look into Pytheas's "tall stories", the more we find that he brought back nothing which was not accurate and scientific fact. His description of the Arctic sludge, for example, would be hard to improve on; his report on the Cornish tin industry was precise and detailed; while his contribution to cartography was fantastic: for he rolled back the map of Europe for over a thousand miles, unveiling in one great voyage the coastline between the Loire and the Arctic Circle.

If a list were made of the half-dozen explorers who have done most to unveil the mysteries of the physical world, then Pytheas—together with Magellan and Cook—would almost certainly be among them.

"OUR MERCHANTS CHASE THE SUNRISE DOWN
THE PATHS OF THE ERYTHRAEAN SEA"

(A first-century voyage from Rome to the Malabar Coast)

KIPLING may have believed that "East is East and West is West and never the twain shall meet", but his conception of a world so divided would have amazed the ancients. For in millennia gone by East and West used to meet, intermingle and trade on equal terms, their intercourse reaching its peak during the halcyon years of the *pax Romana*. And the trade which flourished most in these years was the trade between the Mediterranean and India. For India had everything that was clamoured for by the fashionable world of Rome—silks and muslins, pepper and frankincense, ivory tusks and tortoiseshell, pearls, sapphires, emeralds and beryls, and the bdellium costus and spikenard which made up the "fragrant ointments" beloved of a patrician society.

It is difficult for us to-day to credit the vast scale on which this trade was carried out. Accustomed as we are to regard the opening up of the world as a corollary to the Renaissance, we forget that most of the so-called "discoveries" of the fifteenth and sixteenth centuries were in fact *rediscoveries*: that the Phoenicians, for example, rounded Africa long before Dias, that the Irish and Vikings landed in America long before Columbus, and that the trade route to India was pioneered not by Vasco da Gama but by a multitude of unknown seamen in the first century A.D. For in those far-off days more than a hundred and twenty vessels a year were engaged in regular trade between the Mediterranean and the East, and these vessels included not only freighters and cargo ships but also passenger ships running to a fixed schedule.

The purpose of all this voyaging may have been trade rather than discovery. But discovery, in time, came about as a by-product. For inevitably the eastbound seamen included in their number an adventurous handful who longed to "go

> *Always a little farther: it may be*
> *Beyond that last blue mountain barred with snow,*
> *Across that angry or that glimmering sea."*

We do not know the names of these seamen, nor of their ships; their adventures have been recorded on neither stone nor papyrus; but we can judge the magnitude of their voyages by the customs records, cargo inventories and sailing manuals which have come down to us through the ages. And the most informative of these is a unique document known as *The Periplus of the Erythraean Sea*.

This *Periplus* is a concise and detailed pilots' guide to the inshore waters of the Indian Ocean. Written about A.D. 60 by the merchants of Berenice, it has the great virtues of being based on personal knowledge and of being devoid of literary pretensions. It is, in short, a simple mariners' aid, written by seamen for seamen; and as such it gives a mass of practical information about the location, harbour facilities, weather, inhabitants, exports and imports of the various trading ports between the Red Sea and the Bay of Bengal.

By following this *Periplus* step by step it is possible for us to reconstruct a typical first-century voyage from Rome to the Ganges.

Such a voyage may not rank, by itself, as an epic of exploration. But the cumulative effect of thousands of such voyages was that during the first and second centuries A.D. the confines of the known world were pushed steadily east, and the splendours of Persia, Pakistan, India, Burma and Malaysia were successively made known to the West, until at last even the distant land of Thinae (China) was drawn into contact with the civilizations of the Tiber and the Piraeus. This flowering of intercourse was too precocious to last. With the almost simultaneous crumbling of the Roman Empire and the great Han Dynasty of China, the ebb of commerce between East and West weakened in the fourth century and died in the fifth. Soon only the memory of it remained, a memory which lay quiescent until the days of the Renaissance. Yet while they lasted, these early voyages were both enriching and inspiriting; for they drew East and West together into a union which may have been tenuous and transitory, but which was, nevertheless, endowed with a refreshing innocence and a happy freedom from suspicion or fear.

* * *

The Mediterranean part of our voyage will be unremarkable, the sort of routine trade-run made by literally thousands of vessels during the *pax Romana*. We can picture our ship as a smallish all-purpose merchantman of some 400 tons; our crew as a cosmopolitan fraternity of Egyptians, Phoenicians, Arabs and Greeks—for the Romans were no lovers of the sea and preferred not to soil their hands with the bustle and sweat of trade; and our route as direct from the Tiber to Alexandria, a port about to emerge as the hub of the commercial world.

At Alexandria passengers for the east disembark and travel up-Nile to Coptos (the modern Koft), and thence across the desert to the great emporium of Myos Hormos on the shore of the Red Sea. Of this route Strabo tells us: "*In the old days merchants used to travel between Coptos and Myos Hormos by camel, usually at night, plotting their course by the stars and carrying with them supplies of water as do vessels at sea. But of late, road and water have been provided—the latter being drawn up from wells of a great depth and pumped into wayside reservoirs—so that travellers can now reach Myos Hormus in four easy days from the Nile.*"

Not a trace can be seen to-day of this great emporium, once one of the principal ports of the Red Sea. Even its location is a matter of dispute, some scholars placing it on the Gulf of Aqaba and others on the Gulf of Suez—the latter site being, I think, the more probable. In any event, it is here that we board the merchantman which is to carry us deep into the sunrise waters of the Erythraean Sea.

What do we know of this vessel, which, in the dawn of history, was about

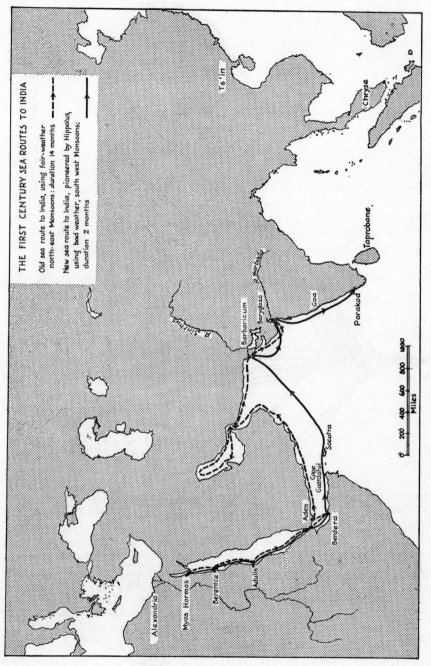

THE FIRST CENTURY SEA ROUTES TO INDIA

Old sea route to India, using fair-weather
north-east Monsoons; duration 14 months - - - - →

New sea route to India, pioneered by Hippalus,
using bad weather, south west Monsoons;
duration 2 months ───────→

Ts'in

Chryse

Taprobane

Barbaricum

R. Indus

Barygaza

R. Narbada

Goa

Porakad

R. Sinthus

Aden

Cape
Guardafui

Socotra

Berdera

Alexandria

Myos Hormos

Berenice

Adulis

0   200 400 600 800 1000
Miles

FIG 11.

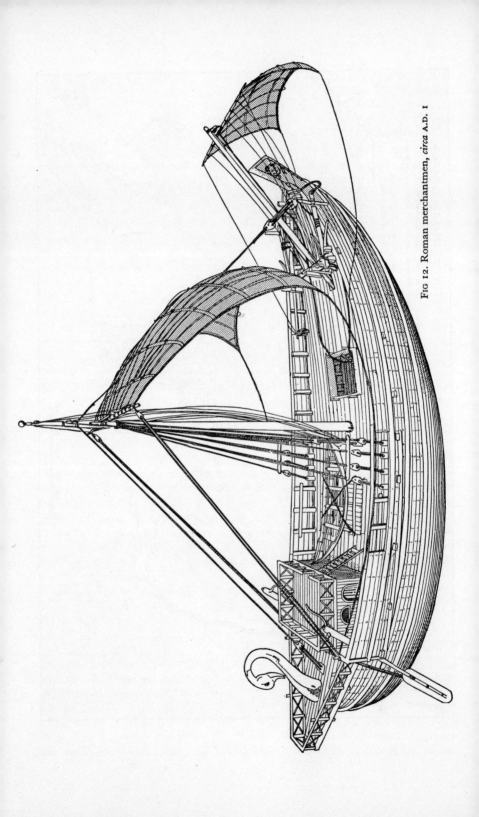

FIG 12. Roman merchantmen, *circa* A.D. I

to embark on so hazardous a voyage? We know she was large, because contemporary cargo inventories prove that she carried a substantial cargo. We know she was seaworthy, because there is evidence that she regularly crossed the Indian Ocean during the south-west monsoons—a season of violent storms and heavy seas. We know she was square-rigged, because this is the type of sail depicted on contemporary coins, bas-reliefs and vases. And in view of the route she traded over, I think it is safe to assume that her design was hybrid, incorporating the better features of both East and West. Thus she was built of Indian teak, which is extremely durable and which when seasoned does not split, crack, shrink or in any way alter its shape; but she was nailed with nails of Egyptian iron, which were far stronger than the Eastern stitches of *ginbar*. She had the big square sail of the Mediterranean, giving stability in bad weather and good speeds with a following wind; but she also had the Arabian sprit or storm sail, giving her added manoeuvrability in winds that were contrary or light. If asked to hazard a guess at her vital statistics, I would put her displacement at 750 tons, her length at 140 feet, her beam at 35 feet, her draught at 12 feet and her sail-area at something over 400 square yards. In other words, the vessel in which we leave Myos Hormus (*vide* Figure 12) is no mere coaster, but a fine ocean-going ship, double the size and six times the weight of the cockleshell *Santa Maria*.

The season, the *Periplus* tells us, is late summer, and our first port of call will be Berenice, about 300 miles from Myos Hormus, on the western shore of the Red Sea.

Berenice is silted up to-day; but here in the Bay of Umm-el-Ketef we can still see the ruins of this once flourishing port, the outline of streets, temples, warehouses and quays bearing silent witness to the busy days of the past. After Berenice we "stand south down the coast of the Fish-Eaters, who live in scattered caves among the wadis"; then on to Ptolemais of the Hunts, a port on the border of Eritrea and the Sudan. Here, the *Periplus* tells us, the natives put out in small boats selling "true land-tortoise shell and a little ivory". But I doubt if a merchantman bound for India would do much trading so close to home. Indeed, I suspect that the calls at Berenice, Ptolemais and the next mentioned port of Adulis (Massawa) were made only to top up with water and provisions and to land the occasional passenger. Not until our vessel has passed the "gate of tears" and debouched into the Gulf of Aden will the bales of cloth and the barrels of wine be hauled up from her hold and exchanged for the fabulous spices and jewels of the East.

It will be early August as our vessel moves slowly down the Somali shore, trading, while she waits for favourable weather to stand east into the Indian Ocean.

The *Periplus* gives us a vivid description of these Somaliland harbours and their imports and exports ... "*We come next to the market-town of Malao* (the modern Berbera), *where the anchorage is no more than an open roadstead, sheltered by a sandspit running out from the east. The natives here are peaceable. Imported into this place are undressed cloth from Egypt, iron, a little coin, wine from Italy, olive oil and a quantity of tunics and cloaks both dressed and dyed. Exported are myrrh, a little frankincense, the harder type of cinnamon, Indian copal and slaves. Two or three days' sail beyond Malao is the market-town of Mundus (Bandan Hais), where ships can lie at anchor more safely behind a projecting island close inshore. The traders living here tend to be quarrelsome. Beyond Mundus, another two-or-three days' sail to the east, is Mosyllum (Ras Hantara) situated on a beach with a poor anchorage. From here vast quantities of cinnamon are shipped, together with fragrant gums, spices, and a small amount of tortoise-shell, ivory and myrrh."*

These are valuable commodities. But our merchantman, mindful of the even-more-fabulous treasures to be found in India, would trade only sparingly, skimming the cream and ignoring the dross. And so we push slowly east, past the Little Nile River with its groves of laurel and frankincense, past the red-brown cliffs of Cape Elephant, until we come at last to the Cape of Spices (Cape Guardafui), the horn of Africa, a headland perpetually scoured by tide rips and a-dance in heat haze.

Cape Guardafui is the hub from which three classic trade routes radiate into the Erythraean Sea. South down the coast of Africa: north to the shores of the Aden and the Oman Protectorates and thence *via* the Persian Gulf to Pakistan: and eastwards across the open sea to India.

The first route is described somewhat sketchily in the *Periplus*, as though the authors regarded it as either too well known or insufficiently important to merit detailed attention. The voyage south, we are told, takes us parallel to a shore which consists first of *"barren bluffs"*, then of *"small and great beaches"*, and then of *"several rivers"*; it terminates at a cluster of offshore islands (Mafia, Pemba and Zanzibar) full of crocodiles and sewn boats, where the natives *"catch fish and tortoise in a peculiar way, using wicker baskets which they fasten across the channel-openings between the breakers"*. The exports are listed as *"cinnamon, ivory, slaves of the better sort, rhinoceros horn* (famous then, as now, as an aphrodisiac) *and tortoise-shell"*. The outward journey is helped by a favourable current and takes three-to-four weeks. And with a few such perfunctory comments the once fabulous route to the golden land of god is dismissed in a couple of pages.

The second route is followed in far greater detail, and with a wealth of information about the interim ports and their trade. We have vivid descriptions, for example, of the coast of Saudi Arabia —*"mountainous and forbidding, wrapped in pestilential clouds of fog, and yielding frankincense from its trees"*: of the Zenobian Islands —*"inhabited by Fish-Eaters, a villainous lot who wear girdles of palm leaves"*: and finally of the river Sinthus —*"greatest of all the rivers that flow into the Erythraean Sea, from whose mouth serpents come forth to meet incoming ships"*. According to the *Periplus* trade was brisk all along this route, a point which the table opposite substantiates.

The items listed here are luxuries, worth a fortune in any age. But for all its potential wealth this coastal route to India had one great disadvantage: it was, the *Periplus* tells us, *"slow and difficult on account of the unfavourable winds"*, and the voyage from Myos Hormus to Bombay took anything up to *"fourteen or even fifteen months"* —a very long time indeed even by the standards of first-century travel.

And it was because of this time factor that our third route from Cape Guardafui came to be pioneered: the direct route across the Indian Ocean.

Goods Exchanged on the Coastal Run to India

Imports	Exports
Wheat	Frankincense
Wine	Aloes
Cloth { Common clothing	Tortoiseshell
Figured linens	Cinnabar
Egyptian linen	Female slaves
Blankets and robes	Sandalwood
Copper	Ebony
Red Coral	Teak
Tin	Pearls
Amber	Gold
Brass	Dates
Gold coin	Rice
	Bdellium

Now so much nonsense has been written about the early voyages between Africa and India that it is difficult to-day to see the wood for the trees. We used to be told that "one Hippalus, a Greek navigator of the first century, was the man who discovered the secret of the monsoons (which is proved by the fact that the south-westerly monsoon is called Hippalus in his honour); and this same man was the first ever to make a direct crossing of the Indian Ocean using the winds that bear his name". This sounds far more convincing than it really is. For common sense ought to tell us that Hippalus could not have *discovered* the secret of the monsoons—the Arabs in their dhows had been sailing the Indian Ocean before him for over two thousand years, in every one of which the monsoons had blown with clockwork regularity! So our original quotation should at least be altered to "Hippalus was first *to make use of* the south-westerly monsoons". But this theory, too, has recently come under critical fire. For practical seamen like Alan Villiers have pointed out that "the south-westerly monsoon is a season of bad weather, and when it has set in conditions are unfit for primitive craft to sail in . . . One gets tired (writes Villiers) of reading that the Arabs sailed one way across the Indian Ocean with the south-west monsoon and then sailed back again with the north-east; for the truth was, and still is, that the north-east monsoon is the sailing season, and that their ships use it to sail *both* ways. I ought to know, for I've spent a year sailing with them". Yet the *Periplus* and other contemporary documents state quite categorically that in the first century A.D. merchants used to sail from Africa to India in August: i.e., at the very height of the south-westerlies. We seem to have reached an *impasse*. But the solution in fact is simple. The Arabs, in their lateen-rigged dhows, crossed the Indian Ocean during the north-east monsoon; the Graeco-Romans, in their heavier square-rigged cogs, crossed it during the south-west. An elementary knowledge of sailing rigs and local weather conditions will explain why. The south-west monsoon (which blows from June to October) is indeed a season of violent storms, heavy rain and high seas; and in these conditions the Arabs in their fragile hand-sewn dhows seek shelter, putting to sea only during the balmier north-easterlies (which blow from November to April). And because the Arabs only put to sea when the winds were north-easterly, they were obliged to evolve a rig capable of making headway both with the wind and against it: hence their lateen sail, which may look cumbersome to western eyes, but which in fact gives their dhows—to quote Alan Villiers—"the characteristics of a modern yacht and enables them to sail right round the compass". In other words, in the first century A.D. Arab dhows could ply quite happily both ways across the Indian Ocean during six months of the year. But as soon as the square-rigged vessels of the West appeared in the Indian Ocean they were in trouble; for they could sail only *with* the wind. Imagine then the predicament of a Graeco-Roman merchantman nosing out from the shelter of Cape Guardafui *en route* for India. If the season was November to April she would be met by the north-easterly monsoons: i.e., headwinds, against which she could make no progress. If the season was June to October she would be swept away by the violent south-westerly monsoons and driven on to a lee shore. No wonder, then, the coastal route to India was described as "difficult" and took anything up to fifteen months. No wonder too that the merchants of the west searched anxiously for a route both shorter and safer.

And the man who found such a route was Hippalus.

His "discovery" is related succinctly enough in the *Periplus*. "*Now this voyage from Aden to the Indus used to be made in small vessels sailing close inshore. Then the pilot Hippalus, by observing the location of the ports and the conditions of wind and sea, discovered how to lay his course direct across the ocean. And from his day on, vessels bound for India have kept not to the shore, but at the time of the south-westerly monsoon have headed boldly out to sea, throwing the ship's head considerably to the south. And so the south-westerly monsoon came to be known as Hippalus, after the name of him who first made the direct passage across.*"

It sounds simple to-day. With our knowledge of the monsoons and the shores of the Indian Ocean it *is* simple. But it must have taken courage two thousand years ago to strike out into the open sea, in the season of storms, continually hauling the vessel's head away from land and into the unknown waters of the south.

And the point about Hippalus's discovery is this. It cut the sea voyage to India from four hundred days to forty.

The stimulus this gave to trade was fantastic. For in those days as in our own, time was money and insurance was heavy. Roman merchants who had hesitated to send their vessels on a three years' voyage down a hazardous shore, looked far more favourably on a voyage of three to four months over open sea. Within a generation of Hippalus's discovery, the number of vessels trading between east and west had doubled; within a lifetime it had increased ten-fold; and by the time of the *Periplus* over a hundred and twenty vessels a year were trading direct between Cape Guardafui and the ports of the Kutch and Deccan.

And this direct sea route is the one which our merchantman is about to follow.

On leaving Cape Guardafui sometime towards the end of August we do not immediately haul away to the south, but head first for the island of

Socotra, a hundred and fifty miles offshore. Here is what the *Periplus* tells us of this last outpost of the western world. "*Well out to sea is an island called Dioscorida which is large, but consists mainly of desert and marsh; it has rivers in it and crocodiles, and many snakes and giant lizards, of which the flesh is eaten and the fat melted and used instead of butter. The few inhabitants live on the north coast—they are mostly Arabs, Indians or Greeks who have come to the island to trade. Here are found both sea tortoise and land tortoise, also white and mountain tortoise, the latter being preferred because of their enormous and very hard shells. Also produced on the island is cinnabar, which is collected in drops from the trees.*" The giant lizards (*varanus niloticus* and *varanus salvator*) are there to-day, still being eaten and melted down by the natives—although, when they are cooking, most Europeans keep well clear of the stench. The land, sea and white tortoises are there too; but the mountain tortoise (*testudo grandidiari*) is extinct. Cinnabar, of course, is a red dye, and not to be confused with the eastern *kinnaberi* or dragon's blood which is mineral rather than vegetable; it is collected to-day much as it was two thousand years ago by the globules of dried juice simply being knocked off the tree and caught in a muslin bag.

On leaving Socotra we head into the open sea.

It is the season of storms. No matter how carefully our captain has picked his time, the winds are liable to strengthen any moment to a full gale and the thunderheads to coagulate. There is no land ahead for a thousand miles, no sextant or compass on the bridge, and no comforting chart in the wheelhouse. But among our crew are a number of Arab seamen, men whose forebears have been sailing the Indian Ocean for generations. And they know where we are. *How* they know they cannot begin to explain. "*Ana baref*" they will say if we ask them: "I just know." And dhow skippers to-day who still cross the Indian Ocean with neither compass, sextant nor radio, will give the same explanation of a skill that is old and instinctive as a bushman's knowledge of his desert's wells.

So our merchantman runs before the high seas, with a succession of helmsmen ahaul on a kicking tiller, forcing our bows continually to starboard, towards the unknown south. The sky is a sheet of leaden grey, darkening to black at night and in the occasional thunderstorms which come rolling up from astern: our speed is a good six or seven knots; and our course is a great southward-bulging arc across the wastes of the Erythraean Sea. A long, lonely voyage across 1,300 miles of open ocean; but for a sailing ship a far less hazardous voyage, in fact, than a coastal run down a lee shore. And in less than a month we shall be nearing the coast of India.

This, if the weather is bad, will be the trickiest part of the voyage; and very likely our merchantman will haul round into wind, waiting for a favourable opportunity before she heads in to make a landfall. On our decks specially trained archers will be keeping a sharp look-out for pirates—as notorious in the first century as the eighteenth; shore-sighting pigeons will be released at intervals and their course watched and followed; and the colour and composition of both sea and sea-bed will be carefully analysed. And if our navigation has been accurate, we shall soon be sighting the vast schools of "sea serpents" swimming out to meet us from the mouth of "the greatest of all the rivers that flows into the Erythraean Sea".

This is what the *Periplus* says of these serpents. *"From a marshy hinterland flows the Sinthus, greatest of all the rivers that flows into the Erythraean Sea, bringing down an enormous volume of water, so that a long way out, before reaching this country, the water of the ocean is fresh from it. And as a sign of approach, to those coming from the sea, there are serpents in great number coming forth from the depths to meet you . . ."* And this is no fo'c'sle yarn. For seamen to-day can judge their proximity to the Indus delta by the size and colour of the gold-green *graca* or water snakes which live in the sediment-mud washed out of the river's seven mouths.

We have now arrived in India after a voyage from Myos Hormus of little more than two months; and the *Periplus* gives us a vivid and accurate description of the coastline now opening up ahead.

"The Sinthus has seven mouths, very shallow and marshy, so that only the one in the middle is navigable. On this stands the market-town of Barbaricum, whence cargoes are ferried up-river to the capital. Imported are clothing of poor quality, figured linen, coral, frankincense, gold and silver plate and coin, and a little wine. Exported are costus, bdellium, lycium, turquoise, lapis lazuli, furs, silks and indigo", a two-way luxury trade of no mean value. The authors of the *Periplus* go on to mention the teredo worm and the mud flats which evidently, then as now, were the two features of the delta of most interest to mariners. For the teredo worm is more virulent off the Indus than anywhere else on earth, boring through half an inch of seasoned teak in under six weeks; while the delta mud-flats shift and accumulate at a startling rate—a silt island of over sixty square miles being formed one year and washed away the next.

On leaving the Indus we soon find ourselves off the Gulf of Baraca—the modern wilderness of Cutch—a vast saline plain which is to-day criss-crossed by caravan routes (the camels travelling by night to avoid the terrible heat, refraction and mirages), but which was shoal-water two thousand years ago, with a clear opening to the sea. It seems to have been a terrifying place: *"The water is shallow with shifting sandbanks occurring continually and a great way from the shore, so that often when land is not even in sight ships run aground and are wrecked. Those who approach the Gulf may avoid it if they put about and stand out to sea but those who are drawn inside are lost: for the waves are very high and violent, and the sea tumultuous and foul with eddies and whirlpools. The bottom is rocky, uneven and sharp so that anchors will not hold. And a sign to those approaching are the serpents, very large and black, in the sea."*

Giving the wilderness of Cutch a wide berth, our merchantman heads south into the Gulf of Cambay. We shall need skilful seamanship here to reach the emporium of Barygaza (the modern Broach) high up the gulf at the mouth of the Narbada River. But once there our rewards will be fabulous.

Here is what the *Periplus* says of the approaches to Broach—then one of the leading emporiums of the east. *"We come next to another gulf, exposed to the sea-waves, and running up to the north. Those sailing to Barygaza (Broach) pass across this gulf, leaving behind and to their left the island of Bacones, and thence sail straight to the river mouth. But the gulf is very narrow and hard to navigate. The passage to the left is better, since to the right is a shoal, long and narrow and full of rocks. And even if the gulf is passed safely, the mouth of the river is found only with difficulty because the*

JAN MAYEN ISLAND discovered by Irish monks in the seventh century

NOVAYA ZEMLYA where Barents' ship's company became the first crew to survive being frozen in by the Arctic winter

THE SOUTH-WEST COAST OF GREENLAND

shore is low and the passage full of shoals. Because of this natives are stationed at the entrance in large fishing boats, and they pilot strangers through to Barygaza, towing them to fixed stations, going up on the flood tide and lying through the ebb in basins. Now the whole of India has many rivers and a great ebb and flow of tides; but off Barygaza the tides are especially violent, so that the bottom is suddenly seen, and all in a moment parts of the dry land are sea, and the rivers (under the inrush of the flood tide) are pushed back and driven inwards against their natural current for many miles. For this reason the standing-in and putting-out of vessels is extremely dangerous to those who are inexperienced. For so great is the rush of waters at the incoming tide that anchors are not able to hold against it; large ships are caught, turned broadside on, driven on to the shoals and wrecked; smaller ships are overturned; and even those that have turned aside among the channels left by the receding waters, if not held on an even keel by props, the flood tide comes upon them suddenly and under the first head of the current they are filled with water and sink. For there is so much force in the rush of the sea, especially during the flood tide at night after a full or new moon, that if you begin the entrance at the moment when the waters are still, there is borne to you at the mouth of the river, a noise like the cries of an army heard from afar, and on an instant the sea itself comes rushing in over the shoals with a hoarse roar."

Now this is a vivid first-hand description of the tidal bore which twice a day still sweeps up the Cambayan Gulf. To seamen accustomed to the all but tideless shores of the Red Sea and the Mediterranean, this bore must indeed have been a frightening phenomenon. But not so frightening that its traits went unobserved; for the account in the *Periplus* ties up exactly with Findlay's modern and definitive *Directory for the Navigation of the Indian Ocean*. For now as then the best way of entering the Gulf of Cambay is by the left-hand passage after leaving Pimam (Bacones) Island astern and to port; now as then the natives pilot strangers up through the estuary "with coolness, courage and skill"; and now as then the tidal bore sweeps up-gulf "starting as a wave only three feet high, but terminating as a great comber of twelve feet, quite perpendicular, scouring away the sandbars as it races past them at a speed of some fifteen knots and breaking with a thunderous roar over anything that lies in its path".

So hazardous a passage would only be attempted if the rewards at the end of it were great. And great they certainly would be for those with the courage and skill to get through. For Barygaza in those days was the principal port of the Gujarat, the richest and most fertile district of India, ruled by the Saka princes who were famous for their wealth and their encouragement of trade. And here at Barygaza the riches of East and West changed hands, on how great a scale the table overleaf shows.

This list is, in fact, rather more intriguing than appears at first sight. For the long-pepper, spikenard, costus, bdellium and lycium are drugs and medicinal herbs which commanded, in those days, a fabulous price in the markets of the West; the costly silks almost certainly came from the distant mulberry trees of north-west China and are our first definite link with "the far-off land of Ts'in"; while the beautiful maidens for the harem are one of the first references in history to the white slave trade.

Our vessel stays some weeks in Broach, loading its cargo which would be

Imports to Barygaza	*Exports from Barygaza*
Fine Italian wine	Muslins
Arabian copper	Fine Indian cloth
Tin	Coarse mallow cloth
Coral	Agate
Topaz	Cornelian
Thin clothing of the finest weave	Spikenard
Bright coloured girdles	Costus
Glass	Bdellium
Antimony	Lycium
Gold and silver coin	Long pepper
Very costly vessels of gold and	Sesame oil
silver	Ivory
Singing boys	Rare skins
Beautiful maidens for the harem	Costly silks

worth by this time something over £1,000,000; then we head south down a *"coast comprising many deserts and mountains in which live all manner of wild beasts — leopards, tigers, elephants, enormous serpents, hyenas and baboons of many species"*. We probably put in at Suppara (the port of Bombay) and maybe Saigarh; but we give Goa a wide berth *"for the coast here"*, the *Periplus* tells us, *"is infested with pirates"*. And we come at last to Porakah, on the Colchin Backwaters, close to the southernmost tip of India.

Here an even more fabulous cargo awaits us; *"pepper, which is produced in the hinterland in great quantity; ivory; precious silks; spikenard and malabath-rum; tortoise-shell; and transparent stones of every kind—beryls, diamonds, pearls, rubies, sapphires, spinel, topaz, turquoise, garnet, jade, lapis lazuli and tourmaline"*. Here indeed are the riches of the Orient, in exchange for which our merchantman unloads cloth, wine, Red Sea coral and vast quantities of gold and silver coin. Times do not change. Fifteen hundred years later a prince of these same Colchin Backwaters gave Vasco da Gama a letter to be handed to the king of Portugal: "In my kingdom" the prince wrote, "is an abundance of cinnamon, pepper and precious stones. What I ask from thy country in return is coral, cloth and gold and silver coin."

Most of the goods exported from Porakad were local products—the pepper (*piper sigrum*) growing wild in the forests of Travancore and Malabar; the pearls being prised, then as now, from fisheries in the Straits of Manar; and the jewels coming from *"the fabulous island of Taprobane"* (Ceylon). But two articles, the *Periplus* tells us, were imported from abroad: *"tortoise-shell from Chryse"* and *"fine silks from the distant land of Ts'in"*. And we have here the hint of a trade route reaching far beyond the confines of the Indian Ocean. For Chryse was the *Aurea Chersonesus*: Malaysia: known as "the golden" on account of the auriferous mines east of Penang. While Ts'in, of course, was the powerful state in north-west China whose capital Hienyang on the river Wei dominated the outlets to the Yellow Sea for nearly a thousand years. And it was the princes of Ts'in who built the great wall and who monopolised the export of silk, an export which reached its heyday in the first three centuries A.D. And there is conclusive evidence that a great deal of Chinese silk reached India not by land but by sea: *via* the Bay of Bengal, the Sunda Straits and the South and East China Seas.

Our particular merchantman, however, will not venture so far to the east. For at the time of which we are writing Graeco-Roman vessels seldom sailed beyond Porakad, and never beyond the Ganges. Indeed, the detailed portion of the *Periplus* ends with a vignette of Porakad, and the coast of Eastern India is described only briefly and obviously at second hand. We are therefore given no more than a hint of the marvels of the Bay of Bengal: of *"the mighty and holy Ganges"*, of *"the people with flat faces who live under the Lesser Bear"*, and of *"the great cities from which is exported raw silk, silk yarn and silken cloth"*. These marvels, however, were drawn into closer contact with the West during the second century. For in about A.D. 120 a merchant named Alexander did for the Bay of Bengal what Hippalus had done for the Arabian Sea —he pioneered a route directly across it, from Ceylon to Malaysia—so that before long Roman merchants were visiting the Chinese trading ports not perhaps regularly but at least as often as two or three times a decade.

East and West had made contact.

And the contact was friendly. In all the accounts that have come down to us of first and second-century trade, there is hardly a hint of a hand raised in anger; and it is one of the tragedies of history that this early and friendly intercourse had to be broken off before there was time for it to develop into an abiding union. But the barbarian invasions, striking near-simultaneously at both East and West, brought trade to an end. The Roman and Chinese empires crumbled. The centuries of chaos which followed are known in both Europe and Asia as "The Dark Ages". And for the best part of a thousand years the flame of exploration burned low.

Yet in the countries of Europe a memory of the East survived: a memory kept alive by the occasional caravan of jewels and silks and spices which managed to struggle through to the Mediterranean. And it was this memory which later acted as a spur to the post-Renaissance voyages of the Spanish and Portuguese.

For this reason our Graeco-Roman merchantman is worthy of an honoured place in the story of exploration. For the first-century merchants who pioneered the sea route to India were the forerunners of the fifteenth-century explorers. Vasco da Gama is known and honoured to-day all over the world; he was indeed a great explorer; but we should never forget that he had a host of unknown precursors, men who pioneered a sea road to the Indies fourteen hundred years before he was born.

ODYSSEUS OF THE NORTH

(The semi-legendary voyages of Saint Brandan in search of America: circa A.D. 570)

THE Dark Ages were not a propitious time for exploration. For exploration flowers most freely when men have time to devote themselves peacefully to the pursuit of knowledge and trade; and in the Dark Ages these pursuits were seldom practicable, since the inhabitants of the civilized world, faced by wave after wave of barbarian invasion, had a full-time job simply to keep alive.

Yet there was one corner of Europe which managed to escape the centuries of chaos which followed the break-up of the Roman Empire—Ireland.

Here, "for several hundred years the torch of learning burned with a steadier flame than anywhere else on earth". Here, an inherited *Romanitas* became grafted on to a native culture recently revitalized by Christianity, so that from the sixth to the tenth century the arts flourished as nowhere else in Europe, erupting into a glorious flowering of metalwork, book-illumination and sculpture. And here, most important of all, man could live in peace, shielded from the wrath of the barbarians by distance and by the Arthurian counter-offensive which held up the hordes in England and Wales. Here, in other words, was the one European country where conditions were ripe for exploration.

But it was a peculiar type of exploration which took place from Dark Age Ireland. The Phoenicians and Carthaginians, a millennium earlier, had explored the world in search of trade—and they had discovered the Cape of Good Hope and the Azores. The Greeks, more recently, had explored it in search of knowledge—and they had discovered the Arctic. Now, about A.D. 500, the Irish began to push deep into the Atlantic in search of a retreat, an island sufficiently remote to remain for ever inviolate against the barbarian hordes which threatened to engulf the civilized world—and they discovered America.

Both motive and destination need to be proved to be believed.

The motive, at least, of the Irish voyages is not hard to establish. We can rule out trade, for there is no reference in contemporary literature to the crews ever having taken out or brought back cargo; also they sailed due west, into the open Atlantic, where there was, of course, no one for them to trade with. We can discount, too, the possibility that the Irish were motivated by the same pure thirst for knowledge as the Greeks; for Irish culture was essentially practical and parochial rather than theoretical and cosmopolitan; and again contemporary records contain no reference to any philosophical or

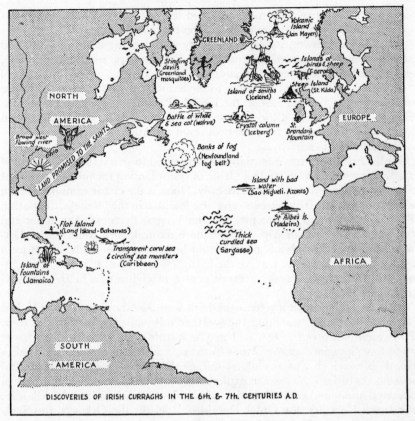

DISCOVERIES OF IRISH CURRAGHS IN THE 6th. & 7th. CENTURIES A.D.

FIG 13.

geographical theory which the voyagers might have been trying to prove. Economic necessity can also be ruled out. The Vikings may have been forced to leave their fjords because of Norway's scarcity of arable land; but Ireland has been described as "one big farm", and no one can seriously believe that the small number of sixth-century Erse were driven seaward by a shortage of either livestock or crops. In other words, none of the more usual reasons for exploration can be accepted in the case of the Irish, and in our search for a motive we are obliged to take a look at the voyagers themselves.

And as soon as we do this, one thing about them becomes immediately apparent: their aura of Christian sanctity. Their captains were always saints: Saint Ailbe, Saint Brandan and Saint Columba. Their crews were always monks: Brothers Chorra, Snodgus and MacRiagla. On their way, they invariably met a variety of religious phenomena. Their voyages often took the conventional forty days of the Bible, and they always seemed to end at the gates of either Paradise or Hell. Even allowing for the fact that the voyages were subsequently written up by churchmen, it is clear that a strong religious *motif* was inherent in their make-up. And the question at once arises: what were all these clergy doing in their voyages into the Atlantic?

The obvious answer, surely, is that they were looking for something; and here contemporary records give us a clue. For the voyage of Saint Brandan, and indeed almost every other voyage, starts off with a vision: a vision of "sailing west to the Land Promised to the Saints", of "discovering the Island of Promise", of "setting foot on the Earthly Paradise where dwelt Man Unfallen". So it seems as if the Irish were seeking a remote and undiscovered land somewhere deep in the sunset waters of the Atlantic.

It is not hard to see why.

Irish Christianity was essentially monastic and itinerant, being built up of small communities who made a virtue of transplanting themselves to distant places—the more distant, the more holy. (Iona is the classic example of such a community; but Irish retreats were also founded in the Orkneys, Shetlands, Faeroes and Iceland, not to mention the Vosges, Pyrenese, Apennines and the Swiss and Austrian Alps.) What more natural, then, than that a last-word-in-retreats, a holy-of-holies, should be sought deep in the Atlantic: a retreat remote enough to survive the barbarian holocaust that was, throughout the Dark Ages, ravaging every centre of civilization in the already-discovered world?

And for finding such a retreat the Irish were ideally placed. They looked out over the ocean, watching the weather roll endlessly in from the west. Fishermen blown out to sea, and maybe a little delirious with thirst, must often have imagined strange lands in the soft mists and sunset gulfs—hallucinations convincing as any desert mirage. We know that in the sixth and seventh centuries Irish seamen explored the archipelagoes north and west of Scotland and found skein after skein of islands scattered far into the Atlantic: the Inner Hebrides, the Outer Hebrides, Rockall; the Orkneys, the Shetlands, the Faeroes, Iceland. And beyond?

Beyond, they must have hoped, lay the land of their dreams: the land whose pastures green they always expected to sight beyond the crest of the next wave: the land in search of which, in the sixth and seventh centuries, their cockleshell curraghs made a series of voyages as spectacular as they are little known.

How far did they get?

I think to America.

But before we try to reconstruct the most famous of their voyages—that of Saint Brandan—we should assess the trustworthiness of our sources.

Our basic difficulty with the Irish voyages is that there are no first-hand reports by the seamen themselves; everything was written up later—sometimes as much as two or three centuries later—by churchmen. For this reason fact is constantly gilded with fancy. Indeed, our records of the earliest voyages from Ireland are pure *immarama*: that is to say, they are works of imagination, the counterpart of the science-fiction written late last century by Wells and Verne. But just as the works of Wells and Verne reflect the interests of their age and contain germs of both prophecy and truth, so the fifth century *immarama* indicate the interest Irishmen took in those days in the Atlantic—

an interest due in no small part to the development of the curragh, a primitive but magnificently seaworthy vessel constructed of skins. And gradually, as these curraghs pushed farther north-by-west, fact caught up with fiction. For we have definite proof (archaeological, literary and etymological) that by the end of the eighth century A.D. the Irish had established religious foundations as far afield as Iceland. Soon it becomes hard to disentangle legend from truth: to distinguish between *immarama* and authentic fact. And this is precisely our difficulty with the voyage of Saint Brandan.

We have a full account of Brandan's voyage (the *Navigatio Sancti Brendani*), written *circa* 870 by an anonymous and extremely gifted cleric. It was fashionable at one time to dismiss this *Navigatio* as a hotch-potch of tall stories—in fact as *immarama*. Then scholars began to notice that the *Navigatio* had an atmosphere of peculiar authenticity, that it hit off exactly the Atlantic's vastness and solitude, and, above all, that many of the saint's "tall stories" were in fact capable of a perfectly rational explanation. So the wheel turned suddenly full circle, and attempts were made to fit all the events of the *Navigatio* into a single voyage, carried out by the saint himself during seven consecutive years at sea. Now this *can* be done—just—by overlooking one or two awkward facts and by making him sail hither and thither non-stop over something like 100,000 miles of the open Atlantic! But common-sense boggles at such a prospect. It is one thing to believe that a cockleshell of hides might reach, say, Jan Mayen Island once in a hundred years; it is another thing altogether to credit that one such boat could voyage non-stop the length and breadth of the Atlantic, visiting in a single voyage Greenland, the Canaries, the Faeroes, the Bahamas, Tenerife and Chesapeake Bay—which are only some of the places mentioned in the *Navigatio*.

So we arrive at the conclusion that the *Navigatio Sancti Brendani* must in fact be a collection or miscellanea: that the voyages themselves are authentic, but that the thread linking them together is fictional and related to the one semi-legendary hero—Saint Brandan—for the sake of making a good story. (There *was* a real Saint Brandan. He lived in the sixth century A.D. We know that he founded monasteries in Galway, the Hebrides and Brittany, and he very likely visited the Orkneys and Shetlands as well. He *was*, in other words, famous for his voyaging; and doubtless in time he became a sort of father-figure to Irish seafaring: a hero like Odysseus, to whom other people's adventures came to be attributed.)

When, therefore, we come to reconstruct the *Navigatio*, we must not expect to follow one man on a single journey. We must not ask ourselves "Did Saint Brandan in such and such a year really set foot in America?"; but rather "Was America really discovered some time in the Dark Ages by an unknown Irish seaman?" The question is fascinating enough for us to feel we need not stretch the truth by trying too hard to particularize.

* * *

The *Navigatio* has been succinctly translated by Denis O'Donoghue. I have summarized the half-dozen most intriguing passages and offer an interpretation, based on common sense, research and a practical knowledge of most of the places concerned.

*1. *Précis of* Navigatio Sancti Brendani, *pp. 111–119.*

Saint Brandan is visited by the monk Barinthus who recounts his voyage to "the land promised to the saints". Brandan decides to make a similar voyage. He chooses fourteen men to accompany him; they establish a camp on the shore of the Dingle Peninsula, and set to work building a curragh. They use iron tools; but the curragh itself has only a wood and wickerwork frame, and is covered with "cow-hides tanned in oak-bark"; its seams are tarred. They put aboard provisions for forty days, including butter to grease the hides, and set sail in midsummer.

All this is quite straightforward. The monk Barinthus was probably a literary invention to get the story started—the equivalent of a Greek chorus. The most likely building-site would be where Brandan Creek runs down from the upper toe of Dingle Peninsula to join the Atlantic. There is a quay here to-day, and beside it black-framed curraghs with bottles of holy water dangling from their bows lie bottom-up on the sand, much as they lay there thirteen hundred years ago.

The curragh itself would have been about thirty feet long, with a single square-sail, unhampered by standing rigging. It would have had a bottom runner of timber (to prevent the hides being damaged when the boat was hauled ashore); its transoms would have been wickerwork, its skin three or four specially treated cow-hides, and its oars bladeless (to prevent shearing). Such a vessel may have looked pitiably small for venturing into the open Atlantic. But its frailty would have been more apparent than real. For curraghs are magnificent sea-boats: light enough to ride the waves like the

Fig 14. Irish Curragh

* The references are to Denis O'Donoghue's text in *Brendaniana*.

proverbial cork, able to sail a little to windward, and capable of lying hove-to in the teeth of even a violent gale without shipping a drop of water. Small, yes: primitive, certainly: cramped and uncomfortable, without a doubt. But the same could be said of *Kon-Tiki*, and it crossed an even wider ocean.

2. *Précis of* Navigatio Sancti Brendani, *pp. 120–132.*

Brandan sets course "straight into the Atlantic"; but after twelve days his curragh is becalmed and his crew lose their bearings. The calm is broken by a gale from the south-west; they run before the gale, and forty days after leaving the Dingle Peninsula sight "a steep rocky island, with rivers cascading down its vertical cliffs". They sail round the island, and after much difficulty disembark at the only possible place—a tiny cove in the south-east. Once ashore they find a dog and follow it to an empty house, where harness and utensils are neatly laid out; but of the occupants there is no sign. They stay here only a few days, then sail "for some time in divers directions" before sighting another island. This second island is inhabited by a vast number of sheep of the "most extraordinary size"; it also has streams which are full of brown and exceedingly tasty fish. Brandan christens it "The Island of Sheep", and his crew spend the winter here before passing in the spring to an adjacent island only a few miles to the west. This third island is grassy, is "full of purple flowers and is peopled by a great multitude of white birds", one of which talks to Brandan, advising him to return home.

Can we identify these three islands? I think we can.

If you sail a curragh west from Kerry for twelve days and are then blown north-east by a gale you will probably find yourself off the Outer Hebrides. And the outermost of the Outer Hebrides is Saint Kilda: an island surrounded by cliffs rising sheer from the sea, and with only one place where it is possible to land—a tiny cove on its south-east tip. After rain (and it rains most days in Saint Kilda!) the cliffs glisten with cascading water. And on the island there are ruins of monastic cells and a chapel dedicated to Saint Brandan. So I think we can safely deduce that their first port of call was Saint Kilda.

The Island of Sheep is equally easy to place. If you drift from Saint Kilda "for some time in divers directions", the odds are that the prevailing winds and currents will bring you to the Faeroes. Now the name Faeroes is derived from the Danish *Faar*, a sheep; and here from time immemorial these animals have flourished, growing to a phenomenal size on account of the peculiarly nutritive grass. Streymoy, the largest island of the group, also has streams which are full of brown trout. There is no need to search farther for their second port of call.

A few miles to the west of Streymoy is the island of Vagar. And Vagar is covered with heather and is famous as a bird sanctuary. It is the breeding and resting ground of over two hundred species, most numerous of which are skuas, kittiwakes and Arctic tern. These birds are white. They may not be able to talk, but they *could* have given Saint Brandan advice. For by watching their migratory pattern, he would have seen that Vagar was the northern terminus of a great many species. This would have led him to believe, quite correctly, that there was no land to the north for a considerable distance; hence the prudence of retracing his steps.

Now all this may not prove anything very spectacular—we already knew that the seventh-century Irish were able to sail their curraghs as far afield as the Hebrides and Faeroes. But it *does* give us confidence in the *Navigatio*, which opens not with the sort of woolly fancifying characteristic of the *immarama*, but with solid facts: and, what is more, the sort of facts that are clearly based on first-hand observation.

3. *Précis of* Navigatio Sancti Brendani, *pp. 133–143.*

For three months after leaving the Faeroes Saint Brandan's curragh "tosses to and fro on a southerly course", the crew seeing nothing but sea and sky. They fast on alternate days so as to eke out their provisions. At last they come to an island "with a balmy climate". They land, and are met by an ancient white-bearded man who leads them to a monastery: the man tells them that this is the island of Saint Ailbe (their first abbot), and that their community have lived here for eighty years. They spend Christmas on the island. On leaving "they drift for two or three weeks using neither oars nor sail", till they come to another island which is rocky and rich in vegetation. Here they find many springs. But the water turns out to be "unsafe"; and some of the crew who have drunk too deeply are taken ill. They leave the island quickly, and after three days come to an area of calms where the sea "resembles a thick curdled mass". They drift about help-lessly for twenty days, then work clear of the "mass" with their oars, and are able once again to hoist sail.

This passage, too, can be interpreted quite logically. The fact that the curragh tossed to and fro for three months—the lengthiest period ever mentioned in the *Navigatio*—presupposes a long-distance voyage with a destination far from the Faeroes. The fact that their course was southerly and the fact that the island they first came to had a "balmy climate", leads us to suppose that they ended up near the Tropic of Cancer: say in Madeira, the Canaries, the Azores, or even as far south as the Cape Verdes. Now Saint Ailbe's Island is hard to identify. But Madeira is an obvious possibility, for few places in the world have a balmier climate. And if we assume for the moment that the first island they sighted was indeed Madeira, then the rest of this part of the *Navigatio* makes sense. For Saint Brandan, you will re-member, spent Christmas in Saint Ailbe's monastery, then, in "two or three weeks", drifted to the island with bad water. Now, after Christmas, winds and currents would take two to three weeks to drift a curragh from Madeira to the Azores. And here, in fact, we find about the only island in the Atlantic which *has* springs with bad water: Sao Miguel.

Sao Miguel, the largest of the Azores, is a rocky, fertile and volcanic peak thrust up from the bed of the ocean. In its craters (especially those in the Furnas Valley) mineral waters gush out of a plethora of springs, some of them hot, some of them cold, and most of them tainted with sulphur and iron. Tourists to-day are expressly warned against drinking these waters; so small wonder that Brandan's crew were taken ill.

Further evidence that we are in the right locality is the reference to the area of calms where the sea resembles a "thick curdled mass". For here surely is the first description in history of the Sargasso Sea. (The Phoenicians almost certainly sighted the Sargasso; but they—characteristically—brought back no information about it, only a series of tall stories of octopus-arms writhing out of the waters to imprison vessels and drag them into the depths.) For the floating patches of Sargasso weed exactly resemble a thick curdled mass; also the Sargasso begins in the doldrums exactly three days' sail from the Azores, and the account of Brandan having to use his oars to clear the area is exactly what one would expect.

Here, then, is proof that Dark-Age curraghs from Ireland penetrated as far south-west as the Azores: nearly half way across the Atlantic. The vital question is—did they penetrate even farther? Our next extract from the *Navigatio* seems to indicate they did.

4. *Précis of* Navigatio Sancti Brendani, *pp. 151–157.*

One day they sight "an island afar off. This island was remarkably flat, almost level with the sea and without a tree or anything that waved in the wind; it was of wide extent and was covered with white and purple flowers, but had no rivers". (There follows a piece of *immarama*, about three choirs who greet the voyagers with hymns.) *On going ashore, the crew are given baskets containing enormous fruit which yield a pound of juice apiece. When it is time to leave this island, one of the monks elects to remain behind.*

Soon afterwards the curragh gets becalmed, and the crew notice that the water is "marvellous clear". Peering down, they can see the bottom, and watch the great fishes moving about like flocks of sheep. Saint Brandan sings Mass, and the fish rise up from the depths and circle the curragh.

After twelve days they sight a bird of magnificent plumage, bearing a bunch of huge red grapes, and four days later they come to a luxuriant well-watered island with trees growing remarkably close together. They explore the island, noticing the "wonderful fragrance of the air, like a house stored with pomegranates". They finally camp at a place where six great fountains well out of the ground, and the vegetation is prolific and brilliant in colour. They stay here for the conventional forty days before loading up with fruit and again putting to sea.

A flat island almost level with the sea: a largish island with no trees, no rivers and enormous juicy fruit. Search the eastern Atlantic with the proverbial tooth-comb, and you will never find it. For without exception the islands of the east Atlantic are volcanic in origin and therefore hilly, they rise steeply out of the sea, and all the larger ones have rivers and trees. We must therefore widen our search. We can, I feel sure, rule out the Arctic, for the whole of our passage has a tropical atmosphere. Which brings us to the south-west Atlantic, and hence to the Caribbean. And here one group of islands fits our description exactly: the Bahamas, and in particular Long Island, which is a coral formation and is therefore "flat and almost level with the sea", which is devoid of natural bush, and which has no rivers—the inhabitants drawing their water entirely from wells. And there is nowhere a larger or juicier fruit than a Bahaman melon. Now the parallels between Saint Brandan's description and Long Island are certainly striking. But so is the thought of a curragh sailing the five thousand miles from Dingle Bay to the Caribbean! And if our evidence rested on this passage alone, I should be inclined to dismiss it as coincidence.

But we also have the clear water and the fragrant island of fountains. The passage about the water is so intriguing that I quote it in full. *"As Saint Brandan was celebrating the festival of St. Peter, they noticed the sea was so clear that they could plainly see what was at the bottom. Thus they beheld beneath them the*

various monsters of the deep, and so transparent was the ocean that it seemed as if they could touch with their hands its greatest depths, and the fishes were visible in great shoals, like flocks of sheep in the pastures, swimming head to tail. The brethren entreated the saint to say Mass quietly, lest the monsters of the deep, hearing a strange voice, might be stirred up to attack them; but he said, 'I wonder at your folly. Why do you dread these monsters which the Lord has created? . . .' Then he began to sing the Mass in a loud voice, while the brethren were still gazing at the fishes; and these, when they heard the voice of the man of God, rose up from the depths and swam round the curragh in such numbers that the brethren could see nothing but the swimming fishes, which, however, came not close to the boat but circled it at some distance until the Mass was ended, when they swam away in divers directions. For eight days, even with a favourable wind and all sail, they were scarcely able to pass out of this pellucid sea."
This description of a sea of peculiar clarity does not fit any European waters. It is, however, an exact and exceedingly graphic description of a coral sea — for it is coral dust which makes water transparent. And the only extensive coral sea in the Atlantic is in the Caribbean. Further evidence that we are dealing with the West Indies is supplied by the surfacing and circling "monsters of the deep". These, clearly, are not the harmless dolphins and porpoise of the East Atlantic (for the crew were frightened of them), but the larger and fiercer barracuda, tuna, sailfish and swordfish of the West. There is, too, the point about the great extent of the pellucid sea; it could "hardly be crossed in eight days' sail, even with a favourable wind"; this puts its extent at over six hundred miles, far larger than any coral formation off Africa, but exactly the width of the coral reefs of the Caribbean.

Finally, we come to the fragrant island of fountains. And here we have the perfect description of Jamaica. The colourful birds, the prolific close-packed trees, the fragrant air, the brilliant colours, the intense green of the vegetation, and, above all, the fountains welling out of the earth; for the very name "Jamaica" stems from the Arawak *Xaymaca*—"a multitude of waters".

Taken singly, neither the flat island, the clear sea nor the land of fountains would be conclusive. But together, I feel they constitute a body of evidence which goes far to prove that some time in the Dark Ages Irish curraghs penetrated as far afield as the Caribbean.

And there is corroborative evidence of this which has nothing to do with the *Navigatio*.

In 1519 when Cortez began his conquest of Mexico he found that the Aztecs worshipped, among other deities, a light-God named Quetzalcoatl. Quetzalcoatl was white, bearded and born of a virgin; he was averse to human sacrifice and taught that men should live "in charity and in peace"; his robes were white and his symbol the cross. Long ago, according to Aztec legend, Quetzalcoatl had come from the east in a vessel with a great square sail; for centuries his teaching had prospered; but eventually his followers had taken to rafts and sailed west (i.e., across the Pacific), leaving a promise that one day his descendants would return.

Here, surely, is evidence of an early Christian contact with Central America; so it is, perhaps, significant that one of Saint Brandan's monks elected to stay behind in the Bahamas.

We come next to the more sensational parts of the *Navigatio*. These have often been scoffed at: but a close examination of them will, I feel, lead us to some surprising conclusions.

5. *Précis of* Navigatio Sancti Brendani, *pp. 147–149 and pp. 158–163.*

One day the voyagers sight an immense column in the sea, "great, bright and be-jewelled like a crystal temple". It takes them three days to come alongside it; then they ship oars, lower the mast, and slide under its silvery canopy to the base of the column itself. They take four days to explore this phenomenon, noting the coldness and the brilliant reflections in the sea, then they sail away to the north.

Soon they come to a high black mountain, wreathed in mist and rising sheer from the sea. A great column of smoke is pouring out of its summit. As they pull away from this terrifying sight, the mists roll back and they see the whole of the upper part of the mountain shooting great banners of flame into the sky.

Next, they arrive at a large barren island covered in slag and devoid of grass or trees. As they pull inshore they hear the hammering of giant smiths at work in subterranean forges. Suddenly one of the smiths comes striding down to the shore; he sees the curragh and flings a great mass of blazing slag at it. Saint Brandan makes the sign of the cross, and tells the brethren to "pull away manfully for we are now on the confines of hell". But soon all the smiths crowd on to the shore "bearing each of them a large mass of burning slag which they fling, every one in turn, after the servants of God; they then returned to their forges which they blew up into mighty flames so that the whole island became transformed into a globe of fire and the sea boiled up like a heated cauldron". The curragh flees; but long after the island is lost to sight the brethren notice a great grumbling and a "noisome stench".

They head west; but their troubles are far from over, for they are soon pursued by a ferocious whale. Saint Brandan prays; and another monster—"a huge be-whiskered sea-cat big as an ox"—rushes up and attacks the whale. There is a terrifying battle, during which the curragh nearly capsizes; but at last the whale is killed and its carcass drifts on to a nearby island. The monks land on this island, but are then detained there by storms and sleet for three months, during which time they are plagued by "stinging devils". They manage to keep alive by eating the whale and by grubbing for herbs and roots. Finally the weather clears and they stand away to the south.

These more spectacular parts of the *Navigatio* have long been the butt of historians. "Bejewelled temples!" they have cried. "Giant smiths tossing lumps of slag into a sea that boils!" "A bewhiskered sea-cat big as an ox!" What civilized man could be expected to believe such nonsense? And yet it is possible in each case to find a perfectly logical explanation of the passage concerned.

The bejewelled temple, of course, would be an iceberg: one of the magnificent edifices squeezed each spring off the Greenland glaciers. These bergs are often creations of great size and unbelievable beauty, well worthy of the poetic description of "temple"; while if one examines them closely their two most distinctive features are indeed their coldness and the beauty of their reflections.

The black island with its column of smoke would almost certainly have been Jan Mayen, which is in the right area (i.e., close to the iceberg zone), and which consists chiefly of the volcanic cone Beerenberg, rising in shale-black cliffs, 7,000 feet high, sheer from the sea. Beerenberg has been quiescent in modern times—except for a minor eruption in 1818—but geologists think that fifteen hundred years ago it was sporadically active. Mist is prevalent off Jan Mayen; and the flame-tipped volcano looming out of the murk on the confines of the known world would indeed have been a terrifying sight.

But it is the island of smiths which has provided most ammunition for the sceptics. This is certainly a purple passage, and on the face of it pretty far-fetched. I quote the *Navigatio* in full. *"One day they sighted an island which was rugged and rocky, was covered all over with slag, and had no trees or herbage but a multitude of smiths' forges. Saint Brandan said to the brethren: 'I have no wish to land on so desolate a shore, yet the wind is driving us straight towards it. O Lord, deliver us from this malign island.' But they continued to drift towards the land, until they could hear the rumble of the smiths' bellows and the beating of their giant hammers on the anvils and iron. As they approached the shallows, one of the smiths came out of his forge. He was all hairy and hideous, begrimed with fire and smoke. 'Woe! Woe! Woe!' he cried, on seeing the servants of Christ. Whereat Saint Brandan armed himself with the sign of the Cross, and cried: 'Put on more sail and ply your oars more briskly, that we may draw away from this place.' But the smith heard this saying, and came rushing down to the shore, bearing aloft a burning mass of slag, of great size and heat, which he flung at the servants of Christ; but it did them no harm (for they were protected by the sign of the Cross) but passed about a furlong ahead of them; and where it fell into the sea it fumed up like a heap of burning coal, making a great column of smoke. Then the rest of the smiths came crowding down to the shore, bearing each of them a great mass of burning slag which they flung, every one in turn, after the servants of God; then they returned to their forges which they blew up into mighty flames, so that the whole island seemed like a globe of fire, and the sea on every side boiled up and foamed like a heated cauldron. But Saint Brandan cried 'Soldiers of Christ, be strong in faith and put on the armour of the Spirit. We are now on the confines of hell. Watch, therefore, and act manfully'. And they drew away from the island. But even after a day's rowing, when it was no longer in sight, they could hear the grumbling of the inhabitants, and could smell from a great distance a noisome stench."*

Now this, surely, is the description of a volcanic eruption written up by someone who knew the classical myth of Etna and its Cyclopean forge. And it is worth bearing in mind here that the *Navigatio* was written by a ninth-century Irish clergyman, and that Irish clergy were at this time among the few people in Europe who had a working knowledge of the Greek classics. Once this interpretation is accepted, a number of details fall convincingly into place. The identification of the island, for instance. We know it must have been somewhere in the far north—because the description of it is sandwiched between the sighting of Jan Mayen and the "bejewelled temple" —and an obvious choice is Iceland. For the passage quoted is an exact description of the Icelandic coast south of Mount Hekla: an area of volcanic, slag-like rock devoid of vegetation. And Hekla, in the Dark Ages, was frequently and violently active—*vide* a contemporary chronicle: *"A fire broke out in Mount Hekla so powerful that the mountain was split asunder. Great boulders moved about in the fire like charcoal in a blacksmith's hearth, crashing together with a noise like thunder. While burning pumice stone, cast out in vast quantities, set fire to the roofs of the Naefurhold farms."* . . . And these slopes of Hekla, the chronicle adds, *"were regarded for centuries as the region of chaos surrounding the gates of hell".* So the beating of hammers in the *Navigatio* could have been the subterranean rumblings of a volcano about to erupt; the burning slag could have been the upflung lumps of pumice stone; the flames of the forges, the tongues of lava seeping out of the craters; and the "stench", the suffocating odour of sulphur which is the aftermath of every volcanic eruption. In other words, far from being a farrago of nonsense, the account of the island of smiths combines accurate on-the-spot observation with a nice knowledge of Greek mythology.

Finally, in this part of the *Navigatio*, there is the battle between the sea-monster and the whale, followed by a landing on the sleet-swept island of stinging devils and herbs. The monster is described as "a powerful animal with huge eyes, bristles, tusks like a boar's and a mouth bewhiskered as a leopard's: a veritable sea-cat, large as an ox". Now this is recognisably a walrus—walrus and whales do sometimes fight, and when they do it is usually the former who comes off best. As for the island, we have three clues to help us identify it. The sleet and the fact that it was storm-swept for three months indicate that it was well north in the depression belt; the "stinging devils" which plagued the crew *could* have been mosquitoes; while the fact that Brandan says they had to exist on roots and herbs points to the fact that the island was barren and uninhabited. And with these three factors in mind I think their only possible landing-place would have been in or around Sardlog, on one of the cluster of islands off south-west Greenland: a theory supported by the fact that this is an area famous for both walrus and whales.

So this part of the *Navigatio* adds up to the fact that some time in the seventh or eighth century Irish curraghs sighted icebergs, sailed past Jan Mayen Island, stood off the coast of Iceland and landed in south-west Greenland. In other words, the Irish pioneered most of the classic sea routes to America several centuries *before* the Vikings.

Can we go further and say that they pioneered it all: that they discovered not only the Bahamas and Greenland, but the American mainland as well? I think we can.

Saint Brandan's story opened, you may remember, with the Monk Barinthus recounting his voyage to "the land promised to the saints"; it ends with Brandan reaching this land, and thus coming at last to his longed-for goal after nearly a decade of perilous voyaging. Here is a summary of this last part of the *Navigatio*.

6. *Précis of* Navigatio Sancti Brendani, *pp. 173–178.*

After Pentecost, Brandan is told to fill his water-skins as full as possible and again head west. And this time, he is told, he will reach the land of his dreams.

For the conventional forty days his curragh stands into the open sea, till it comes to a thick cloud—"bank after bank of vapour pressed low against the water". Brandan stands boldly into this cloud; and at last, emerging from its darkness to the light beyond, he sights the Land of Promise. It is a warm and fruitful land, bathed in eternal autumn sunlight. The monks disembark and push inland for forty days, "viewing the countryside in various directions"; but they can discover no end to the mountains, forest and plain, and come to the conclusion that the land they have reached is "no island but might best be called a continent". Eventually they come to the banks of a great river flowing from east to west and too broad to cross. Here they are met by a celestial messenger, who tells Brandan that Christ has now disclosed to him all the mysteries of the Atlantic, and that the newly discovered Land of Saints will be revealed later to Brandan's successors and subsequently to all mankind. The monks then return to the coast, load up with provisions and set course for Ireland which they reach after an uneventful voyage.

The salient points here are the "bank after bank of vapour", the affirmation that they had discovered not a new island but a new continent, and the river that was too big to cross flowing from east to west.

"Banks of vapour" is a pretty fair description of the Newfoundland fog-belt, formed by the meeting of the Gulf Stream and the Labrador Drift; for here a kaleidoscopic blanket of mist is indeed "pressed low against the water"; and the description of the cloud drifting hither and thither in "bank after bank" rather than consisting of a uniform layer is peculiarly apt.

On landing the monks are said to have pushed inland, "viewing the country in various directions"—which suggests a reconnaissance through terrain both hilly and reasonably open. And the impression one gets from the *Navigatio* is of a fairly thorough exploration; so we must, I think, attach due weight to the opinion that they had discovered "no island . . . but . . . a continent". For nowhere else in the *Navigatio* is such a claim put forward. The Irish had previously sighted some pretty big islands—Iceland, for example, and Greenland—but never before had there been the slightest suggestion that these lands formed part of a new continent. When therefore the claim *is* made to have discovered a new continent it deserves, to say the least, to be taken seriously.

And this claim is strengthened by the great river which is described as being too broad to cross and flowing from east to west. For if you sail from Ireland and explore literally every island in the Atlantic you will not find such a river. It does not exist. The first uncrossable westward-flowing river west of the Irish Shannon is the American Ohio.

So we can visualize Saint Brandan's monks landing somewhere not too far from Chesapeake Bay, pushing inland, crossing the Appalachians and finding their way barred by the mighty branch of the Mississippi.

And this is neither a tall story nor a piece of *immarama*. For the evidence of the *Navigatio* is backed by other evidence which is too explicit to be ignored.

For the Vikings, writing of their eleventh-century exploration of North America, repeatedly state that when they got to the New World they found the Irish already there. There is, for example, the story of Ari Marson which is related independently by two of the most reputable Icelandic chroniclers. *"Greenland"*, one of them says, *"is known to be inhabited. Immediately next to it are deserts, uninhabited places and glaciers* (Baffin Island), *then Markland* (Nova Scotia), *then the Skraelings* (Indians), *then Vineland the Good* (Massachusetts) *and next Hvitramenaland or White Man's Land, which is sometimes called Great Ireland, because thither was sailing, in former times, from Ireland. And here was recognized Ari* (*son of Mar and Katla of Reykjanes*) *of whom nothing had been heard for a long time, but who had been baptized in Great Ireland by a priest and who had been made a chief there by the inhabitants.*" Which is a story that seems to me too explicit and detailed to be disregarded. There is also the evidence of the Viking explorer Karlsefni, who, early in the eleventh century, captured two young Red Indian boys who told him that "*in the country adjacent to theirs, there lived men who wore white garments and who carried in front of them poles festooned with rags and who chanted loudly, and whose country was known as Great Ireland*". Irish monks, of course, wore white gowns; and what better description could a native give of an ecclesiastical procession?

Norse literature is full of such stories. And their inference is plain. When the Vikings got to North America they found that the Irish had been there before them.

And why not? The evidence of these Irish voyages may be circumstantial but it is also cumulative. For the man who wrote the *Navigatio* must have got his facts from somewhere; he could hardly have conjured so many phenomena which in fact exist out of his imagination; and we must therefore assume that he collected together true stories of seafaring and wove them into a tapestry: a tapestry which for long proved too exotic for posterity to believe in, but which was made up, nevertheless, of the strands of truth.

And this Irish discovery of the New World is perhaps the classic example of truth being stranger than fiction. For seldom in the history of seafaring have such long and hazardous voyages been made in such frail and primitive craft.

VI

"BEYOND THE SUNSET AND THE BATHS OF
ALL THE WESTERN STARS"

(*The eleventh-century Vikings attempt to colonize the New World*)

THE ship edged cautiously through broken water towards a shore that was well timbered and fringed by white beaches. After a while she grounded among the plethora of sandbars; but her crew rowed ashore in their pinnace, and later, when the tide rose, managed to tow their vessel to safety. They were enchanted with the land they had come to. It seemed to them "*beautiful . . . the forest dropping down to the water's edge, the rivers full of salmon, and the grass green and well able to pasture cattle*". They decided to winter here, and after a brief reconnaissance set up camp close to a reed-fringed lake.

The year was A.D. 1003; the place Nantucket Sound, Massachusetts; and the ship a Viking *knorr*, commanded by Leif Eriksson, the man who deserves to go down in history as the first authenticated discoverer of the New World.

VIKING PENETRATION INTO THE NEW WORLD

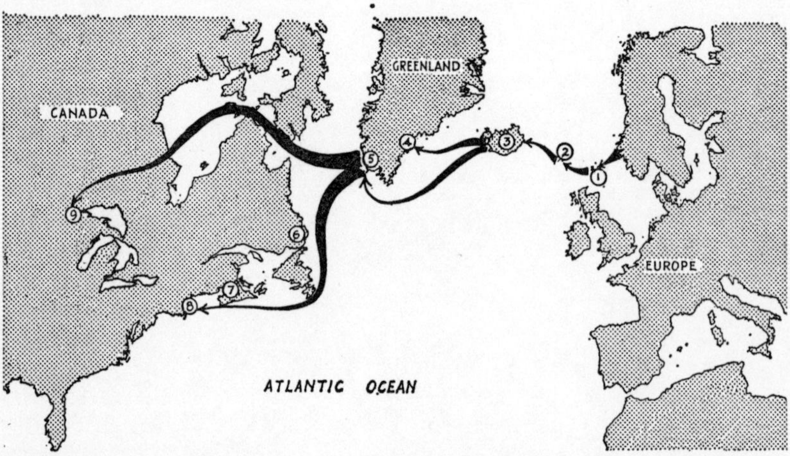

1 NORWAY to SHETLANDS : circa A.D. 650
2 SHETLANDS to FAEROES: circa A.D. 750
3 FAEROES to ICELAND: A.D. 863
4 ICELAND to EAST GREENLAND: A.D. 900
5 ICELAND to WEST GREENLAND: A.D. 985

6 WEST GREENLAND to HELLULAND (LABRADOR) A.D. 1003
7 WEST GREENLAND to MARKLAND (NOVA SCOTIA) : A.D. 1003
8 WEST GREENLAND to VINELAND (CAPE COD) A.D. 1003
9 NORWAY - GREENLAND to MINNESOTA: A.D. 1361/62

FIG 15.

These facts, I believe, should dispose, once and for all, of the myth that Columbus discovered America. For far from being, as was once believed, "the first European ever to set foot in the New World", Columbus was in fact preceded there by the Irish, the Norse and—as we shall see later— quite possibly by the Portuguese and the Danes. And it is high time this fact got into our history books.

A glance at the map of the Atlantic ought, long ago, to have disproved the Columbus myth. For the central and southern Atlantic, where Columbus made his crossing in 1492, is roughly 3,000 miles in width; in these latitudes the prevailing currents and winds are westerly, and there are virtually no islands at which a ship can call *en route*. It is a very different story in the far north. For here, on and around the Arctic Circle, the Atlantic is less than 2,000 miles in width, the prevailing winds and currents are easterly, and a wealth of islands are scattered so symmetrically across the ocean that a vessel can pass from Europe to America, island-hopping, without ever being more than 175 miles from land—Norway to the Shetlands (250 miles), the Shetlands to the Faeroes (300 miles), the Faeroes to Iceland (350 miles), Iceland to Greenland (300 miles), Greenland to Baffin Island (300 miles) and Baffin Island to Labrador (100 miles). Ancient ships which fought shy of a deep water voyage of two-to-three thousand miles with adverse winds, could take a voyage of two-to-three hundred miles with favourable winds in their stride. No wonder then that the Atlantic was first crossed by this northerly route: was crossed, island to island, by the Vikings nearly five hundred years before Columbus was born: and was crossed not merely once or twice, but on many occasions.

The evidence of this is both circumstantial and documentary.

It is well known that the Norsemen were great seafarers, voyaging as far afield as Sicily, the Black Sea and Novaya Zemlya. (This was a case of necessity. For then as now over ninety per cent of Norway was incapable of cultivation, and the sea was her people's natural outlet.) We know that between the seventh and tenth centuries vast bands of emigrating Norsemen crossed the Baltic and North Seas and founded kingdoms in Russia, France and the British Isles. We also know that they took gradual possession of the North Atlantic Islands: first of the Orkneys and Shetlands, then of the Hebrides and Faeroes, and finally, *circa* 863, of Iceland.

To start with, Iceland provided a reasonable home for the Norsemen. In the valleys pasture was good, and the rivers and inshore waters teemed with fish. So it is hardly surprising that a positive flood of immigrants was soon arriving from Norway. But after a while the flood got out of control. Within three generations of the Vikings' arrival, Iceland had become overcrowded, and a shortage of arable land was again forcing the Norsemen west. And once they had reached Iceland, the Norse were more than half way across the Atlantic, *and* had put behind them the longest and most dangerous island-to-island crossing. In other words, as soon as Iceland became overpopulated it was only a matter of time before first Greenland and then America was visited by the questing *knorrs*.

Greenland, in fact, had been sighted by a trader named Ulfsson Gunnbjorn early in the tenth century; but Gunnbjorn had reported only a series of ice-coated skerries, and since there was no land-hunger in Iceland at the time, his discovery was not followed up. Things were very different in 982 when Leif Eriksson's father, Erik the Red, left Iceland in search of new lands in which he could settle.

Erik the Red has been treated none too kindly by historians, many of whom have expressed pious horror at the fact that in his early years he was found guilty of homicide and was exiled. But in fact it would be hard to find a tenth-century Viking who was *not* technically guilty of homicide, and it strikes me as being Erik's misfortune rather than his crime that the men he killed happened to be the sons of an important chief. For this he was banished from Iceland for three years. Most men in Erik's position would have taken his ship and his followers east, back to Europe; but Erik chose to stand west, into un-known waters, searching for the lands first sighted by Gunnbjorn more than fifty years before. Like his predecessor he made an initial landfall among the ice-coated skerries off Eastern Greenland—one of the bleakest and most desolate shores in the world; but on pushing round Cape Farewell (Green-land's southernmost tip), he came to a more promising littoral, the deeply indented fjords of King Frederik VI Land. Nor did his discoveries end here. For in one of the most hazardous and remarkable voyages in history he pushed up the west coat of Greenland for nearly a thousand miles—an amazing feat in his tiny undecked vessel. After spending two winters ashore and one frozen-in in the ice, he returned to the fjords north-west of Cape Farewell and decided—quite rightly—that the coast here was suitable for a permanent settlement. In 985, his banishment over, he returned to Iceland where a land-hungry population received the news of his discoveries with enthusiasm. The following year he again set course for Greenland, this time taking with him no fewer than twenty-five ships and over one thousand five hundred would-be colonists. They settled in and around Eriksfjord (the modern Tunugdliarfik), and soon a prosperous and contented colony was established.

A great deal of nonsense, it seems to me, has been written about this Norse settlement of Greenland. Some historians, armed with hindsight, have pointed out that only a few centuries after the colonies were founded, the last of the Greenland Vikings perished miserably of malnutrition and exposure, and they have therefore condemned the settlement as "a venture foredoomed to failure . . . an ill-starred sortie into a blind alley". But this interpretation does not entirely fit the facts. For until the twelfth century, when a shift in the course of the Gulf Stream led to a sudden deterioration in northern climate, the Greenland colonies flourished—in their heyday the settlers numbered over 4,000, boasted a score of churches not to mention a cathedral, and exported walrus tusks, furs and white falcons to the tune of nearly £1,000,000 a year! Greenland also served as a vital stepping-stone on the route to America, and as the base from which America itself was first colonized.

The very year this Greenland colony was founded there took place an important milestone in Viking penetration into the New World: the first indisputable sighting, by Europeans, of the American mainland.

Here is what the sagas tell us of this dramatic event.

A young Norwegian named Bjarne Herjulfson was in the habit of spending every other winter with his family in Iceland; but in the autumn of 986, on sailing as usual from Norway to their home in Eyar, he found his parents had emigrated during the summer with Erik the Red. He decided to follow them to Greenland. He warned his crew that their voyage would be hazardous, "*seeing that none of us knows exactly where Greenland is*", but they agreed to follow him; and after getting all possible descriptions and sailing directions, Bjarne set sail. Soon after they left Iceland the fair winds died, and a violent storm swept down from the north. They ran before it for many days, till they came to an area of dense fog. Here they were becalmed for an unknown period, unable to see where they were going but drifting generally south by west. At last the fog cleared, they got their bearings, hoist sail and headed north. And that evening they sighted land. They discussed what land it could be, and Bjarne told them he doubted if it was Greenland. On standing inshore they saw that the coast was "*without mountains, well timbered and with little knolls on it*"; this confirmed their impression that it could not be the land they sought, and leaving it on their port quarter they ran before a light south-westerly breeze. Two days later they sighted more land: "*a flat country, covered with woods*". Bjarne said he did not think this was Greenland either, for Greenland, from all accounts, was a country of fjords and glaciers. After they had followed the land for some time, the crew suggested they put ashore for wood and water; but Bjarne told them "*you are in no want of either*", and ordered them to hoist sail. They held course for three more days before the same south-westerly breeze, then sighted a third land "*high and mountainous, with ice on it*". They followed this land for several days, Bjarne again refusing to land "*because the country seemed to him to be good for nothing*", and eventually they discovered it was an island. Once again they headed out to sea —much to the dissatisfaction of the crew. After a while the south-westerly breeze strengthened to a full gale before which they ran close-reefed for four days. They then sighted yet another land. "*Now this,*" Bjarne said, "*is most like what was told me of Greenland, and towards this land we will hold our course.*" So they stood inshore; and that evening they came to the mouth of Eriksfjord, where Bjarne's family had set up house.

This account, which is taken from the *Flateyiarbok*, "the most perfect and reliable of all Icelandic manuscripts", has been variously interpreted; the most persuasive and erudite interpretation, to my mind, being that of Hjalmar R. Holand who identifies Bjarne's first three landfalls as Cape Cod, Nova Scotia and Newfoundland; and bearing in mind their initial run to the south-west before the storm, and their drift in what was obviously the Newfoundland fog-belt, these three areas do indeed seem to be the only places which fit both Bjarne's descriptions and his sailing directions. But no matter how the details of this historic passage are explained, I think that the basic fact is beyond dispute. Bjarne sighted America, and took the news of his discovery to Greenland.

Scholars have often expressed surprise that as long as seventeen years elapsed between this first sighting of America (986) and the first landing there (1003). But this surprise is based, I think, on the fallacy that Greenland was a bleak, unpleasant place from which the Norsemen were anxious to escape. Quite a lot of evidence points to the contrary. To a people brought up among the infertile plateaux of Iceland, the shore of south-western Greenland must have seemed a veritable Eden. I quote Hjalmar R. Holand. "Here (around Eriksfjord) was pasture land in abundance covered with rich grass. Fuel was also present in the form of large tracts of birch and willow of which many trees had big trunks, although the trees themselves were seldom more than ten feet high. The rushing streams were filled with salmon, the waters of the fjords abound in cod, bass and other fish, seals, walruses and wild duck; while on land were reindeer, polar bears, rabbits, grouse and other game birds. To him (Erik) these verdant fields, seen against the background of the great glaciers, must have seemed far more green than the volcanic soil of Iceland." To supplement Holand's picture, the *Encylopaedia Britannica* tells us that "in south-west Greenland flowering plants like aster and mignonette do well; vegetables such as broccoli, spinach, turnips and lettuce flourish, while strawberries and cucumbers can be ripened under glass". In other words the Norsemen, at first, had plenty of reasons for being contented with life in Greenland, and there was little incentive for them to desert their new-found colony.

There were, however, two important commodities which they found after a while that Greenland could not provide: metal and good quality timber. And it was probably in the hope of finding these that in 1003 Leif Eriksson decided to investigate Bjarne's report of lands to the west. Which brings us to an important point. Leif's discovery of America was not an affair of chance; it was a planned event, prepared for and carried out with foresight and skill.

We know quite a lot about the man who made this historic voyage. Leif Eriksson is the first great explorer in history to step out of the past not as a semi-legendary shadow but as a man of flesh and blood. He was born in 980; which means that he must have accompanied his father on Erik's hazardous exploration of western Greenland. What an upbringing! In the first five years of his life Leif must have been aboard ship more often than ashore; he must have seen snow more often than grass; cold and blizzard, hunger, frostbite and mist were the syllabus on which he was reared; no wonder he is described by his contemporaries as "*a man of iron*". Yet there was far more to Leif than physical toughness. The sagas tell us he was "*intelligent, capable and most just in all his dealings*"; he possessed that elusive quality known as leadership—before his twentieth birthday he had already pioneered an important new sea-route, the direct crossing from Norway to Greenland. He was also a devout Christian, having been baptized in 1001 during a visit to King Olaf's court in Norway; and the following year he returned to Greenland and proceeded, with quite astonishing rapidity, to spread the Gospel throughout the newly-founded colony—helped no doubt by his father's influence and his own prowess with main-sail and broadsword. It was during his proselytizing that he first met Bjarne Herjulfson.

Leif Eriksson, like everyone else in Greenland, would have heard by 1002 of Bjarne and his discoveries; but I doubt if up to now the two men had met, for the Herjulfsons' farm was isolated and well over a hundred miles from the centre of the colony at Brattahlid where Leif lived with his father. But when they did eventually get together their meeting made history. For after he had heard the story of the sightings at first hand, Leif bought Bjarne's *knorr*, got together a crew of thirty-five (including several seamen who had made the earlier voyage) and set out to try to retrace Bjarne's route in reverse.

And he succeeded.

We know this because we have a detailed account of his voyage: an account which is indisputably authentic and was written reasonably soon after the events described. I quote the relevant part of the *Flateyiarbok in toto*.

"*There was now* (in Greenland) *much talk of land seeking. And Leif, son of Erik the Red from Brattalid, went to visit Bjarne Herjulfsson and bought his ship of him and hired a crew, so that there were three tens and a half men together. Leif begged his father, Erik, if he would lead the expedition. At first Erik excused himself, saying he was too old and no longer able to endure the hardships of life at sea; Leif, however, argued that he (Erik) would still bring his kinsmen luck, and Erik at last yielded, and when they were ready rode with them from his home to the ship nearby. But the horse stumbled which Erik rode, and he fell off from its back and hurt his foot. Then quoth Erik: 'I am not fated to find more lands other than this where we now dwell; no longer may we voyage together.' So Erik was carried home to Brattalid, and Leif went to his ship and his followers with him.*

"*When the ship was provisioned and ready they put to sea, and after a voyage of several days came they first to that land which Bjarne had sighted last. They stood in to the land and cast anchor and put out the boat and rowed ashore, and saw they there no grass, only large ice-mountains inland, and all was like one stonefield from mountains to the sea, and seemed to them this land to be good for nothing. Then quoth Leif: not to us has it happened as with Bjarne, that we have not set foot on the land; so I now give a name to this country and call it Helluland* (The Land of Flat Stones).

"*Then went they to their ship and sailed out upon the sea until they came to another land. Again they cast anchor, put out the boat and rowed ashore. This land was low and level, with many woods, not steep at the shore and covered with wide white sands wherever they went. Then quoth Leif: 'after its quality shall this land have name, and be called Markland* (Woodland).' *Went they then to their ship as fast as possible, and sailed from thence on the sea before a north-east wind for two days ere they saw more land.*

"*They closed with this land and came to an island which lay to the north of the land, and went they ashore there and looked about in fine weather, and found there was water on the grass; and when they touched this water with their hands and brought it to their mouths they thought not to have known anything as sweet as this was. After a while they boarded their ship and sailed north into an adjacent sound which lay between the island and that cape to the north. It was very shallow at ebb-tide, and ran they aground their ship even though it was far from ship to land. Yet so very curious were they to go ashore that they could not bide that the tide rise under their ship, but ran to the land in their boat to where a river fell into the sea from a lake. And as soon as the tide rose under their ship they rowed back and conveyed it up the river and afterwards into the lake and cast their anchor there and brought from the ship their sleeping-bags, and afterwards took the resolution to make a large house and abide the winter there.*

"*They wanted salmon neither in the lake nor in the river, and larger salmon than ever before they had seen. So good was the land that it seemed to them might no cattle fodder be needed in wintertime. There came little frost in winter so that hardly withered was the grass. Days and nights were of more equal length than in Greenland, and sun had they both at Eykerstad (3 p.m.) and Dagmelastad (9 a.m.) even on the shortest day.*

"When they had finished their home-building, Leif said to his followers: 'Now shall our company be divided into two, one party remaining at home and the other party exploring the land but not becoming separated and not going so far away that they cannot return to the house at night.' And did they this for a while, Leif alternately exploring and staying at home. (Now Leif was big and strong and noble looking: a wise commander, and very just in all his dealings.)

"One evening came the tidings that a man was missing: Tyrher the southerner. Now Leif was very troubled, for Tyrher had been long with his father and had loved and cared for Leif in his childhood. So he rebuked his followers and ordered a search party to seek him. But ere they had gone far from the home, came Tyrher to meet them. Leif saw at once he was excited (now Tyrher was small and insignificant-looking, with a high forehead and restless eyes; but a fine craftsmen). Leif said to him: 'Wherefore are you late coming back, and how did you become separated from your companions?' At first spoke Tyrher in his southern tongue, rolling his eyes and grimacing; but after a while he said in Norse: 'I have not walked much farther than the others but I found something new: vines and grapes.' Leif asked if he was sure, and Tyrher said: 'It is true. For I was born in a land full of grapes and vines.' Now went they back to their house and slept through the night, and the next morning Leif said to his crew: 'Now we have two works, which we shall do alternate days; one work will be to pick grapes, the other will be to cut timber for our cargo when we return home.' Now was hewing and picking until pinnace and storage space were full.

"When spring came they made ready, and sailed away and got a fair wind . . . And Leif named this country Vineland, after its special product." (The saga goes on to describe the voyage home, ending with the rescue of a shipwrecked crew from one of the skerries off Greenland.)

This passage has been the subject of countless books, articles and lectures: some sceptical, some scholarly and some dogmatic. In the old days the sceptics doubted if Leif's landfalls could ever be identified with accuracy; but in recent years a more positive attitude has been adopted, and thanks to some excellent research the location of Vineland is now a matter of fairly general agreement. So let us reconstruct Leif's voyage, step by step, in as much detail as we can.

*   *   *   *

The *knorr* weighed anchor a little before sunset and stood quietly seaward between the hills of willow and birch. It is never, at this time of year, completely dark in Greenland; and while most of the crew slept a skeleton watch took the ship down-fjord; by early morning they had come to the open sea. Once clear of the inshore skerries, the Pole wind filled their sail, the Labrador Drift creamed white under their bow, and they stood handsomely south-west in search of the lands which Bjarne had told them lay far *"beyond the sunset and the baths of all the western stars"*. For a long time, that first day, the Greenland ice-cap glinted in the sun in their wake. But by nightfall the ice-cap had vanished under the waves, and they were alone.

Their ship was a square-rigged trading vessel: straight stemmed and sterned with a cutwater both fore and aft, a single sail with a *beitas* (a spar for keeping the sail taut when sailing close to the wind) and a number of refinements such as a windlass, a ship's boat and anchors both fore and aft. Her measurements, I think, would have been roughly 90 feet in length, 20 in width and 30–40 tons in weight, and she would have drawn about 3½ feet. She was smaller, in other words, than the Phoenician traders which a millennium earlier had also dared the Atlantic; but she was probably just as seaworthy, more stoutly built and better able to ride out a storm. Figure 16 shows a reconstruction of her; and the thing that leaps to the eye is her classic simplicity of line—the hallmark, in any field, of a thoroughbred. She may not have been a comfortable ship in which to cross the Atlantic, but she was wonderfully safe and resilient.

FIG 16. Viking longship: *circa* A.D. 1000

The men who manned her were resilient too. And they were all volunteers; for in eleventh-century Greenland there was none of the press-ganging which was later to bedevil the crewing of vessels from allegedly more civilized countries. Some of them had been with Bjarne on his previous voyage, some were followers of Erik and Leif, some were Christians, and two were Hebridean runners, Hekja and Haki (round whose adventures Nevil Shute wrote his delightful novel *An Old Captivity*). And they were all fine seamen: men skilled in the lore of the Atlantic, able to interpret the changing patterns of wind and cloud, able to judge their whereabouts by the set of the waves, the density of marine life and the course of the migrating birds; able too to orientate themselves by the sun and the Pole Star—*lad steorra* they called the latter, guide-star or lodestar. Food and water were no great problem to them —for fish are plentiful in the North Atlantic and rain frequent. Their greatest hazards were ice, blizzards and the great fifty-foot combers which sometimes come sweeping in the wake of depressions.

Whether or not Leif met these hazards on his voyage from Greenland to America we do not know. The sagas only tell us that he retraced Bjarne's route in reverse, and "after a voyage of several days came to that land which Bjarne had sighted last".

It is 730 miles from Greenland to Newfoundland. A *knorr* would reckon to average some one hundred and twenty miles a day; so Leif must have been out of sight of land for at least five days before a range of snow-capped peaks rose over the western horizon. They stood thankfully towards them, watching in wonder as a magnificent chain of mountains unfolded in growing detail. They didn't put ashore at once, but spent the first day in search of a safe anchorage. It was an iron coast, mile after mile of low, windswept cliffs; but at last they came to a reasonably sheltered inlet, and here they dropped anchor and rowed ashore.

It was an historic moment. The first fully authenticated landing of Europeans in the New World.

But it was a desolate land that Leif and his Vikings had come to—far more desolate than their native Greenland. They found there was no grass; nothing but great slabs of rock stretching without a break "*like one stonefield*" between the shore and the "*ice mountains*" of the interior. There was no incentive for them to linger here and after only a few hours ashore they returned to their ship, Leif christening the country Helluland (The Land of Flat Rocks).

Now there is something in this account that does not quite add up. The land which Bjarne had sighted last was "*a hilly island with ice* on it*"; and this we have identified as Newfoundland. Now, seventeen years later, Leif thinks he has come to this same land and describes it as having "snow-capped peaks" and "ice mountains" in the interior. But there are no such mountains in Newfoundland. The explanation, I think, is this. Leif *thought* he had come to the land which Bjarne had sighted last; but in fact his landfall was some fifty miles farther north, in Labrador. This seems likely because Leif's description does not fit Newfoundland particularly well, but it is an exact and extremely graphic description of the desolate Labrador coast a little to the north of Battle Harbour. We can therefore assume that Leif landed in Labrador, took one look at the country, did not think much of it, and stood out to sea without penetrating the Belle Isle Strait, that narrow neck of water which divides Newfoundland from Labrador and which looks from the sea exactly like the mouth of a fjord. In other words, Leif thought that Labrador and Newfoundland were one. If this is accepted the events and descriptions of the sagas fall naturally into place.

---

* The Icelandic word used by the saga is *jokull*, which is a generic term for ice in general and can apply equally well to glacier, ice-field or ice-berg; in this case it probably refers to one of the icebergs which each year ground in their hundreds at the mouth of Belle Isle Strait.

At any rate Leif stood south from his Helluland, and after running for two days before a favourable wind came to Bjarne's second landfall. And here once again he found a harbour, dropped anchor and rowed ashore.

It was a very different country they had come to now: "*flat, well-wooded and fringed by wide beaches of pale white sand.*" It is not hard to place this second landfall. Six hundred years later the explorer Henry Hudson described the southern tip of Nova Scotia as follows: "a low land, well covered with timber and with a multitude of white sandy beaches." And it was here, probably not far from Sable Point, that Leif and his crew went ashore. It was the trees which took their attention most: the vast forests of spruce and pine, fir and birch, maple and oak which in those days ran in primeval riot right down to the water's edge. One would have expected them to spend some time exploring these forests—especially since timber was one of the things they had come to the New World to find. But they did not. They christened the country Markland (Land of Woods), then "*went they to their ship as fast as possible and sailed from thence on the sea before a north-east wind*". They went as fast as possible, I think, because north-east winds are rare off the Atlantic seaboard, and Leif was anxious to push on to Bjarne's first landfall while conditions were favourable.

The sagas are quite explicit about what happened next—they came to an island north of the mainland where they landed and found sweet water; they then put to sea again, headed north and ran aground, but subsequently towed their vessel ashore and wintered beside a lake; in the spring they sailed home, having christened the country Vineland, after the wild vines which they had found there. This passage has puzzled scholars for generations, especially "*the island which lay to the north of the mainland*"—for on all the Atlantic seaboard no such island exists! And because of this apparent anomaly even the approximate whereabouts of Vineland was for long a matter of dispute. But now, thanks to the painstaking research of men like Hjalmar Holand and Frederick Pohl, we are able with reasonable certainty to identify the island, the sound, the river and even the lake beside which, nearly a thousand years ago, the Vikings wintered.*

If you sail for two days from Cape Sable before a north-easterly wind, you will come to the vicinity of Cape Cod. And we can picture the Vikings, with a following wind, coming to the conglomeration of capes, isthmus, islands and shoals which make up the South Massachusetts seaboard. The day was fine, with good visibility, but a Cape Cod north-easter knocks up a fair sea, and Leif must have realized he was coming to dangerous waters. We would expect him, therefore, to run for shelter into the first available anchorage. Now a ship standing in to this stretch of coast from the north-east gets the impression that Nantucket Sound is a fjord; for the islands to the south of the sound—Nantucket, Martha's Vineyard and No Man's Land—have the appearance of forming a continuous chain, joined to the mainland. What more natural, then, than that Leif should stand into this "fjord". And as he

---

* A summary, with maps, of the evidence which enables us to identify Vineland is given in Appendix A.

entered it, the first thing he would see is the sandy protuberance of Great Point, sticking out from the northern shore of Nantucket. Now Great Point, to-day, is joined to Nantucket Island by a sandbar ten feet high; but even within living memory it has been cut off from the island in time of storm or high tide, and those who study coastal erosion and accretion believe that a thousand years ago it was completely separated from Nantucket. Here, in other words, is our *"island which lay to the north of the land"*. And here, too, is our sweet water. For close to the centre of Great Point, among the gnarled cedars, briars and sedge grass, there is a small hollow surrounded by lush vegetation; and here, all the year round, water that is crystal clear and curiously sweet comes welling up from an underground spring: a miniature oasis in the heart of the sand dunes.

But apart from its sweet water and its sheltered anchorage Great Point has little to commend it, and certainly Leif had not sailed for two thousand miles to end up on an oversized sand-hill. We should therefore expect him to push farther afield as soon as conditions permitted. And the sagas indeed tell us that *"after a while they boarded their ship and sailed north into the adjacent sound"*. The wind must have moved to the south-east by this time and the tide begun to ebb; for Viking ships could make progress only with a following wind and Viking seamen had sufficient know-how not to explore unknown waters when the tide was rising—if a ship runs aground when the tide is rising it is liable to be firmly embedded by inshore currents, but if it grounds when the tide is ebbing the odds are it will embed gently and be easy to refloat later when the flood tide will lift it clear. And this, in fact, is exactly what happened to Leif. Soon after leaving Great Point he saw the hills of Cape Cod to the north. He steered towards them, and ran aground, "even though it was far from ship to land". Assuming the *knorr* drew three-and-a-half feet, she would very likely have run on to Kill Bond Bar or Dogfish Bar, about a mile and a half off-shore. But the Vikings were in no way put out at running aground. They rowed ashore in their pinnace, found a river (the Bass) with a good deep channel, and later that evening, when the tide rose, rowed back to their ship and towed her up the river and into a lake (Follins Pond) some couple of miles inland. We can identify the river and lake because they tie up exactly with the directions and descriptions of the saga. Here they built a house which served first as the base from which they explored the neighbourhood and then as their winter quarters.

The country they had discovered must have seemed almost too good to be true. There were salmon in the rivers and lakes, an abundance of timber and wild grapes, a remarkable amount of good pasture and a pleasant climate. Here indeed was a land as flowing with milk and honey as any promised to the saints: a paradise found, only, alas, all too soon to be lost.

Which brings us to the big problem about the Viking discovery of America. We know that in 1003 Leif Eriksson landed in Massachusetts; we know he found the country pleasant and fertile; we know he took the news of his discovery back to Greenland, and that glowing reports of Vineland-the-good soon spread like wildfire through the kingdoms of the north. Why, then, was discovery not followed by colonization? Why did not the Vikings settle on the

American seaboard as their ancestors had settled before them on far bleaker and less promising littorals?

The answer, I think, is that they did try to. But that their garden of Eden turned out to have its serpent: the "Skraelings", or North American Indians.

And we are faced here with a new and unwelcome factor in the history of exploration. Violence. The opposition of the people living in the lands to which the explorers had come. The Hottentots of Punt had showered the visiting Egyptians with gifts. In all the travels of Necho's Phoenicians and Saint Brandan's Irish there is no hint of a hand raised in anger. But at the very first meeting of Norsemen and Skraeling, men were killed. And they went on being killed, with increasing frequency, whenever the two made contact.

The sagas are full of evidence on this point. Take what happened to Leif's successors; men like Thorfinn Karlsefni and Thorwald Eriksson.

Karlsefni, we are told, was a man of great wealth and sagacity. In 1012 he gathered together a hundred and sixty men and five women, together with a large number of domestic animals, *"intending to try to settle in Vineland"*. They reached America safely and spent four years on the mainland, two years in and around Nantucket Sound and two years on the Hudson River. But wherever they went they ran foul of the Skraeling. The very first summer *"a great band of savages came out of the forest . . . and tried to enter Karlsefni's house"*. There was some desultory trading and the Skraeling went away. But Karlsefni had seen the writing on the wall. He ordered a stout palisade of logs to be built round his house. And sure enough, that winter, the Indians came again *"in larger numbers than before"*. One of them tried to steal some weapons. There was the inevitable fight, *"and many Skraelings were killed"*. Later, when the Vikings pushed farther south, there was another and fiercer battle in which men of both sides were killed. And—to quote the saga—*"it now seemed obvious to Karlsefni that although the land was attractive they could live there only with fear and warfare because of the natives. Accordingly they decided to return to their own country"* (Greenland).

Leif's younger brother Thorwald had even less luck. While exploring the Gulf of Maine in his ship's pinnace, he came across a headland of remarkable beauty and fertility, possibly Cape Ann. *"Here it is beautiful,"* he said to his men, *"and here I will build my home"*—not my house, you will notice, but my home. A few days later he and his crew were surprised by a fleet of Skraeling canoes. The Indians surrounded them, firing their arrows thick and fast, while Thorwald and his crew sheltered as best they could behind their shields. At last the Skraeling withdrew; but not before an arrow had found its way between shield and gunwale and pierced deep into Thorwald's side. Realizing he was about to die, he told his men to bury him on the headland where he had hoped to make his home; and this next day they did, setting up a cross at both the head and foot of his grave. How many other Norsemen whose names have not come down to us must have met a similar fate in their efforts to settle the Atlantic seaboard!

The truth would seem to be, then, that the Vikings did try to colonize America—and tried very hard—but they were neither numerous enough nor powerful enough. And in this connection I quote an interesting passage from Cary and Warmington's classic work *The Ancient Explorers*. "Of all disadvantages under which ancient explorers laboured, the greatest was their deficiency in the matter of weapons. The margin of strength which the more civilized peoples of antiquity possessed over the more primitive ones in regard to lethal instruments was so narrow that exploring parties must often have been more or less at the mercy of the folk whose countries they discovered. Even with firearms the earlier modern settlers in North America had difficulty in holding their own against the Indians. While the Norsemen who settled in these parts about A.D. 1000 were definitely unable to make good their footing with such means of defence as they possessed, and had to abandon their otherwise promising colonies."

So what are we left with? A taste of failure? The vision of a great Dark-Age empire which came so very close to linking the New World with the Old but which at the last moment was forced back into its northern fastnesses, subsequently to perish unremembered on the edge of the known world? This is one's first impression.

But scholars are now beginning to think that the scale of the Viking settlements may well have been far greater than was once believed;* also that the Viking voyages to America were no mere flash in the pan, confined to a few decades, but were part of a sustained and continuous effort spanning many centuries and culminating in the classic Atlantic crossings of the fifteenth century. In support of this theory they advance three types of evidence: archaeological, literary and ethnological.

Norse relics have been found by archaeologists all over North America: as far south as Long Island, as far north as the Arctic Circle, and as far west as Minneapolis. The relics include Viking swords, axes, spears, halberds, boat-hooks and mooring-stones, all of which have been subjected to the most exhaustive investigations before being pronounced genuine. And it is worth bearing in mind, here, how rare such archaeological finds usually are when one race had superimposed itself temporarily on another. The 80,000 Goths, for example, who overran Italy were frequently buried in their robes, and invariably holding these robes in position were *fibulae*; yet in all Italy, after centuries of searching, less than thirty *fibulae* have been unearthed. With this as our yardstick, it would certainly seem that Norse colonization may well have been fairly extensive.

Literary evidence confirms this. For there are references, throughout all the latter part of the Dark Ages, to a continuous if tenuous contact between the New World and the Old. Vatican records, for example, speak of bishops visiting Vineland; cargo ledgers mention turkeys (birds which are peculiar to North America); the Icelandic sagas are full of casual references to "ships arriving from Markland" and "voyages to the lands south-west of Greenland"; while the Norwegian state archives hold records of the great Paul Knutson missionary expedition, which, as late as 1361–2 penetrated to the western shores of the Great Lakes: the very heart of the American continent.

Finally, there is the fascinating evidence of ethnologists with their reports

* The recent discovery of Viking settlements in Newfoundland substantiates this.

of Blond Eskimos and Mandan Indians: men whose skins were pale, whose hair was fair, whose features were Nordic, who lived in square Scandinavian-style houses built of wood, whose mythology taught of a kindly god who was born of a virgin and who died a death of expiation, and who had already been living for generations in the mid-West when the first of the post-Columbian settlers came pushing over the Appalachians. And the only satisfactory explanation of the presence of these so-called "White Indians" is that they were the last, partially-assimilated remnants of the Viking colonists.

We are in controversial waters now, but at least it would seem that we can be reasonably certain of this. In A.D. 1003 the Vikings discovered America. They were not able to colonize the lands they discovered. But—and this is the important point—they did preserve a tenuous contact with them; and so the Atlantic was never regarded in Northern Europe (as it was in the South) as a limitless expanse of ocean stretching away to the edge of the world; it was always known or at least suspected that there was land to the west. No wonder, then, that when in the late fifteenth century there was a renascence of deep-water voyaging, the Atlantic was most probably crossed once again not in the south but in the north, by the classic route of the eleventh-century Vikings (see Chapter VIII). Leif Eriksson's voyage in other words deserves to go down in history not as a "brave but fundamentally useless leap into a blind alley"; but rather as the first and greatest of those epic voyages of discovery which bound together the Old World and the New.

TWO

The Golden Age of Discovery

Introduction to Part Two

BETWEEN the years 1470 and 1770 the discoveries of the ancients, which had been for the most part forgotten during the chaos of the Dark and Middle Ages, were again brought to light; while the remaining coastlines of the world—except for the areas around the poles—were delineated for the first time with reasonable accuracy. This magnificent flowering of deep-sea voyages, the geographical facet of the Renaissance, was motivated by a wide variety of factors—economic, national, religious and scientific—and was accelerated by cumulative progress in the fields of navigation and cartography. Nearly all the voyages of this period are well documented (the exception being those of the fifteenth-century Portuguese); and the historian is now faced with a glut of material rather than a scarcity. The basic problem shifts therefore from interpretation to selection. Which were the really important voyages? Which were the explorers who did most to unveil the secrets of the world?

I have chosen six: Gil Eannes, João Vaz Corte-Real, Magellan, Barents, Quiros and Cook; if asked to increase my list, I should have added Dias, Columbus and either Davis or Roggeveen. Any such selection is bound to be controversial. Some readers, for example, may liken a history of exploration which includes neither Columbus nor Da Gama to an egg that is eaten with neither pepper nor salt. So perhaps some explanation is called for as to how the selection has been made.

I have selected voyages which, it seemed to me, were not only exciting and important in themselves, but also set in motion some new and significant trend in the history of exploration.

When, for example, Gil Eannes rounded Cape Bojador, he triggered off that great series of Portuguese voyages which pushed down the coast of Africa, around the Cape of Good Hope and reached finally to the gates of India. For two thousand years the Saharan headland of Bojador had been regarded as the edge of the world; no ship's company had sailed beyond it and lived; and Eannes's rounding of it was considered by his contemporaries a greater feat than Columbus's crossing of the Atlantic. As the precursor of Dias and Da Gama, Eannes ill merits the obscurity into which he has recently fallen.

João Vaz Corte-Real, I believe, rediscovered America some twenty years before Columbus. His voyage is typical of a whole series of Portuguese forays into the Atlantic—controversial and shrouded in mystery and ambiguity. Yet if it did indeed take place (and a very strong case can be made out for it), then it was surely one of the most significant voyages in history; for it establishes a direct link between the Viking expeditions to America and those of the fifteenth- and sixteenth-century Spanish and Portuguese.

Magellan was not only the first man to circumnavigate the world; he was also first to open up the greatest of the oceans, the Pacific. His is probably the only name which would appear automatically on everyone's short-list of the world's greatest explorers. And rightly so. For his voyage was not only an epic of tenacity and endurance, but it added enormously to man's knowledge of the configuration of the world.

The voyage of William Barents in search of a North-East Passage ended in failure, Barents dying and his crew losing their ship. Yet this voyage had important historical consequences; for by the very nature of its failure it diverted the energies of the Dutch to Australasia and the energies of the British to the north-west. In addition, Barents's was the first expedition in history to survive an Arctic winter; and this patient and resourceful Dutchman can therefore claim to be the precursor of a distinguished line of polar explorers— men such as Parry, Franklin, Nordenskjold, Amundsen and Nansen—whose exploits were made possible only by their ability to remain continuously in the polar regions year after year, lying up in the winter and pushing on with their exploration during the few brief weeks of the Arctic summer.

It was Quiros, or to be exact his second-in-command Torres, who first sighted the north-west coast of Queensland, thereby fixing the position of *Terra Australis Incognita* a hundred and fifty years in advance of Cook. His discovery was little heeded by his contemporaries and has been done less than justice by historians; yet his voyage was not only remarkable in itself, it also triggered off that search for the Great Southern Continent which was to last for over two hundred and fifty years.

Cook has three claims to fame: he delineated the world's largest ocean, the Pacific; he was the first explorer to conquer scurvy; and he recorded his discoveries with an exactness which raised exploration to the dignity of a science. On any one of these counts he is worthy of a place in our history.

These therefore are the explorers who, in my opinion, epitomize the golden age of discovery. Their voyages, taken in conjunction with those dealt with in Parts I and III, span every ocean, represent the achievement of almost every seafaring nation, and form a reasonably continuous narrative of the gradual unveiling of the world.

VII

OUT OF DARKNESS

(The rounding of Cape Bojador by Gil Eannes marks the end of the Middle Ages)

I DOUBT if one person in a thousand to-day has heard of Gil Eannes or could place Cape Bojador on the map. Yet these names were considered of more account in the fifteenth century than Columbus and his Indies — and with good reason; for in those days the rounding of Cape Bojador was a more daring and novel feat of seamanship than crossing the Atlantic.

Cape Bojador lies on the coast of the Spanish Sahara, a little way south of the Canaries. It is by no means remarkable in appearance: a bluff headland, terminating in an unstable cliff of sandstone about sixty feet high: not, you might think, an especially terrifying place. Yet for more than a thousand years this cape was regarded as the last outpost of the habitable world; beyond it, it was widely believed, lay the Sea of Darkness, the Inferno and those undiscovered countries from whose bourne no traveller had ever returned. For not since the days of the Phoenician galleys had a ship's company ventured south of Cape Bojador and lived.

What was the peculiarity of this headland that for thirty-five generations it had acted as a barrier no ship could pass?

Some historians have dismissed the mariners' reluctance to stand south of Cape Bojador as "mere superstition — a legacy of the monsters and glutinous seas of Phoenician legend". But such a view is unrealistic; there is never smoke without fire, and to get at the truth we must turn not to historians but to practical seamen, men who have themselves sailed off this particular stretch of the African shore. Such a seaman is Ernle Bradford who in his book *Southward the Caravels* writes: "The Sahara coast is one of the bleakest and most uninviting parts of the world . . . Barren and burned, devoid of almost all vegetation the land runs down in a glow of ocherish sand to the sea. In places it ends in sandy cliffs, which, disturbed by strong winds, fall with a rumbling crash into the Atlantic and stain the sea with red. The waters are shallow, the depths constantly shifting, and . . . after one of the (frequent) cliff falls, the sea seems to boil until the débris dissolves. Currents are strong and uncertain, the winds light — or hot and violent when the harmatten whirls off the desert. It is a cruel landscape, and it is not difficult to believe that in this region life comes to an end." While Pancho Pereira, another practical seaman, goes on to tell us why of all the headlands that jut out from the Sahara, Cape Bojador in particular was so greatly feared: "This cape, low and covered with sand, is most dangerous; for a reef of rocks runs out from it into the sea for more than fifteen miles . . . The bottom here

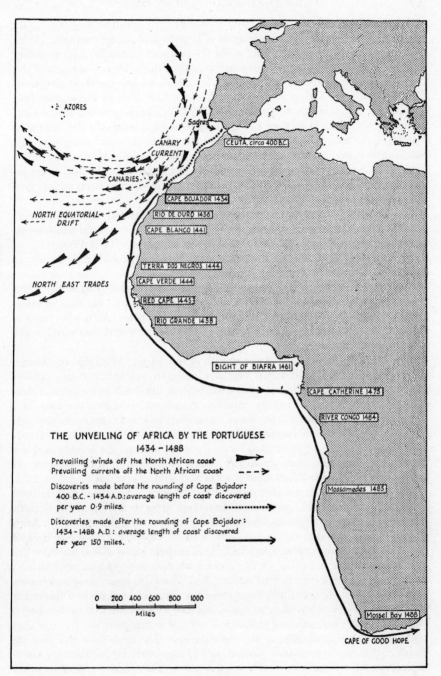

.AZORES

Sagres

CANARY
CURRENT

CEUTA, circa 400 B.C.

CANARIES

CAPE BOJADOR 1434

NORTH EQUATORIAL
DRIFT

RIO DE OURO 1436

CAPE BLANCO 1441

NORTH EAST TRADES

TERRA DOS NEGROS 1444

CAPE VERDE 1444

RED CAPE 1445

RIO GRANDE 1458

BIGHT OF BIAFRA 1461

CAPE CATHERINE 1475

RIVER CONGO 1484

THE UNVEILING OF AFRICA BY THE PORTUGUESE
1434 – 1488

Prevailing winds off the North African coast
Prevailing currents off the North African coast

Discoveries made before the rounding of Cape Bojador:
400 B.C. – 1434 A.D.: average length of coast discovered
per year 0.9 miles.

Discoveries made after the rounding of Cape Bojador:
1434 – 1488 A.D.: average length of coast discovered
per year 150 miles.

Mossamedes 1485

0   200 400 600 800 1000
Miles

Mossel Bay 1488

CAPE OF GOOD HOPE

Fig 17

is full of shoals, and seamen as they approach the cape find shallows—only three fathom of water as many leagues offshore—and strong currents." Why could not these seamen, you ask, avoid the reef and its shallows by standing well out to sea? And here we come to the crux of the matter. For south of the Canaries the winds and currents change both their tempo and their direction. To start with, to a ship pushing south down the African coast, they are favourable; but opposite Cape Bojador they veer abruptly to the south-west, gathering momentum as they swing away from land and into the unknown reaches of the mid-Atlantic. And a vessel forced offshore and caught by this combination of wind and current would be swept helplessly away from the land and carried by the North Equatorial Drift and the North-East trades into the dreaded Sargasso (the Phoenicians' glutinous sea) from whose grip there was no return.

The mariners' fears, in other words, were well founded. For a thousand years they had drawn back from the Bojador reefs. They would continue to draw back from them until there once again appeared off the West African shore a vessel which, like the Phoenician galleys of old, could make headway against an adverse combination of wind and sea.

Early in the fifteenth century such a vessel was evolved. And at the same time a man was born whom scholars have described as "the first oceanographer in history". It was the rapport between these ships—Portuguese caravels—and this man—Prince Henry the Navigator—which ushered in the golden age of discovery.

You can see them to-day at the mouth of the Tagus, Mondego or Douro: broad-beamed, shallow-draught *frigata* (wine-boats), their lateen sails billowing out from a stumpy mast. These wine-boats are both ancestor and descendant of the fifteenth-century caravels: vessels which within the span of a hundred years quadrupled the size of the known world. It was these caravels which took Columbus across the Atlantic, da Gama and Dias round the Cape, and Magellan (in a sophisticated form, the *naos*) around the world; and if a list were made of the most seaworthy vessels in history, then caravels would vie for first place with Phoenician traders and Viking longships.

The word caravel derives from the Moorish *caravo*, which in turn is derived from the Greek χάραβος; and this terminology gives us a clue to the vessel's ancestry. It was conceived in the east, its rig being lateen, like that of an Arab dhow. Now Arab dhows (as we have seen in Chapter 4) have a unique capacity for sailing against the wind. This is their *raison d'être*, for they are obliged to cross the Indian Ocean from both east to west and west to east during the same fair-weather monsoon. And when this eastern rig was superimposed on to a western hull, contemporary chroniclers described the result as follows: "*These caravels have no topsail and their yard-arms are not fixed at a right angle to the mast, but suspended obliquely. Their sail is triangular and its lower edge comes down almost to the level of the ship's gunwale. The yards are rigged from the deck . . . it is easy to move them forward, and by simply crossing the ship they can be shifted from left to right or from right to left in a trice. The sails then open at one corner according to the direction from which the wind is blowing, and they are soon fully extended. All winds are favourable to them, and even with a breeze from the side they*

FIG 18. The Evolution of the Caravel
(a) Two-masted Caravel (1490)   (b) Three-masted Caravel (1500)   (c) Caravel (1520)
(d) Arab Boom (present day)   (e) River Tagus Frigata (present day)
(f) A late fifteenth-century Caravel of the type used by Dias, Da Gama and Columbus

will sail on a bowline as if with a following wind (they can in fact head as much as five or six points—55 to 65 degrees—into the wind): *and for the ship to sail in the opposite direction all that is necessary is to reverse the rig, and this is rapidly done".* Sailing ability alone, however, does not make a good vessel. You need seaworthiness as well, and this was a quality ensured by the design of the caravel's hull.

The word "caravel" has passed into everyday English use as "carvel", a shipbuilding term which denotes a hull constructed with flush as opposed to overlapping planks. This is a form of hull design peculiar to the Portuguese *frigata*, whose keels were—and still are—made of flush oak; whose ribs, strakes and stems were made of local stone-pine; whose planking was of cluster-pine and whose rudder was axled after the fashion of a Baltic cog. Caravels, in other words, were brilliant composites, adapting local methods of hull design to the rig of the east and the rudder of the north; and their capabilities have been nicely summed up for us by the Venetian navigator Cadamosto—*"I see no reason why these ships should not go anywhere in the world. For I believe they are the best sailers that ever travelled upon the sea."*

But the caravels would never have rounded Cape Bojador without an incentive; they needed a spur to drive them south into the unknown; and this spur was provided by Henry the Navigator.

Henry was born at Oporto in March 1394, the third surviving son of King John I of Portugal and Philippa the daughter of John of Gaunt. He is one of the great if enigmatic figures of history: part-mystic, part-saint and part-practical scientist; and his passion for exploration touched off an era of deep-sea voyaging which was to unveil the configuration of the physical world. For Prince Henry dedicated his life to a god no one had ever worshipped before: the sea; and to-day the trade-routes of the world are both his epitaph and his panegyric. It is difficult to be certain of the motives which lay behind his love-affair with the sea. Some historians, seizing on his militant Christianity, have described him as "the last of the Crusaders, a throwback to Godfrey de Bouillon"; others, conscious of the strain his programme of exploration imposed on a small and by no means wealthy nation, have dismissed him as "a misguided fanatic who bled his country to exhaustion". There is a grain of truth in both judgements. Yet the grandeur and clairvoyance of Henry's vision cannot be denied: the vision of a militant Christendom, enriched by trade, extending its domain beyond the confines of Europe and into the unknown corners of the world—which was in fact the very warp and woof of history in the five hundred years that followed his death.

So Henry built his *tercona naval* at Sagres, and from this remote headland on the south-west tip of Portugal, he proceeded to send out ships to every point of the compass—but particularly to the south, down the coast of Africa. These south-standing ships, however, were invariably brought up short by the reefs of Bojador. Henry, we are told by his biographers, argued *"most patiently and reasonably"* with his captains, sending them out again and again with orders to push even a few miles south of the dreaded headland. But his orders were disregarded. For the fears of a thousand years were not brushed aside lightly.

For more than a decade Henry's dreams hung fire. It must have been a frustrating time for him. He knew instinctively that away to the south treasures beyond compare were his for the taking. But Cape Bojador stood in the way. In his book *The Caravels of Christ* Gilbert Renault gives us a glimpse of Henry's thoughts as his ships, like migrating birds, went winging south — but never far enough to the south to turn his dreams to reality: "*Twice a day the tides come beating against the promontory of Sagres. To the Prince their waves seemed to whisper the words: 'Portugal! Portugal! Your destiny lies not among the mountains of the east, but on my flowing plains whose infinite spaces I shall reveal to you . . . Portugal! Portugal! Your plough is not that drawn by the straining ox, but the rapid prow of the ship cleaving a double furrow of foam from which new worlds shall spring. Oh, Portugal, I behold your Prince gazing silent upon me, his countenance brooding on the great ambition that shall one day open the gates of India! Do you know what wares ships shall then bring to your shores? Listen and I will say. From the shores of Africa you shall draw gold and slaves, ivory, ebony and amber; from the Red Sea pearls; from Aden madder; from Socotra aloes; from Arabia incense and myrrh; from Ormuz precious carpets and the fiery stallions of Persia; from Hindustan sugar, alum, wax and opium; from Chaul silk; from Manganor ginger, saltpetre, iron and precious woods; from Cochin pepper whose every grain is weighed as gold; from the Maldives wine, coral and amber; from Ceylon the most splendid rubies, the finest sapphires, the purest topazes and pearls of the most perfect quality; from Ceylon too the great fighting elephants for which all the ports of India compete, and the finest cinnamon, brazil-wood and dye . . . Let us go even farther. From the coast of Coromandel your ships shall bring back the finest cloth, white or dyed; from Bengal cotton, rice and sugared fruit, from the kingdom of the Pegu rubies, musk and gum lac; from Sumatra gold and silk, pepper and aloes, camphor and gum; from Borneo camphor, tortoiseshell, gold and pearls; from Macassar gold and sandalwood; from the isle of Amboina cloves and plumes of the birds of paradise; from Siam brazil-wood, lead, saltpetre, silk and leather; from the kingdom of Cathay, that other world, musk, silks, heavier than the damasks of Syria, porcelain, lacquer and jade; and from the island of Jypen, at the uttermost end of the earth, wrought silverware, silk, lacquer, gold dust and seed pearls . . .' The Prince listened to the voice of the sea, which was neither more nor less than the echo of his dreams, and bent once more over his maps.*" All these things, he knew, would be the heritage of his faith and his country, if only he could pass the reefs of Bojador.

Henry's assault on the Cape could be said to have begun in 1415 with the capture of Ceuta, the Moorish stronghold opposite Gibraltar. This gave him a foothold in Africa: a foundation-stone on which further schemes of expansion could be solidly built. (In the years to come Ceuta was to be Henry's cynosure; he had captured it in the golden hour of his youth; subsequently he left his younger brother to die the most appalling death, unransomed, in a Moorish prison rather than hand the city back; for he realized it was the lynch-pin without which his more distant conquests would be of little value.) Having captured Ceuta he set about establishing a court the like of which had never been seen in history. On the bleak headland of Sagres, where the very rocks seem to tremble to the thunder of wind and sea, he gradually accumulated round him a coterie of all the nautical talents: the Jews of Mallorca, famous as map-makers; scientists and inventors of every nation who were skilled in the use of lodestone, windrose or astrolabe; and shipwrights from the nearby Tagus and Douro and the distant Rhine and Loire. By 1419 Sagres had become his operations room: the nerve-centre from which his voyages of discovery were planned and prepared for, and the base to which his captains reported back with their findings.

But for fifteen years how meagre these findings were! Between 1419 and 1433 Henry sent out more than forty expeditions. But of all this great armada of ships not one had the courage to penetrate south of Cape Bojador. Some, seduced by the easy pleasures of piracy, turned aside to plunder the Moorish ports of Morocco. Others, fearing to stand south, stood west. But these latter vessels at least achieved something; they rediscovered Madeira and the Azores.

These archipelagoes had been known to the Phoenicians in the first millennium B.C.; but then for a thousand years they had disappeared from the maps of the Atlantic. It was in 1419 that two of Henry's captains, Zarco and Teixeira, were blown by storm and by chance on to the islet of Porto Santo, five hundred miles south-west of Cape Saint Vincent. And the following year those who had been sent to explore Porto Santo discovered the neighbouring and far larger island of Madeira. Henry now made an important decision. He ordered the colonization of his discoveries. This to-day sounds so commonplace and commonsense a directive that it is hard to realize it was something of an innovation in the 1420s. For many of the ancient discoverers—the Phoenicians and Carthaginians in particular—had kept the whereabouts of new lands a secret—there is, for example, evidence that Madeira was visited by a vessel from Genoa in the early 1330s; but apart from a handful of Genoese merchants—who, incidentally, never went near the island because it was too far from their usual trade-routes—no one knew this, and so for all practical purposes the discovery might never have taken place. In contrast, Henry's reaction on finding Madeira was immediate and positive; and a thriving colony was quickly established; a colony which supplied its mother country with wood, sugar and wine, and whose inhabitants so rejoiced in their "earthly paradise" that they christened the first Madeira-born children Adam and Eve. The finding of these islands shed the first glimmer of light on the Sea of Darkness. And a decade later the discovery of the Azores turned this glimmer into a steady shaft. For the Azores, like the Madeiras, were quickly colonized, and soon a regular two-way trade came into being, Henry's caravels year after year making the thousand-mile voyage to westward through waters in which a generation earlier they would have feared to venture a hundred miles.

But to the south Cape Bojador remained inviolate, its reefs the wrecking ground of Henry's dreams.

The Prince bided his time. It is said that "everything comes to him who waits"; and in the summer of 1433 his patience was at last rewarded. For in June of that year we have our first mention of the "most eminent and obedient of his sea captains", Gil Eannes.

We know little about Eannes except that he was a native of Lagos, was a "squire" at Henry's court at Sagres, and was "young" at the time he made his epic voyage. But I think we would be safe to assume that he was a member of the poorer nobility, a class which provided Henry with most of his sea captains, much as the West Country squirearchy of England provided Elizabeth I with most of hers. Eannes's orders as he set sail in the summer of 1433 were the usual ones: to round Cape Bojador, "even if only for a few miles". But like so many captains before him he failed. He passed Cape Not on the thirtieth parallel, but then turned west to the Canaries where he sacked a couple of towns and captured some natives.

Inured by this time to disappointment, Henry did not castigate Gil Eannes. The Prince's biographer, Gomes de Azurara, makes this clear: "*Now the Infant always received home again with great patience those whom he had sent out, never upbraiding them with their failure but listening to the story of their voyage, giving them rewards if they were due and then either sending them back to search again or despatching other picked men of his Household . . . Now in the year of Jesus Christ 1434 the Infant made ready the same vessel* (as last year) *and calling Gil Eannes apart again urged him earnestly to strain every nerve to pass Cape Bojador, saying that even if he did nothing else this would be enough. 'You cannot find', said the Infant, 'a peril so great that the hope of reward will not be greater. And in any case I wonder that you take seriously the stories you have been told about this Cape. If there were any authority for them, I could find an excuse for you. But indeed the stories are spread by men of little repute: the type of seamen who know only the coast of Flanders and how to enter well-known ports, and are too ignorant to navigate by compass and chart. Go forth, then, and heed none of their words; but make your journey straightway. For by the grace of God you can gain from this voyage nothing but profit and honour.'*"

So Gil Eannes stood his *barcha* south.

It was late May. Behind him the Algarve can seldom have looked more beautiful, a riot of blossom and sweet-scented cistus; ahead was the Sahara, a wilderness of burning sun, collapsing sand and ever-shifting shallow. But greater by far than Eannes's fear of the Sahara was his fear of the unknown. For he had made up his mind that this time, come what might, he would venture over the edge of the world, into sea-lanes no vessel had sailed in for more than a thousand years.

When winds and currents were favourable a *barcha* could average seventy miles a day; so it would not have taken Eannes more than a week to cover the five hundred miles to Cape Not. This was the easiest part of his voyage: the ship running free down a familiar coast, with well-known landmarks appearing at regular intervals. But on leaving Cape Not astern, the crew must have grown uneasy as their vessel still held course to the south, with the mid-day sun growing ever higher and fiercer, and the pitch in their seams first turning tacky and then welling out through the topsides in glistening bubbles of black.

There is, unfortunately, no existing log or diary to give us the day-by-day details of Eannes's progress south; but by unearthing a host of small contemporary references it is possible to piece the story together.

We know quite a lot, for example, about his ship. It was a *barcha*: a prototype caravel: a cross between the traditional square-sailed barques which for generations had been the mainstay of Iberian coastal trade, and the currently evolving lateen-rigged caravels which were soon to roll back the map of the world. It would have been about 55 tons, half-decked, high-pooped and twin-masted; its length a shade over 60 feet, its beam a shade over 20 and its draught shallow. Such a vessel was eminently suitable for coastal work and sufficiently seaworthy to ride out an Atlantic storm; but it would have had difficulty in making headway against a strong combination of wind and current; and I suggest the fact that Eannes *was* able to make such headway indicates that his *barcha* was probably one of the first to carry the experimental lateen rig of the Arabs.

Navigation for the most part would have been by the classic standbys log, lead and lookout, with the *barcha* seldom venturing far from land. This is not to say that Eannes would not have had aboard a fair number of "scientific" aids, chief of which would have been the astrolabe and the compass. The astronomer's astrolabe in those days was a delicate and elaborate instrument, ill-suited for use from the heaving deck of a ship; but the simplified seaman's version, with its easily read arc of degrees for measuring the height of sun or star, was accurate enough for calculating an approximate latitude (longitude, however, could not be fixed with any degree of certainty for another three hundred years). The *barcha* would also have carried a variety of tables and pamphlets, though some of these were probably more fanciful than accurate —one can imagine, for example, poor Eannes struggling with the complexities of "*Regimento do estralabio e do quadrante perer saber ha declinacem e o logar do soll em ceda huum dia e asy pera saber ha estrella do norte*", (Rules of the astrolabe and the quadrant to tell the declination and position of the sun for each day and so determine the whereabouts of the Pole Star). The compass aboard a *barcha* was kept in a special *bitácula* (or little dwelling), a wooden box illuminated at nights by an oil-burning lantern. This compass was sometimes known as the Stella Maris—a name that has come to be associated nowadays with the Pole Star itself. This confusion in nomenclature is brought out very clearly by the Diary of Felix Faber, a fifteenth-century monk describing his voyage to Palestine: "*They have a compass, a Stella Maris, near the mast, and a second one on the topmost-deck of the poop. Beside it all night long burns a lantern. There is a man constantly watching the Star* (the compass card) *and he never takes his eyes off it. He sings out a pleasant tune, telling that all goes well, and in the same chant directs the man at the tiller, telling him how to turn the rudder. The helmsman dares not move the tiller in the slightest degree except at the orders of him who watches the Stella Maris . . .*" The actual lodestone of this "Stella Maris" was the subject of many a fifteenth-century fo'c'sle yarn: if placed under the pillow of an adulterous wife it was said to make her confess, while some seamen valued it as a contraceptive and others as a cure for venereal disease. Another much-used instrument was the hour-glass, which was the only ships' timekeeper in those days and was usually housed in the same *bitácula* as the compass. It was the job of the ship's boy to look after this hour glass, reversing it every couple of hours when the sand had run through and ending his watch by singing the ditty:

The watch is changed,
The Glass is running:
We shall make a good voyage
If God is willing.

If a boy was caught "warming the glass" by holding it against the lantern or under his shirt, he was flogged; for when the glass was warmed it expanded, the sand ran through more quickly, and the boy's tedious watch was shortened; but at the same time the ship's timekeeping and hence her navigation was jeopardized.

Food was not a serious problem for Henry's caravels; for fish and sea-fowl have always been plentiful off the Atlantic seaboard, and his vessels seldom ventured far from land. Their voyages, too, were of relatively short duration; and the problem of preserving food did not therefore arise, the ships simply carrying the provisions of a usual fifteenth-century commissariat: butts of wine, barrels of olives, lemons, dried fish and salted meat, cases of cheese and vast quantities of ship's biscuit—the royal ovens in Lisbon alone produced more than a thousand tons of these biscuits a year, and the daily ration aboard Gil Eannes's *barcha* would have been over a couple of pounds per man.

As for the crew, we know very little about them. A few may have been coastal fishermen, but the majority were probably peasants: tough, hardy men who had survived centuries of Moorish oppression and civil war. Not, you might think, ideal material out of which to create a seafaring hegemony. Yet if one goes back far enough the Portuguese have both Phoenician and Viking blood in their veins, and Lisbon is said to have been founded by the most famous seafarer of all: Ulysses. So perhaps it is not altogether surprising that Portuguese seamen soon came to be eulogized as *"possessing tenacity and resourcefulness"* and to be *"fortified by both constancy and courage"*.

Gil Eannes's crew were to need these traits in abundance.

We can picture them standing south, that May, down the desert shore. They were too late to run into the clinging mists which shroud the coast of the Sahara in winter; but the swell, piled up by the north-east trades, must have been unpleasantly heavy—often as much as forty feet from trough to crest—and even well offshore they would have heard the ceaseless roar of great waves pounding the littoral: an ever-present reminder of their tenuous mortality.

South of Cape Not, new hands aboard the *barcha* must have held their breath as the ship headed straight into what was apparently shoal water: a knocked-up sea, thick and red as a field of blood. But Eannes knew what he was doing. The leadsman continued to call a full thirty fathoms under their keel. For the appearance of shoal water was due to nothing more than the red sand and mud washed seaward by the Tensift River and the offshore breeze. So their *barcha* stood safely into an ochre sea, her wake snaking out astern like the trail of a stick dragged through mud.

Soon the colour of the water changed again. South of Mogador it was a strange bottle-green; for the sea-bed here is made up of coarse grey sand, quite unlike the rest of the Sahara shore. By day the ship was followed by shoals of flying fish and schools of porpoise. By night the stars were brilliant, and their wake a pathway of phosphorescence.

About ten days out from Sagres the island of Fuerteventura rose dark on their starboard bow. They were level with the Canaries now, and the crew waited for Gil Eannes to alter course to the west, to the easy and familiar haunts of piracy. But the *barcha* continued to the south.

The seamen began to murmur. Where was Eannes taking them? Soon they would be at the edge of the world, on the brink of the Sea of Obscurity where great monsters lay in wait, where the sun was so fierce that the sea boiled and men were burned black, where magnetic rocks would spin their Stella Maris out of its casing and the iron fastenings out of their keel, where the pitch would melt and run out of their seams, and where, if by some miracle they survived all these hazards, they would in the end be swept helplessly away by the great race of waters which poured endlessly over the edge of the world and into the Ocean of Darkness.

Yet still Eannes held course.

The desert wind struck them in blasts, like heat from a furnace; the sun grew fiercer; the pitch began to rise out of their seams in shining bubbles of black; the coast became increasingly arid; and soon they could see ahead of them the very edge of the world—the reefs of Bojador.

As one stands nowadays on the deck of a liner and peers landward at the distant and somewhat nondescript Cape Bojador, it is easy to dismiss the fears of the fifteenth-century mariners with a smile. Yet even in the twentieth century those with a close acquaintance of Bojador have found it a place of unnerving phenomena: witness this account of how the Frenchman Jean Mermoz flew his biplane over the cape in the mid-1930s: "In the last glimmer of daylight Mermoz saw the black wall of the coast, wreathed in cloud, rise steeply out of the Atlantic. He headed his plane towards a gap between sea and cloud. But he soon realized that to slip through would be difficult; for sea, sand and sky appeared to merge in a witches' cauldron of darkness. In the ochre light he could make out great columns of water and strange black shapes which whirled about in endless gyration . . . Craters yawned, in a few seconds filled up with cloud, then spewed out avalanches of steaming water." A present-day yachtsman gives us this even more graphic picture: "The sea off Bojador really does appear to be boiling. For from the foot of the cape there juts out a fifteen-mile reef of rock: and here, where the northerly swell meets the offshore wind, the breakers seethe and burst as if from blowholes, and are tossed skyhigh like geysers in clouds of apparently boiling foam . . . (while) offshore great shoals of sardine dapple and flicker in the water like molten fire."

As their *barcha* came into the shallows she began to lift awkwardly in the knocked up sea. The men huddled together in the bow, peering ahead, crossing themselves and trembling. And soon, to their horror, they saw that the water under their keel was milk-white and bubbling.

"Turn back!" the helmsman cried. "The sea is boiling!"

But Gil Eannes lowered an empty wine butt over the side, hauled it aboard and made the crew plunge their hands into the water.

"The sea is no more boiling here," he chided them, "than off the coast of the Algarve. The whiteness and bubbles are nothing but spindrift, the backwash of the reef."

Soon, however, the leadsman was reporting bottom at less than three fathoms, and Eannes was forced to alter course. It was now that he made the decision which was to usher in the golden age of discovery. He did not—as every sea captain before him had done for a thousand years—take the easy way out and alter course to the north, back to the safe and familiar sea lanes of the Canaries; instead, he altered course to the west, standing parallel to the reef and into the very heart of the Sea of Darkness.

Again the men murmured. For they knew that away from the shelter of land, the winds and currents were likely to gain strength, swing west and sweep them away to where the sea, in a great glittering curve, rushed down-hill faster and faster until it avalanched over the edge of the world. Yet Eannes must somehow have managed to calm their fears; for we are told that his *barcha* "*sailed west for a day and a night until the coast could no longer be seen*". And this statement gives us a clue which does much to account for Eannes's success. When he rounded Cape Bojador the weather was misty and un-usually calm. It must have been calm or he would not have needed to sail west for as long as "*a day and a night*". For in a day and a night, with the usual sort of following wind and sea, one would expect his *barcha* to have covered a good seventy miles; yet Eannes would hardly have stood seventy miles into the dreaded Sea of Darkness when the reef projected only fifteen miles; and it is therefore reasonable to assume that the winds were so light and variable that it took him the full "day and night" to clear the reef. As for it being misty—we are told that at one stage "*the coast could no longer be seen*"; yet a cliff sixty feet high *could*, in normal visibility, have been seen from a *barcha's* masthead when she was off the tip of the reefs; therefore at the time of Eannes's voyage visibility was less than normal; i.e., bearing in mind that there was little wind, it must have been misty.

So we can picture the *barcha*, with no more than a wayward breeze to fill her sail, inching west along the edge of the reef. At first the ochre headland of Bojador loomed out of the mist astern. But towards nightfall it disappeared. And they were alone: alone in the Sea of Darkness from which, to their knowledge, no men had ever returned.

I doubt if the crew slept much. Their nerves strung taut, they more than likely spent the night in prayer or peering anxiously at the mist-wreathed ocean, whose very calmness—so unusual off the Sahara coast—must have added to their apprehension.

After a while Eannes calculated they must be well clear of the Bojador reefs, and at dawn they went about, standing in towards the unknown shore to the south. As the *barcha* settled on to her new heading they watched the sail anxiously, knowing their lives depended on how it filled. And the lateen rig, which a thousand years earlier had carried Arab dhows the breadth of the Indian Ocean into the eye of the wind, came to their aid. Though breeze and current were both from their port bow, the *barcha* stood steadily east, sailing "*as if on a bowline, 60° into wind*". Progress was slow, but it was also sure; and at last, dead ahead, the sand cliffs of the Sahara rose hazily out of the mist.

Here is Ernle Bradford's description of their historic landfall—and its consequences. "As they ran in, on a hot midsummer day with only the sound of the sea and the sigh of the wind in the shrouds, the sailors gathered in the bows and shaded their eyes. Slowly the coast came up ahead, the same coast, it seemed, that they had known for days. But as they drew nearer, they saw that there was one great difference. Away to the south the land ran on, flat, sandy and shining under the sun—a level land with no cape breaking its steady sweep. They looked north and saw that they had passed the impassable limit! They had rounded Cape Bojador!

"It was almost as if a wall had fallen down—a barrier to man's progress that had held him back for centuries. Sailing down this coast to-day, Cape Bojador seems no more than another bleak headland interrupting a coastline as momentous as the desert dunes. But it was what the cape had represented that was important . . . (For) the rounding of Bojador altered man's whole approach to life. More than a cape was passed by Gil Eannes. A whole era of superstition fell away—much as the sand cliffs along this coast sometimes collapse and vanish without trace" into waters which had long been known as the Sea of Darkness but were soon to become one of the great trade-routes of the world.

A couple of miles offshore they passed the hundred-fathom line and came into soundings. Slowly the water ahead changed colour: from sapphire to topaz to aquamarine and then, as surf churned up the sand, to speckled yellow-and-white. Where the water was aquamarine they dropped anchor in a silence so absolute it could almost be felt, and Gil Eannes was rowed ashore. As he climbed the sand-dunes where almost certainly no foot had trod since the dawn of creation, his crew peered at him fearfully, half expecting some terrible fate to dart at him out of the wilderness of sand. But there was no movement: no sign of life. As far as the eye could see the desert lay seared and sterile under a sadic sun. Then Eannes noticed a faint shadow near the crest of one of the dunes. Moving awkwardly through the loose sand, he clambered up; and, as he neared the shadow, he caught his breath. For there, clustered in the shade of a sandstone ledge, was a line of small twisted plants. And, what was more, plants he could recognize: the frail little starlike flowers known in the Algarve as the roses of Saint Mary. He picked them, boxed them carefully, and took them back to Prince Henry.

After this nothing was ever quite the same again. For out of darkness had come forth light. The thousand-year-old legend that the world ended at the reefs of Bojador had been discredited; and life, and what is more familiar life, had been found to exist beyond the point where for so long life had been thought impossible. This discovery ushered in a new conception of the physical world. For it was realized, quite suddenly, that lands and peoples hitherto undreamed of might exist beyond the present confines of men's knowledge. So the horizon stopped being a barrier and became a challenge. And this represented a renaissance in geography as fundamental and far-reaching as Luther's in religion or Leonardo da Vinci's in the arts.

As for Gil Eannes, after his epic voyage his name all but disappears from history. All we know is that on his return to Sagres he was handsomely rewarded by Henry, and that he subsequently led two other expeditions south, in the first penetrating as far as Bir Rouin and in the second rounding Cape Verde and discovering the wide-mouthed estuary of the Gambia. His

THE STRAITS OF MAGELLAN

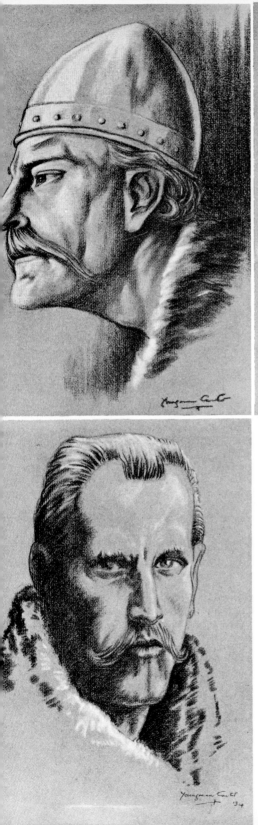

Ferdinand Magellan

Leif Ericsson (*top left*)

THREE OF THE WORLD'S

GREATEST EXPLORERS

Fridtjof Nansen

from drawings by Youngman Carter

immediate rewards for daring the reefs of Bojador were honour and wealth; Prince Henry's biographer, Gomes de Azurara, is quite explicit about this: "*As Gil Eannes purposed, so he performed; for in his great voyage he doubled Cape Bojador, despising all danger, and found the lands beyond quite different to what he, like others, had expected. And on account of its daring this deed was reckoned very great . . . And on his return Eannes was exceeding well received, and given a very considerable increase in both rank and material possessions.*" Certainly in his day Eannes seems to have been more highly regarded than Columbus; and it is one of the injustices of history that his name has been allowed to slide into oblivion. For it was his voyage which triggered off the great Portuguese drive to the south: a drive which was soon to flood round the Cape of Good Hope, surge east to the very gates of India and turn Prince Henry's dream to the most fabulous reality. Before Eannes's voyage Europeans had taken over a thousand years to push nine hundred miles down the coast of Africa (exploring on an average a mere 0.9 miles of coast per annum); but after his voyage they covered the remaining ten thousand miles of coast in less than seventy years (exploring on an average a hundred and fifty miles of coast per annum). A glance at the map on page 101 will show how rapidly Africa was explored the moment the physical and mental barrier of Bojador had been breached. It would therefore be no exaggeration to say that Eannes's voyage, more than any other, marks the end of the Middle Ages and the beginning of that sudden flowering of deep-sea voyages which was the geographical facet of the Renaissance.

VIII

THE REDISCOVERY OF AMERICA

(A joint Danish–Portuguese expedition reaches the New World twenty years before Columbus)

"IN 1492," the history books would have us believe, "Columbus discovered America." It is not true.

We have already, I think, established the fact that between the seventh and eleventh centuries Irish curraghs and Viking longships more than once beached on the shores of North America; so Columbus's achievement, to say the least, should be classified as *rediscovery*. Yet even this more modest claim is very much a matter of dispute.

In the course of the last hundred years a number of new and controversial theories have been advanced as to who may have first set foot in the New World. Most of these theories were championed with more erudition than common-sense, and have now been discredited. The stone, for example, which was unearthed in Brazil and was said to be inscribed with Phoenician lettering is now generally agreed to be a fake; the sixth-century Buddhist monks who were once thought to have sailed from China to Vancouver are now known to have reached no farther than Fusang; while the Welsh Prince Madoc, son of Owain Glyndwr, who was once believed to have met his death in the Mississippi valley is now known to have died in his bed in North Wales; but one theory has refused to be demolished, and has, on the contrary, gained in credibility over the years. This is the theory that America was rediscovered in 1472 by a joint Danish–Portuguese expedition: an expedition which was piloted by Johannes Scolvus, was led by Pining, Pothorst and João Vaz Corte-Real, and which followed the classic northern sea-route, Iceland-to-Greenland-to-Labrador.

An unlikely notion, you think? Yet Corte-Real is to-day regarded as the discoverer of America in a surprisingly large number of countries—in Portugal, Denmark, Norway, Sweden, Brazil, the Argentine and Angola, to mention only a few. As witness of this the visitor to Lisbon who walks down the *Avenida da Liberdade* will see a prominent mosaic pavement inscribed with the words "DESCOBERTA DA AMÉRICA, 1472"; and if this visitor for a moment supposes that a seven has been inadvertently substituted for a nine, he will be quickly disillusioned by the sub-heading "JOÂO VAZ CORTE-REAL, DESCOBRIDOR DA AMÉRICA". While in every Portuguese-speaking school, college and university in the world Corte-Real is eulogized with the enthusiasm that in English-speaking centres of learning is lavished on Columbus. We are dealing, in other words, not with some crankish fancy adhered to blindly by a handful of fanatics, but with a belief that has gained

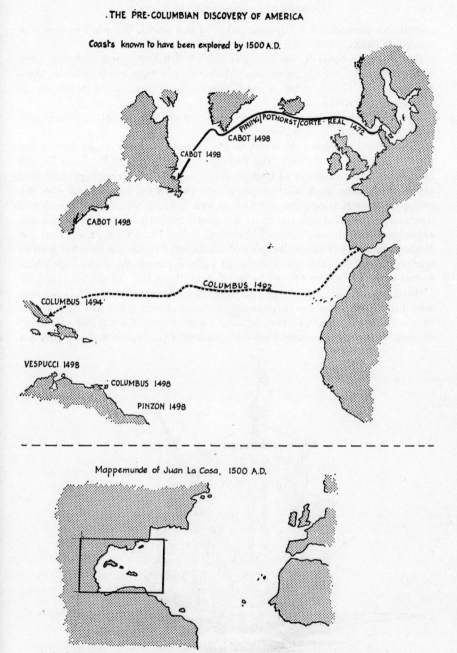

THE PRE-COLUMBIAN DISCOVERY OF AMERICA

Coasts known to have been explored by 1500 A.D.

PINING/POTHORST/CORTE·REAL 1472

CABOT 1498

CABOT 1498

CABOT 1498

COLUMBUS 1492

COLUMBUS 1494

VESPUCCI 1498

COLUMBUS 1498

PINZON 1498

Mappemunde of Juan La Cosa, 1500 A.D.

It is difficult to see how Juan La Cosa could have drawn the area enclosed by the box, unless he had access to the reports of secret Portuguese voyages which enabled him to delineate Cuba as an island and to enclose the western side of the Caribbean with the land mass of Central America.

FIG 19.

acceptance throughout a fair proportion of the world. On what evidence is this belief based?

And here we come to the rub. For the Danish-Portuguese claim to have rediscovered America is based on evidence that is more circumstantial than documentary. That is to say, a pre-Columbian crossing cannot be proved: it can only be proved probable.

However, let us look at the facts: first the circumstantial evidence, and then the evidence of documents.

Who would one have expected, in the fifteenth century, to be first across the Atlantic? Without doubt the Portuguese. For to quote Professor Davies (Reardon-Smith Professor of Geography) "by about 1480 Portugal had fifty years' experience in Atlantic exploration; the Portuguese caravel was the swiftest and most seaworthy vessel afloat; while in the science and practice of navigation Portugal was the most advanced nation of Europe and her sea captains the most experienced". As proof of this Davies points out that the Portuguese voyages down the coast of Africa were by far the greatest feats of seamanship of the fifteenth century; in 1487, for example, when Dias penetrated into the Indian Ocean he sailed four times the distance covered by Columbus and was out of sight of land three times as long. "If Columbus with little experience and three indifferent ships could reach the West Indies at the first attempt," Davies argues, "then surely Portuguese efforts in exploring to westward must have been at least equally successful." This is a

Fig 20. The *Santa Maria*—the type of Portuguese Caravel which rediscovered America

cogent point. In the 1460s Portugal ruled the sea as effectively as in the 1960s America and Russia rule the air; and one would no more have expected an Hispano–Genoese first crossing of the Atlantic in those days, than one would expect an Anglo–French first landing on the moon to-day. And this is the first link in our chain of circumstantial evidence: that in the latter half of the fifteenth century Portugal's maritime supremacy was so indisputable that one would have expected it to be her seamen, in the normal course of events, who were first to cross the Atlantic.

When and by what route were they most likely to have crossed? I think the most probable date would have been between 1460 and 1480, and the most probable route *via* the Viking sea-lanes of the north.

Up to 1460 the Portuguese directed their voyaging almost entirely south down the coast of Africa. But in that year, on crossing the Bight of Biafra, they discovered that the African shore did not swing east—as all the maps of the ancients had led them to suppose—but continued mile after hundred mile to the south. This was a great disappointment. For years the Portuguese had hoped that by rounding Africa they could reach the orient, and in particular the fabulous Spice Islands, the Moluccas, on whose produce the economy of fifteenth-century Europe depended.* But Africa, it seemed, was going to be difficult to round; beyond the equator its shore still stretched away to the south; and in 1460 the Portuguese, temporarily discouraged, took the logical step of seeking another route to the treasures of the east. So the years 1460–1480 saw a sudden recession in voyages to Africa and a boom in voyages west into the Atlantic. "From 1462 onwards," Davies tells us, "many letters patent were issued by Portugal for the discovery of Antilia and other islands in the Atlantic." These letters patent, however, ceased abruptly in 1480; in that year the death penalty was introduced for those who betrayed the secrets of Portuguese expeditions west, and Portugal, on conclusion of a successful war with Spain, strengthened her monopoly in Africa but *waived her claim to a monopoly in the Atlantic;* next year, 1481, African voyaging was resumed, the Cape being rounded six years later. Portuguese historians have a logical explanation of all this. They claim that by 1480 Portugal knew that there was no easy westward route to the Moluccas, and were therefore willing to eschew Atlantic sailings and concentrate once again on their efforts to round Africa. And the corollary of this is inescapable. The Portuguese would only have known for certain that there was no westward route to the Spice Islands if they had been brought up short by the mainland of America: i.e., by 1480 they must have already crossed the Atlantic.

In support of this theory we can produce three fragments of evidence: (i) In 1481 the Florentine cosmographer Toscanelli produced cast-iron proof that Asia could be reached by sailing west; yet the Mathematical Junta of Lisbon (the most eminent maritime specialists of the day) refused to follow his advice to finance an expedition across the Atlantic; (ii) In 1484 King John rejected Columbus's plea to finance his expedition west with the words that *"the King of Portugal has information regarding the western lands more positive than*

---

* Please see Appendix B.

the visions of the Genoese". And (iii) In 1486 the Portuguese government issued a charter to Fernâo Dulmo of the Azores for colonization of "*the islands and mainland* (the emphasis is mine) in the west". This evidence, of course, is far from conclusive; but it adds plausibility to the theory that by 1480 the Atlantic had already been crossed.

By what route? There are three possibilities: by the southern route *via* the Canaries and Cape Verdes as followed by Columbus; by the direct and shortest route across the Central Atlantic *via* the Azores; or by the northern route *via* Iceland and Greenland which had been pioneered by the Norse.

The events of September/October 1492 rule out the first possibility. For every scrap of evidence leads us to suppose that when Columbus allowed the *Santa Maria* to be borne away by the Equatorial Drift and the North-East Trades he was pioneering a *new* sea-passage, well to the south of any that had been attempted before—and herein lies his great contribution to the history of exploration: that he discovered this comparatively easy seaway which was to become the classic route not only to the Americas but also subsequently to the Pacific. If anyone before Columbus had already sailed by this southern route it would have been realized how easy crossing the Atlantic was and a whole spate of voyages would inevitably have followed.

The central route looks the obvious place for a crossing; for the Azores lie a thousand miles from the coast of Europe, and an expedition standing west from Terceira or Sâo Miguel would be already a third of the way across the Atlantic. Yet hardly ever, in all the history of sail, has a ship passed from Europe to America *via* the Azores. For in the central Atlantic winds and currents are contrary; the Gulf Stream and the westerlies run strongly and persistently all the year round from west to east, and ships attempting to stand due west from Europe invariably meet the fate described by William of Worcester—"*On the 15th day of July, 1480 a ship belonging to John Jay Junior of 80 tons burthen sailed from the King's Road of Bristol in search of the island of Brasil beyond the westernmost part of Ireland . . . and news reached Bristol on the 18th day of September that they had sailed about the sea for nine weeks and found not the island but had been repeatedly forced back by tempests till they were obliged to seek harbour in Ireland for rest of ship and crew.*" So on grounds of meteorology we can rule out the central route.

Which takes us north. It seems at first unlikely that the Portuguese, who are one of the most southerly nations of Europe, should have sailed to America by the same route as the Scandinavians, who are among the most northerly. Yet the more one examines this theory the more attractive it becomes. For this northern route was both easy and familiar. Winds and currents north of the sixtieth parallel are generally favourable for a ship sailing from Europe to America, and it is possible to island-hop without ever being more than one hundred and seventy-five miles from land; while there is abundant evidence that throughout the Middle Ages Europeans *knew* that there was land to westward of the Atlantic—the king of Norway, for example, sent an annual trading vessel to Greenland and the occasional missionary to America, the Vatican traded in Greenland falcons and appointed bishops to Vineland. What more natural then than that fifteenth-century Portuguese seamen should have sailed in the wake of Herjulfson and Eriksson and reached America *via* this classic sea-route of the north?

It has sometimes been argued that by the end of the fifteenth century memory of the Viking voyages had faded, and that the Portuguese, isolated in the south of Europe, had neither knowledge of nor interest in what happened in the North Atlantic. It is possible to prove to the contrary. And we come now to a cardinal factor in our case for a pre-Columbian crossing: the fact that in the latter half of the fifteenth century, in the matter of Atlantic voyaging, there was collaboration between the Portuguese and the Danes.

The royal houses of Portugal and Denmark had much in common. They were both militantly Christian, and they were both, by the latter half of the fifteenth century, eagerly reaping the benefits of seaborne trade. Also they were united by marriage, Henry the Navigator's cousin Philippa being the wife of Eric II of Denmark. The two dynasties had good reason therefore to exchange correspondence and visits. In particular it has been established by Professor Sofus Larsen that round about 1445 King Eric sent his cousin-in-law a copy of Claudius Clavus's famous series of northern maps. These maps infer the existence of a sea-lane running parallel to the west coast of Greenland and leading direct from the Atlantic to China. A translation of Clavus's text is: "*The peninsula of the island of Greenland extends southwards from an unknown land to the north, which is inaccessible on account of ice. Nevertheless, as I have myself seen, the Eskimos frequently descend on Greenland in large hosts, doubtless from the land beyond the Pole. Hence the ocean does not lap the shores of a continent immediately below the Pole—as all the early authors assert; and the knight Mandeville did not lie when he said that he had sailed through from China to one of the islands of Scandinavia.*" This is the first reference in history to that North-West Passage, the quest for which was to last for more than four hundred years and cost an unknown multitude of seamen their lives. It would have been strange indeed if Henry the Navigator, who was probably more anxious to reach the orient than any of his contemporaries, had not followed this clue up. And his first step, according to Larsen, was to invite a Danish observer to sail in a Portuguese expedition down the coast of Africa, his objective being to establish a precedent whereby he could subsequently place a Portuguese observer aboard a Danish expedition to Greenland. And there is documentary evidence that this exchange took place. Several contemporary Portuguese writers, including Azurara and Barros, give a full account of how, in 1448, a Danish nobleman named Vallarte (probably Wollart in the vernacular) took part in Fernand-affonso's expedition to Cape Verde, and how the Dane, "*being a man of small prudence*", allowed himself to be captured by the natives. And the thing that stands out from every account is that Vallarte was *not* obliged to smuggle aboard a Portuguese ship *incognito;* he was an accredited representative of the Danish court travelling with the official blessing of Henry the Navigator — witness Azurara: "*And when Vallarte had been staying for some time at the court of the Infante, he requested that a caravel might be equipped so that he could make a voyage to the land of the Negroes. The Infante at once ordered a caravel to be made ready, and set Vallarte the task of sailing (with Fernandaffonso) to Cape Verde to see what information could be obtained about the king of that country* . . ." This, I think, is the only instance in fifteenth-century history of the Portuguese inviting a foreigner to take part in one of their voyages, and it is indisputable evidence of Dano–Portuguese collusion.

Thus far our argument has proceeded smoothly. We have established that the best qualified nation to have rediscovered America were the Portuguese: that the most likely date for their discovery was between 1460 and 1480: and that the most likely route for their crossing the Atlantic was *via* Iceland and Greenland —with Danish co-operation.

But we now come to an *impasse*. There is no contemporary record of any Dano–Portuguese expedition having crossed the North Atlantic between 1460 and 1480. There are several references to such an expedition which were either written or discovered at a later date. But the complete lack of contemporary documentation—the "silence of history" —has long been a powerful argument of those who reject a pre-Columbian discovery. Look what a fuss was made of Columbus, the doubters say in effect; if some other explorer had really crossed the Atlantic before 1492 then surely his exploits would have enjoyed the same sort of coverage as those of the Genoese?

To this, Portuguese historians have a sophisticated answer. They claim that the Danes did not publicize their discoveries because the Pining–Pothorst–Corte-Real expedition touched only the far north of America which was of no commercial potential, while the Portuguese for their part were bound to silence by their official policy of secrecy. Most British and American historians dismiss this argument as casuistry. They point out that although the Portuguese would doubtless have liked to keep their voyages secret, they were not in fact able to do so—witness the number of "foreigners" who stowed away in Portuguese ships and the rapidity and regularity with which Portuguese discoveries *were* in fact made known in other countries. Yet the Portuguese point of view does not deserve to be dismissed too summarily; and I think it is only fair to differentiate between Portugal's attitude towards discoveries in Africa and her attitude towards discoveries in the Atlantic. As regards Africa, after about 1450 Portugal was by no means loath to publicise her voyages, because an almost yearly succession of Papal Bulls confirmed her monopoly in these waters, and the more voyages she made the more this monopoly (by right of discovery and usage) was strengthened. As regards the Atlantic, her position was entirely different. Here the Canary Islands belonged to Castile, and by mid-century Spanish ships were venturing west in fair numbers. Portugal was not strong enough to claim, let alone maintain, an Atlantic monopoly as well as an African one, and the last thing she wanted to do was to pioneer an Atlantic route to the Moluccas only to find that Spain reaped where she had sown. So on Portuguese voyages west the order of the day was the strictest secrecy. This is confirmed by Professor Davies: "No Portuguese charts or maps of Atlantic discoveries exist before 1502, and even the Royal Historians were forbidden to record discoveries. For *it was entirely contrary to Portuguese interests to publicise the possibility of reaching Asia by sailing west.*" The Portuguese, in other words, had good reason to keep Corte-Real's discoveries secret. And the silence of contemporary history is not a completely convincing argument that a pre-Columbian crossing did not in fact take place.

But if there is no contemporary record of Pining, Pothorst and Corte-Real having crossed the Atlantic, then on what evidence, you ask, is their claim advanced? The answer is, on a series of scattered references in documents, letters and maps which have been unearthed in Scandinavia, Portugal and the Azores, all of which are genuine but all of which suffer the disadvantage of having been written some time after the voyage took place.

These references can be divided into three groups: those relating to Johannes Scolvus; those relating to Pining and Pothorst; and those relating to João Vaz Corte-Real. And we pass now from evidence that is circumstantial and deals with the likelihood of a pre-Columbian crossing in general to evidence that is documentary and deals with an actual crossing in particular.

EVIDENCE OF A PRE-COLUMBIAN DISCOVERY BY JOHANNES SCOLVUS

There are a fair number of references in Scandinavian literature to a certain Johannes Scolvus (possibly Jon Scolp in the vernacular), a pilot, who, in the 1470s, made a voyage of discovery in the waters of the far north. I quote four of these:

(a) In 1537 Gemma Frisius and Gerhard Mercator collaborated to produce their famous globe. This shows a great polar strait running parallel to the west of Greenland and marked with the words: *"Fretum trium fratum, per quod Lusitani ad Orientem & ad Indos & ad Moluccas navigare conatisunt* (there follow some corrupted Portuguese names, then to the west of Greenland the words) *. . . quig populi, ad quos Johannes Scolvus Danus pervenit circa annum 1476."*

(b) In 1552 the Spanish author de Gomara wrote in his book *Primera y Segunda Parte de la Historia General de los Indias: "To this place* (Labrador) *there came also people from Norway under Johannes Scolvus and Englishmen under Sebastian Cabot"*, and a little later there occurs the passage *"Britons and Danes have also visited Stockfishland"* (Newfoundland).

(c) In his classic work *In Northern Mists* Fridtjof Nansen quotes an English document, dated 1575, which reads *"And this passage is called The Narowe Sea or Streicte of the three Brethren in which passage, at no tyme in the yere, is ise wonte to be found. The cause is the swifte ronnyng downe of sea into sea. In the North side of this Passage, John Scolvus, a pilot of Denmarke, was in anno 1476.* (It seems probable that this *"Streicte of the three Brethren"* is the *"fretum trium fratum"* referred to in (a) above, the three brothers probably being the sons of João Vaz Corte-Real who subsequently perished in their efforts to explore the passage discovered by their father.)

(d) In *Wytfliet's Descriptionis Ptolemaicae* (1597) there occurs the passage *"Secundum detectae hujus regionis decus tulit Johannes Sclolvus Polonus, qui Anno reparate salutis MCCCCLXXVI octoginta et sex annis a prima eius lustratione navigars udtra Norvegiam, Groenlandiam, Frislandiamque, Boreale hoc fretum ingressus sub ipso Antico circulo ad Laboratois hanc terram Estolilordiamque delatus est."*

These passages are unlikely to have been copied one from another, and the point they establish is that round about 1476 a Scandinavian pilot named Scolvus pushed into a *fretum* or "strait" to the west of Greenland. But how could this Scolvus have known he was in a strait, as distinct from the open sea, unless he had made contact with land to the west? Johannes Scolvus, in other words, must surely have rediscovered the mainland of America some twenty years before Columbus.

EVIDENCE OF A PRE-COLUMBIAN DISCOVERY BY PINING AND POTHORST

Hans Pothorst and Diderik Pining were freebooters, the Danish counterparts of Frobisher and Drake. In an age when war-hero and pirate were all but synonymous it is hardly surprising that Pining and Pothorst were alternately rewarded with governorships and condemned to be hung in chains. There are several references to them in contemporary British and Danish literature, and Pothorst has a plaque in his honour in the vault of Elsinore church; but the most interesting fact about these Danish sea-captains was not brought to light until 1551. In that year King Christian III of Denmark commissioned the burgomaster of Kiel to buy him a number of maps, books and pictures to add to the maritime museum he was building up in his palace. In the course of this commission the burgomaster visited Paris, and here he was offered a map which was similar to Olaus's famous *Carta Marina* but which evidently contained additional material provided by an unknown source. This map so excited the burgomaster that he wrote King Christian a special letter about it.

"Your Royal Highness can be assured that your land of Greenland extends well towards the New World and the countries discovered by the Spaniards and Portuguese. I have recently seen a map, made in Paris, which relates to Your Majesty's land of Iceland and all the wonders to be seen there. In the text accompanying this map it is stated that Iceland is twice the size of Sicily. It is also stated that in the reign of Your Majesty's grandfather King Christian I, two skippers Pynink and Poidthorsth were sent forth with several ships, at the request of the king of Portugal, to search for new islands and continents in the north. These were the skippers who set up a great beacon on the rock of Wydtszeick off the coast of Greenland opposite Sniefeldsickel in Iceland, to warn people of the Greenland pirates (the Eskimos) who attack in large numbers in little keelless boats."

There are two points of special interest here. The objective of the expedition is clearly stated: "to search for new islands and continents in the north." And the motivation is made equally clear; the expedition set out "at the request of the King of Portugal". There is one simple explanation of this surprising statement. Here is Portugal's long-deferred *quid pro quo* for Vallarte's voyage down Africa. Here in fact is evidence of that joint Dano-Portuguese venture which we should have expected to take place in the north between 1460 and 1480 but which contemporary chroniclers, for reasons we have already noted, failed to mention.

EVIDENCE OF A PRE-COLUMBIAN DISCOVERY BY JOÃO VAZ CORTE-REAL

João Vaz Corte-Real is one of those shadowy almost legendary explorers, like Pytheas of Marseilles, about whom we know tantalisingly little. He is first mentioned as holding the position of "head porter" to Fernando, Duke of Viseu; then in 1474 he was suddenly awarded the governorship of Angra and Sâo Jorge, the largest and richest provinces of the Azores. He must surely have done something fairly spectacular to deserve such promotion, and this is confirmed by the letters-patent announcing his appointment—"in consideration of the services that Joâo Vaz Corte-Real, gentleman of the household, has performed for the Infante my Lord . . . is conferred on him the captaincy of Angra in the Island of Terceira . . ." In his *History of the Azores* Antonio Cordeiro gives us a clue as to what this feat might have been. *"About the time,"* he writes, *"that the viceroyship of Terceyra became vacant on account of the death of Jacome de Bruges, there landed at Terceyra two gentlemen who had recently returned from stockfish-land (terra do bacalhao) which they had gone out to discover by order of the Portuguese king. One of these gentlemen was Joao Vaz Corte-Real . . . and he petitioned that he might have the governorship as a reward for his services."* Cordeiro admits that his source for this story is Gaspar Frutuoso, a not very reliable collector of local gossip who lived in the Azores in the sixteenth century. But gossip is frequently based on a substratum of truth, and it is surely no coincidence that Frutuoso's story ties up so exactly with the facts we have already established. For Joâo Vaz Corte-Real was surely the Portuguese observer placed by order of the king aboard Pining and Pothorst's expedition to the north.

To accept this we must account for the discrepancy in dates. Corte-Real is said to have taken up the governorship of Terceira, as a reward for his voyage, in 1474; yet on all the documents we have examined the voyage is said to have taken place *"circa anno 1476"*. Now it is unlikely, to say the least, that there were two voyages to Newfoundland, one in 1472–3 and the other in 1476, and I therefore suggest that what happened was this. The voyage took place in 1472–3; Corte-Real wrote his report of it as soon as he had settled in the Azores, say *circa* 1474–5; this report reached the King of Portugal *circa* 1476 and was placed in the royal archives of that year, and when historians subsequently unearthed the report they erroneously assumed the voyage had taken place in the year under which it was filed.

The account of Cordeiro is by no means the only evidence we have of Corte-Real's voyage. We have already mentioned the Gemma Frisius globe and its entry: *"Strait of the Three Brothers, through which the Portuguese attempted to sail to the Orient, the Indies and the Moluccas . . . to which neighbourhood came Johannes Scolvus in about 1476."* Assuming that Joâo Vaz Corte-Real accompanied Scolvus, this gives added weight to his claim to a pre-Columbian discovery. In addition, on the maps of the Portuguese cartographer Dourado (1534) we find the following entries on a stretch of the Labrador coast: *"teso de Joâo Vaz"* and *"baia de Joâo Vaz."* It is true that both Joâo and Vaz are common names in Portugal; but it would surely be a surprising coincidence if the headland and bay in question were called after another discoverer who had the same names.

Lastly, Corte-Real's claim is supported by two pieces of circumstantial evidence: the family tradition of Labrador voyaging that was perpetuated by his sons; and the *mappemunde* of Juan de la Cosa which shows a long reach of American coastline that no explorer is known to have sighted.

Joâo Vaz Corte-Real had three sons (Vasqueanos, Gaspar and Miguel) who dedicated their lives to North Atlantic voyaging. Time and again, between 1493 and 1503, these three brothers set sail "to seek out the lands to northward, holding that others had by now discovered all that lay in the south". It is arguable that their dedication to the North Atlantic had its roots in their father's voyage of 1472–3, and that by following his footsteps the young Corte-Reals were hoping to penetrate the strait that was believed to lead to the orient. Be that as it may, they died in the attempt, their ships being lost one after another, in the bleak sub-Arctic waters of the Davis Strait. It has been said that Portugal gained little honour or wealth from these voyages of the Corte-Reals. But this is not so. Their discoveries were in fact worth more to Portugal than were those of Cortes and Pizarro to Spain. Salt cod may lack the romantic attraction of Aztec gold, but in terms of hard cash it was to prove a more profitable investment. For Spain had an average annual income of less than £400,000 from her South American treasure ships, while Portugal's average income from her Newfoundland fisheries rose quickly to over £1,000,000 a year; she still sends a fleet of seventy vessels a season to fish the Banks, and the coast of Newfoundland is studded with names that are memorials to her seamen—Cabo Raco, Bacalhan, Conception Bay, Fogo, Boavista and Portugal Cove. So whatever the extent of Joâo Vaz's discoveries, the Corte-Reals could not be said to have died in vain.

Finally we come to Juan de la Cosa's map, which tends (like so many other fragments of evidence) to prove the likelihood of a pre-Columbian discovery.

Juan de la Cosa was a Basque. In 1500 he drew his famous *mappemunde* (*vide* page 115). This map was definitely not based on guesswork; for its outlines, though crude, are fundamentally correct. In particular de Cosa depicted Cuba as an island nine years before it was officially circumnavigated, and he accurately delineated the coast of Central America a decade before its official sighting. Whence did he get his information on these points? It has been conjectured by Davies that he had access to secret Portuguese documents. This theory is strengthened by the fact that letters, written by Pasqualigo and Pereira also lead us to suppose that the Portuguese were in fact aware of the outline of Central America long before it had been officially discovered by the Spaniards. (The text of these letters is: from Pietro Pasqualigo to the Venetian Signory, dated October 18th, 1501: "*the Corte-Reals have run along about six hundred miles of Labrador without finding the end thereof, which leads them to suppose it is part of the continent they visited last year. They say also that this continent is connected to the Antilles and to the land of parrots (Brazil).*" From Pacheco Pereira to King Manuel of Portugal, dated 1505: "*therefore, most fortunate Prince, we have known and seen how a very large and continuous mass of land, with many large islands adjacent, extending from 70° north of the equator to 23½° south of it, has been found and navigated.*") Yet more weight is given to Davies's argument by the fact that when de Cosa visited Lisbon in 1503 he was promptly arrested—for disclosing state secrets?— and was only released after he had drawn and sent to Queen Isabella of Spain two new maps which showed open sea to the west of the Caribbean: i.e., maps which would encourage Spain in her search for a passage west to the Moluccas.

Now it is not claimed that Joâo Vaz Corte-Real in his voyage of 1472-3 discovered the coast of Central America as well as the coast of Labrador — that would be tantamount to accrediting to a single voyage all the alleged discoveries of Saint Brandan. But de Cosa's map does indicate, I think, that a number of unknown Portuguese seamen may well have visited the mainland of Central America on several occasions prior to its official discovery by Spain. What happened in the south could have happened just as easily in the north.

Such is the case for a pre-Columbian discovery of America. It is not a cast-iron case. There is no single piece of evidence that we can point to and say "Here is irrefutable proof that the Danes and the Portuguese reached Labrador in 1472", but the cumulative effect of so many scraps of circumstantial and documentary evidence strikes me as almost overwhelming, and I hope that the hitherto unknown Pining, Pothorst and Joâo Vaz Corte-Real may at last be accorded their rightful place in the galaxy of the world's greatest explorers.

IX

THE GREATEST VOYAGE OF ALL

(Magellan, first round the world: A.D. 1519–1522)

IT was October, 1516, and outside his palace in Lisbon King Manuel the Fortunate was enthroned in state on his dais of ebony and gold. All day a succession of applicants had knelt at his feet, humbly begging in public those favours for which they lacked the influence to petition in private. By the time the evening sun was streaming into the courtyard and a herald was announcing the name of the last supplicant, Dom Manuel was tired.

"Fernào de Magalhàes!"

A stir of surprise ran through the assembled court. For Ferdinand Magellan was a man of substance, a *fidalgo escudeiro*, not the type of person expected to go down on his knees in public. Heads craned forward as the short, thickset figure limped awkwardly up to the dais. And Dom Manuel frowned; he cordially disliked Magellan.

In a low voice the mariner made his petition. He outlined his twenty years in the king's service—years in which he had done as much as anyone to extend Portugal's empire in the far east—he mentioned the three times he had been seriously wounded, and begged that he might now be raised in rank to *fidalgo da casa de El Rei*. Brusquely Dom Manuel refused. But Magellan stayed on his knees. He was making another petition now: that he might be given command of one of the royal caravels soon to set sail for the Moluccas, the fabulous Spice Islands of the east. Again Dom Manuel refused, adding maliciously that he had no use for Magellan's services either in a caravel or anywhere else. Magellan had not expected this; he was humiliated and indignant.

"Then may I be permitted, El Rei," he cried, "to seek service under another Lord?"

Dom Manuel rose from his throne. He was a commanding figure, towering majestically over the crippled and insignificant Magellan. "It is a matter of indifference to me," he said loudly, "whence you go or whom you serve."

Automatically Magellan leaned forward to kiss the king's hand, a ritual which loyal *fidalgos* had followed for generations at the end of their audience. But Dom Manuel put his hands behind his back.

It was an expensive gesture.

For a year later Magellan was outlining to another and more sympathetic monarch, Charles V of Spain, his scheme for reaching the Moluccas by sailing not south-east down the coast of Africa but south-west across the Atlantic.

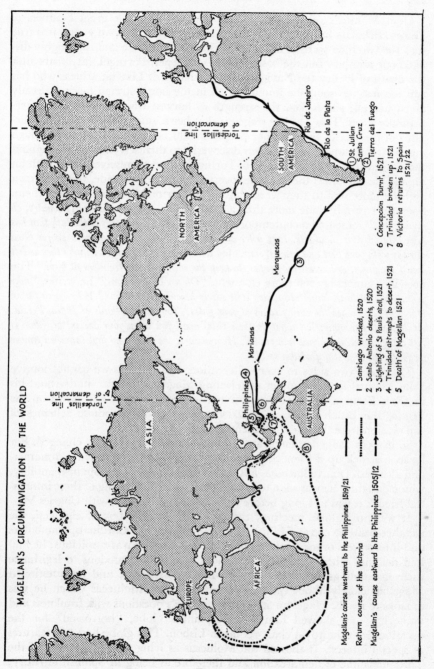

MAGELLAN'S CIRCUMNAVIGATION OF THE WORLD

Tordesillas line of demarcation

NORTH AMERICA

SOUTH AMERICA

Rio de Janeiro

Rio de la Plata

① St. Julian
Santa Cruz
② Tierra del Fuego

Marquesas

③

Marianas

ASIA

AUSTRALIA

AFRICA

EUROPE

④ Philippines
⑥
⑤
⑦
⑧

"Tordesillas" line of demarcation

1 Santiago wrecked, 1520
2 Santo Antonio deserts, 1520
3 Sighting of St Paul's atoll, 1521
4 Trinidad attempts to desert, 1521
5 Death of Magellan 1521
6 Concepción burnt, 1521
7 Trinidad broken up, 1521
8 Victoria returns to Spain
   1521/22

Magellan's course westward to the Philippines 1519/21
Return course of the Victoria
Magellan's course eastward to the Philippines 1505/12

FIG 21.

Dom Manuel's rejection of Magellan was one of the great blunders of history. Scholars have often put it down to personal antipathy, and it is true that the two men were as different as chalk from cheese and thoroughly disliked one another. But the basic reasons go deeper. Portugal, fifty years after the death of Henry the Navigator, was exhausted. Like an athlete who has run too fast too soon she found herself in the home stretch having already given her all; she lacked the strength to harvest where she had so enterprisingly sown. This was her tragedy: that her seamen should discover fourfifths of the world, but that her people should be neither numerous enough nor powerful enough to keep their discoveries to themselves. Thus throughout the sixteenth century the rulers of Portugal found themselves faced with an impossible dilemma: the more discoveries their seamen made, the more men and the more wealth they were obliged to pour out to try to preserve them. Soon the strain became more than a small nation could bear. "*My country, oh my country,*" lamented a contemporary chronicler. "*Too heavy is the task that has been laid on your shoulders. Day after day I watch the ships leaving your shores filled always with your best and bravest sons. And too many do not return . . . who then is left to till the fields, to harvest the grapes, to keep the enemy on our frontiers at bay?*" The poet De Camões is even more eloquent. "*Oh my beloved sons,*" he writes, "*why venture out on to the cruel sea which will surely become your shroud? Why go so far in search of foes, when the enemy rages at your gates? You may be Lords of India, Persia, Arabia and Ethiopia; but what do these titles avail you when your ancient kingdom is left depopulated, weakened and ruined. Heaven curse the man who first launched timber on to the sea or first unfurled a sail!*"

There are two sides to every altercation. And though we cannot forgive Dom Manuel for his manner of rejecting Magellan, we can understand his motives. Portugal by 1516 was satiated with discoveries; and down on the *Restelo*, the Beach of Tears, grizzled seamen with grandiose schemes of exploration were thick and pestilential as flies.

So in 1517 Magellan emigrated to Spain. And here his luck changed. For he soon struck up a friendship with Ruy Faleiro, a fashionable astronomer, and also with Duarte Barbosa, a Knight Commander of the Spanish nobility, whose daughter he was soon to marry. And with the backing of these influential friends it was not long before he secured an audience with Charles V.

It was an historic meeting: the pale slightly-built boy of eighteen, the weather-beaten veteran of forty, and round them the Cardinals, councillors and interpreters of the Spanish court. At first Charles was suspicious; he had had dealings with Portuguese renegades before, men anxious to legitimize their maraudings into Portugal's far-flung possessions; and he questioned Magellan closely about the exact location of the Moluccas which he was anxious to reach. Magellan answered the king's questions with frankness and authority, and showed him a hand-painted globe, "borrowed" for the occasion from the royal chart-rooms in Lisbon. This globe had two features of special interest. It showed the Moluccas as lying well to the east of the Tordesillas line of demarcation and therefore as being in Spanish territory; it also contained an enigmatic reference, in code, to a strait passing east-to-west through America and so linking the Atlantic and Pacific. On the

THE COAST OF THE SAHARA

strength of this globe and his favourable impression of Magellan, Charles commissioned the voyage on the spot.

It is easy to see how the king's approval was won—with the body of a middle-aged invalid and the mind of a youth of action, Charles was peculiarly susceptible to adventurous projects. What is not so easy to understand is the confidence with which Magellan put forward his theory that the Moluccas could be reached by sailing not east but west. This was a revolutionary suggestion. And unless we realize just *how* revolutionary it seemed to his contemporaries, it is difficult for us to-day to appreciate the full significance of Magellan's voyage. Let us therefore take a brief look at man's knowledge of the world on the eve of Magellan's departure.

It was known at least in theory in 1518 that the world was a sphere, but its circumference was still in dispute and was generally much underestimated. It was known that there was land to the west of the Atlantic, land which formed part of a large continent which was not Asia; but the extent and continuity of the continent was a matter of conjecture. It was known that beyond this continent lay another ocean—Balboa had sighted it in 1513—but the extent of this ocean too was something at which cartographers were loth to hazard a guess; nor was there any proof that this unknown ocean was connected to the Atlantic by sea—indeed, all available evidence pointed to the fact that the intervening land-mass of America stretched impassably from pole to pole. How then can we account for Magellan's confidence?

The explanation lies, I think, in his friendship with the little-known Portuguese navigator John of Lisbon. In the summer of 1514 John of Lisbon had pushed far down the coast of South America and had made a reconnaissance of the estuary of the River Plate. And having sailed due west into this estuary for over 150 miles without having sighted land, he not unnaturally imagined that he had discovered a strait: a strait which if followed would lead to the unknown ocean beyond. John of Lisbon, at the time of this voyage, was in the service not of the Portuguese crown but of the Fugger Bankers. He did not, therefore, divulge his discoveries in Lisbon. But he *did* divulge them to Magellan, as an act of friendship to a colleague who he thought had been shabbily treated by Dom Manuel; and he gave Magellan not only copies of his logs and charts, but also exact details of the bearings, soundings, anchorages, shoals, currents and landmarks of the La Plata estuary. And it was on the strength of this secret but erroneous information that Magellan made plans for his voyage.

What great deeds are sometimes conceived in misapprehension! A generation earlier Columbus had tried to sail west to Asia—and had reached America. Now in 1518 Magellan tried to sail *via* the River Plate to the Moluccas—and he circumnavigated the world.

*   *   *

At dawn on Monday, August 10th, 1519, five ships were moored to the Dock of Mules in Seville.

For over a year these ships had been preparing for their great voyage. They had been recaulked, refitted and almost entirely recanvassed. They had been provisioned in theory for three years—although in practice Portuguese agents, attempting to hamstring Magellan's departure, had pilfered so extensively that supplies for only two years were actually aboard. In their forward holds were spare timbers, forges, anvils, bellows and a whole armoury of weapons; also the *bric-à-brac* of trade—bars of copper, flasks of quicksilver, bales of cloth, together with 5,000 cheap German knives, 10,000 fish-hooks and over 20,000 bells. In their sail-lockers were six spare sets of canvas. Lashed to their decks were their three *bergentym*, shallow draught pinnaces for exploring close inshore. In their forecastles and cabins were a plethora of navigational aids: twenty-four parchment charts, six pairs of compasses, twenty-one wooden quadrants, seven astrolabes, thirty-five compass needles, eighteen hour glasses and Faleiro's tables for calculating latitude. In their after holds were provisions on a scale hitherto undreamed of—21,300 pounds of biscuit, 1,120 pounds of cheese, 570 pounds of meat, 480 pounds of oil, 200 barrels of sardines, together with vast quantities of good quality wine, peas, beans, lentils, rice, sugar, radishes, garlic, onions, raisins, figs, honey and salt. Their armament was comprehensive. Their crews were in good heart. And the only note of discord was in the relationship of their captains; for four were Spaniards of noble birth who disliked taking orders from *"the upstart Portuguese"* whom the king had placed over them, and although these captains had publicly sworn *"to follow the course ordered by their Captain-General and to obey him in everything"*, yet even before their ships left Spanish waters they were plotting mutiny and murder. But their dissensions were veiled for the time being in the bustle and excitement of departure. The ropes were cast off. Tugged at by an ebb-tide the vessels drifted slowly away from the Dock of Mules. One by one as they came to mid-river they hoisted their foresails. And as the sun rose red over the banks of the Guadalquivir, they stood west for the open sea: first Magellan's flagship the 110-ton *Trinidad*, then the *San Antonio*, then the *Concepcion*, then the *Victoria* and finally the diminutive 75-ton *Santiago*. The greatest voyage in history was under way.

Soon the armada came to the open sea. Night fell and Magellan hoisted an oil-burning lantern high on the *Trinidad's* poop. The ships fell into line astern, standing quietly west into the Atlantic swell. Five ships and 268 men setting out with high hopes into the unknown. But only one ship and nineteen men were to see their homeland again.

We know surprisingly little about the ships and the men who left Spain early that August on their historic voyage.

The ships' names have come down to us, also their tonnage, but no model, painting or drawing of them is known to exist. The details of their construction and rig are therefore conjecture. Bearing in mind, however, that they were described by the Portuguese consul as being *"of poor size and quality"*, with *"ribs as soft as butter"*, we must assume they were relatively old. I suspect, therefore, that they were a cross between Columbus's *Santa Maria* and the graceful high-sterned galleons of the mid-sixteenth century. That is to say, they would have been three-masted, square-sailed and with a relatively simple deck structure. Their displacement we are told averaged some hundred tons, and I would estimate their dimensions roughly as follows: length stem to stern 80–85 feet, length of keel 65–68 feet, breadth 27–30 feet,

Fig 22. Sixteenth-century Naos of the type used by Magellan

sail area 3,600 square yards, draught 7–8 feet. They probably had a crew of between forty and forty-five, and plenty of space for cargo. In other words, they were more complex but decidedly smaller than the Phoenician traders of the first millennium B.C. Figure 22 shows Fouille's reconstruction of such a vessel.

As for the men, they were a polyglot collection: Spaniards, Portuguese, Basques, Genoese, English, Sicilians, Negroes and Malaysians. Many of them were "the scum of the waterfront", a few were criminals, and about twenty or thirty were absolute landlubbers —family retainers brought aboard as personal servants of the high-ranking Spanish officers. Some seventy of the crew, however, were first-class seamen (about half of whom had served under Magellan before), and these men formed in each vessel a professional core from whom the rest of the ship's company were quick to learn. Apart from Magellan, few of the officers were men of much ability or integrity —with one exception. Shortly before the *Trinidad* sailed she was joined by an Italian named Antonio Pigafetta, a young man of good education who joined the expedition solely because he was "*desirous of seeing the wonderful things of the ocean*"; he certainly had his desire fulfilled; and he kept a diary, a remarkably full and unbiased account of his experiences, which has been of the greatest value to historians. And it is because of Pigafetta's diary that we are now able to follow Magellan's fortunes day by day.

To start with the armada enjoyed fair weather. The ships standing west into a placid sea, the *Trinidad* leading, the others copying her course and the set of her sails. By night, oil-burning *farols* were hung in the poops, and lighted torches gave warning of alterations of course. Magellan was happy to be at sea, emancipated at last from the drudgery and paper-work of commissioning; but he knew that serious difficulties were still to be faced. For he feared that the Portuguese might try to waylay him. And he mistrusted his captains.

After a week the ships put in to Tenerife, where they topped up with firewood and stores. And here Magellan's suspicions were confirmed. For no sooner had the *Trinidad* berthed, than a fast despatch boat came racing up to her with a letter from Dom Barbosa. This letter warned Magellan that a triumvirate of the captains, led by Juan de Cartegna of the *San Antonio*, were planning to take over command; if Magellan opposed them they intended to kill him.

Magellan handled the situation with a subtlety that would have warmed the heart of Machiavelli. The triumvirate planned to provoke a quarrel which, they hoped, would trigger off violence. But Magellan refused to be provoked. For several weeks he meekly endured the snubs and insults to which the would-be mutineers subjected him. Juan de Cartegna publicly insulted him, disputing his course and refusing to salute him. But Magellan did nothing. He bided his time. Then, when his ships were again at sea and his opportunity came, he struck hard. It was a court-martial which gave Magellan the chance he had been waiting for. The *Victoria's contramaestre* had been caught in the act of sodomy, a crime usually punished by flogging but technically carrying the penalty of public hanging. Magellan ordered a full-dress trial, for which he summoned all four captains aboard the *Trinidad*. After the hearing, Cartegna, as Magellan had expected, began to taunt him, trying once again to precipitate a crisis. He succeeded. To start with, Magellan listened passively to his captain's tirade of insults; then Cartegna overstepped himself.

"No longer," he shouted, "am I prepared to obey the orders of such a fool!"

Magellan raised his hand. Before the captains realized what was happening a file of marines moved swiftly into the cabin. Cartegna was pinioned before his sword was out of its sheath.

"Rebel!" Magellan cried. "You are not prepared to obey me. This is mutiny."

Cartegna lost his head.

"Stab him! Stab him!" he cried to his fellow-captains.

But they too were surrounded by the *Trinidad's* men at arms.

Magellan had the mutineers at his mercy. In front of officers assembled for a formal court-martial, Cartegna had shouted his refusal to obey orders and had incited his fellow-captains to kill their commander. He was dragged away, screaming threats and abuse, and clamped into the forecastle stocks.

Here he was left, to be gaped at by the crew and to await the Captain-General's pleasure.

If Magellan had ordered the triumvirate to be hanged and drawn on the spot, he would have been within his rights. But he was merciful. He stripped Cartegna of his command, then set him free on parole under oath of his future obedience.

There was no question now as to who was in command: no querying of Magellan's course, as the five ships headed south by west down the coast of Africa, keeping unusually close inshore.

Magellan had good reasons for holding this peculiar course. He had dealt with the mutineers, but the threat of the Portuguese remained. He therefore decided to avoid the usual trade-routes: to hug the African shore as far south as the equator, then strike westward into the unfrequented Sargasso Sea. It was a reasonable plan. But as events turned out it was bedevilled by bad weather.

On October 18th, off Sierra Leone, the armada ran into a series of terrifying storms, with violent head-winds. Magellan's ships, with their rounded hulls and shallow draught, were not at their best in a heavy sea. Soon they were rolling their guts out. They rolled so viciously in fact that their yard-arms actually touched the crests of the waves, the seas sluiced green over their decks, and the seamen could only huddle helplessly into the forecastle and pray. And eventually, Don Antonio tells us, their prayers were heard. For the sacred fire of Saint Elmo* lit up their masts, and a little later the storms began to abate.

But their troubles were not over. For after the storm came the rain.

For twenty days as they beat slowly up to the equator, torrential rain poured without respite out of a leaden sky. The crew grew dispirited; and their spirits were not improved when Magellan, alarmed at his lack of progress, ordered a cut in their rations. But eventually the rain—like the storms—died away, the sun reappeared, and Magellan was able to check his position and alter course to the west.

For a while progress was good. Then came an ordeal even more searching than rain or storm: the doldrums, the windless cauldron of the Sargasso. Magellan's men had a foretaste now of what was to lie ahead of them in the Pacific.

In mid-November the winds weakened and died, the atmosphere turned oppressive, and the sea took on a peculiar sheen, like oiled glass. The swell, however, remained; and although there was no wind to fill their sails the five ships were never still, but spun and pitched this way and that, to the groaning of timbers and the rattling of spars. They were athwart the equator now, and the sun blazed down on them day after day with cruel intensity. The tar melted in their seams, their timbers split open, and the pumps had to be continually manned—yet so intense was the heat that after ten minutes pumping the seamen fainted. Their stores were not packaged to withstand

---

* Saint Elmo is the patron saint of seamen, and the luminous discharge which sometimes glows on masts and spars during an electric storm used to be known as his "fire".

these conditions; their wheat parched, their meat turned putrid and the hoops of their water- and wine-casks warped and burst. But the crew were too enervated to care; they lolled listlessly in what little shade they could find, grumbling at the shortage of water and cursing the day they had been foolish enough to enlist. The nights were as sultry and airless as the days. If Magellan had been becalmed for long in the Sargasso, his fleet would have perished. But after three weeks of purgatory a whisper of wind stirred their canvas and the ships, slowly at first and then with increasing certainty began to get under way. The South Equatorial Current had drifted them through the doldrums, and they were able thankfully to set course for Brazil.

The next month, in contrast to what had gone before, was one of the pleasantest of the voyage. Magellan knew that the shores of Brazil were dangerous—the Portuguese had lost many caravels here, and John of Lisbon had expressly warned him of the flat underwater reefs extending more than seventy miles offshore—so when his dead-reckoning plot indicated they were nearing land, he ordered a round-the-clock watch and took frequent soundings. Early in December a brightly coloured land-bird was sighted, and soon the earthy scent of the great Brazilian forests came drifting out of the west. Magellan doubled his watch by day and furled his sails by night; and at dawn on December 8th a low forested littoral rose green over the horizon. They hit the coast a little south of Cape Roque: a perfect landfall after a voyage of nearly five thousand miles. They were, however, in Portuguese waters; landing would have been impolitic; so the armada stood south-south-west, keeping well offshore to avoid the reefs. And on December 13th they put in to the most beautiful harbour in the world: Rio de Janeiro: well to the south of the last Portuguese settlement.

Rio was idyllic, in more senses than one. The scenery was beyond compare: the fantastic Sugar-loaf peak, the Mediterranean blue of the sea, and the emerald green of the primeval forest with its riot of flowers. The delights of the palate were incomparable too—fresh fruit and sugar-cane after eleven weeks of putrefying stores would have satisfied the most exacting gourmet. But the delights most keenly appreciated of all were those of the flesh. For no sooner had Magellan's ships dropped anchor than they were surrounded by a swarm of native canoes; friendly relations were quickly established; and soon, we are told, "*a plentiful supply of young virgins was made available to the crew*". When it was discovered that the white men were willing to offer such luxuries as jack-knives and beads in exchange for a girl, whole bevies of beauties came swarming aboard eager to offer themselves in exchange for trinkets. "*They wear*", writes Don Antonio, "*no clothes at all except their hair, and in exchange for a knife or an axe we could obtain two or even three of these delightful daughters of Eve, so perfect and well shaped in every possible way.*" Before long every seaman could boast a veritable and extremely willing harem.

For a fortnight there was an orgy of feasting and making love; even the priests went ashore and had to be brought back by squads of marines, while the careening and reprovisioning of the ships made little headway. It was all very reprehensible no doubt. But at least there was no violence, no extortion and none of the frenzied searching for gold which in subsequent expeditions was to lead to so much misery and bloodshed. And when, on Christmas morning, Magellan's ships pulled slowly out of Rio bay, the natives wept.

Once in open waters the armada crowded on sail, a north-easterly breeze and a south-flowing current lent them wings, and soon they were running free down the South American coast at the rate of a hundred miles a day. Their holds were crammed with fresh meat, pineapples and sugar-cane; their crews were in good heart, and we can tell from the entries in Pigafetta's diary that Magellan himself was optimistic, believing his ships were drawing each day nearer to John of Lisbon's strait, their gateway to the orient.

And indeed after ten days of fast and pleasant sailing the South American coast swung west. Here, clearly, was the entrance to *el paso*, their short-cut to the Moluccas.

For over a week Magellan's vessels edged into the path of the setting sun. Progress was slow, for the winds were light and contrary. But no one, it seems, doubted they were on the threshold of success; no one drew any inference from the muddy water or from the gradual waning of the flood tide; and no one bothered to lower a mug over the side and taste the water. But eventually sailing conditions became so difficult that Magellan's suspicions were aroused; the vessels hove to, and their *bergentym* were lowered and ordered to reconnoitre ahead. The soundings grew progressively more shallow, and at last the helmsman of the leading *bergantym* flung out his arm. "I see mountains," he cried—hence the name Montevideo—and next morning the truth became clear. Ahead lay not a channel but a river, a great river flowing into a land-locked bay. Their strait was a chimera: their short cut to the Spice Islands a myth.

It was the bitterest moment of Magellan's life. For four years all his hopes and dreams had been based on finding John of Lisbon's strait. And now, it seemed, the strait did not even exist. That night, as he paced his cabin, Magellan's cup of disillusion must have been full to overflowing. Yet it was now, in his darkest hour, that he gave proof of his greatness.

"We shall go on," he told his assembled ships' companies the next morning. "The strait is not here, but assuredly we shall find it a few leagues farther south."

The captains shook their heads and grumbled; but the seamen—more loyal or perhaps more credulous—were won over. And early in February Magellan left the estuary of the Plate and set course for the unknown and storm-lashed approaches to Cape Horn.

For eight weeks his ships fought their way south, through waters as difficult and dangerous as any on earth. They were battered by gale force winds, bludgeoned by heavy seas, lashed by hail and sleet, and towards the end of their passage weighed down with ice. But they did not give up. Time and again the clumsy square-sailed *naos*, with their high prows and poops, were driven literally backwards by the furious winds, several times they were scattered by antarctic hurricanes, and once a blizzard caught them inside a tiny gulf where there was no holding ground and for six days they were forced to beat frantically to and fro between the cliffs, like frightened swallows trapped in a windowless room. It was a voyage of appalling hazards, brilliant seamanship, and tenacity of the sort that makes history: a voyage all the more remarkable because Magellan was continually cramped for sea-room — for he had to keep close inshore in order to investigate every tiny inlet and bay in search of the longed-for strait. Modern vessels, in spite of their radar and detailed charts, avoid these waters which are known to this day as "the sea of graves". For a sixteenth-century sailing ship to have pioneered them for over a thousand miles, at the approach of winter, was a fantastic achievement: an achievement due principally to Magellan's personal skill.

For after leaving La Plata it was always the *Trinidad* which was in the lead, and always Magellan who piloted her. His alone was the responsibility of picking a course through the uncharted reefs, sandbars and shoals which lay in seemingly endless succession across their path. For six weeks he was never out of his sodden clothes; for five weeks he never slept for more than two or three hours at a stretch; and for three weeks he never had a hot meal — for in the near-perpetual blizzards the galley fires could not be kept alight. In these terrible conditions Magellan's cheerfulness and fortitude earned him the admiration and respect of his crew. But his captains, day after day lurching awkwardly in the *Trinidad's* wake, were less charitable in their judgement. "The *capitana* will surely lead us all to destruction," Cartegna is reported to have cried. "He is obsessed with his search for a strait. On the flame of his ambition he will crucify us all."

Cartegna was right. Magellan *was* determined to find the strait or perish. And as his ships reeled south through mountainous seas and gale-force winds, with the ice thick on their rigging, the latter alternative must have seemed by far the more probable.

But by the third week of March even Magellan could see that his crew were at the limit of their endurance, and that to have gone on would have been suicide. His captains urged him to give up, to retrace his steps at least as far back as the estuary of La Plata. But Magellan remained adamant.

"We winter here," he said, "and in the spring we continue our search for *el paso.*"

Wintering in Patagonia, however, was easier said than done; and for day after day the ships reeled on through blinding snow squalls, searching in vain for a harbour. Then at last, on March 31st, the lookout of the *Trinidad* reported a break in the coast. They headed towards it, scraped over a foaming bar and found themselves in the bleak but well-watered and reasonably sheltered bay of Saint Julian.

Magellan must have hoped, as the armada dropped anchor, that the worst of his troubles were over. In fact they were about to begin. For that first evening in Saint Julian there was an unusual amount of coming and going between the ships of the Spanish captains, and much muttering and dissatisfaction among the men.

The events of the next few days are recorded, factually and impartially, in Pigafetta's Diary.

"Now in this harbour (Saint Julian) much dissatisfaction and mistrust rose up against Magellan. Immediately after we had dropped anchor, Magellan gave orders

for dwellings to be erected on land; he also ordered a cut in daily rations, in order to ensure that our food supplies lasted the winter. The captains and the crews objected to both these orders, and the dissatisfied demanded to return home. Magellan refused to discuss the matter, and, when some of the crew persisted, he had them arrested and punished. But this only exasperated the men. On April 1st, when Magellan ordered everyone ashore for Mass, the captains Cartegna, Mendoza and Quesada did not appear; and soon afterwards there was open revolt. Cartegna was the ringleader. On the night of April 1st/2nd he boarded the San Antonio (whose captain was loyal to Magellan) and forced her ship's company to acknowledge him as their leader. So that on the morning of April 2nd Cartegna was in command of three ships (the San Antonio, Victoria and Concepcion), and Magellan of only two (the Trinidad and the Santiago). However, by means of a cunning ruse, the Admiral managed to get possession of the Victoria, and he then placed his three vessels across the mouth of the harbour. (Fate then played into his hands.) During the night the San Antonio dragged her anchor and came drifting towards the flagship. She was taken with hardly a blow—for on finding themselves boarded the crew quickly declared for Magellan. As a result Cartegna, the next morning, found himself hopelessly outnumbered and had no option but to submit to the Captain-General. The rebels were speedily punished. Mendoza had been killed during the retaking of the Victoria; Cartegna and his chaplain were marooned (and never heard of again), and Gaspar de Quesada was executed. Members of the crews who had taken part in the rising were condemned to work in chains . . ."

The facts set out above are clearly beyond dispute; their interpretation, however, is a matter of opinion. For Magellan's champions see the rising as a product of the jealousy and intrigue of the Spanish captains, while his detractors see it as a result of the unreasonable hardships which his crew had been forced to endure. There is truth in both points of view. And we will not, I think, get to the heart of the matter until we understand something of the relationship which existed in the sixteenth century between a captain and his crew.

When historians deal with the many occasions on which fifteenth- and sixteenth-century seamen refused to follow their leader, they are prone nowadays to condemn the crew's behaviour as "mutiny". But the word is inapt—and was never used by contemporaries. For the Oxford Dictionary tells us that mutiny is "the refusal of five or more members of the armed forces to obey the orders of a senior officer"; and sixteenth-century seamen, of course, were not members of the armed forces, they were cosmopolitan bands of drifters scraped together from the waterfronts of a dozen countries and bound not by King's Rules and Admiralty Instructions but by the far more loosely-framed Medieval Maritime Laws of Rhodes and Oleron. And these laws expressly state that "*a ship's company are entitled to refuse to undertake a voyage which will jeopardise their lives*". Bearing this in mind, we clearly cannot apply the word "mutiny" to the *fracas* at Saint Julian—for the Captain-General *was* endangering the lives of his crew, and they were perfectly within their rights in refusing to follow him. Magellan, in other words, dealt with the malcontents over-harshly and in a manner both high-handed and technically illegal.

Yet if he had acted otherwise he would never have circumnavigated the world. Fame is more often achieved by breaking rules than by keeping them, and those dedicated to an ideal are obliged all too frequently to trample their less exalted associates underfoot. *El paso* had become Magellan's grail. Those who refused to follow him in search of it must, to his way of thinking, be taught the error of their ways. In other words, it was not enough for the "mutiny" merely to be crushed; those who opposed him had to be given a lesson which they would never forget.

Beneath the towering cliffs of Saint Julian Magellan assembled the ships' companies. Dark clouds obscured the sun; a chill wind moaned endlessly down from the snows of the Andes; in the centre of the beach was an executioner's block. And here, on the morning of April 7th, 1520, Gaspar de Quesada was publicly executed, the axe that severed his head being swung, on Magellan's orders, by his own foster-brother. His body (and that of the dead Mendoza) was then drawn, quartered and strung up on the gibbets which had been erected at strategic intervals around the bay. The crew dispersed. But for three months the gibbets stayed in place, their gruesome remains an ever-present reminder that the Captain-General was not a man to be trifled with.

Saint Julian was a place of unhappy memories—fifty years later Sir Francis Drake was also to execute his second-in-command here, literally in the shadow of the gibbets raised by Magellan—and there must have been widespread relief when, in mid-winter, quarters were shifted to the nearby harbour of Santa Cruz. Here fresh huts were built on a less forbidding terrain, the ships were hauled up and careened, and large numbers of seals, fish and sea-fowl were killed and preserved in an effort to eke out stores.

For food had suddenly become a major problem. Magellan had expected his supplies to be more than adequate; but when the foodstuffs were carried ashore and reinvoiced serious deficiencies came to light—the result of Portuguese chicanery during the commissioning at Seville. Magellan concealed the losses as best he could, and supplemented the men's diet with local produce. There was no shortage of fish or meat in Santa Cruz; but vegetables were scarce; and before long the crew were suffering from a deficiency of vitamin C, and in particular of the ascorbic acid ($C_6H_8O_6$) which is the sole preventative of scurvy. This shortage of vegetables did not strike anyone as being especially serious at the time. But events were to prove it fatal.

For six months the armada was forced to lie up, while winter storms and seas of unbelievable fury lashed the Patagonian shore. Then at the beginning of October the days began slowly to lengthen and the storms to decrease in violence. Magellan prepared to put to sea. His captains and pilots again implored him to retrace his steps, or at least to seek the Moluccas by sailing east rather than west. But Magellan brushed their arguments aside. And by October 18th his fleet was again at sea, probing the bays and inlets at the approaches to Cape Horn.

On October 21st they hove-to in what appeared to be the entrance of a large bay. The water was light green—and hence, it was assumed, shallow— and away in the distance the ships' companies could make out a range of

snow-capped peaks. It seemed a most unlikely place to search for *el paso*.
Magellan, however, was taking no chances; and he ordered the *San Antonio*
and the *Concepcion* to head straight into the bay, while he and the other ships
explored its southern and northern shores. The captains of the *San Antonio*
and the *Concepcion* grumbled at such an obvious waste of time. But a sudden
and violent storm from the east cut short their dissent, and drove them
willy-nilly into the bay. Magellan himself had just sufficient sea-room to run
for open water; but the luckless *San Antonio* and *Concepcion* were driven
violently shoreward into a frenzy of breakers, shoals and spindrift. They
vanished from sight behind a daggerlike reef of rocks, and Magellan gave
them up for lost.

For a couple of days Magellan's two surviving vessels rolled and pitched
into the teeth of the storm, their waist decks awash and their pumps continually manned. Then the weather cleared, and the Captain-General was
able to lead his ships back into the bay in search of survivors.

After a while the *Trinidad's* lookout reported a column of smoke deep in
the bay; and this confirmed Magellan in the hope that at least some of the
crew of the *Concepcion* and the *San Antonio* were alive. Then, as the flagship
rounded a promontory, her lookout gave an excited shout.

"A sail! A sail!"

The crew scrambled into the rigging, peering west.

"Two sails!" the lookout repeated. And a while later, "The *Concepcion*
and the *Antonio*. They're fully dressed! They're flying flags from every halyard and spar!"

Under a great press of canvas the beflagged vessels bore down on the
Trinidad, guns booming, and seamen cheering and waving. And the truth
came to Magellan, so suddenly and unexpectedly that he fell to his knees in tears.

They had discovered *el paso*.

Soon the exultant captains were reporting aboard the *Trinidad*. And what
a story they had to tell! Here is Charles McKew Parr's* account of their
dramatic and almost miraculous discovery of the straits of Magellan.

"The (captains) reported how, after tacking frantically in the storm and
exhausting every manoeuvre to escape the lee shore, their two ships had
been miraculously swept around the promontory by a strong current and
then had been again blown helplessly by the gale towards the breakers.
Suddenly they saw a narrow passage, like the mouth of a river ahead of
them in the surf, and managed to steer into it. Driven on by the wind and
swept ahead by a rushing flood tide, they raced through these narrows into
a wide lake. Still driven by the storm, they were carried west for some hours,
across this lake and into another narrow passage, although now the current
had reversed, and what appeared to be a great ebb tide came rushing at
them. They debouched from this second strait into a broad body of water
that stretched far towards the setting sun, and, excited and triumphant,
they had boldly sailed across this to where it discharged into several westward channels.

"They entered one of these and observed that it bore the marks of a

* Taken from his biography of Magellan, *So Noble a Captain.*

forty-foot tidal drop along its precipitous shores. Taught by their previous disillusionment when they had assumed the Rio de Solis to be the *paso*, they this time made continuous tests of the water . . . to see if its saltiness decreased. They found, however, that it continued to be sea brine throughout. Another lesson which they had learned was to check the comparative flow of the ebb and flood tides to see if the ebb was the stronger, as it would be if augmented by the outflow of a river. Their observations, however, showed that the flood tide from the Atlantic each time was as strong as the ebb or even stronger; hence they were sure there must be an outlet westward. Frequent soundings indicated a deep channel without sandbanks or shallows, and every test and check convinced the pilots that this was a genuine strait, opening westward into the Great South Sea . . . They had seized upon a change of wind and raced back to Magellan with the news."

Next day the armada stood west into *el paso* — all except for the *San Antonio* whose pilots had no stomach for further adventures and who deserted Magellan in the hour of his triumph and slipped quietly back to Spain, taking with them, incidentally, over half of his already inadequate stocks of food.

At first the strait was not too difficult to navigate; but after a while it split into a maze of tortuous channels hemmed in by towering cliffs. A longboat was sent ahead to reconnoitre, while Magellan's vessels followed in single file, close-reefed to their storm-sails. And as they pushed deeper into the wilderness of channel, island, fjord and shoal, their passage became increasingly hazardous. Soon the ships were hemmed in by four thousand foot walls of rock rising sheer from the water; the fantastic ebb and flow of the tides swept them this way and that like straws in a mill-race; the winds shifted violently and unpredictably through every point of the compass; great rollers surged in from both Atlantic and Pacific to meet in a frenzy of backwash and whirlpool; sleet fell without respite out of a cold grey sky; while layers of mist rolled down from the ice-cap, and there were no beaches or safe holding-grounds where the vessels could anchor. By day there was no sign of life. But at night the darkness was pinpointed by a host of flickering flames, the camp fires of the Patagonian Indians (hence the Spanish name for the lands to southward of the strait, *Tierra del Fuego*).

For over three hundred miles the armada groped through these hazardous channels, their survival being a testimony to Magellan's genius as a navigator.

And at last, in mid-November, they fought through to the unknown ocean beyond: the substance of so much speculation and doubt, the desideratum of their Captain-General's nightly dreams.

Here at the gateway to the Pacific Magellan rested awhile, and made an inventory of his stores. When he discovered how low his supplies had become, he swore his officers to secrecy. But having come so far, he was determined to push on to the Moluccas, which, he fondly imagined, he would now sight any day above the horizon.

And so on November 28th, 1520, his fleet again stood west into unknown waters. They were making now a leap in the dark such as no mariners had ever attempted before in the history of the world. And Magellan may have

suspected this. For as his ships stood into the Great Southern Ocean, cruci-
fixes were raised, the chanting of the *Te Deum* drowned the cries of the sea
birds, and the lions and castles of Castile broke free from their mastheads.

"Gentlemen," Magellan said, "we are now standing into waters where
no ship has ever sailed before. May this sea always be calm and peaceful as
it is this morning. In this hope I name it the *Mar Pacifico*."

The Pacific did indeed remain calm for Magellan. But before he had
crossed it more than half of his men were to die in agony.

They died in agony of a disease which was to claim more victims in the
next 250 years than the combined toll of lee shore, tempest and shoal.

Scurvy.

We know to-day that scurvy is due to a lack of vitamin C: to be exact,
to a daily deficiency in diet of .05 grammes of ascorbic acid. But this is a
recent discovery. In the sixteenth and seventeenth centuries scurvy was
regarded as an infection; that is to say it was bracketed in men's minds with
such diseases as malaria, leprosy, typhus and cholera. No one connected its
incidence with a shortage of fresh vegetables. Magellan therefore was not
unduly worried that spring by the fact that his crew had been short of green-
stuff for the last eight months, nor by the fact that the only vegetables left
aboard were a few odd pounds of garlic, raisins and figs.

But here were the seeds of tragedy.

To start with, the *Mar Pacifico* must have seemed like the waters of Paradise.
Magellan stood his vessels north-west, slanting away from the coast of Chile
with a following wind and a favourable current. Soon the weather grew
milder, the sea became alive with fish, and the crew peered eagerly ahead
expecting any moment to see the longed-for Moluccas. But after a while the
vastness of the Pacific began to make itself felt. As the *naos* forged ahead for
week after week with never a sight of land, the crew became worried—
Atlantic voyages had never lacked a landfall as long as this. The monotony
frayed their nerves: day after day the same blustering wind from astern, the
same unclouded sky, the same blazing sun, and the same hunger a-gnaw at
their bellies—for Magellan, alarmed at his failure to make a landfall, had
cut their rations. But worse was to come. For as they stood deeper into the
tropics, the little food they had began to deteriorate. Their penguin and
seal meat was the first to go. Under the burning sun of the equator it turned
putrid, breeding long white maggots which crawled everywhere and ate,
with impartial voracity, clothes, leather and hull. Then the water in their
casks turned yellow; soon it stank so overpoweringly that the men had to
hold their noses before they could drink it. And soon the nine months' shortage of vegetables began to tell. The crew became listless; dark circles
appeared under their eyes; their limbs started to ache and their gums to
turn blue and swell. And early in the new year, six weeks out from the
Straits of Magellan, men began to die. They died painfully and without
dignity, their bodies emaciated, their breath foetid and their joints gro-
tesquely swollen. Padre Valderrama heard their confessions, Pigafetta wrote
their last messages to parents, sweetheart or wife, and their bodies were
tipped unceremoniously into the Great South Sea, far from their Basque

and Andalusian homes. And still, week after week, the ships ran on beneath skies that were unclouded blue by day, and filled by night with stars of unbelievable beauty. Magellan threw away his charts. They were useless. *"With the pardon of the cartographers,"* he wrote, *"the Moluccas are not to be found at their appointed place on the map."*

Then, as if in answer to their prayers, they sighted land: a tiny atoll, the green of its lagoon reflected on the under-surface of a circle of cloud. They dropped anchor, rowed ashore, and fell down on their knees and gave thanks to God.

The island they had come to was small; it had little vegetation except for a stunted magnolia-type of shrub, and no water except for a series of brackish wells sunk deep in the sand; but along its shore were vast numbers of sea-birds and shellfish, and these provided the men with food of a sort, though not with the vitamin C which alone would have alleviated their scurvy. Magellan stayed on the atoll for the better part of a week, then weighed anchor and headed for the Philippines—which he had visited from the east in 1512 and which he now thought might make a nearer and safer landfall than the elusive Moluccas. In the holds of his *naos*, as they pulled away from the atoll, there was food for less than a month. Magellan was confident, however, that from now on they would make frequent landfalls where they could top up with water and food; for he thought they had all but traversed the *Mar Pacifico* and that the atoll disappearing astern was an outrunner of the great archipelagoes which he knew lined the shore of Asia. But in this he was wrong. Far from having traversed the Pacific, he had crossed barely half of it.

To start with, hopes were high as the armada again stood west-north-west. But as the days lengthened into weeks and no more islands were sighted, the spectre of scurvy returned. With the unrelenting wind from astern there could be no turning back, and the *naos* now had no choice but to reel on and on through a sea of glass, watched by a brazen sun by day and a haloed moon by night. By the end of February not a single particle of food was left. And their crews were dying.

Aboard the *Trinidad* they scraped the maggots out of the barrels and pounded them into "gruel"; they baked cakes of sawdust soaked in the urine of rats (the rats themselves were luxuries, selling at the equivalent of half of a seaman's annual pay); they unwound the leather from their main-mast, soaked it and grilled it and served it to the few of the ship's company whose teeth had not yet rotted free of their gums. Men lay curled on the deck, dying of starvation, their palates too enlarged to swallow even the spoonfuls of water left in the casks. In the wake of each vessel followed a shoal of sharks. And with increasing frequency men went scrambling into the gunwales with shrieks of "Land! Land!", as the dream-islands of hallucination swam vividly in front of their eyes. So when a *grumate* named Navarro clawed up the ratlines in the early morning of March 6th and screamed "Praise God! Praise God! Land!" quite a few of the *Trinidad's* ship's company did not even look up.

Then a cannon boomed in ecstasy, the flag of Castile broke from the *Victoria's* mast, and a mountainous peak, etched clear in the gathering light of dawn, rose on their starboard bow.

Magellan had crossed the Pacific.

He had circumnavigated the world.*

* * *

The aftermath was tragedy and anticlimax.

It was in fact the Marianas which Magellan had come to. Here, after an unfortunate skirmish with the natives, he took aboard water and food, including stocks of the yams, coconuts and bananas which his crew so desperately needed. He then sailed on through a maze of islands to the Philippines, where he landed on March 16th, 1521.

He was in familiar territory now; his Malaysian slave Enriques could talk to the islanders in his native tongue, and the fabulous Spice Islands which he had voyaged so far to find were only a stone's throw over the horizon. But Magellan was never to see them. A month after his landfall he became involved, quite unnecessarily, in a feud between two native chiefs. Deciding to give a demonstration of the white men's powers, he landed with a handful of seamen and set fire to a village. But the land was a far less happy environment for Magellan than the sea. Three times already, when serving the Portuguese, he had been wounded in forays ashore. This time he was killed: his handful of seamen being hacked to pieces by the bamboo spears of an army of three thousand natives.

FIG 23. The *Victoria*—the first ship to circumnavigate the world—
from a contemporary woodcut

* Some historians hold that the first man physically to travel round the world was not Magellan, but his slave "Malaccan Henry", whom Magellan had bought in the East Indies and who accompanied his master ten years later on his epic voyage. But I think Magellan himself has an equal claim; for it is now generally believed that in 1511 he made a secret voyage to the Philippines, the islands where he was later killed.

And so, Pigafetta lamented, *"they killed our mirror, our light, our saviour and faithful guide"* : a tragically wasteful death for the man who had voyaged so far and through such appalling hazards to within sight of his goal.

With Magellan's death his armada broke up; he alone of the captains possessed the necessary knowledge and force of character to hold his vessels together. On their long trail home some of the remnants of his fleet were wrecked, some were scuttled and some were captured; they all indulged in piracy, and among their ships' companies losses through scurvy, fever and skirmishing were appalling. But at last one sole survivor struggled back into Seville. On September 8th, 1522, after a voyage of almost exactly three years, the *Victoria* tied up at the Dock of Mules. Of the 268 men who had set sail with Magellan, nineteen had returned.

*   *   *

Magellan has been depicted by some historians as a serpent—a tyrant of Machiavellian subtlety, and by others as a saint—a simple seaman dedicated unselfishly to his calling. These different views are not to be wondered at, for great men are often figures of controversy, and greatness is a quality which even Magellan's detractors admit he possessed. He was a leader: a man of decision—although his decisions were not always right: a good friend but a dangerous enemy. Such men frequently earn the hatred of their contemporaries, but the pages of history ring out their praise. Yet perhaps the last word on Magellan should be left with someone who was completely unbiased: the level-headed and matter-of-fact Pigafetta, who wrote: *"His main virtues were constancy and perseverance in even the most difficult situations; for example he bore hunger and fatigue better than all the rest of us. He was well versed in the art of reading nautical maps, and he understood navigation better than all his pilots. The best proof of his genius is the fact that he circumnavigated the world, no man having preceded him in this."*

It has been argued that "Magellan's circumnavigation was in fact of little value, since the passage he discovered was too dangerous for sea traffic"; but this is a narrow view. Magellan *proved*, in the most practical way possible, what had previously been only a theory: the fact that the earth is a sphere; and with this knowledge a whole millennium of legend and superstition fell into disrepute. He added a new ocean to the maps of the world, and the flag he hoisted on it was the flag not of Portugal but of Spain, and the Philippines to this day are the only country in Asia that is both Catholic and Spanish.

Dom Manuel the Fortunate, when he heard of the circumnavigation, ordered the seizure of Magellan's estate and the obliteration of his coat of arms; his achievements were not obliterated so easily.

X

"ALL NIGHT THE ARCTIC FOXES PATTERED
ACROSS OUR ROOF"

(The voyage of William Barents in 1596-7 in search of a North-East passage. A voyage "so strange and woonderfull that the like hath never been heard of before: done and performed by Shippes of Holland and Zeeland, on the north sides of Norway, Muscovia and Tartaria, towards the Kingdomes of Cathay and China; shewing the discoverie of Noua Zembla, where never any man had bin before: with the cruell white Beares and the unsupportable and extreame cold. And how in that last voyage their Shippe was so inclosed by the Ice that . . . the men were forced to build a house in the cold and desart Countrie of Noua Zembla, wherein they continued 10 monthes together, and never saw nor heard of any man, in most great cold and extreame miserie: and how after that they were constrained to Sayle above 1,000 English miles in little open Boates over the Maine Seas in most great danger and with extreame labour, miserie, and hunger")

THE summer of 1871 was unusually mild in the Arctic; by August the pack-ice had receded far towards the Pole, and the sealing and whaling skippers were able to stand their vessels into waters that had not been fished for generations. One of these skippers, the Norwegian Elling Carlsen, managed to push his sloop the *Solid* as far north as Novaya Zemlya. By mid-August he had rounded the island's north-eastern tip and was working the virgin waters of the Kara Sea. The fishing here was good, but after a while the weather took a turn for the worse, the ice began to close in, and Carlsen was forced to run for shelter. On Friday, September 8th, he dropped anchor in a little bay on the east coast of Novaya Zemlya. It was a desolate, uninviting place, wreathed in mist and half choked with grounded ice, and to start with Carlsen had little incentive to put ashore. But as he stared at the plethora of floes piled higgledy-piggledy along the arc of beach, he saw, to his amazement, what looked like the outline of a house.

It was too late to investigate that evening, but early the following morning Carlsen and three of his crew struggled ashore. He half expected the house would prove a mirage—a trick of light and shadow among the floes—but it turned out to be very real and very old: four timber walls, with the roof caved in and the snow piled up inside over an internal chimney and a line of primitive bunks. Wondering, the sealers fossicked among the ruins, unearthing tankards, books, clocks and pieces of navigational equipment. It seemed to them incredible that men should have built a house on this uninhabited island, far north of the usual hunting and fishing grounds. "On the nearby beach," Carlsen wrote in his diary, "we found pieces of wood which had once been part of a ship. And I therefore formed the opinion that a vessel must have been wrecked here: that her crew built the house with materials from the wreck, and afterwards took to the ship's boats . . ."

Carlsen's surmise was correct. What he had no inkling of was the incredible age and historical interest of the building he had stumbled across. For what he had discovered was the *behouden-huis* (house of safety) built nearly three hundred years earlier by William Barents, whose ship's company was the first in history* to survive an Arctic winter.

The sealers erected a cairn alongside Barents' house, and took the relics they found inside it—some seventy articles—back to Norway. The news of their discovery spread quickly; and a couple of years later Charles Gardiner, an amateur explorer with plenty of money and a penchant for adventure, managed to force his yacht *Glow-worm* into the same Novaya Zemlyan harbour. Gardiner made an exhaustive search among the ruins, and managed to unearth more Barents relics: no fewer than a hundred and twelve items: some as small as a stick of sealing wax, some as large as a harpoon, and among them a parchment log which was signed by Barents himself and which told the story of his star-crossed voyage in search of a north-east passage to China.

You can see these relics to-day in The Hague: the shoes of the ship's carpenter whose *behouden-huis* saved his comrades but not himself, the clock that poured away the endless Arctic nights, the quill with which the dying Barents signed his log, and, most evocative of all, the mildewed copy of Mendoza's *China*: symbol of a quest that was foredoomed to failure, but whose failure was more glorious than many a success. From these, and from the handful of contemporary documents, we are able to piece together the story of Barents' epic voyage to the "*cold and desert Countrie of Noua Zembla*".

* * *

One does not immediately associate Dutch explorers with the Arctic. It is their exploits in the Pacific which have caught the eye of posterity: the great voyages of Tasman, and the restless energy of van Diemen. Yet the contribution of the Dutch to Arctic exploration is, I think, the more remarkable. For they discovered Bear Island, Orange Island and Spitzbergen, they founded the ice-free port of Archangel, they mapped (with great accuracy) almost all of Novaya Zemlya, they pushed farther east along the Siberian shore than anyone was to push for over two hundred years, and they pioneered—albeit involuntarily—a technique of Arctic survival which explorers still emulate to-day.

The first Dutchman to pioneer the sea lanes beyond North Cape was Oliver Brunel. In this he had a dual objective: to open up a trade in furs with the recently "discovered" kingdom of Muscovy, and to search for a north-east sea-passage to China. His first objective he achieved in no uncertain fashion, but his second eluded him; for he found the ice a more recalcitrant opponent than his rival traders. In 1584 he made a determined effort to penetrate the Pet Strait, between the southern tip of Novaya Zemlya

---

* Erik the Red may also have been frozen in for one or possibly two winters during his epic exploration of the east coast of Greenland, but there are no detailed records of his experiences.

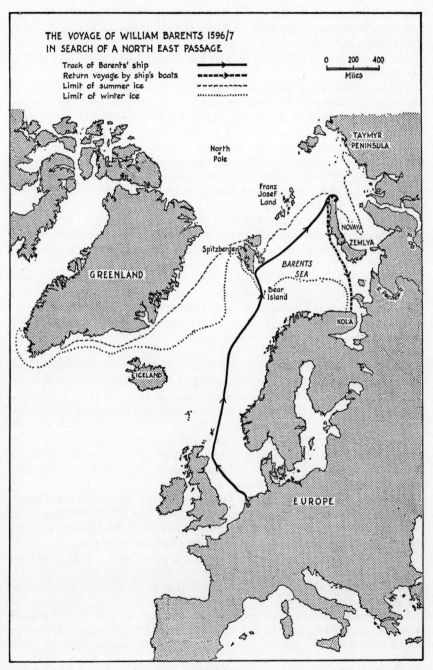

THE VOYAGE OF WILLIAM BARENTS 1596/7
IN SEARCH OF A NORTH EAST PASSAGE

Track of Barents' ship
Return voyage by ship's boats
Limit of summer ice
Limit of winter ice

0   200   400
Miles

North
Pole

TAYMYR
PENINSULA

Franz
Josef
Land

NOVAYA
ZEMLYA

Spitzbergen

BARENTS
SEA

GREENLAND

Bear
Island

KOLA

ICELAND

EUROPE

Fig 24.

and the Siberian shore; but the ice that year was "most frightful to behold", and he said goodbye to his ship, his cargo and his dreams in the icy silt of the Pechora River.

But others were to follow the trail he had blazed, and the greatest of these was Barents.

William Barents was born, *circa* 1548, on the little island of Terschelling off the coast of Friesland. Terschelling is dominated by the sea; and Barents' whole life from birth to death was played out within sound of the Atlantic waves—which probably accounts for the fact that he was, first and foremost, a magnificent practical seaman. We know little about his early years beyond the fact that he progressed steadily through the nautical hierarchy from cabin boy to pilot and finally to master, accumulating *en route* a thorough knowledge of all branches of his calling. And in 1594 he took part in the first of his three famous voyages in search of a north-east passage.

Initially the search for this passage was backed by the States General, who hoped to establish a trade-route to the east which was not already dominated by England, Portugal or Spain. In 1594 and again in 1595 they provided ships, stores and men for a *"voyage of discoverie along the North sides of Muscovia and Tartaria"*; but on each occasion their ships were blocked by the ice at about 60° East (roughly level with the island of Novaya Zemlya). On both these voyages it was Barents who pushed his ship most deeply into unknown waters, manoeuvring among the ice lanes with a skill and daring that his associates viewed with both admiration and alarm. But the ice remained obdurate.

When the vessels returned a second time to Holland without having found the passage, the Dutch parliament began to lose heart. Barents, however, remained convinced that a passage existed; and he now put forward his view that the best route to follow might lie not to the south of Novaya Zemlya but to the north.

The States General considered this too risky a theory in which to invest public funds; but Barents soon found backers among the merchants of Amsterdam; and early in May 1596 two vessels stood out of the Wadden Zee, bound again for the desolate wastes of the north.

The ships were commanded by Jan Cornelis Ryp and Jacob van Heemskerck, with Barents acting as the latter's pilot. By this arrangement the Amsterdam merchants hoped to ensure that Barents' determination to find a passage did not jeopardize the safety of their ships. But their plans went awry. Barents was a stronger and more forceful character than van Heemskerck, and in practice it was he who proved the expedition's leader.

And because of this the ships were doomed from the moment they cleared the Wadden Zee.

For Barents, after two failures, was now determined to force the passage which his instinct (quite rightly) told him existed*; but sixteenth-century vessels were not built strongly enough to survive in the waters of the far north

---

* The north-east passage was not in fact discovered until 1878–9 when the Finn Nils Eric Nordenskiold sailed the *Vega* from Gothenburg to Yokahama, thus realizing a dream which seamen had been pursuing for over three hundred years.

—in particular they were not able to withstand the stresses and strains of being frozen in during an Arctic winter. And in this fact lay the seeds of tragedy.

The expedition left Amsterdam on May 10th.

The winds at first were contrary, and it took them the best part of a fortnight to clear the Frisians; but from then on progress was rapid up to the Arctic Circle. Here the ships all but parted company; for Ryp insisted on heading north, while Barents was convinced that their correct course was north by east. Barents was right. But Ryp's insistence on heading straight for the Pole did at least lead to two discoveries. On June 9th they became the first men ever to set foot on Bear Island, and between June 19th and 30th they discovered and circumnavigated Spitzbergen.

Here is Barents' account of how their first discovery came to be named. *"On our secound going on to this islande, earlie in the morning, wee saw a white beare, which we rowed after with our boate, thinking to cast a roape about her necke; but when we were neare her, shee was so great that we durst not doe it, but rowed backe again to our shippe to fetch more men and our armes, and then made to her againe with muskets, hargubushes, halbertes and hatchets, John Cornellyson's men comming also with their boate to helpe us. And being so well furnished of men and weapons, we rowed with our boates unto the beare and fought with her while foure glasses were runne out (i.e.,* two hours), *for our weapons could doe her little hurt; and amongst the rest of the blowes that we gave her one of our men strake her into the backe with an axe which stucke fast in her, and yet she swomme away with it; but we rowed after her, and at last we cut her head in sunder with an axe, wherewith she dyed; and then we brought her into John Corneolyson's shippe where wee fleaced her and found her skinne to bee twelve foote long: which done, we eate some of her flesh, but we brookt it not well. Our island wee then called the Beare Island."* This encounter was an augury. For in the winter to come the "cruell white beares" were to prove a frequent source of anxiety to van Heemskerck and Barents.

Their impressions of Spitzbergen, which they came to a week later, were less alarming. Here they found *"many red geese egges, also two sea horses teethe that waighed six pounds apiece".* They also noted with surprise that although the islands they had discovered lay astride the eightieth parallel, *"there groweth here leaves and grasse, and are found such beastes as live thereon like harts and buckes".* Their surprise is not to be wondered at. For nowhere else in the world is vegetation found at such a high latitude—Spitzbergen's relative mildness being due to the fact that it lies on the edge of the Gulf Stream.

On leaving Spitzbergen, Ryp and van Heemskerck again disagreed on their course, and on July 1st they parted company, Ryp heading north and van Heemskerck and Barents east. Cornelis Ryp now fades out of the picture for over a year—he soon found his path blocked by ice, and after a somewhat perfunctory attempt to break through, returned to Holland. But van Heemskerck and Barents, men of sterner fibre, pushed on to the unknown waters north of Novaya Zemlya.

On July 17th, in bright sunny weather, they rounded the island's northeast tip. But almost at once they were brought up short by the consolidated pack.

It stretched from horizon to horizon across their bows: a mosaic of soft white floe, thin rubbery pack-ice and inviting sea lanes: a barrier whose frailty was an illusion, for whose defences were in depth.

For four weeks Barents battered away at the ice, running, tacking, twisting among the leads, hauling his way eastward inch by painful inch. But the sea-lanes were teasing jades, promising always more than they gave. Again and again Barents found his way blocked and was forced to retrace his steps. The currents were violent and unpredictable, and soon blizzards and mist were tolling the knell of the brief Arctic summer. The ice, imperceptibly, thickened and began to creep south-west. By August 16th Barents was forced back to the shore of Novaya Zemlya.

The events of the next twenty-four hours were to prove decisive. In the early morning of August 17th a party of ten men went ashore and struggled to the top of the highest of the coastal hills. From the summit they had a commanding view. To the north-east broken ice lay like a shroud from shore to horizon. But in the south-east there was open water: "whereat," wrote the ship's doctor, "we were much comforted, thinking we had won our way through and not knowing how we could get soone enough on board to certifie William Barents."

Next morning they weighed anchor and headed hopefully south-east. But the open water was a trap. After fifteen miles of hazardous tacking to and fro they were again brought up short by an impenetrable barrier. For several days Barents sought a way through, hampered by clinging mists and a "*mightie current which drave the ice violently against the shippe*". But their efforts were in vain. Their frailly-built galleon was not strong enough to force the pack.

On August 23rd the expedition was back at Ice Haven—their original landing-point, some 250 miles from the northern tip of Novaya Zemlya. The weather was worsening now, and they decided that night they had no alternative but to admit defeat and return to Holland.

But they had left it too late.

In the few days they had spent in exploring the "open" water to south-ward, the ice had closed in; Novaya Zemlya was now sealed off from the inhabited world; they were cut off as effectively as if they had been ship-wrecked on the face of the moon.

They did not realize at first that they were trapped. For several days they tried to inch their way up the coast, alternately battered by gales and wreathed in mist. But the ice was too much for them. As a spider's web ensnares a fly, it closed inexorably round them, first hampering them, then immobilizing them and finally squeezing their frailly-built galleon to death. Their tiller and rudder were "*shorne in peaces*", their boats were staved-in, their hull sprang a series of leaks, and it seemed to them that their whole ship "*would soon be prest and crusht to peaces*". But on August 26th a violent storm broke up the pack and drove them back into Ice Haven. Here they piled up among the ice-floes lining the shore.

For a fortnight they struggled to lever and dig themselves clear; then another storm drove them even more firmly aground. And their ship began to break up.

There are few more terrifying experiences than being trapped in pack-ice during a storm—witness the account of Barents' doctor. "*Soon the ice* (floes) *began to drive together one upon the other with greater force than before and to crash against the shippe with a boystrous south-by-west wind and a greate snowe, so that the whole shippe was borne up and inclosed and squeezed, whereat all that was in it began to crack as if about to burst into 100 peaces, which was most fearfull both to see and heare, and made all ye haire of our heads to rise upright with feare. And after this the shippe (by the ice on both sides being joined underneath her) was driven so upright as if she had been lifted with a wrench or vice.*"

Fig 25. "Our Shippe was borne up and inclosed and squeezed as if to burst into 100 pieces"

They realized now that there was no hope of getting their vessel back to Holland: their only chance of survival was to winter ashore, and in the spring, if they were still alive, to take to the ship's boats.

So while great bergs, "tall as the salt hills of Spain", drifted by within crossbow-shot of their ship, they dragged their stores and their two surviving yawls up the ice-strewn beach and into a little hollow among the hillocks lining the shore. For the moment they were safe; but as they looked about them they must have wondered if they had not leapt out of the frying-pan into the fire. For the north-east coast of Novaya Zemlya is desolate as the land God gave to Cain: a wilderness devoid of vegetation, perpetually glazed in ice, and gripped, even in September, by an aching and unrelenting cold: while ahead lay all the terrors of the Arctic winter, terrors which no ship's company had ever faced up to, and lived.

Their first task, Barents and van Heemskerck decided, must be to build a house "*for defence against both the cold and the wild beastes*". And it was while they were reconnoitring a site for this house that they made the discovery which was to save their lives.

About a mile and a half from Ice Haven they came across an enormous pile of driftwood, cast like a benediction on to the iron shore.

We can to-day account for this driftwood quite logically—if we want to; for oceanographers tell us that it must have been borne to Novaya Zemlya from the forests of Siberia by the Westerly Polar Drift. But to the sixteenth century Dutch it was a miracle: "*And here in our need we found certain great trees, roots and all, as if God had purposely sent them unto us, and these served not onely to build our house but also to burn all winter; otherwise without God's mercy we had all, without doubt, died there miserably with extreame cold.*" It took them a week to drag the driftwood to the site they had chosen for their house, and another five weeks to build the *behouden-huis* itself.

All September the hills encircling Ice Haven echoed to the grate and saw and the thud of hammer and adze. The driftwood was first sawn into planks 15 inches broad, 1½ inches thick and 6 feet to 8 feet long. Then the foundations were laid for a single room, 32 feet by 20 feet, with three doors, a central fireplace and a chimney built out of barrels. The walls, 11 feet high, were then carefully caulked and tarred; and finally the roof was constructed out of a sail, supported by a timber frame and coated with alternate layers of sand and frozen snow. It was slow, painful and dangerous work. Slow and painful because of the cold—"*It froze so hard*," wrote the ship's doctor, "*that if we put a nayle in our mouths (as carpenters do) there would hang ice thereon and when we tooke it out againe the blood would follow.*" Dangerous because of the polar bears, which attacked the sledging parties, stole food and interfered with the building of the house. These bears were inquisitive and fearless, their thick fur made them impervious to everything but a well-placed shot at point-blank range, and not till the roof and doors were in place did Barents and his men enjoy a sound night's sleep. But by mid-October the work was nearly complete, and the crew moved in for the winter—all except the carpenter who had died on September 23rd, worn out with cold, exhaustion and the responsibility of building his *behouden-huis;* he was buried in the shingle, "*hard by the sea, for already* (they) *could not dig up the earth by reason of the great cold*".

The story of the next six months is the story of polar exploration in microcosm.

What happened that winter to van Heemskerck and Barents was to be repeated often in the years to come: the sickness, the privation, the suffering and the dying; the courage, the improvisation and the holding-on-to-life against seemingly impossible odds. It is probably true that other and later expeditions sometimes suffered more, or exercised greater ingenuity in their techniques of survival; but nothing can rob the Dutch of their special place in the galaxy of explorers; for they were the first ship's company in history to winter in the Arctic, and survive.

It was October 24th before the sixteen men, one of whom was already dangerously weak, finally moved into the house. Conditions at first were

almost more than they could endure; for their clothing was pitiably inadequate, their bunks not yet built, and their chimney smoked so excessively that
the fire had to be frequently doused. But little by little they turned the bleak
and cheerless *behouden-huis* into a home. Bunks and a porch were built out of
driftwood and ship's timber; an improved chimney was fashioned out of
boarded-up kegs; bears were shot and their skins used as rugs and their fat

FIG 26. "The exact manner of the house wherein we wintered"

to burn in the lanterns; stores, timber and sea coal were manhandled up the
beach and stacked alongside the house; and finally, as an expression of confidence in their survival, the ship's yawls were carefully careened in anticipa-
tion of the spring. They then settled down to endure, as best they could, the
unknown perils of the Arctic winter.

During the last few days of October snow fell endlessly out of a leaden sky,
so that no one could leave the house. Then came a temporary clearance; and
on November 2nd they caught sight—for the last time that year—of the sun.
But the sun by now was hardly recognizable: a dull, heatless disc that did not
rise into the sky, but crawled for a few brief moments along the horizon, then
dropped with sickening finality to the other side of the world. And with this
final disappearance of the sun, the cold increased.

Cold.

The requiem of Arctic explorers.

The enemy who, in the months to come, was to hound van Heemskerck
and his crew to the very threshold of death.

No words written to-day can adequately describe the privations of that appalling winter, nor can those without experience of polar conditions fully comprehend all that had to be endured. But the matter-of-fact entries in the diary of Gerrit de Veer, the ship's doctor, bring us a message whose impact the centuries cannot diminish.

"*November: faire weather: to-day we washed our shirts, but it was so cold that they frose stiffe, and although we laid them by a great fire yet onely the side that lay next to the fire thawed, the other remaining frosen hard as a board . . . December 2nd, foule weather, whereby we were forced to keep still in the house; we heated stones which we put into our bunks to warm our feet, for the cold was unsupportable; but the stones remained not hot for long . . . December 6th, foule weather againe, with an easterly wind and extreame cold almost not to be indured, so that we lookt upon one another, being in great feare that if the extremity of the cold grew more we should all die; for the fire, no matter how great we made it, would not warm us . . . December 12th: faire, clear weather with a bright sky and a north-west wind, but extreame cold, so that the walls inside our house and our bunks were frozen a finger thick with ice; yea, and the very clothes upon our backs were white all over with frost and icicles . . . December 27th: foule weather, and within the house it was so extreame cold that as we sate close before a great fire which seemed to burn our shins on the fore side, yet we froze behinde at our backs, and were all white, like the peasants coming into our towns in Holland with their sledges after they have been travelling the winter night.*"

Nothing saps courage more surely than cold, and many men in these conditions would have quietly lain down to die. But the Dutch clung stubbornly to life. And they did not complain: in all De Veer's and Barents' diaries there is never a hint of self-pity, only a straightforward exposition of the measures they took to survive.

They trapped arctic foxes and ate their flesh (which they compared with venison) and turned their pelts into caps and shoes. They took what exercise they could, out-of-doors playing hockey and a sort of golf, and indoors indulging in that stand-by of all polar explorers, amateur theatricals. They took at least one steam bath a week, in a wine-keg rigged up by De Veer. And they never stopped trying to improve their *behouden-huis*, experimenting with the chimney, recaulking the walls, bringing in supplies of driftwood and rearranging their stores. One of their experiments nearly proved fatal for the whole expedition.

"*December 7th, still foule weather, and a great storme with a north-east wind which brought extreame cold, so that we knew not what to do; but while we sate consulting together one of us gave counsell to burn some of the sea coles that we had brought out of the ship, which would cast a great heat and continue long. And so that evening we made a great fire thereof. (This being done) we were very careful to keepe it in, and the heat being so great a comfort unto us we took care how to make it continue long; whereupon we agreed to stop up all the doores and the chimney. We then went to our bunks to sleepe, well comforted, and lay a great while talking together. But after a while we were taken with a great swounding and daseling in our heads, some more than others and the sick man most of all; so those that were strongest jumped out of their bunks and opened up the chimney and then the doores. And when this was done we recovered our healthes againe by reason of the cold air; and so the cold which had before been so great an enemy unto us was now our reliefe, otherwise without doubt we had all died in that sodaine swound. Afterwards, when we were come to ourselves againe, the master gave every one of us a little wine to comfort our hearts."*

Explorers to-day are well aware of the dangers of carbon-monoxide poisoning. But here—as in so many other things—Barents had to learn from his own mistakes rather than the mistakes of others.

So the winter dragged on: with the cold increasing, their stocks of food and fuel diminishing, and exposure and malnutrition gradually sapping their strength. By mid-December several of the crew, including Barents, were suffering from scurvy; they lost weight and their joints became painful and swollen. It grew so dark they could not tell night from day. Their clock froze solid. The Arctic foxes pattered each night across the roof of their *behouden-huis*, keeping them awake with their sharp staccato barking. Down on the shore the sea ice *"burst and crackt with a hugh noyse, most terrifying to heare"*. And soon it was the shortest day. *"The 26 of December,"* wrote De Veer. *"Wind north-west, and so cold that we could not warm ourselves, although we used all the meanes we could, with greate fires, greate stores of clothes and with hot stones laid upon us; yet notwithstanding all this, in the morning our bunks were frozen white. But we comforted ourselves with the thought that the sunne was now as low as he could go, and would soone be coming to us again. For although it is true that the cold doth strengthen as the days do lengthen, yet hope for the future eased our present paine."**

But it was some time before their hopes were realized; and the last days of 1596 were played out to even fiercer blizzards and even bitterer cold. *"The 31 of December was most foule weather with a violent storme, whereby we were fast shut up in the house as if we had been prisoners; and it was so extreame cold that our fire caste no warmth, and as we put our feete to the flames we burned our stockings before we could feel the heate—indeed if we had not smelt sooner than we felt we should have burned quite away . . . And so, with great cold, danger and hardship we brought the yeare unto an end and entered into ye yeare of our Lord God 1597, the beginning whereof was in like manner to the end of anno 1596. For the weather continued as cold, boisterous and snowy as it was before . . . The 4 of January it was still stormie, with much snow and greate cold and we were forced to keep constantly in the house. To know which way the wind blew we thrust a half-pike out of ye chimney with a little cloth upon it; but we had to look at it quickly, the moment the wind caught it; for no sooner had we thrust it out than it froze as hard as a peece of board and could not stirre with the wind . . . Next day, ye 5 January, it was somewhat calmer. And we diggd our doors open againe that we might carry out all the filth that had bin made during the time of our being shut in the house. And we tookt the middle of our three doors away and diggd a great hole in the snow that lay without, like unto a vault, wherein we might go to ease ourselves . . . And when we had laboured hard all day, we remembered it was Twelvth Night; so we made merry and drunke to the three kings, and made pancakes with oyle, and every man had a white bisket sopt in wine. And so, fancying ourselves in our own countrie and amongst friends, it comforted us as much as if we had sate down to a greate banquet."*

* This is an amalgamation of two Dutch proverbs: *De daghen die langhen zijn de daghen stranghen* (the cold strengthens as the days lengthen), and *dan hoope dede pign versoeten* (hope sweetens pain).

Towards the middle of January the weather began to improve; and on the 16th they were able to go outside *"to stretch* (their) *joynts"*. On the 17th they saw *"a certaine redness in the skie at noone"*, a harbinger of the returning sun; and a couple of days later they were able to cross the ice to visit their ship. They found her low in the water and breaking up fast, but they managed to salvage some timber and half a barrel of biscuit. About this time the arctic foxes began to disappear, and the polar bears to emerge from hibernation. They thought this must be a sign that the Arctic winter was drawing to its close. But their hopes were premature.

Early in February the cold and the storms closed in again, and for six weeks Barents and his men were virtually confined to their house. The snow piled up so deeply they were unable to dig open their doors and their only exit was *via* the chimney; the ice spread over their bunks and the inside walls *"till it were full two fingers thicke"*; their stocks of fuel dwindled to a few lengths of sodden ship's timber, and men began to die.

They died of exposure and malnutrition, *"despairing ever againe of seeing the sunne,"* and worn out by ill-health and their never-ending battle against the cold. Among those who grew dangerously weak was William Barents, the oldest of the ship's company and the least able to withstand sub-zero temperatures. But although some died, the majority clung doggedly to life. And towards the end of March the cold began to lose its edge, and the sun to gain an iota of warmth; until at long last, with the coming of April, the survivors were able to venture out of doors—if only briefly—almost every day. They were pitiably weak to start with and prone to be snow-blind. But fresh air, exercise and the kiss of the sun were the best tonics they could have wished for; and with the maturing of spring those who were able to struggle clear of the *behouden-huis* slowly built up their strength.

Their first concern was to replenish their stocks of fuel. A sledging party fought through to the pile of driftwood, and the *"certaine great trees"* were dug out of twelve feet of snow and hauled laboriously back to Ice Haven. But the effort was almost too much for them—*"It was sore labour unto us, for we were become so weake and feeble that we doubted if we should ever recover our strengths enough to fetch more wood but should all die there miserablie of cold; but the present necessitie and the hope of better weather increased our forces and made us doe more than our strengths allowed."*

Their second concern was their ship. As they were salvaging driftwood they had noticed she was still there. The storms of winter had driven her farther out to sea; she was very low in the water, and was supported only by the ice under her keel. It was obvious she would never sail again. But at least she was a valuable source of wood. They began to dismember her, hauling her timbers ashore—partly for firewood and partly for strengthening their yawls.

All that spring they worked on the two little twelve-foot spritsail boats which they had careened six months ago and which now represented their sole and slender hope of survival. At first they were so weak they could hardly dig them out and turn them over, let alone shift them this way and that to effect repairs. But realizing their lives depended on their efforts, they slowly manhandled the boats seaward, at the same time strengthening their keels, raising their gunwales and repairing masts and sails. In this work they were constantly plagued by polar bears: "*Then came another great bear, as if she had smelt that we would be gone and desired first to have a taste of us; for this was the third day running that the bears set so fiercely upon us that we were obliged to leave our work and run for the house; for if we had lost even two or three men we should never have got away, for we should have been too few to lift our boates.*"

By the end of May the yawls were ready. The ice was breaking up fast, and the crew were anxious to be away.

Barents, by now, was pitiably weak. He was unable even to sit up in bed, and he had not been out of the *behouden-huis* for more than six months. Yet he was still very much the expedition leader; his ship's company still looked to him for advice; and the advice he gave them now was sound as ever. "*Wait,*" he said, "*a while longer, till the ice be more completely broken.*" So they postponed their departure for several weeks, anxious to leave the "*wild, desart, cold and fearefull country wherein* (they) *had bin prisonners for ten months*", yet appreciating the wisdom of Barents' suggestion. And in mid-June they were favoured with fair weather.

June 13th was the day they had been longing for: the day they loaded up their yawls and "*in the name of God began* (their) *voige to saile out of Nova Zembla*". Before they left, Barents wrote a letter, "*shewing how we came out of Holland to saile to the kingdom of China, and all that had happened unto us since; so that if any man chanced to come hither he might know how we had fared . . . and this letter he put in a bandoler and hanged it up in the chimney.*" Van Heemskerck also wrote two letters, in similar vein, and put one in each boat. "*And so committing* (themselves) *to the will and mercie of God, with a west-north-west wind and endifferent open water,* (they) *set saile and put to sea.*"

Two little open boats and fourteen scurvy-weakened men (three of them dying) setting out to sail one thousand miles through the ice-choked wastes of the Arctic. Only a miracle, it must have seemed, could save them.

Almost at once they ran into trouble.

The pack-ice through which they had to pick a course was easy enough to sail through in good weather; but in bad weather it became, all too literally, a death-trap. On the evening of June 16th a sudden storm blew up from the west; and before they could run their boats ashore, they were trapped in a great conglomeration of heaving, disintegrating floes. "*Next morning the ice drave upon us so fearefully that it made the haires stand upright upon our heads. For we could not make fast our boates, and thought verily that our last end had come, since we were borne away so violently by the ice and were so crusht between the floes that we thought our yawls would burst into a hundred peeces; whereat we lookt pittifully at each other, for no counsell nor advice was to be found, and every minute of every hour we saw death before our eies.*" Eventually they managed to escape by jumping with ropes from floe to floe and hauling their boats after them to the shore; but they lost a lot of their stores, and the yawls were damaged.

They spent a couple of days drying out and repairing the boats; then, as soon as the weather cleared, they again headed west. As they passed Ice Point, off the northern tip of Novaya Zemlya, Barents got two of the crew to lift him up. And a little later, as a freshening breeze scattered the floes and opened up a pathway for the escaping ships, he asked the ship's doctor for a drink. *"But he had no sooner drunke than he was taken with so sodain a qualme, that he turned up his eies in his head and died, and we had no time to call the master out of the other boat to speake unto him."*

Barents died as all that winter he had lived: unobtrusively and without complaint. His ship's company were heartbroken: *"he was our chief guide and pilot, the man next only to God in whom we had put our trust."* But now, in their hour of need, the Dutch found another champion—the quiet and unassuming van Heemskerck.

Outside his native Holland van Heemskerck is seldom remembered to-day: indeed I doubt if one person in a thousand could say which expedition he commanded. Yet he was obviously a man of character and ability. For on Barents' death he managed to keep his ship's company together and in good heart: and, what is more, he managed to lead them to safety by making one of the most fantastic voyages in history—eight hundred miles of intricate open-boat sailing through pack-ice, parallel to the Siberian shore.

Progress was never easy. Time and again their tiny, open boats were trapped by the ice—twice they had to haul them several hundred yards over solid floes. Time and again, battered by storms, they were driven on to the bleak Siberian littoral. More than once they capsized; the ice broke under their feet as they tried to struggle to safety; they were pursued by bears and *"greate sea horses"* (walrus); they ran out of food, and lived off the sea-fowl they shot and the eggs they salvaged off a marshy shore. More men died. But the survivors struggled doggedly on: sometimes sailing, sometimes rowing, and sometimes hauling their boats inch by painful inch over the ice. They never gave up. And at the end of July they came to the mouth of the Pechora, where they saw something they had not seen for more than a year. Another man.

Their joy was past our comprehension. For seldom if ever in the history of exploration have men lingered so long in the valley of the shadow of death, and then struggled back to the sunlight and companionship of the world they thought they had lost.

A month later they were in Kola, where they found Jan Cornelis Ryp who had come to search for them—more in hope than expectation. And two months after this they were back in Amsterdam, *"where men wondered to see us, having believed us long ago to have been dead and rotten . . . and in our homes men were wont ever after to call on us to rehearse our journey, both our voyages and our adventures, and marvel".*

*   *   *

The homecoming of van Heemskerck from the north coincided with the return of the first Dutch fleet from the East Indies. The former limped back to Amsterdam with neither ship nor riches, thankful to have escaped with their lives; the latter sailed into port in triumph filled with the treasures of the orient. The lesson was plain. The Dutch turned their eyes and their energies south, to the golden islands of the Pacific whose secrets, in the next hundred years, they did as much as any nation to unveil. The north became a backwater, the domain of the free-traders whose exploits lacked government backing and hence permanence. On Jan Mayen and Spitzbergen whaling stations enjoyed a brief heyday and then fell into decay; and at the mouth of the Hudson the little trading post of New Amsterdam flourished initially and was then handed over to the English with hardly a murmur. For the Dutch had suffered too much in the Arctic to risk burning their fingers again, while their dream of discovering a north-east passage to China had been killed stone-dead. For what had happened to Barents was conclusive—seamen of all nations agreed on that—and for the next 250 years there were no more voyages of discovery along the north-east shores of the Arctic.

It is strange to think that this north-east passage, so long neglected, may eventually prove one of the great sea-routes of the world, with cargo-carrying submarines voyaging from Atlantic to Pacific under the polar ice. If this comes about—and there are signs that it very well may—then William Barents will go down in history (together with De Long, Nansen and Anderson of the *Nautilus*) as one of the first and greatest pioneers of the Arctic Ocean.

XI

AUSTRIALIA DEL ESPIRITU SANTO

(The Voyage of Pedro Fernandez de Quiros to Australasia "for the saving of countless million souls": 1605-6)

ON August 28th, 1601, a pale slightly-built man in pilgrim's dress knelt at the feet of Pope Clement VIII. He was a humble man — humble in both family and character — but he pleaded his cause with eloquence. *"There is a great Countrie south of the Mar Pacifico,"* he told His Holiness, *"a new and undiscovered world, wherein lies an infinity of souls crying out to be saved."* The Pope was first sceptical then impressed; there were two more audiences; the most learned pilots and mathematicians in Rome checked the petitioner's credentials, and at last Clement VIII was won over. He not only wrote letters recommending the voyage to Philip of Spain, but also, as tangible evidence of his support, handed over a number of specially blessed rosaries and a piece of wood from the True Cross; for never before had he given audience to a man so eager and apparently so well qualified to spread the Gospel to the farthest corners of the earth.

The man in the pilgrim's robes was the thirty-six-year-old Pedro Fernandez de Quiros: an explorer whom history has dismissed as an impractical visionary, but whose achievements in fact were those of a humane and exceptionally gifted navigator.

How does a man become dubbed a visionary? Of what stuff are the dreams of a Don Quixote made? Heredity, upbringing, environment and health may all help to shape a man's personality; but in the case of Quiros, his proselytizing zeal can, I think, be attributed to one particular event: his passage to the Philippines in 1595 as chief pilot to Alvaro de Mendana.

When Mendana's armada left Peru on April 9th, 1595, his ships had been stolen by force and provisioned by trickery; his charts were deliberately falsified, his provisions were *"sufficient neither in quality nor quantity"*, on weighing anchor his crew were brawling and drunk, and Quiros admitted to being *"very uncertain what would be the end of the voyage, seeing the beginning was so disorderly"*. The fleet sailed some four thousand miles across the Pacific and on July 28th dropped anchor off Fatu-Hiva in the Marquesas, home of the graceful and gentle Polynesians later immortalized by Gauguin. The islands of the Marquesas were beautiful: palms and golden sands, lagoons full of fish, rich volcanic soil and great groves of breadfruit and bamboo. The inhabitants were beautiful too: *"gentle and graceful creatures, almost white, lovely of leg, hand, eyes, face and figure and with much cause to praise their Creator."* But the grace and beauty of the Polynesians availed them little against the shots of Mendana's arquebusiers. They were massacred as pointlessly and wantonly as so many

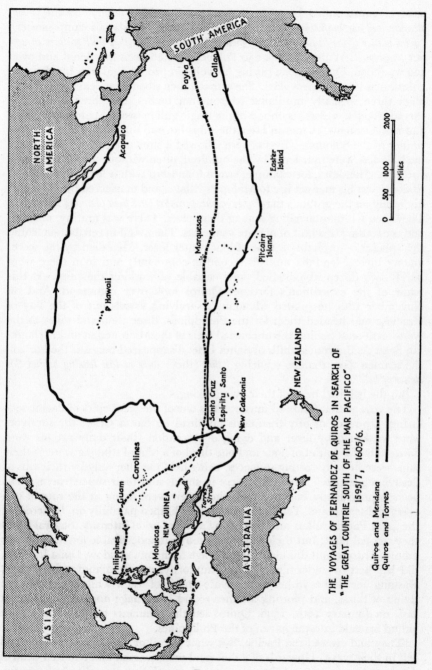

THE VOYAGES OF FERNANDEZ DE QUIROS IN SEARCH OF
"THE GREAT COUNTRIE SOUTH OF THE MAR PACIFICO"
1595/7, 1605/6.

Quiros and Mendana — — — — —
Quiros and Torres ———————

Fig 27.

head of game, killed because (to quote a Spanish soldier) *"to kill is our pleasure and our profession"*, and because (to quote Mendana's camp master) *"what matter if the heathen are consigned to hell to-day since they will go there in any case tomorrow"*. Within a week 250 Polynesians had been murdered and over 400 wounded, Quiros alone raising his voice in protest against a butchery as pointless as it was unprovoked. The armada then stood west, leaving on Fatu-Hiva three specially mutilated Marquesian bodies and three beautifully carved wooden crosses—symbols of the tragic gulf between Spain's intentions and achievements. A month later the ships hove-to off Santa Cruz, an out-runner of the Solomons. Events here followed a similar pattern. Once again the islanders were murdered by the hundred, often without the slightest pro-vocation. Mendana, for example, swore friendship with a local chief named Malope; but his men set fire to Malope's village, and massacred the chief and his family on the grounds that *"they might, perhaps, have been planning treachery"*. They then fell to quarrelling among themselves. There was mutiny, murder, and the settling of a host of private vendettas. Then, as if in retribution, came the "plague"—probably a type of blackwater fever. Men died by the score, among them Mendana and his second-in-command; and soon there were barely two dozen able-bodied crew capable of working the ships. At this nadir of the expedition's fortunes Quiros took over command. And on November 18th he piloted Mendana's surviving vessels out of the Bay of Graciosa and headed them for the Philippines, three thousand miles to the west-north-west behind the uncharted reefs of the Micronesian and Melanes-ian Seas. As the conical hills of Santa Cruz disappeared beneath the horizon the seamen gave thanks, rejoicing *"that (they) were at last leaving behind this corner of hell"*.

But the hell had been of their own making.

The voyage that followed must rank as one of the great epics of Pacific sea-faring. Upwards of fifty Spaniards lay dead on Santa Cruz; the survivors were weakened by fever and dying of starvation (their daily rations were down to half a pound of flour and one third of a pint of stinking water); their ships were literally rotting to pieces, being held together only by their ribs of Peruvian *guatchapeli;* their sails were in shreds and their superstructure had been improvidently burnt as fuel; their crew were dying at the rate of one every eighteen hours. Yet day after day they limped painfully on, battered by the great Pacific rollers and broiled by a sun of cruel intensity. Several times they sighted land; but their ships were too unmanoeuvrable for them to put ashore. Throughout this nightmare voyage Mendana's widow, Dona Isabella, did her best to undermine Quiros's authority, countermanding his orders, washing her clothes in her own private supply of water while the crew were dying of thirst, and plotting another round of carnage and murder. But at last, on January 12th, 1596, Quiros led the remnants of Mendana's once proud armada into the haven of the Philippines.

They had crossed the Pacific. But what a trail of human misery they had left in their wake! Upwards of a thousand men, women and children dead of fever, gunshot or sword-thrust; a record of pointless brutality hitherto un-equalled in the annals of exploration by sea.

Such was Quiros's initiation to Pacific voyaging. One does not need to be a religious fanatic to be appalled at so much suffering and bloodshed; one does not need to be a visionary to dream of a programme of exploration in which the graceful and gentle Polynesians would be not indiscriminately massacred but peaceably converted.

When Quiros had returned to Peru he sought an audience with the Viceroy. If he were given a ship of 70 tons and a crew of forty he would, he said, return to the islands of the south-west Pacific, bring their inhabitants into the bosom of the Catholic Church and then push on to discover and colonize the great southern continent, *Terra Australis Incognita*, which he was convinced lay south-west of Santa Cruz. His scheme was ambitious, but it was by no means the daydream of an impractical visionary. Quiros may have over-estimated the size of Australia (it was inconceivable to a sixteenth-century cartographer that there should not be a vast land-mass in the south to counterbalance the mass of Eurasia in the north); but at least he was intending to search for it in exactly the right place. And if he had been given a free hand he would almost certainly have anticipated the discoveries of Cook by a hundred and fifty years.

But he was not given a free hand. For Spain in 1600 was in the predicament which Portugal had been in in 1500: satiated with discovery, too preoccupied with holding on to her existing conquests to want to accumulate more. This was Quiros's tragedy: that his zeal and fervour were an embarrassment to the establishment: that those from whom he sought support were apathetic if not antipathetic to the dream to which he was now determined to dedicate his life.

The Viceroy of Peru referred Quiros to the court of Spain; the court of Spain referred him to the Papacy; the Papacy referred him back to Philip III; Philip handed him over to the Council of The Indies, and the Council of The Indies passed him on to the Council of State. It was seven years before he was back in South America. And by this time he was a sick man, worn out with the subterfuge and intrigue of politicians and with serious internal injuries caused when a building collapsed on him in Panama. But he had at last obtained permission to make his voyage. He handed the Viceroy instructions from Philip III and Clement VIII which were too explicit to be denied. And in the autumn of 1605 a small fleet began to assemble in the Peruvian port of Callao.

This autumn of 1605 must have been the happiest period of Quiros's life. It is true that there were still obstacles and delays—his route was drastically amended, and several of his crew (including the Chief Pilot) were foist on him against his wishes—but overshadowing these minor pin-pricks was the joy of his impending leap into the unknown. He was given three good ships: the *Capitana*, the *Almiranta* and a small 20-ton *zabra* or launch *Los Tres Reyes Magos*. His crew numbered close on 300; among them were a large number of friars, but a large number, too, of soldiers who had been lured aboard by promises of the unknown continent's gold. His provisions were adequate for more than a year. And all Callao turned out to watch him go.

As the three ships stood slowly out of harbour, the beach and the docks and the rooftops were crowded with spectators. Banners were everywhere. Guns boomed. Quiros and his officers, dressed in sackcloth, were on their knees. And—to quote one of the pilots—"*With our desire to serve God, to spread the True Faith and to enrich the crown of Spain, all things seemed easy to us.*"

Cynics may sneer that Quiros's achievements turned out to be less than his pretensions; but nothing can erase the idealism in which his voyage was conceived. He was a Utopian, sailing in search not of wealth or fame but of a new and better world. It was his tragedy that he was never sure, to the end of his days, whether or not he had found it.

His armada left Callao on the feast of Saint Thomas (December 21st), 1605.

The passage from Peru to Polynesia is generally a pleasant one; for winds and currents are favourable, the weather equable and the sea full of fish; and during this early part of the voyage Quiros had only one anxiety: his health. We do not know for certain what was the matter with him, but his premature death and the frequent references in his diary to "sickness" lead us to suppose the complaint was serious. And herein, I think, lies a partial explanation of the extraordinary course his voyage was to take. For when Quiros was

Fig 28. A sixteenth-century Galleon

well, his command was reasonably effective; but when he was ill, all was in-decision and chaos.

For a month the ships stood west-south-west with following winds and swell. Quiros retired to his cabin at first; but by January 8th he was suffi-ciently recovered to issue a voluminous series of orders. And these orders are another clue to the events of the next nine months, for they epitomize both Quiros's virtues and failings: his mastery of the technicalities of his profession, and his inability to fathom the complexities of human nature. They contain, for example, detailed and extremely sensible instructions on such subjects as rationing, fire precautions and shallow-water pilotage among the reefs of the south seas; but they also lay down a code of behaviour that is almost im-possibly idealistic—"*We must never curse nor blaspheme . . . there must be no playings with dice nor cards . . . gaming tables are to be thrown overboard . . . all crew, each day in the afternoon, are to go on their knees before an altar where there are images of Christ and the Virgin Mary and pray for intercession.*" A Cromwell might have been able to enforce these rules; but Quiros was too lenient and sweetly reasonable to impose on others a code he had laid down for himself. Those who transgressed, he forgave. He was more a saint than a sea-captain.

Towards the middle of January the weather turned squally, with a bitter wind and a great swell from the south. The seamen became disgruntled; "*Whither,*" they asked, "*are the pilots taking us into this great gulf, in the winter season?*" Quiros retired to his cabin, and then made one of his frequent and characteristic changes of plan: they would, he decided, alter course to the west-*north*-west.

Taking the long view this was tragic, for if the ships had held course they would almost certainly have sighted either New Zealand or Australia; but the immediate result was all that Quiros could have wished. For on January 26th they sighted land.

It was an uninhabited atoll they came to first: "*a submerged island*" was their graphic description of it, "*a piece of water surrounded by coral*". Much to their disappointment they found no sign of life and no water (which they were beginning to need badly), only "*coconuts and certain other fruits too unripe to eat*". But they soon discovered that this atoll was only the forerunner of a considerable archipelago; for in the next ten days they passed an endless succession of islands—Dulcie, Henderson, Marutea: the Actaeons, Oeno and Nenonengo; they had discovered The Societies. The weather throughout these ten days was capricious, with high winds and violent storms; and this, I think, accounts for their missing many of the larger islands of the group, including Tahiti. But they did make contact—and friendly contact—with the natives.

And herein lies the vindication of Quiros's high-flown proclamations and orders. Mendana had visited the Polynesians with treachery and violence, and the natives who survived his stay had showered his departing ships with curses and stones; Quiros visited them with fair-dealing and kindness, and when it was time for his ships to leave the natives kissed him and exchanged gifts with his seamen and wept. There are more facets to exploration than the physical act of setting foot on a virgin shore; and the manner in which an explorer makes a discovery is sometimes as important as the discovery itself.

One might have expected Quiros, now, to go back to his original course of west-south-west. But he did not. He was somewhat short of both water and food, having happened to land on only the more barren of the Society Islands; and he therefore decided to head for Santa Cruz, where he knew there were supplies in abundance. All through February and March his armada stood west-north-west. Progress was slow, for the winds now turned contrary and there was a good deal of mist. As the weeks passed and no landfall was made, the crew again became disgruntled and the Chief Pilot openly mutinous. Quiros's fellow-captains urged him to stern action; but action was not Quiros's *forte*. He forgave the incipient mutineers time and again, urging them to read "*good improving books and to learn the arts of fortification and artillery and the spheres of navigation*". He did, however, order an executioner's block to be placed under the yardarm—though his crew probably realized by this time that he would never be capable of bringing himself to use it. It was fortunate that their next landfall was not long delayed.

Early in April they again noticed signs of land: turtles, trunks of trees and random currents. Soon the water grew shallow, so they reefed sails and sent *Los Tres Reyes Magos* ahead to reconnoitre; and on April 7th the *zabra's* lookout reported "*hills to the north-west: high and black*". Next day, "*full of exceeding joy*", they dropped anchor off a fertile well-wooded island.

The landfall was not in fact Santa Cruz, but the nearby and hitherto undiscovered Taumaco, one of the Duff Group. And here again Quiros's behaviour towards the natives was the antithesis of Mendana's.

About 150 Polynesians had gathered on the beach to oppose the Spanish landing. Mendana would have massacred the lot; but the more humane Quiros ordered his men to fire over the natives' heads, and in due course friendly relations were established without bloodshed. The local chief, a handsome grey-bearded man named Tumai, was invited aboard, given presents and dressed in shot silk; the Spaniards promised not to harm his people nor pilfer their possessions, and in return Tumai offered the strangers all the information and supplies they needed. And both kept faith.

There followed a ten days' idyll, all too rare in the history of Pacific exploration.

Relations between Spaniards and natives were excellent; there was no bloodshed and no thieving, but "*goodfellowship abounded and gifts and names were freely exchanged*". Tumai's people, working in shifts with their canoes, supplied all the water and wood that was needed, and in return were given mirrors, fish-hooks and bells. The Spaniards then explored the island thoroughly, marvelling at the white beaches, the prolific fruit trees, the clean airy houses and the magnificent outrigger canoes, some of them forty feet long, beautifully carved and with their prows inlaid with mother-of-pearl. Before many days they were wandering about singly or in pairs without fear of attack; and eventually, to quote Quiros's Diary, "*If any of our belongings such as clothes, pots or kettles were missing we knew for certain they were not stolen but only being washed by natives in a nearby stream.*"

Those who dismiss Quiros as an impractical visionary should remember that few other Pacific explorers were able to establish such a satisfactory *modus vivendi* with the natives; and, quite apart from any ethical considerations, the practical results of such a *rapport* were considerable. For Tumai's people not only loaded the Spaniards with water, food and fuel; they also gave them a mass of valuable information about the cartography of the south-west Pacific. Here is Quiros's account of how this information was obtained and ratified.

"The Captain then asked Tumai whether he knew of other lands, far or near, inhabited or uninhabited. In reply Tumai pointed to his island, then to the sea, then to various points of the horizon; he then began counting on his fingers up to as many as sixty islands, ending with a very large land which he called 'Manicolo'. The Captain wrote down the names, having the compass before him for noting the bearing of each island from Taumaco. To explain which were small islands, Tumai drew small circles, and for larger ones larger circles; while for the very large land to the south-west he opened both his hands and his arms as wide as he could. To explain which were the distant islands and which the nearer, he pointed to the sun, then rested his head on his hand, shut his eyes, and with his fingers counted the number of nights one had to sleep on the voyage. In a similar way he explained which people were white, black or mulattos; which friendly and which hostile. He gave us to understand, by biting his arm, that in one island they ate human flesh, and indicated he disapproved of such people. In this way what he said was understood. He repeated his information many times until he was tired, and showed a desire to return to his house; and then the Captain gave him many gifts for barter, and he departed after embraces and other tokens of love.

"Next day the Captain went to the village, and in order to corroborate what Tumai had said, he assembled the natives on the beach. Holding a paper in his hand, with the compass before him, he began asking them many times respecting the lands to seaward; and all gave the same information. Other persons that same day put the same questions to other natives elsewhere in the island, always with the same result. So it appeared certain to us that the natives were truthful."

Quiros left Taumaco at sunset on April 18th. There was no longer need for him to hold course for Santa Cruz, for his ships were full of provisions and his crew in excellent health. He therefore decided to continue his search for the great unknown continent of the south, his hopes being raised, no doubt, by Tumai's references to the land of Manicolo.

For several days his armada coasted through a veritable maze of atolls, exchanging greetings and gifts with the natives; then a violent storm forced them to heave to. When the weather cleared and the pilots asked Quiros for a course he said simply, "Let the ships run free: God will guide them". And it must have seemed to the Spaniards as if their course was indeed divinely inspired; for in the next three days they sighted no less than eight beautiful and fertile islands (the Banks group). Here again they made friendly contact with the natives, offering them knives, plumed hats and mirrors in exchange for figs, fruit and sugar-cane. A couple of days later, on April 29th, more land appeared over the southern horizon; and soon at every point of the compass between south-east and south-west there seemed to be islands, while in the distance rose a "massive and exceeding lofty chain of mountains, their peaks wreathed in cloud". To Quiros this was "the most

joyful and celebrated day of the whole voyage"; for he believed that at long
last, after a voyage of almost ten thousand miles he was approaching the
shores of *Terra Australis Incognita*, the last of the world's great continents and
the home of countless millions of heathen whom he would now be able to
save from perdition.

He had in fact reached only the outskirts of Australia, the New Hebrides,
where, to those approaching from the north, the overlapping islands of
Pentecost, Ambrim and Aurora have the exact appearance of a mass of
high and continuous land. This, however, was not realized for some time;
and the Spaniards, as they gazed in wonder at the succession of magnificent
headlands and bays now unfolding across their bows, believed that they
had come at last to the land of their dreams and that they now held within
their grasp "*the greatest and most abundant territorie ever to come into the service of
Spain*".

On May 3rd their ships dropped anchor in a deep, well-sheltered bay.
An advance party rowed ashore, marvelling at the exotic woods, the great
rivers, the rich dark soil and the abundance of wild life. A few days later
Quiros himself landed to supervise the building of a church-cum-fort. There
followed a series of pageants and religious ceremonies which may have
seemed apposite at the time but which have in retrospect an air of magnificent futility. Ministries were set up, new religious orders were created,
the foundations of a great city—the New Jerusalem—were dug literally out
of sand; there were processions, the celebrating of special Masses, and a
ceremony of taking possession as ineffective as it was grandiloquent. Quiros—
who appears to have been overfond of making speeches—was swept away
in a frenzy of religious zeal; he knelt and kissed the earth—"*sought for so
long by many and so much desired by me*", and in the names of the Trinity, the
Catholic Church, St. Francis, the Order of the Holy Ghost and Philip III
of Spain, he took possession not only of the island on which he now stood,
but also of "*all the lands which I have sighted and am going to sight, and of all
this region of the South as far as the Pole, which from this time forth shall be called
Austrialia del Espiritu Santo, with all its dependencies and belongings*". The ships
fired their guns, the soldiers their arquebuses; there were rockets and fire-
wheels, dancing and feasting; banners and crosses were set up around the
bay, while the natives peered in wonder at a scene beyond their—and
our—comprehension.

Alas for Quiros's dreams! To-day I doubt if one person in a thousand
could place the tiny island of Espiritu Santo—which belongs, incidentally,
not to Spain but to Great Britain and France—while the great southern
continent which Quiros thought he had discovered has been named not
Austrialia after the House of Austria (Quiros's joint patron) but Australia
after the south or austral wind. Quiros's dreams faded, in fact, almost at
the moment of their conception. For during his brief stay on Espiritu Santo
everything went wrong.

It was the natives who were his first stumbling-block. They did not want
to be saved. And it is unfortunate for Quiros's reputation that his mistaken
landfall coincided with his one and only failure to win the friendship of the

Polynesians. Exactly why good relations were not established on Espiritu Santo is hard to say, for contemporary records are conflicting. But I think the basic reason is that Quiros's men were by this time bored with inaction and had had their fill of piety. They were soldiers, not missionaries; they dreamed more of El Dorado than the New Jerusalem; and Quiros's vision of a heathen continent peaceably converted to Christianity was one they could neither understand nor share. So they disobeyed orders and engineered a *fracas*. That, at any rate, is my interpretation of the events which Quiros describes as follows.

"*Next day the Captain ordered a party of soldiers to go ashore and try by all possible means to catch some of the natives, so as to establish peace and friendship, based on the good work we intended to do for them. The landing party ran their boat high up on the beach, and quickly formed into a squadron; for the natives were coming, and it was not known with what object. Being near, the natives made signs and spoke, but were not understood. Our people called to them in return. The natives then drew a line on the ground, seemingly to indicate that we were not to pass beyond it. As I understood it there was no one in either party who could make himself really intelligible; and it is a great misfortune on these occasions when there is a lack of well-intentioned leadership. Soon, natives were seen in the woods, and to frighten them muskets were fired into the air. But one of the soldiers, who had either lost patience or forgotten his orders, fired low and killed a native. The others, with loud cries, fled. Another soldier, who was the drummer, then cut off the head and one foot of the dead native, and hung the body on the branch of a tree. It then happened that three native chiefs came to the place where our people were; and we, instead of showing them kindness and bringing them on board, showed them instead their comrade without a head and running blood, pretending that they thought this cruelty a means of making peace. The chiefs showed great sorrow. They went back to their people, and after a while the sound of instruments blowing with great force was heard among the trees. Then the natives began shooting arrows and darts, while our people fired on them.*

"*The Captain saw all this from his ship, and great was his regret that peace was turned to war . . . Soon a tall, elderly native advanced by himself, blowing on a shell. He seemed to be indicating that his people would defend their country against the invaders who came to it and killed the inhabitants. And eight of our musketeers were in ambush; and one of them unfortunately — and as he afterwards said by mistake — killed this chief. Whereat the others desisted, and raised their dead on their shoulders and went inland, leaving their villages deserted. Such was the end of the peace that the Captain had hoped for and sought for, and the great good that he had intended was now but a hollow sound.*"

When Quiros rebuked his men for disobeying orders, he was told they "had only killed so as to teach the natives the respect that all peoples should be made to show for the king of Spain".

There followed three weeks of alternate ceremony and skirmish. Quiros made repeated efforts to win back the natives' confidence. He went in person through their deserted villages sowing Peruvian calabashes, maize, melons, beans, lentils and potatoes; he returned the pigs which his soldiers had stolen, and he ordered an endless succession of Masses and prayers. But the evil that had been done could not be undone. And on May 26th he decided, quite suddenly, to leave Espiritu Santo and *"visit the lands to wind-ward"*.

Historians have been unanimous in condemning this decision. "So," writes J. C. Beaglehole, "on the pinnacle of glory, Quiros turned his back; and there began that melancholy retreat the truth of which is so hard to dis-entangle." Yet there seems to me to be a simple and logical explanation of Quiros's behaviour. He had begun to suspect that Espiritu Santo might not, after all, be the unknown continent of his dreams, and in order to seek reassurance on this point he had decided to survey the mountains which had been sighted to the south. His Diary is quite explicit about this being his motive—*"the Captain resolved to weigh anchor in order to obtain a near view of the great and high chain of mountains"*. This strikes me as an advance rather than a retreat. But unhappily for Quiros, at this most critical moment of his career, he fell victim to his recurrent ill-health.

Here again his Diary gives us the sequence of events. When it was decided to leave Espiritu Santo, Quiros's second-in-command, Torres, asked if the ships might spend a last day in harbour fishing and taking aboard provisions. Quiros agreed. But as luck would have it the fish they netted included a number of the bream-like and exceedingly poisonous *fargos*. All who ate the *fargos* were violently ill, with nausea, vomiting and high fever. Among those who suffered most was Quiros, whose health was never robust and who now seems to have lain close to death for several days. Departure was postponed; but even so, Quiros was far from fit when his fleet put to sea on June 8th.

What happened next must have happened many times in the days of sail. As the ships stood seaward the wind appeared to be light from the east; but outside the bay it veered to the south-east and freshened. Now Quiros wanted to head south-east, but his vessels were not able to beat directly into wind—it was a characteristic of Peruvian-built ships that they were difficult to handle under little sail, and in this case Quiros had the current against him as well. All that day they battled against the wind but made no progress; in fact they were blown if anything slightly backwards. In the evening there was a conference of pilots, and Quiros decided to return to harbour. But this was easier said than done. All night the three vessels, on different tacks, beat to and fro, clawing their way inch by painful inch into the teeth of a rising wind. By next morning the *Almiranta* and *Los Tres Reyes Magos* were reasonably close to the bay, but the *Capitana* (which was carrying less sail than her consorts) had made no progress at all. During the afternoon the two leading vessels managed to struggle back into port, and here as darkness fell they lit lanterns to give their flagship a guide. Slowly the *Capitana* beat up to the bay. Soon she was less than an arquebus-shot from safety. Then a particularly violent squall halted her progress. Her pilot now seems to have lost his nerve: confused by the many lights (some of them native) and uncertain of the position of rocks, he decided to stand into the centre of the bay and wait for dawn. But the wind was increasing now, and every time the *Capitana* tacked she was blown further to leeward. By daybreak she was well outside the bay, and being driven slowly but inexorably north. At this juncture Quiros appeared on deck—we can only assume that he had been confined up to now to his cabin. He at once ordered the pilot to hoist more sail, but was told the sea was too high and their bow timbers would split if the ship was driven harder. We shall never know if the pilot was giving a reason or making an excuse. At any rate, though the *Capitana* beat to and fro for the best part of a week off the coast of Espiritu Santo, she could make no headway but was driven hour by hour farther to leeward. "*With great sorrow*" Quiros saw his mountains of the south sink below the horizon; soon even the coast of Espiritu Santo had vanished, and he was alone.

These are the facts; but they do not, I think, tell us the whole story. Quiros was certainly ill, he obviously had little confidence in his crew, and it is quite possible that he was temporarily mastered by wind and wave. But one would have expected him either to return when the wind dropped or else to make for Santa Cruz, the rendezvous which had been agreed in case of just such an eventuality. Instead, he returned to Peru.

His Diary does not say why; it is full of lamentations over his "*many and great sins*", of "*sorrowful discourses*" and of explanations which fail to explain; also, if one reads between the lines, there is the hint of mutiny. And here, I think, we have the key to Quiros's behaviour. There may not have been open mutiny (although more than one contemporary writer states categorically that there was): but there was almost certainly a conspiracy to take advantage of Quiros's sickness. The scene is easy to picture: the men bored with proselytizing and disappointed at the lack of women and gold; the commander ill in his cabin, with his congenital lack of firmness now accentuated by the aftermath of poisoning. I don't think they tried very hard to beat back to Espiritu Santo. This, at any rate, was the opinion of Torres who clearly considered that he had been deserted by his commander—"*From within this bay*," he wrote, "*the Capitana departed at one hour past midnight, without any notice or signal; and although the next morning we went to seek them, we could not find them, for they did not sail on the proper course or with good intention.*"

Whatever the truth, Austrialia del Espiritu Santo and the New Jerusalem now lay behind Quiros; and there was to be no return. The rest of his life was anticlimax.

It took him four and a half months to recross the Pacific. The passage was arduous and full of incident: thirst, slaked by a timely cloudburst; hunger, alleviated by a great shoal of albacore and bonito; an earthquake followed by a tidal wave; an eclipse of the moon, and a fierce storm off the Gulf of California. But at last, on November 23rd, 1606, the *Capitana* again dropped anchor in the shadow of the Andes.

Quiros had been away for nearly a year. He had made a voyage of more than twenty thousand miles (double the distance covered by Columbus in his crossing of the Atlantic). He had discovered skein after skein of islands in the south-west Pacific. He had established friendly relations with the inhabitants of all but one of these islands. Of his ship's company only one man, the aged Commissary of the Friars, had died. And—and this is not generally realized—his ships had sighted the north-east coast of Australia,

160 years before its usually accepted "discovery" by Cook. (For after Quiros had left them, the *Almiranta* and *Los Tres Reyes Magos* continued to the westward; they discovered and explored the south coast of New Guinea, and then passed through the Torres Strait. Here, we are told, they sighted *"many islands, including one very large one to the south"*; and the inhabitants of these southerly islands they described as *"black-skinned and naked"*. And these two adjectives give us a vital clue. For the inhabitants of the islands around New Guinea were neither black nor nude; they were, Torres tells us, *"not very white, and naked except for their private parts which are covered with a cloth made of bark"*. Torres's description can therefore only apply to the Australian Aboriginals, and the islands he sighted must have been the Mulgrave and Banks archipelagoes, with the Cape York mainland beyond.) Such a series of achievements is without parallel in the history of Pacific exploration. Yet Quiros was disregarded by his contemporaries, and his name to-day has been virtually forgotten. Conversion, it seems, brings less kudos than massacre; and the discovery of new continents wins fewer accolades than the discovery of gold.

Back in Peru Quiros was received with sceptical tolerance. His claim to have discovered a "new world" aroused little enthusiasm, especially when he failed to produce tangible evidence of its wealth; and when he sought funds to finance another expedition he was quickly referred to Spain. He was not, however, given passage money, nor did he receive a single ducat for the voyage he had just accomplished. As a result he grew steadily poorer. Soon he was forced to sell even his clothes and his cross of orange-wood which he had hoped to present to the Pope. Indeed, if it had not been for the charity of a fellow sea-captain, who gave him a free passage to Europe, he would probably have spent the rest of his life in South America. As it was he reached Cadiz in the summer of 1607 in poor health and destitute. He gave his last two tiny coins to a beggar, then sold his bed and standards to pay the coach fare to Madrid.

What happened next is an indictment of seventeenth-century Spain. Quiros argued with vehemence—and with much truth—that he had stood on the threshold of a great new continent; and he told the authorities it was now his dearest wish to return there, both to check the extent of his discoveries and to fulfil his dream of converting the heathen. But for seven frustrating years he was passed to and fro between courts and councils, the victim of gossip, intrigue and never-ending procrastination. He submitted a whole flood of documents and maps; he attended an endless succession of audiences and auditions. But to no avail. He had been born a century too late. For the Spain of Philip III was not the Spain of Ferdinand and Isabella. Her drive was spent by now, her virility sapped, and her desideratum had shifted from acquisition to assimilation. To such a nation Quiros and his dreams were an embarrassment. Even the arrival of Torres's despatches, confirming the existence of great new lands in the south, failed to stimulate interest; and it is one of the more remarkable facts of history that Spanish seamen should have discovered Australia in 1606, only for Spanish politicians to hush their discovery up for the better part of a century.

It was this official apathy which killed Quiros. Faced with so unyielding a wall of disinterest, a lesser man would have given up. But Quiros had the tenacity and nervous energy of a fanatic. His flood of petitions did not diminish with the years; if anything it increased. Though he became so poor that he frequently fainted in the streets from hunger and had to kneel awkwardly at Mass for fear men should see the holes in his shoes, he never gave up. And at last, in 1614, he thought he saw a ray of hope. In the autumn of that year a new Viceroy was appointed to Peru, and Quiros was given permission to accompany him. *"Seeing"*, he wrote, *"that my health and patience were by now quite worn out, I decided to put into this man's hands all my life and work. 'Trust me,' the Viceroy said, 'and see what I shall do'."* In November the two men set sail for Callao.

It was as well for Quiros that he died *en route*. For death spared him the last betrayal of the country and faith he had spent his life in serving so loyally. He never knew that among the Viceroy's papers were orders forbidding him ever again to search for the continent of his dreams.

His death marks the end of an epoch. He was the last of the Conquistadors, and with him died the heroic age of Spain.

XII

VENUS, SAUERKRAUT AND YORKSHIRE GRIT

(James Cook delineates the Pacific: 1768–71)

JAMES COOK would probably appear in most people's short-list of the world's greatest explorers—his companions in my own list being Pytheas, Leif Eriksson and Magellan—and for the extent of his cartographical discoveries alone Cook is well worthy of a place among the élite; for not only did he delineate the world's greatest ocean, the Pacific; he also disproved the myth of the world's supposedly greatest continent, the *Terra Australis Incognita* which for two thousand years cartographers had been inking on to their globes to counterbalance the land mass of Eurasia. Yet Cook also made other contributions to the science of discovery: contributions less tangible but not, I think, less important. For he brought to his calling a new and peculiarly modern approach, a searching-after-absolute-truth-for-its-own-sake, a return, after two thousand years, to the spirit which had carried Pytheas to Ultima Thule; while his career was stamped with a humanity and a respect for life which explorers in the last hundred years have taken for granted but which was rare in the eighteenth century.

He was born at Marton in Yorkshire on October 27th, 1728, the second child of a Scottish farm labourer. It is doubtful if he saw salt water before he was seventeen, when his parents took him to the fishing village of Staithes and apprenticed him to a grocer-cum-haberdasher. For a year and a half Cook sold potatoes and lengths of cloth in a cramped little shop—a less auspicious boyhood for an embryo explorer it would be hard to imagine—but the grey expanse of the North Sea lay literally at his doorstep, and in 1746 he decided to try his luck in the nearby port of Whitby. Within a month he was at sea: deck-hand aboard the *Freelove*, a 450-ton brig carrying coal from Newcastle to London.

It was now that Cook first displayed the trait which was subsequently to take him to the very ends of the earth: determination. Having made up his mind that the sea was to be his life, he set about learning his profession with the zeal of an apostate. There is no evidence that he had a particularly quick brain, but he was industrious and gifted with "God's good common-sense that's more than any knowledge". He taught himself pilotage, navigation, surveying and astronomy. For close on ten years he worked his way up the lower-deck hierarchy from able seaman to mate, and in the spring of 1755 he was offered a command of his own, a Whitby brig in trade with the Baltic.

Then, apparently, he threw it all away. On June 17th, 1755, he enrolled as an A.B. in the Royal Navy.

It must have seemed at first a step backward rather than forward. For a master's cabin in those days was a very different place from the fourteen inches of deck space allotted to hands in a man-of-war, and Cook's first impression of the Navy must have been one of unbelievable squalor. Here is Admiral Muir's account of conditions aboard Cook's first ship, the sixty-gun *Eagle*. "The only ventilation was by way of the gun-ports and hatches, which had to be closed in bad weather. The ship leaked badly, the bilge water stank with a nauseating odour which permeated the whole vessel, whilst suffocation from falling into the well was a common accident. The sanitary arrangements consisted of an open space about the heel of the bowsprit, where the men were exposed to showers of spray, and excrement stuck to the bows until washed off in heavy weather. No wonder that cruising, even in home waters, was invariably accompanied by a shocking mortality." In view of these conditions it is not surprising that at the end of Cook's first spell of blockading in the Channel his captain's report made tragic reading — "*Put ashore to the hospital 130 sick men, most of which are extremely ill; buried the last month 22. The surgeon and 4 men died yesterday* . . ." Yet such conditions were the rule in the eighteenth century rather than the exception. Cook suffered them for years. And it is this, I think, which accounts for the almost fanatical measures which he took when he had a command of his own to safeguard the health of his crew—not many naval captains in those days had "enjoyed" first-hand experience of life on the lower deck. But for the time being Cook could only endure what he lacked the influence to reform.

It quickly became apparent to his officers that their new A.B. was several cuts above the usual press-ganged landlubber, and Cook's promotions came steadily: to petty officer, to master's mate, and finally after only a couple of years to warrant officer. Then came the crucial moment of his career. On October 27th, 1757 (his twenty-ninth birthday) he was appointed master to the *Pembroke*, another sixty-gunner commanded by Captain Simcoe. A few days later the *Pembroke* was ordered to the Saint Lawrence. And here, on one of the trickiest waterways of the world, Cook discovered his *métier*.

When he went to Canada Cook had a number of admirers among the ship owners of Whitby, and he had earned the approbation of his immediate superiors in the Navy; but his name was not known either to high-ranking officers or to the public. Within ten years more than one admiral had officially described him as a "genius", and the Royal Society acknowledged him "a man very expert in his own particular business". And the "business" which brought him so suddenly into the limelight was surveying.

His first piece of survey work led to Wolfe's capture of Quebec.

The French defences of Quebec were based on the fact that part of the Saint Lawrence River known as The Traverse was believed to be impassable to warships—and those who know The Traverse can understand why, for a wilder, more rock-strewn race of water would be hard to find. But in the weeks prior to the assault on the Heights of Abraham, Cook and Bissett (the master of the *Stirling Castle*) surveyed and sounded The Traverse and marked

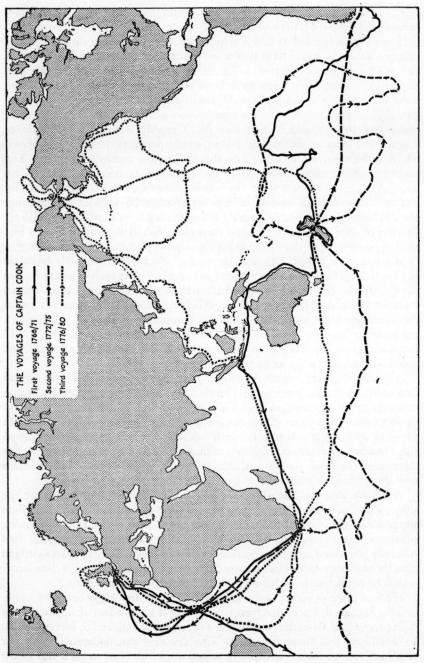

FIG 29.

it so effectively with buoys that on the night of June 24th the entire British fleet was able to pass through without the loss of a single man. This was a fine piece of work by Cook, and it brought him to the attention of the great, and in particular of Lord Colville, who was so impressed with the buoying of the passage that when the fighting was over he arranged for Cook to stay on as "Master-Surveyor" aboard the *Northumberland*, flagship of the North American Fleet.

For several years Cook worked steadily at his surveying, plotting with amazing accuracy long stretches of the Saint Lawrence and the coast of Nova Scotia. It was work for which he was well suited by both temperament and inclination: and in 1762 Colville felt able to write to the Admiralty *"that from my experience of Mr. Cook's genius and capacity I think him well qualified for the* (surveying) *work he has performed and for greater undertakings of the same kind"*.

Cook the mariner was rising to fame. It was as well for Cook the man that he used his six weeks' leave in the winter of '62 to get married. For he was not, in the remaining seventeen years of his life, to spend much time ashore.

After the Saint Lawrence, Newfoundland—which Cook surveyed with such skill and thoroughness that his charts to-day are still the basis for local pilotage. It was during this period that he observed an eclipse of the sun which helped him to calculate with unusual accuracy the longitude of Cook's Rock on the Newfoundland coast; and his observations on this occasion were of sufficient originality and interest to be sent to the Royal Society. This led to important results. For when, a couple of years later, the Society was anxious to send an observer south to witness the transit of Venus, Cook at once came to their minds as a possible candidate.

So it was that on May 25th, 1768, Lieutenant James Cook was appointed to the *Endeavour Bark*, a 368-ton Whitby-built collier which the Admiralty had bought specially for the voyage south. His ostensible object was *"from such a place southward of the Equinoctial Line as shall be judged proper . . . to observe the passage of the Planet Venus over the disk of the sun on the 3rd June, 1769"*. But there was in fact a great deal more to Cook's commission than this. For as well as the scientists of the Royal Society and their plethora of equipment, the *Endeavour* also carried sealed and top-secret orders. These instructed Cook, after the transit had been observed, to *"search for the Great Southern Continent, to observe with accuracy the situation of this and such other lands as you may discover, to make surveys and draughts of such of them as appear of consequence and to take possession of them in the name of His Majesty"*. The existence of these secret instructions has only recently come to light; and they prove, I think, that the observation of the transit of Venus was only an excuse, and that the real *raison d'être* of Cook's voyage was in fact nothing less than the exploration of the South Pacific.

What were the problems posed by such a commission, and what difficulties and dangers lay ahead of the *Endeavour* as late that July she slipped quietly out of Deptford?

Two hundred and fifty years had passed since Magellan's first crossing of the *Mar Pacifico*. Yet the great ocean was still an enigma, its extent only hazily appreciated, its mysteries still largely unveiled. Some dozen explorers had crossed it—Drake, Mendana, Quiros and Le Maire; Byron, Carteret, Wallis and Bougainville—but they had mostly followed the same route, running from east to west along the Tropic of Cancer and returning from west to east along the Tropic of Capricorn. All that lay between and to the north and south of these routes was virgin sea, mile after million square mile that was either blank or cloud-cuckoo-land on the cartographer's spheres. On pages 194 and 195 is a map of the Pacific as it was known in 1750; and one is amazed by the inaccuracy of the coastlines, and in particular by the continued myth of the Great Southern Continent and the hazy outline of Australia.

The reason why the Pacific had not been explored more thoroughly was its size. Its vast area—greater than all the land surfaces of the world put together—presented two almost insuperable problems to the explorers of the sixteenth, seventeenth and eighteenth centuries. And it was these problems which now confronted Cook: the one navigational, the other medicinal.

FIG 30. The *Endeavour Bark* (1793)

By the middle of the eighteenth century ships at sea were able to calculate their latitude with reasonable accuracy, but longitude was still largely a matter of guesswork. This meant that when a new land was sighted in a vast expanse of ocean it was difficult to survey it and place it accurately on a map. It has been argued that "Cook's charting of the Pacific was made possible by the invention of the sextant and chronometer", and it was "because he enjoyed the use of these new navigational aids that he succeeded where his predecessors had failed". But this is not altogether true. On his first voyage, for instance, Cook did not carry chronometers, and yet he was able to survey and orientate the whole of New Zealand and the east coast of Australia with pin-point accuracy. The truth is, I think, that previous explorers in the Pacific had been primarily interested in things other than cartography—in saving souls, in acquiring wealth, in adding to their country's possessions or in the golden girls of the islands—but Cook, to quote his own words, was motivated by a desire simply *"to go as far as it was possible for man to go, and to make an exact recording of all that I saw"*. In other words, it was largely because of Cook's character rather than his instruments that he overcame the navigational problems which had defeated his predecessors.

The medical difficulties he had to face can be summed up in a single word: scurvy.

It was scurvy and the fear of scurvy which for two hundred and fifty years had been the main obstacle to Pacific exploration. For ships' companies who wandered off the shortest and quickest route died: their diet and hygiene being unable to withstand the strain of spending month after month at sea without making frequent landfalls to reprovision. We have already seen that eighteenth-century vessels were prone to disease even when cruising in home waters. And this proneness was increased a hundredfold in the vast reaches of the Pacific, where for a single crossing a crew loss of 50% was normal and a loss of 75% by no means unusual. (For example in 1741 Anson started his voyage round the world with a crew of 961; by the time he reached Juan Fernandez 621 were dead. And in his voyage of 1721–22 across the Pacific Roggeween lost an average of four men a day and has left this heartrending account of his experiences: *"No pen can describe the misery of life in our ships. Only God knows how much we have suffered. Our vessels reeked of sickness and death. The stricken wailed and lamented without respite, and their cries would have moved stones to pity. Some became so emaciated that they looked like walking corpses and death blew them out like so many candles. Others became very fat and blown up like balloons; these were so afflicted with dysentery that they passed nothing but blood except for two or three days before they died when their excrement was like grey sulphur—and this was a sure sign that their hour had come. All were overcome by a fearful melancholy . . . And even those who were not seriously ill, like myself, were left very weak and enfeebled. My teeth were loose in my gums, which were swollen up almost to the thickness of a thumb, and my body was covered with swellings, red, yellow, green and blue in colour and the size of hazelnuts."*) With such a spectre at their yardarms no wonder that vessels in the Pacific hurried as fast as they could along the routes that were known: no wonder the blank spaces on cartographers' charts were referred to as "the seas of death".

And yet in his three voyages to the Pacific Cook was able to criss-cross these blank spaces again and again, in safety. How?

It has been suggested that Cook had aboard an elixir: sauerkraut: and that it was this which kept his ship's company healthy where others had died. It is certainly true that his provisions were far better balanced than those of his predecessors; that due to Lind's and Pringle's experiments the value of vegetables as an antiscorbutic was at last beginning to be appreciated, and that the *Endeavour* had aboard over 7,000 lb. of sauerkraut (i.e., cabbage pickled in brine). What is not so generally realized is that Cook in fact largely nullified the value of his sauerkraut by serving it boiled and diluted as soup—the boiling, of course, ruining its vitamin content and hence its efficiency as an antiscorbutic. In other words, the *Endeavour's* clean bill of health cannot be wholly attributed to her crews' diet; and much of the credit, once again, must be given to Cook himself. For he cared for his men in a way that is unique in the annals of exploration, and the lengths he went to in order to safeguard their health were revolutionary. He kept three watches instead of the usual two; he insisted that every man had at least one cold bath a day, even in the Antarctic; hammocks, clothing and bedding were brought on deck twice a week for airing; once a week the ship was either "cured with fires" or "smoked clean with a mixture of vinegar and gunpowder"; the well was regularly fumigated; coppers were scoured daily; diet was minutely supervised; a carefully worked-out programme ensured there was no idleness, while Cook himself made frequent inspections of every part of his ship and every member of his crew. There was some discontent at first at so overpowering a routine—*"every day is Sunday* (i.e., a captain's rounds day) *with Mr. Cook"* one of his crew complained—but events were to justify the precautions and inspections in no uncertain manner.

It was late August before the *Endeavour* finally cleared Plymouth, for the Royal Society had sent aboard so many scientists and so much equipment that special cabins had to be knocked up to accommodate them. The first part of her voyage was uneventful. Stores were replenished at Madeira and again at Rio, and by early December the *Endeavour* was nearing Cape Horn. Her ship's company landed briefly on Staten Island, off the tip of Tierra del Fuego, where they collected scurvy grass, marvelled at the hundred-and-twenty foot strands of kelp, surveyed the Straits of Le Maire, and noted that the natives were *"as Miserable a Sett of People as are this day upon Earth"* — an opinion endorsed the following century by Darwin—and so on to the Pacific which they entered towards the end of January 1769.

Their voyage to date had been remarkable only for its ease and for the good health of the *Endeavour's* crew. But ahead lay the dreaded *Mar Pacifico* and the spectre of scurvy.

Cook's crossing of the Pacific, however, was to prove as uneventful as his crossing of the Atlantic. He took one hundred and twenty seven days to make the passage from Cape Horn to Tahiti, where the transit of Venus was being observed. This was slightly longer than usual, and considerably longer than the ninety days which was then considered the maximum period for which a ship could remain at sea without her crew developing serious scurvy. Yet when the *Endeavour* dropped anchor in Matavai Bay not a single member of her ship's company was or had been seriously sick.

It is impossible to over-estimate the significance of this achievement. For it opened up a new dimension in the history of exploration by sea: time: the practicability of vessels being able to spend month after month in deep waters, far from land, without deleterious effect on the health of their crew. And this new-found ability Cook was soon to use to good effect.

They spent three months on Tahiti, first setting up an observatory and then, on June 3rd, recording the transit of Venus with meticulous accuracy. The natives proved friendly—too friendly indeed for the Puritanical Cook, whose impression of the South Sea Islands compares amusingly with Bougainville's. *"The young girls,"* (wrote the Yorkshireman) *"whenever they can collect 8 or 10 together dance a very indecent dance which they call Timorodee* singing most indecent songs and useing most indecent actions in the practice of which they are brought up from their earlyest Childhood. One amusement more I must mention, tho I confess I do not expect to be believed as it is founded upon a Custom so inhuman and contrary to the first principils of human nature: it is this, that the inhabitants have enter'd into a resolution of injoying free liberty in love without being troubled by the consequences; these mix and cohabit together with the utmost freedom and the children who are so unfortunate as to be thus begot are smother'd . . . And they are so far from concealing this, that they look upon it as a branch of freedom which they value."* Bougainville, who had visited Tahiti a couple of years earlier, saw these same events in a different light. *"Here,"* he wrote, *"is the only place on earth where the people are without vice. These happy folk, born under eternally blue skies and fed on the choicest fruits of the earth, are governed by wise old men, the heads of families, and the whole island knows only one god: the god of love. Every day they make offering to him, the whole island is his temple, the men are his priests and the women sacrifice themselves on his altar—Et quelles femmes, me demanderez-vous? Les rivales des Georgiennes en beauté et les soeurs des graces, toutes nues!"*

Yorkshire outrage and Gallic sophistication were, however, in agreement on one point. The natives were beautiful: being lithe, surprisingly fair-skinned and even in some cases fair-haired. A twentieth-century serologist could have added another and even more surprising fact about them; they were all of the comparatively rare blood group A: i.e., the same blood group as the Nordic races of Europe. And the mystery of how these "near-white Europeans" came to settle within a well-defined triangle in mid-Pacific is one of the most fascinating problems of anthropology, and a problem which Cook—unwittingly—can help us to solve.

The natives who live within a triangle bounded by New Zealand, Hawaii and Easter Island are known as Polynesians. They are all light-skinned; they are all of the same blood-group; they speak a common language, and have common gods and a common culture; they are a race apart, with almost no affinities with the neighbouring Melanesians, Chinese or Indians. It is generally agreed by anthropologists that they settled in their island homes about fifteen hundred years ago: not much earlier or their language and customs would by now have diversified, and not much later because many families can narrate a direct ancestry and residence dating back to the fifth century. It was thought at one time that they must have emigrated from Indonesia, island-hopping eastward until they were at last brought up short by four thousand miles of open sea. But this theory has serious flaws. For by the fifth century Indian and Indonesian culture was at a high level; Sanskrit was a common language, the wheel was in common use and the arts of pottery-making and weaving flourished. Yet seventeenth-century

---

* Probably a rendering of *te ai moro iti:* mock-copulation.

Polynesia was barely out of the Stone Age; in the language there was no trace of Sanskrit, the wheel was unknown, and in spite of plentiful supplies of cotton and clay the arts of weaving and pottery were undreamed of. It is unthinkable that a race as intelligent as the Polynesians should have suffered a complete cultural collapse; and the inference is therefore plain; the Polynesians could not have come from the south-west, from Indonesia. Nor could they have come from the north-west, from Melanesia; for again they have none of the characteristics of the peoples of these lands—their features are not flat nor their skins yellow; they do not chew betel nut, make palmtree wine nor grow rice—habits which, in fact, are found in all South Sea Islands *except* those within our triangle. Yet if the Polynesians did not come from the west where did they come from? Not surely from the east, across more than four thousand miles of empty sea? A generation ago such an idea would have been dismissed as impractical. But Thor Heyerdahl on his *Kon-Tiki* raft proved that such a voyage *could* have been made—and if our imagination boggles at the idea of such an exodus *en masse*, let us remember that at much the same moment in history Irish curraghs were crossing the Atlantic (an ocean which lacks the ever-favourable winds and currents of the south-east Pacific). Nor is concrete evidence of such a migration lacking. For the Norwegian ethnologist Erland Nordenskjöld has listed forty-nine cultural factors which are common to both South America and Polynesia; and the parallels he has unearthed are too close to be coincidental: the most delicate brain operations are performed in both localities; the arithmetical threads of the Incas known as *guipus* correspond to the knotted strings used by the Polynesians for astronomical measurement; both people use conch-shells, pan-pipes, feathered headgear and the poncho; they brew exactly the same type of intoxicating liquor; their fish hooks, paddles and nets are almost identical, and their calendars have the same peculiarities. Nor does the evidence of a connection end here. In his magnificent book *The World Unveiled* Paul Herrmann has brought to light even more remarkable similarities, perhaps the most fascinating of which concerns the chromosomes of the cotton-seed. Botanists tell us that there are two types of cotton in the world: the Asiatic type which has thirteen large flat chromosomes, and the American type which has twenty-six smaller ones. In the western islands of the Pacific the only type of cotton is that of the Old World; in Polynesia the only type is that of the New. How did the New World cotton-seeds get to Polynesia? They could not have been carried there by birds, for birds never touch cottonseed; they could not have been drifted there by ocean currents, for salt water at once kills the chromosomes. Only one conclusion is possible: the twenty-six-chromosome cotton was imported into Polynesia from America by people travelling in boats.

And this is where James Cook comes into the argument. His Diary supplies yet another piece of evidence of the link between Polynesia and South America. For Cook mentions several times that the natives of Polynesia cultivated the sweet potato. His Diary contains between twenty and thirty references to these plants, most of them being quite unambiguous—"*The soil (in New Zealand) both of the hills and vallies is light and sandy and very proper for producing all kinds of Roots, but we saw only sweet Potatoes . . . these they plant in little round hills, and have plantations of them containing several acres neatly laid out and kept in good order fenced in with low pailing.*" But the potato is a plant of American origin. It was not widely cultivated in Eurasia in the eighteenth century. So how can we account for the fact that Cook found it in New Zealand in 1769? It certainly cannot have drifted there accidentally, because salt water rots it in a matter of hours; and once again only one conclusion is possible: it was carried there by ship. And as final evidence that this was indeed so, the sweet potato is known by the same name (*kumara*) in both New Zealand and Peru.

So Polynesia was almost certainly settled from South America. But even if this is accepted, much of the mystery remains—the Polynesians' fair skins, their A blood-group and their legends of ancestors who were bearded, blue-eyed and taught the blessings of peace. Now we have already put forward the suggestion (in Chapter V) that by about the fifth century A.D. Irish missionaries had reached South America. Is it possible to go further and suggest that the descendants of these missionaries later sailed in balsa-wood rafts across the Pacific? The idea sounds far-fetched at first; but the more it is thought about the better it seems to fit the facts. It fits, among other things, Thor Heyerdahl's account of how the God Kon-Tiki came to Polynesia: "Tiki came sailing across the sea from a mountainous land in the east which was parched by the sun . . . He was the high-priest or sun-king of the Inca's legendary white men, who had left the enormous ruins on the shores of Lake Titicaca (in Peru). The legend runs that these mysterious white men with beards were attacked by a chief named Cari who came from the Coquinbo valley. In a battle on an island in Lake Titicaca the fair race were massacred, but Kon-Tiki himself and his closest companions escaped and later came down to the Pacific coast, whence they finally disappeared overseas to the westward." This, it should be noticed, ties up exactly with the Aztec legend of the god who "taught that men should live 'in charity and peace' and who took to rafts with his followers and sailed west across the Pacific leaving a promise that one day his descendants would return". And as a final thought it is quite remarkable how the sail plan of Thor Heyerdahl's *Kon-Tiki* raft resembles that of an Irish curragh. But all this is conjecture, and a long haul from the deck of the *Endeavour*.

Cook left Tahiti on July 14th, 1769. His ostensible object, the observation of the transit of Venus, had been achieved; but the secret and more important part of his commission, the search for *Terra Australis Incognita*, still lay ahead.

The *Endeavour* cruised quietly through the Southern Societies, new islands being sighted at frequent intervals and friendly contact being established with the natives—this contact being facilitated by the fact that a Tahitian chief named Tupia had agreed to accompany Cook on his voyage south, so there was none of the language problem which had so bedevilled previous expeditions. Week after week the *Endeavour* stood south, the weather becoming gradually colder, the wind stronger and the seas more boisterous. As he watched the great swell rolling endlessly out of the south, Cook became increasingly convinced that *Terra Australis* was a myth; but he went well below the 40th parallel laid down in his instructions before he hauled round to the west-north-west and stood for New Zealand. (The west coast of New Zealand had been sighted more than a hundred years earlier by Tasman; but such were the difficulties inherent in exploring the Pacific that no one had subsequently returned to survey the island, or indeed to determine if it were an island at all or part of the fabled Southland.) For a month the *Endeavour* held her new course, with nothing to break the monotony of the great waves, the circling albatross and the steady roar of the adverse trades. Few ships in those days cared to venture so irrevocably into the unknown; but the health of the *Endeavour's* crew was still excellent, with not a sign of scurvy, and early in October their patience was rewarded. The water paled, seaweed and land-birds were sighted for the first time in months, and on October 7th land rose over the western horizon.

Cook's Journal gives no indication of the excitement he must have felt; it merely gives us a sober record of wind and wave, anchorage and sounding—but he must at heart have been deeply satisfied. For here at last was a virgin coast on which he could exercise his skill, a new land which he could transcribe for the first time on to a map.

Cook spent six months off the coast of New Zealand, with only a couple of short breaks ashore; and in this time he surveyed the coastline with the most remarkable accuracy. When he arrived, New Zealand was nothing but a strip of disjointed west-facing coast. But when he left, all the islands' principal features were transcribed on to his charts, accurately and in detail. Never before in history had a country been so thoroughly surveyed at its first discovery.

Late in the evening of October 8th Cook wrote in his Diary: "*Seeing the opening of a Bay that appeared to run pretty far inland,* (we) *hauld our wind and stood for it. We saw in the Bay several Canoes, People on the shore and some houses in the country. The land on the Sea Coast is high, with Steep Cliffs; and back inland are very high mountains. The face of the country is of a hilly surface, and appears to be cloathed with wood and Verdure.*" This passage provides the clue to events in the next six months; for it tells us the problems which Cook had to face in New Zealand: a shore that was indented and precipitous, and a hinterland that was fertile and thickly populated—and populated moreover by one of the bravest and most warlike races on earth.

The Maoris were completely without fear, and they had the proverbial Irish love of a fight. Fortunately, they also had an inherent generosity and a highly developed sense of fairness, and once they found that the strange "white goblins" were friendly and could stand up for themselves they soon responded to Cook's advances. But the two races' initial exchanges were hair-raising; for when the *Endeavour's* pinnace first put ashore to load water, the Maoris tried to steal it, and when Cook tried to capture a Maori canoe (with the object of Tupia opening up negotiations) the rowers defended themselves to such effect that Cook had to open fire to safeguard his men's lives. After a few weeks, however, relations improved; and the Maoris were soon selling the *Endeavour* fresh vegetables, etc., and flocking aboard in large numbers. A

Maori chief has left this delightful account of one such visit—an account which, incidentally, gives us an all too rare glimpse of Cook's character:

*"*We three children sat on the deck of the ship where we were looked at by the goblins who with their hands stroked our mats and the hair of our heads, and made much gabbling noise in talking. There was one supreme man in the ship. We could tell he was the chief by his noble demeanour. He seldom spoke, but handled our mats and weapons, patted our cheeks and very gently touched our heads . . . We had not been long aboard before this chief made a speech, and took some charcoal and made marks upon the deck of the ship, pointing to the shore and then looking at our warriors. One of our old men said, 'He is asking for an outline of our land', and he stood up, took the charcoal and marked the outline of Ika-a-Maui (The North Island) . . . After a while the chief goblin came to where I and my two companions were sitting and put his hand towards us, holding out a nail. My companions were afraid and sat in silence; but I laughed, and he gave the nail to me. I took it in my hand and said 'Ka pai' (That is good). And my companions said: 'This man is fond of children, and you can tell he is a chief by his kindness. For is it not written 'E hore te tino tangata e ngaro i roto i te tokomaho' (A man of noble birth cannot be lost in a crowd)."*

Cook's original landfall in New Zealand had been in Poverty Bay, about half way up the east coast of the North Island. For the next week he followed the coastline south, passing the curious Mahia peninsula and the magnificent sweep of Hawke's Bay. Then, acting apparently on impulse, he hauled round and headed back to the north. This decision typifies Cook's flair for exploration; for had he been perfectly aware of the outline of New Zealand he could not have hit on a better and more economic way of surveying the islands. And so with a favourable breeze from the south-west the *Endeavour* first retraced her steps and then, keeping close inshore, worked her way up the unknown coast of the North Island. The country was "*covered with woods and hath all the appearance of a very pleasant and fertile land*"; it was also thickly populated and the *Endeavour* was often followed by a veritable armada of canoes, one especially interesting visitor being a magnificent catamaran, carrying two hundred men, which kept abreast of Cook's vessel hour after hour with the greatest ease. On November 4th they put into a bay on the Coromandel Peninsula to observe the transit of Mercury—which enabled Cook to determine their longitude with the greatest accuracy. And so north by east up a deeply indented shore, fringed by islands and alive with natives "who trafficked with us in the most friendly manner imaginable".

Towards the end of the year, as he neared the northerly tip of New Zealand, Cook was confronted by a series of summer storms. For three weeks, from December 13th to January 5th, the *Endeavour* battled through mountainous seas and sixty-mile-an-hour winds as she fought her way round the promontory of North Cape. It took her twenty-three days to cover fifty miles. And by a curious coincidence the winds which split the *Endeavour's* sails and carried away her rigging were at the same time doing even more damage to another vessel approaching North Cape from the opposite direction—the *Jean Baptist* commanded by Chevalier de Surville. But what a contrast the two ships made! The *Endeavour* with her holds full of fresh and well-balanced

* This account is taken from *Life of Captain Cook* by Hugh Carrington.

provisions and her crew one hundred per cent fit: the *Jean Baptist* desperately short of supplies, with her crew dying of scurvy and with hardly enough fit men to work her sails; yet of the two it was the *Endeavour* that had been at sea nearly a year the longer. At about 3 p.m. on December 16th the two ships passed within thirty miles of each other; then they drew gradually apart, the one destined for oblivion and the other for immortality.

The New Year brought better weather; and with a following wind Cook ran free down the west coast of the North Island, covering four hundred miles in a fortnight. The *Endeavour* was on a lee shore now. Cook recognized this, noting in his Diary: "*Nothing is to be seen but long sandhills; and the great sea which the prevailing westerly winds impel upon the shore must render this a very dangerous coast.*" Nevertheless, he managed to chart the shoreline with fair accuracy. On January 15th the *Endeavour* entered what appeared to be a large bay, and finding "*a good snug cove*" Cook decided to put ashore, partly to stock up with fresh provisions and partly to make good the damage caused by the storms.

Queen Charlotte Sound is an anchorage of rare beauty: gently sloping beaches, mirror-like water alive with fish (it is no angler's yarn that two are frequently pulled in on the same hook), and a delightfully wooded hinterland. In these pleasant surroundings the *Endeavour* was dragged ashore—you can still to-day see the tree stump that was used for warping her up the beach—and for three weeks there was all the activity of a thorough spring-clean. The ship was careened, scraped free of barnacles, retarred below the waterline and repainted above; the blacksmith assembled his forge and set to work rewelding the tiller and other ironwork; the armourers laid out their gunpowder to dry in the sun, and the coopers cleaned and tightened their water-casks; wood was cut from a hinterland that was "*one intire forest*"; sails were re-patched and rigging respliced; while large quantities of fish and vegetables were bought from the Maoris. While his crew were thus engaged, Cook made an important discovery. Reconnoitring in the ship's pinnace he found that what he had taken at first to be a large bay was in fact a strait, a twenty-mile-wide strip of water dividing the North Island of New Zealand from the South. And as soon as the *Endeavour* was ready he made the surveying of this strait—which bears his name—a first priority.

He found the passage none too easy, a combination of wind and tide-rip all but driving the *Endeavour* aground; but by February 8th he was again in open water, having passed between the two islands from the Tasman Sea to the South Pacific. There was still a faint possibility that the North Island might be a peninsula jutting west from *Terra Australis*, and to disprove this Cook followed the coastline north until he came to landmarks that he could recognize from his exploration of the previous October. Then, having satisfied himself that he had circumnavigated the North Island, he turned his attention to the South.

It took the *Endeavour* less than six weeks to sail round the South Island. Cook's survey was less accurate here than it had been in the north; for he kept farther offshore, deeming it prudent to give himself plenty of sea-room in case he was suddenly brought up short by the land mass of the Great Southern

Continent; and this, I think, accounts for his mistaking Banks Peninsula for an island and Stewart Island for a peninsula.

The Maoris had apparently told Cook that he would come to the southern extremity of New Zealand in "about three or four days"; but at the end of a couple of weeks the *Endeavour* was still edging south down a shore that became increasingly barren and sparsely populated. Once a rumour of land to port took her nearly a hundred miles out to sea before Cook was able to convince the lookout that his "mountains" were in fact no more than cloud; but by early March they were at last running parallel to Stewart Island. The gales off this southern extremity of New Zealand were almost as bad as they had been in the north. The *Endeavour's* top gallant was carried away, her foresail was "*split all in pieces*", and she was nearly wrecked on The Traps, a reef that knifes viciously out of deep water some fifteen miles offshore. But by March 10th they had rounded the last obstacle and could see the coastline in front of them stretching away to the north. "*Blew fresh all day,*" the scientist Banks wrote in his diary, "(and) *we were carried round the point to the total destruction of our aerial fabric called continent.*" Cook was more cautious, merely observing that: "I began now to think that this was the southernmost land, and that we should be able to get round it; for we have had a large swell from the S.W. ever since the last gale from that quarter, which makes me think there is no land in that direction." As the days passed these impressions were confirmed. For it became increasingly clear, as the *Endeavour* continued her run to the north, that New Zealand was an island and the Great Southern Continent— at least in this part of the world—a myth.

It took them less than a fortnight to run the four hundred miles back to Queen Charlotte Sound, and by March 25th the whole of New Zealand had been circumnavigated. Banks and his fellow-scientists had badly wanted to land on the west coast of the South Island, where they had observed that "*the rocks appeared to be full of the most interesting minerals*"; but Cook, viewing the coast with the eye of a seaman, recognized the danger of being pinned by the prevailing winds against a lee shore as precipitous as almost any in the world, and he rightly kept well out to sea. They did, however, put ashore as soon as they came to the gentler and more sheltered littoral at the approaches to Queen Charlotte Sound, where they topped up with water and fresh vegetables. Cook then called a meeting of officers to discuss their next move.

They had been away from home now for close on twenty-one months; they had observed the transit of Venus; they had exploded at least in part the myth of the Great Southern Continent, and they had put New Zealand firmly and accurately on the map. It might be thought they had already done all that could reasonably be expected of them; but Cook's yearning "to go as far as it was possible for men to go" was not yet sated, and he now persuaded his crew to return home *via* a hitherto unexplored route. His Diary tells us how this decision was arrived at. "*Upon my return in the evening I found the water etc. all on board and the ship ready for sea, and being now resolved to quit this country and to bend my thoughts towards returning home by such a rout as might conduce most to the advantage of the service I am upon, I consulted with the officers upon the most eligible way of putting this in execution. To return by way of Cape Horn was what I*

most wish'd because by this rout we should have been able to prove the existence or non
existence of a Southern Continent which yet remains doubtfull; but in order to ascertain
this we must have kept in a high latitude in the very depth of winter, and the condition of
the ship was not thought sufficient for such an undertaking. The thought of proceeding
directly to the Cape of Good Hope was laid aside, as no discovery of any moment could
be hoped for in that rout. It was therefore resolved to return by way of the East Indies by
the following rout: upon leaving this coast to steer to the westward untill we fall in with
the East coast of New Holland and then to follow the direction of that coast to the
northward or what other direction it may take untill we arrive at its northern extremity,
and if this should be found impractical then to endeavour to fall in with the lands or
Islands discover'd by Quiros. With this in view, at day light we got under sail and put
to sea having the advantage of a fresh gale from the S.E."

Early on Sunday April 1st the promontory of Cape Farewell disappeared
in a belt of slanting rain. And New Zealand lay astern, Australia ahead.

Cook's choice of a route home strikes us to-day as being eminently reasonable; yet judged by eighteenth-century standards it was an amazing act of
faith. For in those days the making of even a single voyage through the
unknown regions of the *Mar Pacifico* was considered daring, and the making
of two in succession must have seemed little short of foolhardy. But Cook
knew what he was doing. The health and morale of his ship's company was
so good that the prospect of making yet another leap into the unknown had
few terrors for him. For the first time in history man could claim to feel almost
at home in the vast reaches of ocean.

So the *Endeavour* stood boldly west.

The Tasman Sea was kind that autumn—"*gentle breezes*", Cook's Diary
records, "*with very pleasant weather*"—and the days and the miles slipped
gently by. Even now, after twenty-one months at sea, the crew were showing
no sign of scurvy. Their good health, however, was not preserved without a
very considerable effort on Cook's part; and inspections, fumigations and
disinfectings were carried out as frequently and sedulously during their
eighty-eighth week in the Tasman Sea as they had been during their first
week in the Atlantic.

There had been some difficulty at first in convincing the men that a diet of
lean meat and sauerkraut was a beneficial exchange for their traditional
quota of fat pork, butter and biscuit—a marine had been given twelve lashes
for refusing his meat, and the crew had complained that the "noxious vegetables" gave them flatulence! But Cook had then proved himself no mean
psychologist; he increased his allocation of the hated sauerkraut to the officers,
with the result that the men promptly did a complete *volte-face* and began to
clamour for it voraciously: "*for such*," Cook wrote, "*are the temper and dis-*
position of seamen in general that whatever you give them out of the common way—
altho' it be every so much for their good—it will not go down, and you will hear nothing
but murmurings against the man that first invented it; but the moment they see their
superiors set a value upon it it becomes the finest stuff in the world and the inventor an
honest fellow."

With so much being written on the subject of food it is surprising that no
record exists of an eighteenth-century vessel's dietary. But neither among the

Endeavour's logs and victualling instructions, nor among the documents relating to any other ship can we find an answer to the simple question: "What did a crew eat?" The following table, however—which has been pieced together from a wide variety of contemporary references—will act as a rough guide.

	Weekly rations aboard an average 18th century man-of-war	Weekly rations aboard the Endeavour
Bread and Biscuit	6 lb	5 lb
Butter	¼ lb	—
Cheese	½ lb	—
Beef	4 lb (including fat)	3 lb (no fat)
Pork	2½ lb („ „)	2 lb („ „)
Oatmeal	1 pint	1 pint
Sauerkraut and fresh vegetables	Less than ½ lb	4 lb
Peas	2 pints	2 pints
Portable soup	—	3 oz
Wort and orange-and-lemon conserve	—	As needed

It has been suggested by several writers that the last of these items was the clue to Cook's clean bill of health: that the combination of wort and fruit juice which was given to the crew at the first symptom of scurvy acted as a preventative. But this is too glib a judgement. For the wort and orange-and-lemon conserve was invariably boiled before it was drunk (which destroyed ninety-nine per cent of its value as an antiscorbutic), also the lemons in fact were limes! (for owing to an error in the victualling yards' nomenclature West Indian limes, which contain comparatively little Vitamin C, had been shipped in place of the health-bringing lemons). The *Endeavour's* dietary, in other words, was by no means as beneficial in practice as in theory; and without Cook's other measures his crew would have been in no shape, twenty-one months after leaving England, to have set about exploring the coast of Australia.

They sighted this coast at dawn on Thursday, April 21st: the first white men in history to set eyes on the land dreamed of and so nearly realized by Quiros a hundred and fifty years before.

Their landfall was Point Hicks Hill, about midway between Sydney and Melbourne; and their first impression was "*of an agreeable and pleasant aspect . . . a land of sloping hills, covered in parts with trees and bushes but interspersed with large tracts of sand*". The *Endeavour*, standing close inshore, followed the coast-line north. Through his telescope Cook could make out smoke from the natives' fires, and on one occasion the Aboriginals themselves. He wanted to land; but for several days this proved impossible because of "*a large hollow sea from ye S.E. rowling in upon the land which beat everywhere very high*". But on April 30th he lowered his boats in the shelter of Botany Bay. His landing was opposed by two naked Aboriginals, who waved their spears threateningly at the thirty to forty well-armed Europeans. Tupia failed to make himself understood, every overture of friendship was spurned, and the firing of muskets into the air had no apparent effect; even when one of the natives was slightly wounded first in the leg and then in the arm, he refused to give ground, but ran back to his hut to fetch a wooden shield. At last, however, a volley of gunfire frightened the spirited defenders into the bush; and Cook's nephew-in-law stepped ashore: the first European to land on the east coast of Australia.

Cook thought the country "pleasent", and noted with prophetic insight that the soil appeared suitable for grain and sheep. Banks was even more enthusiastic; he described Australia as *"completely fascinating, a veritable treasure trove of strange plants and insects"*; in Botany Bay alone he collected over two hundred specimens, and he deserves to go down in history as the first man to appreciate the unique interest of Australia's flora and fauna. After spending a week in Botany Bay, the *Endeavour* continued to run to the north. The weather was fine, the sea calm and the unknown coast that unfolded before them peacefully uniform: mile after hundred mile of sandy beaches and gently rolling hills. But towards the end of May they came to waters that were anything but peaceful, that were in fact the most dangerous in the world: the rocks and ever-shifting shallows and shoals of the Great Barrier Reef.

The north-east coast of Australia is flanked for more than twelve hundred miles by the largest continuous growth of coral in the world: a reef rising sheer from the seabed, its ocean face an unbelievable riot of colour and life (starfish, clams and mother-of-pearl; *bêche-de-mer*, sea-urchins and sponges), its landward face tapering away into a plethora of islands, rocks and sub-sidiary growths of coral. Even now that it has been charted, the passage between reef and shore is recognized as one of the most treacherous in the world; and two hundred years ago as Cook edged cautiously into its unknown hazards his seamanship must have been tested as never before. With a pinnace sounding ahead and a leadsman constantly in chains, the *Endeavour* felt her way north through a maze of ever-shifting shallows and sandbars, reefs and shoals. For several weeks, by a combination of luck and judgement, she managed to keep out of trouble. But on the night of Monday, June 11th, her luck ran out.

It was moonlit, calm and coming up to high tide as soon after 9 p.m. their lookout reported broken water ahead. Cook shortened sail and hauled round into what little wind there was, intending, in the words of his Journal, *"to stretch off all night to avoid the danger"*. His account of what happened next is aggravatingly matter-of-fact; but in between the unemotional lines of his Journal we can catch a glimpse of a desperately close shave: a vessel in danger of becoming a complete loss on a desert shore more than two thousand miles from the nearest known land.

"A breeze of wind and a clear moonlight night," writes Cook. *"In standing off we deepen'd our water from 14 to 21 fathom, when all at once we fell into 12, 10 and 8 fathom. At this time I had everybody at their stations to put about and come to anchor, but in this I was not so fortunate, for meeting again with deep water I thought there could be no danger in standing on. Before 10 o'clock we had 20 and 21 fathoms and continued in that depth untill a few minutes before 11 o'clock when we had 17 fathom,*

and before the man at the lead could heave another cast the ship struck and stuck fast. We took in our sails, hoisted out the boats and sounded round the ship, and found that we had got upon the S.E. edge of a reef of coral rocks. We struck yards and topmasts and carried out the stream anchor upon the starboard bow and the casting anchor upon the starboard quarter and hove it upon a very great stream, which was all to no purpose, the ship being quite fast. Upon this we went to work to lighten her, which seemed to be the only means we had left to get her off, since we went ashore about the top of high water. We throw'd overboard our guns, iron and stone ballast corks, hoops, oyle jars, decay'd stores etc. . . . All this time the ship made little or no water. At 11 o'clock a.m., being as we thought high water,* we tried to heave her off without success, she not being afloat by a foot or more, notwithstanding by this time we had thrown overboard 40 or 50 Tun weight. As this was not found sufficient we continued to lighten her by every method we could think of. But when the tide fell the ship began to make water as much as two pumps could free. At noon she lay with 3 or 4 Strakes heel to Starboard . . . Fortunately we had little wind, fine weather and a smooth Sea, which gave us an opportunity to carry out the two Bower Anchors, the one on the Starboard quarter and the other right astern. Got blocks and tackles upon the cables, brought the falls in abaft and hove taught. By this time it was 5 o'clock in the p.m., the tide began to rise and the leak increased upon us which obliged us to set the 3rd Pump to work. At 9 o'clock the Ship righted. But the leak at once gained upon the Pump considerably. This was an alarming and I may say terrible circumstance, and threatened immediate destruction to us as soon as the Ship was afloat. However I resolved to risk all and heave her off, and accordingly turned as many hands to the Capstan and windlass as could be spared from the pumps and about 20 past 10 o'clock the Ship floated and we hove her off into deep water, having at this time 3 feet 9 inches water in the hold."

There was real danger, now she was off the reef, that the *Endeavour* would fill up and sink under their feet; but this was prevented by a superhuman stint at the pumps, and by Midshipman Munkhouse's skill in fothering the leaks by means of a sail soaked in wool, sheep's dung and oakum.

The pumping was a combined effort "*at which every man on board assisted, the Captain, Mr. Banks and all the officers not excepted, relieving one another every quarter of an hour*". And here is Cook's description of how they stopped the inrush of water: "*. . . we at once got the sail ready for fothering. The manner this is done is thus, we Mix oakam and wool together and chop it up small and then stick it loosely by hand-fulls all over the sail and throw over it sheeps dung or other filth* (the *Endeavour* had a number of sheep aboard). *The sail thus prepared is hauld under the Ship's bottom by ropes and if the place of the leak is uncertain it must be hauld from one part of her bottom to another untill the place is found where it takes effect; while the sail is under the Ship the oakum etc. is washed off and part of it carried along with the water into the leaks and in part stops up the hole. Mr. Munkhouse, one of my midshipmen, was once in a Merchant ship which sprung a leak and made 48 inches water per hour, but by this means was brought home from Virginia to London; to him I gave the direction of this* (operation) *and he exicuted it very much to my satisfaction.*"

So the water was kept at bay. The *Endeavour* limped for the shore, and after an anxious search was beached not far from the present site of Cooktown.

---

* The daylight tide off Australia does not rise as high as the night tide, a fact which Cook noted for the first time during this emergency.

Not till they had warped her ashore, stayed her up and exposed the bottom of her keel, did they find what had saved them. A great splinter of coral, sheared off the reef, had jammed tight in the hole in her hull. But for this, she would have gone down like the proverbial stone.

Cook had been lucky. But he had also been skilful in extricating himself from danger; while his ship's company had behaved magnificently—"*No crew,*" Cook wrote, "*ever behaved better; every man seem'd to have a sence of the danger we were in, and exerted himself to the utmost.*" And this opinion was endorsed by Banks: "*No grumbling or growling was to be heard throughout the ship, not even an oath—though the ship was in general as well furnished with them as most in His Majesty's service! And I must say for the credit of our people that I believe every man exerted his utmost for the preservation of the ship.*" Cook's unusual care for his men, which had already been justified by their clean bill of health, had now been vindicated again by the way they had faced emergency.

It took them seven weeks to repair the *Endeavour*. For their false keel and sheathing had been extensively damaged and four mainplanks had been sheared clean through, "*as if cut away by an instrument*". The ship was also scrubbed and repainted, both inside and out; while fresh vegetables and turtle and kangaroo meat were taken aboard. The meat was especially welcome; for apart from the occasional bird their diet for the last twelve months had been exclusively vegetable and fish (there are no edible animals indigenous to New Zealand).

By August 4th repairs were complete, and the *Endeavour* was again heading north. But for several days she made little progress. For in the seaway between mainland and reef conditions were appalling, with rocks and islets multitudinous as the galaxies of the Milky Way, and the water shoaling steeply and without warning. Cook himself went to the masthead and saw "*that* (they) *were surrounded on every side with dangers, in so much that* (he) *was quite at a loss which way to steer*". For a couple of days they inched painfully north; but on August 11th they were forced to drop anchor, being completely embayed with islands and reefs.

Cook then took a decision which must have seemed reasonable enough at the time, but which brought his expedition nevertheless to within a hairsbreadth of disaster. Seeing a gap in the reef, he decided to escape the shallows and make for the open sea.

So with her pinnace ahead and her leadsman reporting deeper water at every cast, the *Endeavour* crept out through one of the rare breaches in the reef. "*The moment*", wrote Cook, "*we were without the breakers, we had no ground at 100 fathoms of line, and found a large sea rowling in from the S.E. By this I was well assured we were got without all the Shoals, which gave us no small joy, after having been intangled* (therein) *ever since the 26th May, in which time we have sailed above 360 leagues by the lead without ever having a leadsman out of the chains—a circumstance that perhaps never happened to any ship before.*" But for all his joy Cook was now in a dilemma. He knew instinctively that the seaward edge of the Barrier Reef was a place of death; yet he was obliged to keep within sight of land—i.e., close to the reef—in case he missed the passage west between Australia and New Guinea. For although this passage had been pioneered by

THE GREAT BARRIER REEF

Torres over a hundred and fifty years earlier, its existence was still in dispute, many maps not only tacking Quiros's Espiritu Santo on to the coast of New Holland but also running the New Holland coastline north to join New Guinea. Cook had therefore to keep the land in sight for fear of missing a strait which, if indeed it existed at all, might well be as narrow and difficult of access as Magellan's.

Thursday, August 16th, was the day on which everyone aboard the *Endeavour* missed death by a matter of yards. Cook describes the incident in his usual laconic style; but not much imagination is needed to picture the fate that his ship's company avoided by the width of no more than a single wave.

"*Soon we saw breakers between us and the land extending to the Southward farther than we could see, and (a little later) we saw the Reef also extend away to the North-ward; upon this we hauld close upon a wind which was now at E.S.E. We had hardly trimed our sails before the wind came to E. by N., which was right upon the Reef and made our clearing of it doubtfull.* (There follows a somewhat technical account of their efforts to beat or tack out of trouble.) *But before long it fell quite Calm. We sounded both now and several times in the night, but had no ground with 140 fathoms of line. A little after 4 o'clock the roaring of the surf was plainly heard, and at daybreak the vast foaming breakers were too plainly to be seen not a mile from us, towards which we found the Ship was carried by the waves surprisingly fast. We had at this time not an air of wind, and the depth of water was unfathomable, so that there was not a possibility of Anchoring; in this distressed situation we had nothing but Providence and the small Assistance of our boats to trust to. The Yawl and the Longboat were hoisted out and sent ahead to tow, which together with the help of sweeps abaft got the ship's head round to the northward which seem'd to be the only way to keep her off the reef or at best to delay time. Before this was effected it was six o'clock and we were not above eighty yards from the breakers, the same sea that washed the sides of the ship rising in a breaker pro-digiously high the very next time it did rise, so that between us and distruction was only a dismal valley the breadth of one wave; and even now no ground could be felt with 120 fathoms. We had hardly any hopes of saving the Ship and full as little our lives, yet in this truly terrible situation not one man ceased to do his utmost and that with as much calmness as if no danger had been near. All the dangers we had escaped so far were little in comparison of being thrown upon this Reef, where the Ship must be dashed to pieces in a Moment. A Reef such as is here spoke of is scarcely known in Europe; it is a wall of Coral Rock rising almost perpendicular out of the unfathomable Ocean, and the waves meeting with so sudden a resistance make a most terrible surf breaking great mountains high, especially as in our case where the trade wind blows directly upon it. At this critical juncture when all our endeavours seem'd too little, a small air of wind sprung up, but so small that at any other time we should not have observed it, and with this and the assistance of our boats we could observe the Ship to move off the Reef in a slanting direction, but in less than 10 Minutes we had as flat a Calm as ever. Then a small opening was seen in the Reef which I sent one of the Mates to examine . . .*" (This was their salvation. With the boats towing and helped by a favourable current, the *Endeavour* was swept through the channel.) . . . "*depth 30 to 7 fathom,*" writes Cook, "*with very erregular soundings and foul ground until we were quite within the Reef where we anchored in 19 fathom, a corally and shelly bottom,*

CARTE PHYSIQUE
DE LA GRANDE MER
ci-devant nommée MER DU SUD ou PACIFIQUE;
Où se voient les Grandes Chaînes de Montagnes
qui traversent les parties les plus Orientales de l'ASIE et les Occid.les
de l'AMÉRIQUE; et leurs continuations dans le fond de la MER,
Indiquées par les Isles, Bancs &c.
Avec la représentation de ce que l'on conjecture
Sur la Mer Glaciale Antarctique.
Dressée et Présentée à l'Acad. des Sc le 5 Sept.bre 1744
Par Philippe Buache

Drawing from
a map prepared
in 1744

Publiée sous le Privilège de l'Académie du 4 Sept.bre 1754

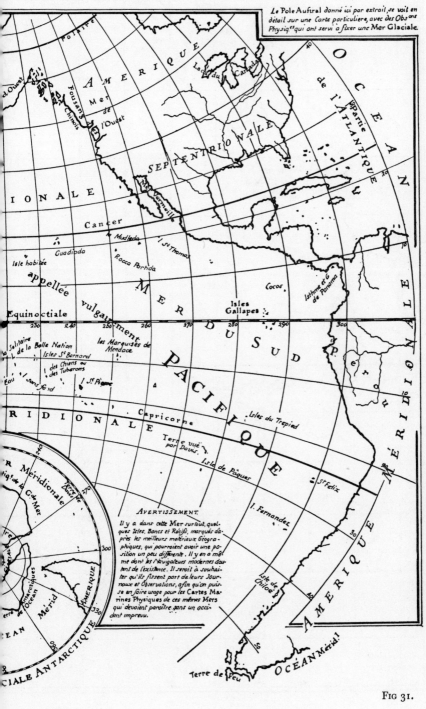

AMÉRIQUE

Lac du Canada

O C É A N

de l'Atlantique

Mer de l'Ouest

Foulang

Chinois

SEPTENTRIONALE

Partie de l'ATLANTIQUE

20

IONALE

Mer Vermeille

Cancer

Muilleda

Guadiopa

Rocca Partida

1. St. Thomas

Isle habitée

appellée vulgairement Equinoctiale

M E R   D U   S U D

Cocos

Isthme et G. de Panama

Isles Gallapes

10

Perou

230   240   250   260   270   280   290   300

Solitaire de la Belle Nation

les Marquises de Mendoce

Isles St. Bernard

des Chiens ou des Tuberons

Eau Sans Fond

1. St. Pierre

P A C I F I Q U E

RIDIONALE

Capricorne

Isles du Trepied

Terre vuë par Davis.

Isle de Pâques

MÉRIDIONALE

r Meridionale

qu. de la Gde. Mer

300

Isle Antarctique

AMÉRIQUE

330

St. Felix

20

AMÉRIQUE

I. Fernandez

AVERTISSEMENT.

Il y a dans cette Mer surtout, quelques Isles, Bancs et Recifs, marqués d'après les meilleurs materiaux Géographiques, qui pourroient avoir une position un peu différente. Il y en a même dont les Navigateurs modernes doutent de l'existence. Il seroit à souhaiter qu'ils fissent part de leurs Journaux et Observations, afin qu'on puisse en faire usage pour les Cartes Marines Physiques de ces mêmes Mers qui devoient paroitre sans un accident imprevu.

Terre d'ocarctiques

OCEAN Merid.

Isle de Chiloe

30

ALE ANTARCTIQUE

Terre de Feu

OCÉAN Mérid.l

50

Fig 31.

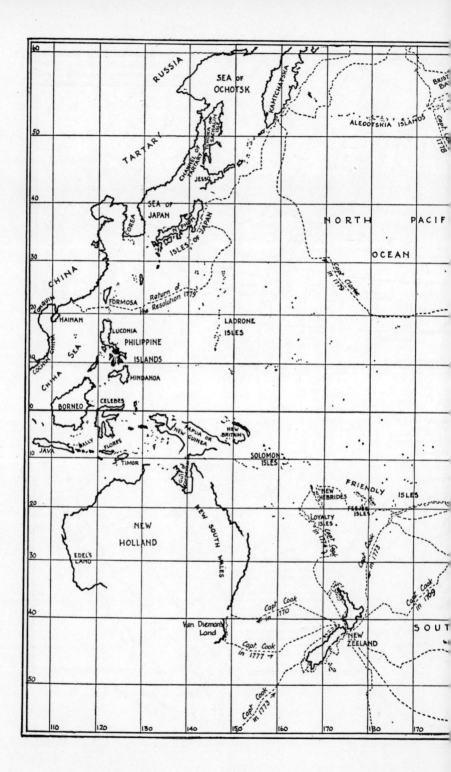

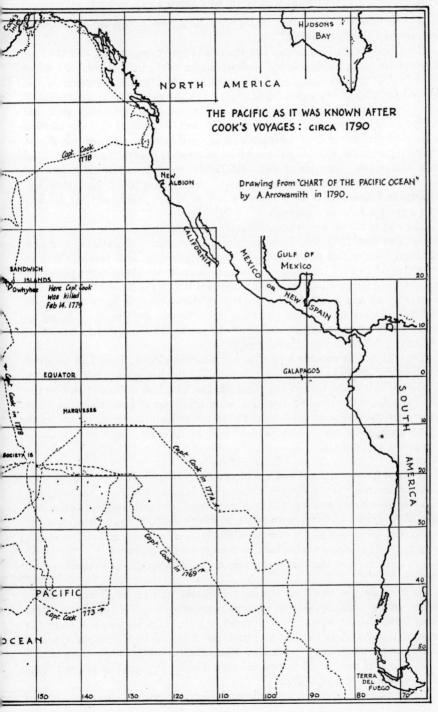

THE PACIFIC AS IT WAS KNOWN AFTER
COOK'S VOYAGES : CIRCA 1790

Drawing from "CHART OF THE PACIFIC OCEAN"
by A. Arrowsmith in 1790.

HUDSONS
BAY

NORTH AMERICA

Capt. Cook.
1778

NEW
ALBION

CALIFORNIA

MEXICO

GULF OF
MEXICO

MEXICO OR NEW SPAIN

SANDWICH
ISLANDS
Owhyhee   Here Capt. Cook
was killed
Feb 14. 1779

EQUATOR

GALAPAGOS

MARQUESES

Capt. Cook in 1774

SOCIETY IS.

SOUTH AMERICA

Capt. Cook in 1769

PACIFIC

Capt. Cook 773

OCEAN

TERRA
DEL
FUEGO

150   140   130   120   110   100   90   80   70

20

10

0

10

20

30

40

50

FIG 32.

happy once more to incounter those shoals which but a few days ago our utmost wishes were crowned by getting clear of.''

Cook had learned his lesson. For the rest of his voyage round Australia he hugged the coast, preferring the obvious danger of the inshore reefs to the less obvious but greater dangers of the open sea. And at last he came to the longed-for strait. On August 23rd, 1770, rounding the northernmost point of the Cape York Peninsula, he saw to the westward nothing but open sea. Adept in his interpretation of wind and wave, he realized that the sudden advent of the gentle south-west trades and swell could mean only one thing: that they were approaching the confines of another ocean: the Indian. *"And this,"* he wrote, *"gave me no small satisfaction, not only because the danger and fatigues of the voyage were drawing to an end, but by being able to prove that New Holland and New Guinea are 2 separate Lands or Islands, which until this day hath been a doubtful point with geographers."*

The rest of his voyage was anticlimax. And tragedy.

On October 10th the *Endeavour* dropped anchor off Batavia, her first civilized port of call since leaving Rio twenty-two months before. Cook at once despatched all journals, diaries and charts to the Admiralty; prefacing his covering letter with the modest comment that *"The discoveries made in this Voyage are not very great"* and ending it with the words: *"in justice to the officers and crew, I must say they have gone through the fatigues and dangers of the voyage with cheerfulness and allertness, and I have the satisfaction to say that I have not lost one man by sickness during the whole voyage."*

Yet within four months a third of his crew were dead. They had survived the perils of scurvy in the Pacific only to fall victim to the fever and dysentery of the malarial East Indies. For these ills Cook had no panacea; and by the time the *Endeavour* reached England, after a voyage of almost exactly three years, her complement had been cut from ninety-four to fifty-six: a sad finale to an expedition which had been blessed in its early stages with unusual happiness and success.

*   *   *

It is not hard to assess Cook's achievements. In a single voyage he revolutionized the map of the Pacific, proving the insularity of New Zealand, disproving the existence of a Great Southern Continent and completing the outline of Australia. He also revolutionized man's attitude towards deep-water voyaging; for although the spectre of scurvy was by no means conquered, it would be true to say that after the voyage of the *Endeavour* it never again shone with such malignancy—an enemy once defeated loses much of his terror.

Cook made two more voyages to the Pacific, sailing in all over 200,000 miles—or eight times round the circumference of the world. Countless volumes have been written about these voyages, which ranged from Macao in the west to Vancouver in the east and from north of Alaska to south of Graham Land; but a single map can tell us more than a plethora of words, and a comparison of the Pacific before and after Cook's voyages (see pages 194–7) is his most eloquent panegyric.

As for Cook's character, he has been depicted by some writers as hard and humourless, a man who inspired admiration rather than love. But such a view does him less than justice; for his essential characteristics were reserve and humanity.

He was reserved, I think, by nature; and this reserve was heightened by the circumstances of his life—it was difficult for a man in the eighteenth century to cut through the class hierarchy and keep the friends he made *en route*; also the captain of a ship is congenitally lonely, for the mystique of command is a burden that cannot be shared. As for his humanity, it shines through his every action, from the care he took of his crew to the consideration he habitually showed to the people whose lands he discovered.

He died at the age of fifty, his life's work completed, stabbed to death on the fine white sands of Hawaii in a death reminiscent of Magellan's. And those who describe him as "stern and unloving" might remember that his last words were to order his men not to fire at the natives who were about to kill him.

THREE

The Farthest Ends of the Earth

Introduction to Part Three

BY the end of the eighteenth century the pattern of continents and oceans had been delineated with some accuracy over four-fifths of the surface of the world; only the poles remained an enigma.

The exploration of these farthest ends of the earth posed special problems.

The Antarctic is a continent, ringed in places by an ice-free ocean which is ringed in turn by a belt of ice—much as a coral island is enclosed first by its lagoon and then its reef. The problem in the south, therefore, was how to penetrate the belt of consolidated pack-ice, which, by and large, remained constant around the sixty-fifth parallel. Not till a ship had been designed that was strong enough to butt her way through this ice could the veil be lifted from the last of the continents.

The Arctic, in contrast, is an ocean ringed by land, but with a number of straits linking it to the navigable waters of the south. The problem here was more complex. In some areas the ice reached south to the sixtieth parallel, in others it receded to the eighty-fifth (a difference of over a thousand miles); its extent and behaviour varied considerably from one year to the next; while the channels which seemed to lead most promisingly northwards were in fact blocked by outward flowing ice. The problem here, therefore, was to find a way into the Arctic. For several centuries explorers directed their efforts mainly up the Davis Strait, with occasional forays into the Barents Sea; but these approaches were irrevocably blocked. Not until the American De Long stood north through the Bering Strait and became involuntarily enmeshed in the ice-drift of the great polar current was the last of the oceans approached, let alone explored.

And this final phase of exploration has a selflessness that was not to be found in many of the earlier voyages of discovery. As long ago as the eleventh century the Norse author of *The King's Mirror* listed the three motives which have led men to explore the unknown: love of fame, love of wealth and love of knowledge. Of these motives it was the last, and noblest, which inspired the explorers of the Arctic and Antarctic. The men who drove their ships again and again into the unyielding fields of ice, who suffered cold, boredom, hunger, physical exhaustion and all too frequently death in the polar wastes, had little hope of material reward; they were motivated by the desire for knowledge, drawn on by the lure of the unknown. And it is, I think, only fitting that the final chapter in our long saga of exploration should have been written by men such as Nansen and De Long; men whose triumphs were those of character as much as achievement, and whose exploits bear witness for all time to the indomitable spirit of man.

XIII

ON THE EDGE OF A DREAM

(Parry's discovery in 1819 of a strait reaching deep into the heart of the Arctic gives new life to the quest for a North-West Passage)

THE search for a North-West Passage is one of the great sagas in the history of exploration. It was a long search, spanning five centuries; it was a search foredoomed to failure, for the ice of the Canadian Arctic was too formidable a barrier ever to be breached by ships under sail; yet it was a search which demonstrates more clearly perhaps than any other phase of exploration the unconquerable spirit of man.

Again and again explorers were to drive their vessels north by west into the great fields of ice and struggle forward, foot by painful foot, only in the end to be brought up short by an impenetrable barrier. They were battered by storms, these explorers, enveloped in fog, blinded by blizzards, and frozen all too frequently to death by the wind and the cold. But those who survived never gave up. They came back again and again. And the great pioneers of the Canadian north-west—Parry and Franklin, Ross and Back—spent virtually the whole of their lives in the frozen wastes of the Arctic, finding here a challenge which drew out of them all those qualities—courage, patience, endurance and technical expertise—which will one day take mankind to the stars.

The search for a passage got under way as soon as it was appreciated that the great land-mass of America lay between Europe and the treasures of the orient. It was an entirely logical search, for anyone with a globe and a piece of string can satisfy himself that the shortest distance from Europe to China is *via* the Pole; it was also a search that was of peculiar interest to Great Britain; for the Spaniards and Portuguese had a monopoly of trade-routes in the south, and if a route in the north *could* be pioneered England was ideally sited to benefit from it.

It was therefore the Elizabethan seamen—Davis, Frobisher, Hudson and Baffin—who made the first attempts to reach the Pacific *via* the sea-lanes of the Canadian Arctic. And the greatest of these was Davis. His work was sound rather than spectacular; he came back with no sensational stories of gold, like Frobisher; and he was far too able a seaman to die a sensational death, like Hudson. But his work was cartographically sound. He delineated the west coast of Greenland and the east coast of Canada with surprising accuracy as far as the seventieth parallel, lighting (as Sir Clements Markham succinctly puts it) Hudson into his strait and Baffin into his bay. But after his death his discoveries were largely forgotten. For the British government, concluding quite rightly that a North-West Passage to the Pacific could never be a com-

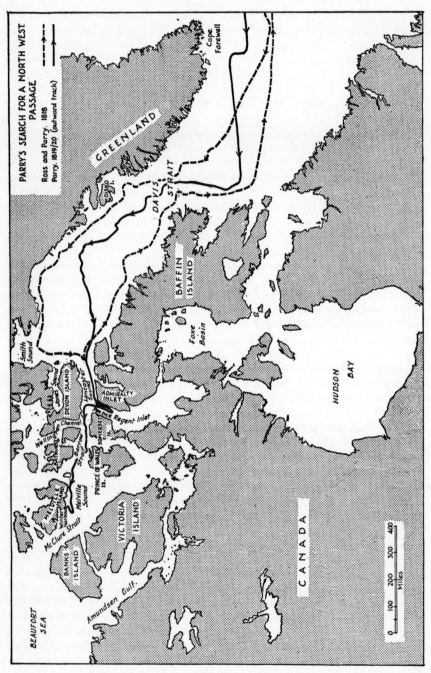

Fig 33.

mercial proposition, declined to finance further expeditions; and not until Cook discovered the Pacific end of the passage by his penetration in 1778 of the Bering Strait did official interest revive.

By this time exploration was coming to be viewed with a more scientific outlook, and the fact that a passage was unlikely to be of commercial use no longer debarred it from being investigated. For some years after Cook's voyage the Napoleonic wars precluded the search being renewed; then in 1815 a number of circumstances combined to usher in the golden age of British polar exploration.

The first of these circumstances was the glut of ships and men who, at the end of the Napoleonic wars, found themselves out of work. This meant that in 1815, for the first time in years, the Royal Navy was able and willing to concentrate its resources on exploration. And the years of the *pax Britannica* which followed the Congress of Vienna formed the ideal background for a century of more or less continuous polar voyaging.

The second circumstance was the appointment of John Barrow as Secretary to the Admiralty. Barrow, a man of great ability and drive, dedicated his whole life to the advancement of polar exploration by sea. His judgement was far from infallible, and being unafraid to speak his mind he made almost as many enemies as friends; but the enthusiasm with which he fathered his cause was of the greatest value to two generations of explorers. For forty years, from his room in the Admiralty, he planned, co-ordinated and set in motion a whole series of expeditions, conceived on the grand scale and organized with meticulous attention to detail. He was the father-figure of British polar voyaging: the man who, more than any other, made the science of exploration a part of our Naval heritage.

The third and last circumstance which helped to bring about a revival in Arctic voyaging was the publication in 1817 of *A Treatise on the Northern Ice*: a pamphlet by William Scoresby. Scoresby was a whaling skipper who was also a qualified chemist and a friend of Sir Joseph Banks, president of the Royal Society. His opinions, backed by both a practical and theoretical knowledge of his subject, carried considerable weight; and the following extract from his treatise was soon brought to Barrow's attention: "*I found on my last voyage about two thousand square leagues of the Greenland sea, between the 74th and 80th parallels, perfectly void of ice, which is usually covered with it. All this ice has disappeared within the last two years . . . And had I been so fortunate as to have had the command of an expedition for discovery instead of for fishing I have little doubt but that the mystery of a north-west passage might have been in some measure resolved. For there would have been no great difficulty in these years in exploring the coast of Greenland, etc.*" This pamphlet of Scoresby's is the first official document to advance the now-proven theory of seasonal fluctuations in the limits of Arctic pack-ice; and the Admiralty were quick to benefit from their new-found knowledge. Within a month of the pamphlet's publication, plans had been drawn up for two expeditions to take advantage of the ice's recession: one to explore the east coast of Greenland and push on if possible to the Pole, the other to explore the west coast and then push through to the Bering Strait and the Pacific.

The expeditions set sail in the spring of 1818.

The ships assigned to the east coast of Greenland were the bomb-boats *Dorothea* and the *Trent*, commanded by Captain Buchan. The logs of these two vessels are a chronicle of near-disaster. North of the Arctic Circle they met a violent gale and were driven into the pack-ice and frozen solid. Fighting clear of the pack, they were then so severely battered by another gale that they all but foundered among the bergs and floes of the Spitzbergen Ridge. They limped back to England in the autumn, thankful to be alive but with nothing to show for their efforts except a map of northern Spitzbergen.

The second expedition consisted of the *Alexander* and *Isabella*, commanded by John Ross. This expedition achieved more—though not nearly as much as Barrow had hoped. Standing north up the Davis Strait, they restored to the map the discoveries of the great Elizabethan seamen—Baffin Bay and the three "sounds" that run out of it: Smith Sound, Jones Sound and Lancaster Sound. Two of these exits—Smith Sound and Jones Sound—were choked with ice, and Ross was brought up short at their mouth by an obviously impenetrable barrier. The third exit, Lancaster Sound, was found to be ice-free. Into this promising lead Ross stood his vessels westward for a day and a night. Then he turned back, saying that ahead of him he "distinctly saw mountains round the bottom of the bay (or sound)". He was so certain these mountains were there that he named them the Croker Mountains, after Barrow's fellow-Secretary to the Admiralty, and then set course for home, convinced that no sea-lane led westward out of the Davis Strait.

It was subsequently proved that the Croker Mountains were a myth, and that Lancaster Sound was open sea.

A great deal of nonsense was written at the time (and has been written since) about Ross's mythical mountains, and all sorts of devious motives have been read into his decision to return home. But anyone who knows the Arctic will realize what must have happened. Ross had seen a mirage: a mass of ice heaved up along the shore and raised skyward by refracted light. Such phenomena are common in very high latitudes, especially when the weather is misty—as it was on this occasion; Baffin had seen a similar mirage in exactly the same spot two hundred years before. Franklin and McClure were subsequently misled by mirages farther west, while the opening up of Antarctica is bedevilled by reports of mountains and snowfields where in fact there is nothing but open sea. It is easy now to look at the map and censure Ross with a condescending smile. But it is worth while remembering that the bulk of his ship's company agreed with him at the time that the mountains were there, and endorsed his decision to head for home.

Among those who did not endorse his decision was his second-in-command William Parry, captain of the *Alexander*.

William Edward Parry was born in Bath on December 19th, 1790, fourth son of a fashionable and successful doctor—Jane Austen's "dear Doctor Parry". He joined the Navy at the age of twelve, and soon earned the approval of his commanding officers. *"He is a fine steady lad,"* wrote Admiral Cornwallis, *"I never knew of anyone so generally approved of . . . and he will, I am sure, soon be fit for promotion."* This judgement was vindicated by events; and by the end of the war Parry was a lieutenant attached to the West Indies station:

a handsome six-footer with dark grey eyes and wavy chestnut hair. In 1817 he volunteered to take part in an expedition bound for the Congo, but much to his chagrin the expedition sailed before his appointment came through. A few weeks later he happened to read of Scoresby's *Treatise on the Northern Ice* and of the proposed expeditions to Greenland. Writing to a friend he added half-jokingly in a postscript that he *"was ready for* (either) *hot or cold"*; and from this small aside stemmed a considerable chain of events. For Parry's letter reached the desk of the omnipresent Barrow. The young lieutenant was summoned to the Admiralty, and a week later was given command of the *Alexander*. In the next ten years Parry was to see Polar floes more often than English fields.

His first voyage north, as Ross's second-in-command, has been described as "little more than a summer cruise", and was an easy initiation to the Arctic. Ross was a good seaman, solicitous for the safety of his ships and the well-being of his crew; but he seems to have had two weaknesses: an exaggerated fear of becoming embayed, and a propensity for filling every blank space on his charts with coastline. Both these weaknesses were brought to light in Lancaster Sound.

On August 29th, 1818, the *Isabella* and *Alexander* were nosing south down the Davis Strait. Not far from the 74th parallel, an opening was sighted in the coast to starboard. This, Ross and his first lieutenant agreed, was undoubtedly the "Sir Jas. Lancaster's Sound" first discovered some two hundred years ago by Baffin. They decided to explore it, and with a following wind stood in through an opening some forty-five miles in width. They were on the threshold now of a great discovery. But within twenty-four hours Ross had turned back. Here is his own account of why:

"Soon after midnight the wind began to shift, and the ship came gradually up, enabling us to stand directly into the bay. I therefore made all sail and soon left the Alexander considerably astern. A little before 4 a.m. land was seen at the bottom of the inlet by the officers of the watch; but before I got on deck a space of about seven degrees was obscured by fog. The land which I saw at this time was a high ridge of mountains, extending directly across the bottom of the inlet. This ridge appeared extremely high in the centre, and the peaks in the north had at times the appearance of islands, being insulated by the fog at their base. Although a passage in this direction appeared hopeless, I was determined completely to explore it, since the wind was favourable, and therefore continued all sail. Mr. Beverly, who up to now had been the most sanguine (of finding a passage) reported to me from the crow's nest that before the weather became thick he had seen land across the bottom of the bay . . . When I went below there was little hope of it clearing, but at 3 p.m. the officer of the watch reported some appearance of better weather. I immediately went on deck; and soon after it completely cleared for about ten minutes, and I distinctly saw land round the bottom of the bay, forming a chain of mountains connected with those which extended along the north and south sides. This land appeared to be at the distance of eight leagues; and Mr. Lewis the master and James Haig leading man being sent for, they took its bearings, which were inserted in the log. At this same time I also saw a continuity of ice, extending from one side of the bay to the other . . . At a quarter past three, the weather again became thick and unsettled; and being now perfectly satisfied that there was no passage in this direction,

nor any harbour into which I could enter to make magnetic observations, I tacked to join the Alexander, which was at a distance of eight miles astern; and having joined her a little after four we stood together to the south east—for the weather appearing yet more unsettled, it became advisable to stand out of this dangerous inlet, in which we were embayed a distance of more than eighty miles."

This account establishes three facts. On the night of August 29th/30th the weather was unsettled and misty: most of those aboard Ross's ship *thought* they could see a chain of mountains across the bottom of the sound: Parry's ship, at the time these "mountains" were sighted, was eight miles astern of her consort. In view of this last fact it is hardly surprising that Parry and the crew of the *Alexander* were incredulous and bitterly disappointed when Ross turned back; for being well astern of the flagship and in thick mist they had not seen the so-called mountains. Parry was especially disgruntled. For all his observations up to this moment had led him to suppose that Lancaster Sound was not a mere inlet but a genuine strait—*vide* his Diary: "*May this be the channel we are in search of! And why should it not be? . . . The swell comes down from the North West and continues just as it does in the ocean, and it is impossible to remark this circumstance without feeling a hope that it may be caused by this inlet being a passage into a sea to the westward of it.*" If Parry had been a Nelson he would probably have turned a blind eye to Ross's signal to put about. As it was he left the Sound unwillingly in his commander's wake. And the moment the expedition had returned to London, he sought an interview with Barrow.

The Secretary to the Admiralty, disappointed by the comparatively meagre results of the voyages of 1818, was quick to find fault with Ross's charts; and he made use of Parry's insistence that Lancaster Sound had not been properly investigated to lay plans for another expedition.

It was unfortunate but perhaps inevitable that two rival schools of thought now came into being: the Ross school which held that there was no exit out of the Davis Strait and hence no North-West Passage, and the Parry school which held that an exit did exist and that somewhere deep in the Arctic a North-West Passage lay waiting to be discovered. Each school had its host of extremely vocal champions—most of whom had never been near the Arctic, and whose dogmatic assertions engendered far more heat than light. It is pleasant to record that neither Ross nor Parry entered the ranks of the mud-slingers. Privately, Parry was convinced that his commander had been guilty of an error of judgement; but he never criticized him in public; and on his next two voyages north he took with him Ross's nephew, the young James Clark Ross, a man destined to become probably the greatest of all polar explorers.

There was no doubt in the minds of the Admiralty about whom to put in command of the expedition which Barrow was planning for the summer of 1819. Parry was only twenty-eight; but he was able, ambitious and had experience of Arctic voyaging; what was more, he had the personal incentive of wanting to prove a theory in practice. On January 16th, 1819, he was officially invited to take command of the vessels *Hecla* and *Griper* "*for the Purpose of Attempting the Discovery of a North West Passage between the Atlantic Ocean and the Pacific*".

James Cook

TWO OF THE GREATEST
EXPLORERS OF THE PACIF

James Clark Ross

*Engraved by Henry Cook from the
original painting by Wildman*

"NOTHING IS MORE BEAUTIFUL THAN THE ARCTIC NIGHT"—*Fridtjof Nansen*

The *Hecla*, a bomb- (or bombardment) vessel, had been launched in the Humber in 1815. She was a big, clumsy ship—length 105 feet, breadth 28 feet, draught 10 feet and displacement 375 tons; she carried a crew of fifty-five to sixty, and her strong construction made her ideal for work in the ice.

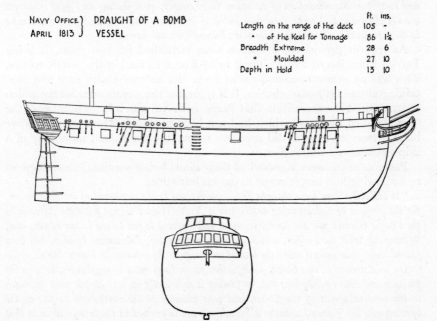

<table>
<tr><td>NAVY OFFICE
APRIL 1813</td><td>DRAUGHT OF A BOMB
VESSEL</td></tr>
</table>

	Ft.	ins.
Length on the range of the deck	105	-
" of the Keel for Tonnage	86	1¼
Breadth Extreme	28	6
" Moulded	27	10
Depth in Hold	13	10

FIG 34. H.M.S. *Hecla*

Under Parry's supervision she was now completely renovated, her keel was reinforced, her bows were strengthened and her rig was altered from fore and aft to square—Arctic whalers having found by experience that a barque or square-rig was the easiest to work and enabled a ship's company to keep three watches instead of the usual two. Parry was delighted with the *Hecla*. *"She is a charming ship,"* he wrote, *"and I really believe she will combine everything we want —great strength, capacity of hold, good sailing, and fine accommodation."* Events were to prove his optimism justified. The *Griper* was an unhappy contrast. An ancient coastguard vessel, she was far smaller than her flagship (length 84 feet, breadth 22 feet, draught 8 feet and displacement only 180 tons) and she had a poor carrying capacity. To try to rectify this deficiency, her deck was raised some six feet during her refit; but this ill-conceived experiment served only to make her top-heavy and so reduced her sailing qualities that the *Hecla* had frequently to take her in tow! She was commanded by Matthew Liddon, a close friend of Parry's who deserves a great deal of credit for keeping up with his commander when handicapped by ill-health and a vessel that was barely seaworthy.

The crew were distinguished by two qualities: their extreme youth and the fact that they were all volunteers. At twenty-eight, Parry was the oldest of the commissioned officers; while the men were carefully chosen from those who had previous experience of the Arctic. "*I believe we are as well manned,*" wrote Parry, "*as any ship that ever went to sea. For besides our own men* (i.e. those who had sailed under Ross) *we have had the choice of a great many of Buchan's, and so have had every possible advantage of selection. Good wages, good feeding and good treatment are not always to be had by these poor fellows! and as we bear a tolerably good character in these respects we have been quite overwhelmed with volunteers.*"

As regards provisions, the ships were victualled for two years, it being Parry's intention to allow himself to be frozen in during the Arctic winter. This was an innovation, and called for a diet balanced with care and containing abundant antiscorbutics. It is typical of the advanced thinking which characterized the expedition that Parry took with him a large number of the "new-fangled tin-cans" which had just been patented. These were to prove ideal preservatives, and did much to relieve the traditional monotony of a ship's company's winter diet.

Parry's orders were a model of their kind: being succinct, unambiguous and allowing him ample scope to use his initiative:

"*WHEREAS we have thought fit to appoint you to the command of an Expedition, for the purpose of endeavouring to discover a North-West Passage from the Atlantic to the Pacific Ocean: you are hereby required and directed to put to sea in the Hecla, and, in company with the Griper, which with her commander, Lieutenant Liddon, has been placed under your orders, make the best of your way to the entrance to Davis' Strait.*

On your arrival in this Strait, your further proceedings must be regulated chiefly by the position and extent of the ice; but, on finding it sufficiently open to permit your approach to the western shores of the Strait, and your advance to the northward as far as the opening into Sir James Lancaster's Sound, you are to proceed in the first instance to that part of the coast, and use your best endeavours to explore the bottom of that Sound; or, in the event of it proving a Strait opening to the westward, you are to use all possible means, consistent with the safety of the two ships, to pass through it, and ascertain its direction and communications; and if it should be found to connect itself with the northern sea, you are to make the best of your way to Behring's Strait."

*   *   *

They stood out of the Nore on the afternoon of May 11th, 1819.

The winds were light and contrary that spring, and it took them over a month to reach the approaches to Cape Farewell, the sluggish *Griper* having on more than one occasion to be taken in tow. On June 18th they sighted their first ice, and a few days later were brought up short by the pack. This was the adversary with whom they were to battle without respite for the next sixteen months. But Parry's first impression of the ice was of beauty rather than malevolence. "*The weather was fine and clear,*" he wrote, "*and nothing could exceed the serenity and grandure of the scene around us. The water was glassy smooth, and the ships glided gently among the numberless masses of ice. Greenland, rugged, high and covered with snow, filled the eastern horizon; and Disko was visible to the north, its hills reflecting the bright redness of the midnight sun.*" But the ice soon lost its charm when they attempted to breach it.

Being anxious to reach Lancaster Sound as early in the season as possible,

Parry was unwilling either to make a long detour round the ice or to wait for it to melt. So at the end of June he stood his vessels straight into the pack. This was a bold move—and one which James Clark Ross was to emulate with spectacular results twenty years later and nine thousand miles to the south— but its success that summer hung for a long time in the balance. For over a month the *Hecla* and *Griper* fought their way west through the stream of southward-moving floes. In days of calm the pack-ice was beautiful: "*the clouds like wool pulled out into lengths, the pure white of the snow on ice, the exquisite rich blue about the waterline, and the numberless shapes the different masses assume all creating in us fresh expressions of admiration whenever we look at it.*" The days of fog were less idyllic, with rime frozen thick on the rigging and having to be shaken to the deck like glass, and the ships keeping in touch by firing muskets; while the days of storm were full of danger—"*the wind and swell caused great destruction this morning among the icebergs, the wrecks of which were scattered in every direction*".

It was the swell that troubled them most: witness Parry's description of the early hours of Sunday, July 4th. "*Towards midnight, the wind having shifted to the south-west and moderated, another extensive chain of very large icebergs appeared to the northward; as we approached them the wind died away, and the ships' heads were kept to the northward only by the steerage-way given to them by a heavy southerly swell, which, dashing the loose ice with tremendous force against the bergs, sometimes raised a white spray over the latter to the height of more than one hundred feet, being accompanied by a loud noise like the roar of distant thunder; this presented a scene at once awful and sublime. We could find no bottom near these icebergs with 110 fathoms of line. A quantity of loose ice was straggling among the bergs, and Hecla pushed into this. But at 4 a.m. it fell suddenly calm. The ship at once became completely unmanageable, and was soon at the mercy of the swell, which drifted us fast towards the bergs. The boats were immediately sent ahead to tow, and Griper was signalled not to enter the ice. After two hours' hard pulling, we succeeded in getting back into clear water and far enough from the icebergs, which it is very dangerous to approach when there is any swell.*"

All through July the *Hecla* and *Griper* inched their way painfully west: sometimes being towed by their boats; sometimes being tracked by their crews (i.e., being hauled along by men on hawsers, like a barge through a canal); and sometimes being warped along on their anchors (i.e., their anchors being laid out ahead, secured in the ice and then wound in on the capstans). It was slow, arduous work. Sometimes a day's progress was measured in yards rather than miles; and sometimes the promising-looking leads into which they ran proved to be *cul de sacs*. But at last Parry's initiative was rewarded. Late in July the ice began to thin and the leads to widen; and finally, on the 28th, they emerged into open sea.

It had taken them nearly four weeks to cross the eighty miles of pack-ice; but they had reached the north-eastern coast of Baffin Land a month earlier than in 1818.

Soon they were at the mouth of Lancaster Sound: the spot where the dream of a North-West Passage would be either rekindled or finally and irrevocably doused.

But for several days, the winds being light and westerly, they were unable to enter the sound. Parry's impatience is revealed in his Diary: "*We are now* (he wrote) *about to enter the great sound which has obtained celebrity on account of the very opposite opinions which have been held regarding it. This was the point of our voyage which was to determine the success or failure of the whole expedition. And it will readily be conceived how great was our anxiety for a change of the westerly wind and swell which set down the Sound and prevented our making progress.*" On the evening of August 2nd Parry was rowed across to the *Griper*. He told Liddon that the moment the wind changed he would stand *Hecla* into the sound under all sail, leaving his slower consort to follow as best she could. In the event of the sound proving a strait, and the ships becoming widely separated, a rendezvous was fixed on the 85th meridian.

At noon the next day, as Parry was tacking to and fro off the mouth of the sound, *Griper*, some couple of miles astern, was seen suddenly to run up her studding sails and come racing towards them. A moment later the wind reached *Hecla*. It was easterly; and by 1 p.m. both ships were running free and fast into unknown waters.

All day and all the following night they ran to the westward, between low snow-covered shores, with no sign of the way ahead being blocked by land. "*It is more easy to imagine than describe our breathless anxiety,*" wrote Parry, "*as the breeze increased to a fresh gale and we ran quickly up the Sound. The mastheads were crowded by officers and men, and an unconcerned observer—if any could have been un-concerned on such an occasion—would have been amused by the eagerness with which the reports from the crow's nest were received—all favourable to our most sanguine hopes.*" Soon they were well past the mythical Croker Mountains; and still the passage lay glittering ahead: wide, free of ice and unblocked by any semblance of land. In the small hours of August 4th they came up to the 84th meridian, more than fifty miles to westward of the spot where Ross had placed his mountains; and here the *Hecla* hove-to, close-reefed in a rising gale, to wait for her consort. The strait, at this point, was still over forty miles wide; it was 150 fathoms deep; and a steady current and swell was running in from the west. This current, Parry believed, was evidence that Lancaster Strait must be connected to the Polar Sea. He was right. What he failed to realize was that almost every sea-lane leading from the Pacific Ocean to the Arctic was chocked, even in midsummer, with ice too thick for a sailing vessel to breach.

This was the tragedy of the North-West Passage: that only a hundred miles of ice blocked the route between the Atlantic and the Pacific; but this hundred miles might as well, to a ship under sail, have been a hundred thousand. Man had no answer, in those days, to the implacable resistance of nature.

As soon as *Griper* had closed with the flagship, the two vessels again stood west. At mid-day on August 4th they sighted an islet to starboard which they christened Croker Bay, to compensate the Secretary for the loss of his mountains, now relegated to the limbo of mythology. And still the wind blew fresh from the east, and still ahead of them the strait reached on and on, mile after hundred mile, deep into the heart of the Arctic. Parry's hopes were high now: "*The water being as free from ice as any part of the Atlantic, we began to flatter ourselves that we had fairly entered the Polar Sea, and some of the most sanguine among us had even calculated the bearing and distance of Icy Cape* (off the Bering Strait) *as a matter of no very difficult or improbable accomplishment.*" But on August 7th, as they came up to the 90th meridian, they suffered a rude awakening. Ahead lay a solid barrier of ice.

"*The prospect from the crow's nest,*" wrote Parry, "*suddenly assumed a very unpromising appearance, the whole of the western horizon being completely covered with ice, consisting of heavy and extensive floes, beyond which no indication of water was visible; instead of which there was a bright and dazzling ice-blink extending from shore to shore.*"

Baulked for the moment in the west, Parry headed his vessels south into Prince Regent Inlet. They were very close now to the magnetic pole, and the ships' compasses became so unreliable that they had to be taken out of their binnacles and put in store. The weather worsened, and for several days the ships groped blindly forward through thick fog and heavy snow-showers. After a while, finding that the inlet continued to the south, Parry decided to retrace his steps and attempt to break the ice-fields that had halted him at the foot of Lancaster Strait. But the passage back up the Inlet was slow and hazardous: "*On August 11th, the weather was so thick with fog that it was impossible to ascertain in what direction we were going; so we made the ships fast to a floe. On August 12th a breeze sprung up, but the weather was so foggy that for some hours we did not know in what direction it was blowing. When at last the fog cleared, we found that the floe to which we had anchored was drifting fast upon a great body of ice to leeward, threatening to enclose the ships between them. We therefore cast off and made sail, endeavouring to beat to northward; but we found great difficulty in doing this owing to the quantity of loose ice with which this part of the inlet was covered . . . At evening the men amused themselves by chasing the white whales which swam round the ships in large numbers, emitting a shrill ringing sound, not unlike that of musical glasses badly played . . . On August 19th the wind and sea increased, with a heavy fall of snow, which, together with the uselessness of the compasses and the narrow space in which we were working between the ice and the land, combined to make our situation for several hours a very unpleasant one. At 2 p.m. the weather being still so thick that we could scarcely see the length of the ship ahead, we suddenly found ourselves close under the land, with very little room to spare in wearing round.*" But by August 21st they had managed to work their way back to Lancaster Strait.

Much to Parry's delight the solid barrier of floes had broken up in the fortnight they had been away in the south, and the *Hecla* and *Griper* were now able to push west through a narrow sea-lane off the coast of Devon Island. Progress was slow, with fitful winds, fog, and a good deal of broken ice. But as they stood west, the ice gradually thinned out; and by August 23rd they were once again in open water, with two broad and ice-free leads stretching ahead of them: Wellington Channel to the north and Barrow Strait to the west. As Parry stood into the latter, he thought he had at last discovered the key to the North-West Passage. "*Though two-thirds of August had by now elapsed* (he says) *I had every reason to be satisfied with the progress made. I calculated on the sea being navigable for another six weeks, or even more. Our prospects were therefore exhilarating: the ships had suffered no injury; we had plenty of provisions; crews in high health and spirits; a sea, if not open, then at least navigable, and a zealous and unanimous determination in both officers and men to accomplish the grand object on which we had the happiness to be employed.*"

But Barrow Strait was to prove a false trail: a *cul de sac* which led not to the promised warm waters of the Bering Sea but to the ice-choked wilderness of Melville Sound.

This sound does indeed form a link between the Atlantic Ocean and the Pacific; but its eastern exits are blocked all the year round by solid ice: a barrier of compacted floes, more than fifty feet thick, which are squeezed each season out of the Arctic Sea like paste from a tube. In 1819 conditions in the Sound were unusually favourable, and Parry was able to push on to the 112th meridian—farther west than any explorer was to penetrate until the passage was finally achieved by Amundsen nearly a century later and five hundred miles to the south. But he had no more hope of breaking this final hundred miles of ice than of sailing the *Hecla* and *Griper* to the moon.

When therefore we come to assess the historical importance of Parry's voyage we must differentiate between his discovery of Lancaster Sound and his discovery of Barrow Strait. The former was of the greatest importance; for it opened up a new and navigable seaway which led deep into the heart of the Arctic and which proved to be the gateway through which a North-West Passage was finally achieved. His discovery of Barrow Strait, on the other hand, led nowhere; it was a barren triumph; a feat of skill and endurance as useless as Mallory and Irvine's assault on the north face of Everest. Usefulness alone, however, is a poor criterion for judging a man's deeds.

The early days of September 1819 saw *Hecla* and *Griper* battling slowly westward. The weather was difficult, with light winds and heavy fogs; soundings were shallow, and a helmsman had to be constantly on watch in the chains; while with the compasses still useless Parry had to resort to steering the ships by each other, keeping their masts exactly in line. "*It was amusing as well as novel,*" he remarks dryly, "*to see the quarter-master conning the ship by looking at the dog-vane.*" On September 4th they crossed the 110th meridian, thereby earning the £5,000 offered by Act of Parliament to the first ship's company to penetrate this far to the west. But their celebrations were short-lived. On September 6th they were brought up short by the ice-barrier.

It was a very different barrier this time to the shallow floes which had barred their way before. Towering high above *Hecla*'s masts, the ice rose green and malevolent out of the swirling mist. The moment he saw it Parry must have known he was defeated. But for ten days he skirted to and fro along the edge of the field seeking a flaw in its defences. But the ice was all too plainly inviolate. On September 16th, with the temperature down to −12°C and young ice forming each night on the face of the sea, they reached their farthest west (112° 51') and next day Parry decided to lay up his ships for the winter.

His decision was arrived at none too soon. For before he could reach a sheltered anchorage, he was all but frozen in off an open shore straight in the path of the advancing ice-field. Here is Parry's account of what was very nearly the end of his expedition.

"*Saturday, 18th September: It was my intention, as usual of late, to sail along the shore till we came to land-ice which would afford shelter to the ships during the night. As we ran along, however, it was soon perceived that the main body of the icefield was very rapidly approaching the land. The ships were immediately stood in-shore to find the best security which circumstances would admit; but the bay-ice had in this place become so thickened that the ships were arrested in their progress about one mile from the land. Every expedient to break the ice was resorted to, without our being able to move the ships a single foot ahead. The field meanwhile continued rapidly closing in on the shore, forcing the ships before it and bringing with it great quantities of berg ice . . ."*

Parry now tried to force his way towards a group of bergs stranded inshore, hoping they might afford at least some degree of protection. Luckily for him he did not succeed. For this was the spot at which a projection of the ice-field hit the shore.

". . . At 8 p.m. the field came in contact with these (bergs) *with a tremendous crash, piling up enormous fragments of ice in the most awful and terrifying manner, and with a force almost incalculable—since we could not see over the field in motion even from our mast-head. We were at this time less than a hundred yards from the point of contact, and had great reason to be thankful for having escaped from being carried into a situation in which no human power or skill could have saved the ships from instant destruction."*

Next morning, luckily for Parry, the ice-field was borne away by a shift in the wind, and the *Hecla* and *Griper* were able to slip out through the broken water of its wake and continue their search for winter quarters.

They found them on September 22nd: a deep, well-sheltered inlet—which Parry had previously taken note of—on the south coast of Melville Island. And here again they were only just in time. For the ice by now was so thick that a passageway had to be cut inshore: a miniature canal, the width of the *Hecla* and more than two and a quarter miles in length. It took them four days of non-stop labour to sound, mark out and cut their canal to the beach, with the vessels being alternately warped and towed down-channel, and the young ice closing in fast behind them. *"The thermometer read 6° this morning,"* wrote Parry, *"and rose only to 9° at noon. For men to be at work in the water in such conditions is very trying; but our crews are composed of no common men: they do everything cheerfully and well . . . and at 3.15 p.m. on September 26th we reached our winter quarters with three loud and hearty cheers from both ships' companies."*

On this desolate shore, farther north than any other men in the world, the crews of the *Hecla* and *Griper* were to remain frozen in for nearly eleven months.

It would be difficult to overestimate the importance of these months to the history of polar exploration. For when Parry dropped anchor that autumn in Winter Harbour he was creating a precedent: never before in history had a ship's company voluntarily let themselves be frozen in by an Arctic winter. Several crews had been frozen in by accident; and of these some had perished and some, with varying degrees of ill-health and suffering, had survived. Parry was now to prove that a well organised expedition could live out an Arctic winter in tolerable comfort and perfect health. And the knowledge that this could be done was of the utmost value to future expeditions. For its effect was comparable to Cook's taming of scurvy: it opened up a new dimension in polar voyaging: time: the prospect of an expedition not having to return each winter to its home port, but being able to spend two, three or even four seasons in the Arctic, pushing on always a little farther from its halting-place of the year before.

But the eleven months' incarceration of the *Hecla* and *Griper* was not achieved easily. It was made possible only by careful foresight, meticulous attention to detail and unceasing vigilance. If Parry and his men had relaxed, even for a moment, they would never have survived; for the Arctic winter takes a quick toll of the careless, the lazy and the casually optimistic.

As soon as the ships had dropped anchor, their upper masts and yards were dismantled and taken ashore and buried together with the sails, boats, loose tackle and running gear. The lower yards were then lashed fore-and-aft amidships so as to form a ridge-pole or framework for the roof; this roof consisted of oak planks which had been specially brought out from England and were now laid between yards and gunwale and covered with wadding tilt — much to Parry's wrath the latter had rotted in places and had to be patched with canvas dipped in boiling tar. As soon as the roof was in place a heating system was installed, both to provide warmth and offset condensation; from the ship's galley and from a portable oven set up in the main hatchway, a system of pipes conducted hot air — at least in theory! — to every part of the ship. And finally the vessels' sides were banked high with snow to help insulation. Within a week *Hecla* and *Griper* had taken on a comforting but distinctly odd appearance (*vide* the picture opposite page 225): half ship, half house, and with smoke rising cheerfully out of their galley chimneys. Parry then instigated a winter routine that was without parallel in its attention to detail. His orders included two daily inspections — both of crew and quarters; the strict supervision of every item of diet; daily airing of bedding and scrubbing down of bunks with heated sandstone, and organized exercise either ashore or on the upper deck. The result was all he hoped for. An uneventful winter. No sickness. No discontent. And a continuous record of scientific observation — *"Care is to be taken* (his orders read) *that every small occurrence is to be noted down at the time; since what appears unimportant then may hereafter prove useful and interesting"*; and the mass of technical information brought back to the Admiralty bears witness to the diligence with which these orders were carried out.

Soon the days began to draw in. On October 4th there was still sufficient sunlight for Parry to read and write in his cabin, and from its stern windows he could watch, in admiration, the ever-changing colours of the Arctic sunrise and sunset. But a month later the sun sank under the horizon with a depressing finality; no one was to see it again for a hundred days; and the temperature almost at once dropped sharply. They were in the grip now of the Arctic winter. Soon an incessant wind was beating out of the north. Condemned to live by the light of candles the crew gradually took on the sallow complexion of troglodytes, and their sleep was broken each night by the howling of wolves and the groan and crack of timbers squeezed by an unendurable pressure of ice. It would be too much to claim that time passed pleasantly that winter. But it passed. February brought back the sun; and soon the ships' companies were busy sawing leads through the ice, and exploring Melville Island. After three months of darkness and candlelight the sudden flowering of the Arctic spring seemed like a miracle: with moss springing green out of the melting snow, and the pink and yellow saxifrage all the more vivid for the drabness that had gone before.

But their term of imprisonment was far from over. For the ice in 1820 was late to melt; and in mid-July they were still held fast in Winter Harbour, with the pack showing not the slightest inclination to shift. "*It is not a very pleasing truth,*" wrote Parry, "*that we have been in this harbour, frozen up, during a part of every month in the year except one (August).*" On July 24th he ordered the sails to be set, but more in defiance than expectation—"*for the truth is that it becomes necessary to make some show of moving, however unpromising the ice looks; for it is impossible to conceal from the men the fact that in eight or nine weeks our season of operations in these regions must once more come to a conclusion.*" But at last, early on August 1st, the pack moved suddenly away in a body, and the next day *Hecla* and *Griper* nosed cautiously out of harbour. They knew that in less than six weeks the ice, once again, would claim them for the winter.

Parry at once stood west to re-investigate the ice barrier. He must have known that he was beaten; yet for four weeks he continued to probe at the field's defences, now struggling a few miles farther to westward, now being driven back again by snow-squalls, contrary winds and broken ice. It was as if he knew instinctively that he was on the edge of realizing his dream: that only a hundred miles to the west was open water through which he could have sailed to the Pacific. But there was no chink in the ice-field's armour; it was a barrier beyond the power of man to breach. And on August 30th Parry reluctantly set course for home. His ships were badly battered by gales off Cape Farewell, and the *Hecla* lost both bowsprit and foresail. But at last, early in November, they limped back to England after a voyage of almost exactly eighteen months.

So ended what was perhaps the most successful of all Arctic voyages. In a single season Parry had penetrated more than halfway to the Pacific; he had accurately charted more than a thousand miles of unknown coast; he had proved that a ship's company could survive the Arctic winter; he had not lost a single member of his crew, and had brought back a mass of useful scientific information. His expedition established a pattern and set a standard which explorers still try to emulate to-day.

XIV

THE LAST CONTINENT

(James Clark Ross discovers Antarctica: 1840–41)

ON September 26th, 1839, a pair of squat little ketches were warped out of the Medway. They were so heavily laden that they were unable to clear the Sheerness flats, and had to suffer the indignity of being towed to the open sea. Nor were their troubles over when they reached deep water; for the winds that September were light, the ketches were slothful sailers, and for nearly a week they lay becalmed while other and more graceful vessels slipped to and fro. It needed the best part of an equinoctial gale to send them reeling awkwardly down Channel.

Such was the inauspicious start to a voyage now recognized as one of the greatest epics in the history of exploration: Ross's discovery of Antarctica.

*   *   *   *

Terra Antarctica, Terra Incognita: the words were synonymous; and for nearly two thousand years they had been spaced out across the bottom of every map of the world. For the ancients' belief that all created things had to be balanced, and that a great land mass comparable to Eurasia existed in the far south, died hard. Even after Magellan and a dozen others had sailed round the world, *Terra Incognita* still appeared on the maps; a vast circular land mass of over ten million square miles, reaching nearly as far north as Cape Horn and the Cape of Good Hope and bulging into the Pacific to within a hand's breadth of Java and Sumatra.

It was not until the seventeenth century that doubts were raised about the extent of this "unknown land". Then, Dutch skippers on the spice run to Batavia discovered that if they kept well to the south of the Cape of Good Hope they could cut their outward voyage from sixteen months to six (for instead of being becalmed among the contrary drifts and counter-currents of the Indian Ocean, they could, in the far south, run free in the roaring forties). To start with, naturally enough, these skippers were nervous when sailing over an area plainly marked on their charts as land; but as voyage succeeded voyage and not so much as an island was sighted, they gained confidence; soon their route was given official blessing, and *Terra Incognita* disappeared from the Indian Ocean. Next century Cook removed it from the Atlantic and Pacific. In his famous voyage of 1772–75 Cook circumnavigated the world from west to east by following a zigzag course either side of the sixtieth parallel. Several times he penetrated as far south as the Antarctic Circle. But he found no land. Pack-ice barred his way. He returned to

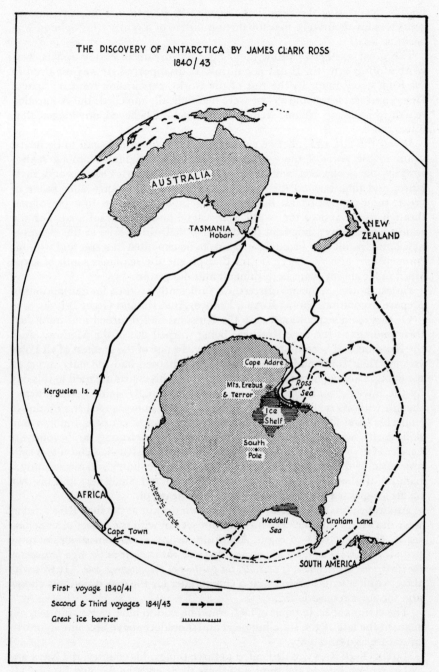

THE DISCOVERY OF ANTARCTICA BY JAMES CLARK ROSS
1840/43

AUSTRALIA

TASMANIA
Hobart

NEW ZEALAND

Cape Adare

Mts. Erebus & Terror

Ross Sea

Ice Shelf

Kerguelen Is.

South Pole

AFRICA

Antarctic Circle

Weddell Sea

Graham Land

Cape Town

SOUTH AMERICA

First voyage 1840/41 ————→
Second & Third voyages 1841/43 ----→
Great ice barrier ⊔⊔⊔⊔⊔⊔⊔

Fig 35.

England expressing the view that *"impenetrable ice extends to the pole"*; and so great was his reputation that for three-quarters of a century his opinion was taken as final.

The great southern continent, so long the dream of cartographers, was written off as a myth. It did not shrink. It disappeared. It was removed *in toto* from every map. In the rest of the world, exploration went on apace. Desert and sea, forest and steppe were methodically unveiled; but Antarctica remained inviolate. No one went there; for no one believed, any longer, that it was there.

It was the late 1820s before rumours of *Terra Incognita* began to be heard again in the ports of the south. These rumours originated among sealers working the Scotia Sea, who reported first the Southern Orkneys and Shetlands, and then beyond them—or so the story went—range after range of great, snow-capped peaks. But for a long time the reports that percolated through to the rest of the world were vague and unsubstantiated. For the sealers were canny; they kept the details of their discoveries to themselves— new lands meant new breeding-grounds to be exploited in secret and without competition; also the fierce storms that plague the sea-lanes south of Cape Horn made survey work both difficult and dangerous.

At last, however, official interest was sufficiently aroused for four nations to prepare expeditions south: Russia, France, America and Great Britain.

Of these four expeditions, only the Russians had returned and published their findings at the time Ross was being warped out of the Medway. And the Russians had been desperately unlucky. In one of the greatest of all Polar voyages their commander Thaddeus Bellingshausen had not only surveyed the Scotian and adjacent seas so accurately that his charts are used to this day by the international whaling fleets, but had actually sighted Antarctica— though without realizing it—for he mistook the snow-capped mountains of Enderby Land for icebergs. Bellingshausen, a man of courage, humour and skill, spent two years in the south, frequently penetrating far beyond the Circle. With a little more luck he would have staked Russia's claim to a sizeable slice of the Antarctic; as it was he left his country's name on only a handful of islands (Alexander, Peter, Borodino and Smolensk) and his own on an ice-girt sea that few people have ever heard of.

Antarctica, in other words, was not known to exist at the time Ross's orders were drawn up; and he certainly did not set sail with the object of searching for it. His objective—to quote Admiralty orders—was something far more prosaic: *"to make an extensive series of magnetic observations in the high latitudes of the south, and to determine, if possible, the position of the magnetic pole."* It was with these requirements in mind that a commander for the expedition was chosen and the ships requisitioned.

The commander, in point of fact, could be said to have chosen himself, one man, in the late 1830s, standing head and shoulders above his contemporaries in stature and suitability.

James Clark Ross was dedicated to three things: his country, the Navy and polar exploration; to the service of these three gods he devoted his life. His portrait gives us a clue to his character: steady eyes, a large hooked nose, a firm, near-obstinate mouth. He is said to have been the handsomest man in the Navy; yet he did not marry until he had turned forty-three, which seems evidence of the strength of his dedication. As a seaman he was supremely competent; indeed, using the word in its strictly technical sense he was probably the greatest sailor England has ever produced. He joined the Navy at the age of twelve. As a midshipman he served under the best possible tutor, Parry, on the best possible voyage, the expedition of 1819. Of his next twenty summers, seventeen were spent in the Arctic, pushing ever north and west in search of the elusive passage. At the end of these seventeen summers what he did not know about icemanship was not worth knowing. His career seemed to have reached its climax when he became the first man to set foot on the north magnetic pole. Then, in April 1839 he was given command of the *Erebus* and *Terror*, the pair of converted bomb ketches earmarked for an expedition south. He was a shade under forty when he was first piped aboard *Erebus*: a man at the height of his physical and mental powers who was already something of a national hero.

And the ships of the expedition were as well suited to their work as the commander.

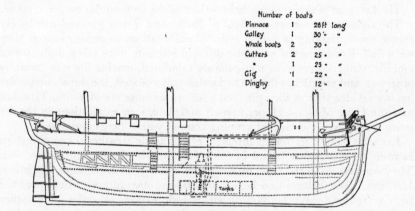

Number of boats		
Pinnace	1	28 ft long
Galley	1	30 " "
Whale boats	2	30 " "
Cutters	2	25 " "
"	1	23 " "
Gig	1	22 " "
Dinghy	1	12 " "

FIG 36. Profile of H.M.S. *Terror* as fitted for Antarctica

Erebus, like most of the vessels used for polar exploration, was a bomb-boat: length 105 feet, beam 28 feet, draught 11 feet, and displacement 370 tons. She rolled badly and was a clumsy sailer; but she had two great assets; her hold was enormous, having been designed for storing mines and mortar shells, and she was stoutly built and able to stand a fantastic amount of buffeting. *Terror* was similar, both in size and characteristics: length 102 feet, beam 27 feet, draught 10 feet, and displacement 340 tons; she was an old hand at polar explorations, having survived several freezings-in in the north-west. Neither ship had anything of the grace and beauty of line so often associated with the swan-song days of sail; but for work in the polar ice-pack they were eminently suitable.

On taking over his new command on April 8th, 1839, Ross's first step was to have his ships strengthened still further. Their decks were taken up and replaced by two thicknesses of special planking with waterproof cloth in between; their bow and stern sections were scientifically shored up with interlacing beams of oak; all protruberances were smoothed off their hulls which were then encased in a new outer skin; and their keels were double-sheathed in copper. This work took most of the summer.

Ross's next concern was victualling and equipping. And here the Admiralty gave their commander a free hand, with the result that Ross's expedition was probably the best provided for of any in the nineteenth century. His supplies were sufficient for three years and included a vast quantity of antiscorbutics — 2,618 pints of vegetable soup, for example, 2,398 lb. of pickled cabbage, and no fewer than 10,782 lb. of carrots; while to quote his own words, "warm clothing of the best quality was furnished to both ships, and every arrangement was made in the interior fittings that could contribute to health and comfort". His crew were hand-picked, many of them having served with him previously in the Arctic. His orders were concise, and yet gave him considerable powers of discretion. And all in all the expedition which stood down-Channel in the autumn of 1839 was well-found, if strictly limited in its intentions.

The first part of their voyage held no hint of the momentous events to come. Throughout the winter of 1839–40 *Erebus* and *Terror* pursued a leisurely course south, making *en route* a series of observations as meritorious as they were dull. Recordings of magnetic dip and intensity were taken daily, water and air temperatures were meticulously tabulated, marine life was carefully observed, and samples of the sea bed sedulously collated, the ships' companies having no idea that as they pursued a leisurely course *via* Madeira, Trinidad and the Cape of Good Hope, French and American expeditions in the far south were making their first groping contact with a new continent.

Early in May they had a foretaste of Antarctic weather when the ships hove-to off Kerguelen Island in thick fog, squalls of snow and heavy seas. They warped up to the head of Kerguelen's one good anchorage, Christmas Harbour, landed stores and began to build an observatory. They spent the next sixty-three days on Kerguelen Island, making a series of complex magnetic recordings. Out of these sixty-three days it snowed or sleeted on sixty-one and blew a full gale on forty-five. But the recordings were made accurately and without a break. And this gives us a clue to Ross's greatest trait as an explorer: his determination to see a job through no matter what the difficulties.

It was mid-July before they left "this most dreary and disagreeable island", and set course for Tasmania.

The bad weather followed them. On July 28th, not far from the fiftieth parallel, they ran into a full hurricane. Both ships were reduced to close-reefed topsails; but even so, the seas broke green over their quarters and kept their decks continually awash to a depth of two feet; while to quote the matter-of-fact Ross, "*it was indeed an unusual sight to see the crests of the great waves driven completely over us in solid sheets of water.*" *Erebus* and *Terror* became separated; but they both survived, and a fortnight later crept battered into the Derwent. It is worth remembering that storms in the fifties are the worst in the world; for the seas in this latitude are enormous, having been driven by the westerly-wind-drift clean round the globe in a 13,000-mile circle unchecked by land. Modern cargo vessels have been known to founder in Antarctic hurricanes; little ketches of under 400 tons could only survive them by their crews' vigilance and skill.

Hobart, a short way up the Derwent estuary, must have been a pleasant change from Kerguelen. The expedition spent ten weeks here, building an observatory and caulking and repainting *Erebus* and *Terror*: a delightful interlude for the crew, but a time of some anxiety for their commander.

The Governor of Tasmania, Sir John Franklin, went out of his way to give the expedition all possible help and hospitality. Kangaroo hunts and opossum shoots were organized daily; trips were made into the interior in search of fossils; there were dinners at Government House, tea-parties and picnics — at one of the latter we are told that young Hooker (the expedition's botanist) gave a yelp of delight at finding a rare plant, *"which put the ladies in a great flutter since they feared he had been bitten by a snake"*. All these social comings and goings Lady Franklin recorded in her diary. She recorded, too, her conviction that Captain Crozier of the *Terror* had fallen in love with her companion, the beautiful Sophia Cracroft, but that the latter *"seems to be setting her cap at Ross himself!"*

Ross, however, had less attractive matters to attend to. For news was waiting him at Hobart that only a few months previously both the French and American expeditions had sighted land in the far south; and, what is more, had sighted it in the very area in which he had been ordered to search for the magnetic pole. What should he do?

This was the turning-point of the expedition. Should Ross keep to his orders and content himself with merely enlarging on the French and American discoveries — which, at best, were sketchy, limited and none too accurate? Or should he strike out elsewhere on his own?

The official report he submitted to the Admiralty gives his answer. *"Fortunately,"* he wrote, *"in my instructions much had been left to my judgement in unforeseen circumstances; and impressed with the feeling that England had ever led the way of discovery in the southern as well as the northern regions, I considered it would have been inconsistent with the pre-eminence she had ever maintained, if we were to follow in the footsteps of any other nation. I therefore resolved at once to avoid all interference with their discoveries, and selected a much more easterly meridian on which to endeavour to penetrate south."*

It was an answer at once bigoted, courageous and full of common sense. For Ross had seen from their reports that the French and American expeditions had in fact achieved little, the former having surveyed only a tiny fragment of coastline and the latter having pencilled "an appearance of mountains" in several unlikely reaches of sea; in fact, so sketchy were their observations that they were not even certain whether they had discovered a new continent or a series of disconnected islands; for the pack-ice had thwarted them — as it had thwarted Cook, Bellingshausen and a host of unknown sealers before them. It now occurred to Ross that with his specially strengthened ships he might be able to *penetrate the ice*, to make for the first time in history an accurate survey of what—if anything—lay beyond, and so solve the age-old mystery of *Terra Incognita*.

Having reached his decision, it remained only to choose a route. His early experience with Parry helped him here. In the north, in the Davis Strait, Parry had taken his lead from those who knew the Arctic, the whalers; and now in the south Ross prepared to take a lead from those who knew the Antarctic, the sealers. He read and listened to their stories of the pack-ice falling away to the south around the 180th meridian, and decided that here, well to the east of the French and American discoveries, he would make his attempt to penetrate the unknown. He felt that great discoveries might well await him, if only he could force a way through the pack-ice. This was the crux of the matter: the imponderable on which hung failure or success. Could he penetrate the pack?

Erebus and *Terror* weighed anchor at 5 a.m. on Thursday, November 12th. It was overcast with low cloud and a gentle breeze as the ships tacked down the Derwent. At noon the pilots were dropped, sea routine was piped, and the voyage to Antarctica was under way.

At first the ships headed east-south-east towards the Auckland and Campbell Islands, which they passed early in December. Then, on reaching the 175th meridian, they stood due south for the pack. As the weather grew colder, both ships' companies experienced a heightening of tension and purpose. "*Our future,*" wrote Robert McCormick (*Erebus*'s doctor) "*promises to be full of interest, for we may soon make great discoveries in a region of our globe fresh and new as at creation's first dawn.*" The more practical and less poetic Ross confined his observations to the state of wind and sea, and the sighting of "*much weed and many albatross*".

As they approached the Antarctic Circle the weather could hardly have been more favourable; the sun shone out of a cloudless sky, winds were light and visibility unlimited. On Boxing Day they sighted their first iceberg. Flat-topped, white-crested, sapphire-based and over a hundred feet in height, it drifted past them streaming water and surrounded by whales and petrels. By the evening, five other bergs were in sight, and the temperature was dropping fast.

In the next couple of days the icebergs increased in size and number— sometimes as many as thirty could be sighted from the crow's nest. *Erebus* and *Terror* picked a course through them without difficulty; they had done this sort of thing before, in the Arctic. They crossed the Circle on New Year's Eve; and after the celebrations the crew were given their special clothing: to each man "*a boxcloth jacket and trousers, a pair of water boots, two pairs of hose, two comforters, a red frock and a Welsh wig*". Next morning they sighted a bar of yellow across the south-eastern horizon, which the old hands identified as an iceblink. They knew then that they were nearing the pack.

The weather chose this inopportune moment to worsen; a northerly gale bringing snow and high seas, and forcing the vessels to shorten sail and haul away from the ice. Visibility was bad during the night; there were many icebergs about, and often the first warning the crew had of their approach was the roar of waves dashing against their sides. The watch was doubled, and

MOUNT EREBUS, ANTARCTICA

H. M. ships *Hecla* and *Griper* in Winter Harbour.
An engraving by W. Westall from a sketch made on the spot by Lieutenant Beechey

The *Erebus* passing through the chain of bergs, 13th March, 1842.
A contemporary engraving from the painting by I. E. Davis

the night passed anxiously. But at dawn the wind shifted, the weather cleared, and the ships were able to stand in to examine the pack.

It stretched away to the south as far as the eye could see: a shimmering damask of white: solid at the edge, but—much to Ross's satisfaction—with occasional leads of open water inside. The ships ran parallel to it for several miles, searching for a place to enter. But there seemed no flaw in its defences.

Ross was in a quandary. The weather was unsettled. At the moment the wind was in the right quarter for attempting a breakthrough; but if he delayed, it could easily shift. He took a chance, ordered *Terror* to follow and ran full-tilt at the pack.

Again and again their bow smashed into the ice. An ordinary vessel would have been staved in; but *Erebus*, with her double skin and her shored-up bow, was relatively unhurt; nor did the great avalanches of dislodged ice damage her hull, for it had been smoothed down and offered no protruberances against which the shattered floes could lodge. But strength alone would never have got the vessels through. It needs fine seamanship to run a sailing vessel's bow again and again into the same place at the same velocity. This seamanship Ross took as a matter of course, and his account of breaking the pack is almost prosaic. *"After about an hour's hard thumping, we forced our way into some small holes of water, connected by narrow lanes, for which we had steered. We found the ice lighter and more scattered than it had appeared, and by no means of so formidable a character as we had been led to expect . . . At noon we were in latitude 65° 55′ S; and the clear sea was no longer discernible from the masthead as we pursued our way through the pack, choosing the clearest 'leads' and forcing the interposing barriers as they occurred, at times sustaining violent shocks which nothing but ships so strengthened could have sustained."* By nightfall they had penetrated fifty miles into the pack, and the omens were more auspicious than Ross could have dared to hope.

Progress in the next few days was equally encouraging. Hour after hour the vessels forced their way south, twisting, tacking, running and occasionally warping a path through floes and sea-lanes. Penguins, whales and the infrequent seal watched them curiously; petrels circled over head; snow fell in sudden flurries, and over all was the great silence of the unknown.

But Antarctica was not to yield her secrets easily nor without a fight.

During the night of January 5th/6th the ice started to close up and thicken; progress became increasingly slow, and dawn found *Erebus* and *Terror* twisting anxiously this way and that to avoid being frozen in. But to no avail. A little before mid-day they were forced to heave-to in a small circle of water out of which they could find no way. Ross was not unduly worried; for a heavy swell was continually shifting the ice, and he had every reason to believe that a lead would eventually open. But that evening the weather took a turn for the worse. Storm clouds came rolling out of the north. And the barometer dropped.

By dawn it was snowing hard, the wind had increased to a full hurricane, and the swell had widened and steepened. It widened and steepened to such and extent that soon, to the horror of Ross and his ships' companies, the pack began to split up, and great combers alive with solid blocks of ice came sweeping down on the imprisoned vessels.

Ross was to learn that day why no ship had ever ventured into the Antarctic pack, and lived.

Hour after hour the storm raged with such frenetic violence that there seemed no hope of survival. They tried to moor to the lee of a floe, but their stoutest hawsers parted like rotten string. They tried to run with the wind, but their sails were split to shreds. Soon they were reduced to rigging staysails, and alternately backing and filling to try to avoid the heaviest conglomerations of floes. But they could not avoid them all. Again and again great blocks of ice, hard as adamant and weighing hundreds of tons, crashed into the labouring vessels. If they had not been so soundly and scientifically strengthened they would have foundered within the hour. As it was, they suffered terrible damage. *Erebus*'s rudder was twisted and split, and the copper sheathing ripped from her hull; while *Terror*'s rudder was wrenched completely away, and the unfortunate vessel drifted helplessly this way and that, at the mercy of the storm. And still the waves increased in size and fury, until they towered *above* the vessels' topsail yards. Even the phlegmatic Ross thought their last moment had come. *"Our ships"*, he wrote, *"rolled and groaned amidst the fragments of bergs, over which the ocean rolled its mountainous waves, throwing huge masses one upon another then burying them deep beneath its foaming waters, the while dashing and grinding them together with fearful violence. The awful grandeur of such a scene can neither be imagined nor described. Each of us could only secure a hold, waiting the issue with resignation to the will of Him who alone could bring us through such extreme danger; watching with breathless anxiety the effect of each succeeding collision and the vibrations of the tottering masts, expecting every moment to see them give way."*

But the storm was too violent to last for long. That night the wind backed and dropped, the waves slowly lost their malevolence, and the ships were able at last to limp into shelter behind a line of mammoth bergs. They had survived partly because of the care and skill with which they had been strengthened, and partly because of the fine seamanship of their crews—*"I must express my admiration"*, wrote Ross with typical understatement, *"of their conduct on this trying occasion; throughout a period of twenty-eight hours, during any one of which there appeared to be very little hope that we should live to see another, the coolness, steady obedience and untiring exertions of each individual were in every way worthy of British seamen."* It was not within Ross's capacity to lavish greater praise.

While the storm blew itself out, the crews set to work on repairs. They were well equipped for such an emergency. Both vessels carried a spare rudder, a blacksmith's forge, and supplies of caulking and seasoned timber; and within thirty-six hours Ross was again heading south. He had been lucky. Not only had he survived; but the storm had broken up the pack, and driven his ships quickly and violently forward in the direction they wanted to go. Next season Ross was to spend two months in the pack, being driven this way and that by contrary winds and being frequently frozen in; this season he was to cross it in exactly a week. For the following evening *Erebus*'s look-out reported a water-blink on their starboard bow; and by midnight the crew could make out ahead of them the southern edge of the pack, and beyond it open sea.

At 5 a.m. on January 9th, 1841, in position 69° 13′ S, 176° 15′ E, *Erebus* and *Terror* fought clear of the ice and emerged into an unknown ocean.

It stretched away in front of them in the bright Antarctic dawn; a virginal world of greens and blues and dazzling white. It was a great moment in the history of exploration. The barrier which had remained inviolate since the day of its creation was behind them, and the last of the continents lay waiting her discoverers.

For two days, in perfect weather, the ships stood south through waters crystal clear and free of all but the tiniest particles of ice. Petrels circled overhead. The waters were alive with whales—blue and sperm, humpback and fin. And Ross's hopes were divided. The prospect of discovering new lands was exciting; but below in his cabin was the Union Jack which he had unfurled ten years previously at the north magnetic pole, and to raise the same flag at the South Pole was his most cherished dream. By the evening of January 10th the angle of magnetic dip had increased to eighty-five degrees, and they knew the pole must be near. But even as they were measuring the dip, an ill-defined land-blink was sighted on the southern horizon, and it became a question of which they would discover first: new lands or the pole.

Their doubts were resolved that night.

As we might expect, Ross's account of sighting Antarctica is brief and undemonstrative—as if in common with many present-day leaders of expeditions he fought shy of displaying any sort of emotion. But Doctor Robert McCormick had fewer inhibitions.

"*Monday, January 11th, 1841*," he wrote. "*At the early hour of 2.30 a.m., land was reported from the crow's nest, and the officer of the watch at once called me . . . It may well be imagined that not a moment was lost on my part in leaving my comfortable bed for the deck. The newly-discovered land at first appeared very indistinctly, through haze and a few light clouds, skirting the horizon on the port bow. I could just trace the outline of the summit of a lofty mountain, having a steep escarpment streaked with snow. After about an hour this became so intermingled with the hazy horizon as to give rise to doubts about it being land at all. But by 9 a.m. the coast had become sufficiently well defined to enable me to get a sketch. It extended from S.E. to S.W.; very high, and was enveloped in a mantle of snow, except for the lower portions of the aforementioned escarpment which were black . . . The whole of the upper part of this vast mountain range appeared to be a glaciation, relieved only at intervals by the apex of some dark hummock or projecting peak . . . And* (it soon became clear that) *we had discovered a new land, of so extensive a coastline and attaining such altitude, as to justify the appellation of a Great New Southern Continent.*"

It was indeed a great new continent which now unfolded peak by peak before their astonished eyes. All day they stood towards it, marvelling at the scale and grandeur of the land they had discovered: at the virginal white of its snows, at the refracted brilliance of its light, and at the great silence which hung like a benediction over their advancing ships. Theirs was the almost unique joy of making a genuine discovery. For most famous explorers—from Pytheas to Columbus—had either enjoyed precursors or else had visited lands already known to somebody. But the crews of *Erebus* and *Terror*, that January afternoon, became the first men in the world ever to sail close inshore to the mountains of Antarctica. And next day they became the first men to set foot on them.

At 9.50 a.m. on Tuesday, January 12th, Captains Ross and Crozier were rowed to an offshore island to take possession of Victoria Land. It must have been an incongruous ceremony. The officers in their gold braid and wing collars, the crew in their red frocks and Welsh wigs: the difficulty of landing through heavy surf on an ice-choked shore: the penguins which "fought" the landing party as savagely as South Sea cannibals: the Queen's health drunk in a glass of sherry: the overpowering stench of guano, and the calling for "three hearty cheers": all interrupted by the boom of recall guns from *Erebus* and *Terror*. For the weather was worsening. Soon fog and low cloud was drifting inshore, and the ships' boats scuttled back and were hoist aboard as the ships stood hurriedly for the safety of the open sea.

This ceremony was the prelude to five weeks of remarkable and hazardous discovery. Remarkable because of the bizarre nature of the coast which unfolded before them; hazardous because they were continually traversing a lee shore devoid of beach or anchorage and lined with continuous cliffs of ice; if, at any time in these five weeks, *Erebus* and *Terror* had been driven ashore they would have stood little chance of survival.

A lee shore. To a generation unaccustomed to the problems of sail, the words have an academic ring. But amateur yachtsmen at least will have an inkling of the problems facing Ross that summer as he sailed, often in thick fog and blinding snow, down five hundred miles of uncharted coast, plagued by icebergs and inshore winds, and in vessels which were cumbersome sailers. The measure of his seamanship is the fact that he charted his discoveries with meticulous accuracy — and survived.

For forty-eight hours after the landing a southerly storm prevented further exploration; indeed, the ships had to carry all sail to prevent themselves being blown far from the coast. Then on January 14th the weather improved, and Ross again stood his vessels south, passing through vast herds of whales — which, he remarked, "*had hitherto enjoyed a life of tranquillity beyond the reach of their persecutors, but would soon, no doubt, be made to contribute to the wealth of our country.*" Next morning, on rounding a small cape, they were greeted by a scene of the utmost grandeur: a great chain of mountains, over 10,000 feet in height, stretching away to the south in a single, unbroken sweep from sea to sky. All day they sailed parallel to the mountains, about three miles off-shore, watching the peaks unfold in a panorama of ever-changing beauty. Ross named them after various Sea Lords and Fellows of the Royal Society, about whom we now know little and care less. Not until they had spent nearly a week off the coast of Antarctica did he name a landmark after his fiancée (Cape Anne); his gallantry in this respect falling far short of that of the leader of the French expedition, who gave his wife's name (Adélie Land) to the whole extent of his discoveries.

For over a week they continued south, following the coast as close inshore as they dared, surveying the mountains, taking samples of the sea-bed, and searching without success for a possible beach on which to winter. By January 23rd they were in latitude 74° 23′ , farther south than men had ever penetrated before. That night in the gunroom they drank to "better luck still", and—since the coastline ahead seemed to bear away to the south-west—to "the discovery of the magnetic pole". But it turned out to be something far more bizarre than the pole which they discovered. For a couple of days later they sighted, dead ahead, a pair of enormous volcanoes, one of them extremely active, rising steeply out of the wilderness of ice.

"*Thursday, January 28th,*" wrote McCormick. "*We were this morning startled by the most unexpected discovery in this vast region of glaciation : a stupendous volcanic mountain in a high state of activity. At 10 a.m., upon going on deck, my attention was arrested by what appeared to be a fine snowdrift, driving from the summit of a lofty crater-shaped peak. As we made a nearer approach, however, this apparent snowdrift resolved itself into a dense column of smoke, intermingled with flashes of red flame, emerging from a magnificent volcanic vent, in the very centre of a mighty mountain range encased in eternal ice and snow. The peak itself, which rises to an altitude of 12,400 feet . . . was named after our ship, Mount Erebus. Adjacent to it, and separated by only a saddle of ice, arose a sister mountain to the height of 10,900 feet, but now extinct. This received the name of Mount Terror.*"

It was, indeed, a sensational discovery. But greater surprises still were in store for them.

All morning they closed with the volcanoes: surveying, sketching and sounding. Then in the afternoon they were faced with an even more astonishing phenomenon. For to the east of Mount Erebus they found their way blocked not by a coastline, but by a vast barrier of solid ice, smooth as onyx and treble the height of their mainmast.

Ross's description gives us a vivid picture, both of the ice-barrier itself and of their feelings at finding that it blocked their way to the south. "*As we approached the land*", he wrote, "*under all studding sails, we perceived a low white line extending east from the volcano as far as the eye could discern. It presented an extraordinary appearance, gradually increasing in height as we got nearer to it, and proving at length to be a perpendicular cliff of ice, between one hundred and fifty and two hundred feet above the level of the sea, perfectly flat at the top and without any fissures or promontories on its seaward face. What was beyond it we could not imagine, but it was an obstruction of such a character as to leave no doubt upon my mind as to our future proceedings; for we might as well try to sail through the cliffs of Dover as penetrate such a mass. This was a great disappointment to us all . . . At 4 p.m. (just as we were hauling round to follow the barrier east) Mount Erebus was observed to emit smoke and flame in unusual quantities, producing a most grand spectacle. A volume of dense smoke was projected at each successive jet with great force, in a vertical column, to a height of about two thousand feet above the mouth of the crater; and as the smoke cleared away the bright red flame that filled the vent was clearly perceptible . . . That evening, favoured by a fresh north-westerly breeze, we made good progress along the lofty cliffs of the ice barrier. It would be impossible to conceive a more solid-looking structure; not the smallest appearance of a rent or fissure could we discover throughout its whole extent. But many small fragments lay at the foot of the cliffs, broken away by the force of the waves, which dashed their spray high up the face of them.*"

They had hoped, at first, that the barrier might either diminish in size or else fall away to the south. Instead, it became, if anything, loftier and more impenetrable than ever; and after they had skirted it for nearly 250 miles it began to curve north, back towards the pack.

The weather, all this time, was fickle: fog and violent snow-storms alternating with days of lyrical calm. Ross knew that the short Antarctic exploring season would soon be drawing to its close, and he began to search anxiously for a place to winter. But without success. To port lay the pack, to starboard the barrier, and soon "young" ice—the harbinger of winter—began to form on the water ahead. Ross pushed on for as long as he dared; then on February 13th, he did the only possible thing; he hauled round and retraced his steps, back towards Mounts Erebus and Terror. He had very nearly left it too late. Three times that February his vessels were all but frozen in in the fast-narrowing sea-lane between barrier and pack; twice they were almost driven on to the cliffs of ice.

These cliffs became a nightmare to Ross as he fought his way back to safety. At first their novelty had been intriguing—"They are quite unlike any formation known in the Arctic", wrote one of Crozier's officers; while the *Erebus*'s blacksmith had been inspired to launch into verse:

> *Awful and sublime, magnificent and rare,*
> *No other earthly object with the Barrier can compare!*

But as the weather worsened and the inshore winds gained strength, the Barrier began to take on the malevolence of an ever-present hazard: a Scylla and Charybdis lying in wait for the opportunity to splinter Ross's labouring vessels to matchwood. And as summer gave way to autumn, two other hazards began to make their presence felt: sea mist and icebergs. Soon Ross found himself in the same *impasse* as Coleridge's Ancient Mariner:

> *And now there came both mist and snow*
> *And it grew wondrous cold;*
> *And ice, most high, came floating by,*
> *As green as emerald.*

The aptness of these lines, incidentally, has been remarked on by many writers who have expressed surprise that Coleridge's description should fit the polar scene so exactly. The explanation is that Coleridge lived in Bristol and had read the seventeenth-century classic of his fellow townsman, *The Strange and Dangerous Voyage of Captain Thomas James*; James had spent a season exploring the exits from Hudson Bay, and the experiences of Coleridge's mariner are directly based on James's adventures on his "Strange and Dangerous Voyage".

It was March before *Erebus* and *Terror* fought clear of the dangers of the barrier, and were able to head north for the pack. They made a last search for winter quarters off Capes Anne and Adare, but without success. They then spent several days searching for the mythical mountains which Wilkes had placed off the tip of Victoria Land, but again without success. Not until young sea-ice was forming round them to a thickness of two to three inches, did they finally set course for Tasmania.

One last danger had to be overcome: they had to recross the pack. It is usually said, in the few existing accounts of Ross's expedition, that the pack was crossed in about ten days "without undue difficulty"; and certainly Ross himself devotes only two or three pages of his report to this part of the voyage. Yet one extract from his report is significant.

"*March 7th. We found ourselves embayed in a deep bight of the pack, stretching across our bows. Much hampered by fields of pancake ice, we tried to haul to the wind. But at noon it fell quite calm, and the heavy easterly swell began to drive us on to a line of large bergs—from the mast head we counted eighty-four large ones and some hundred of smaller dimension. (After a while) we found we were fast closing this chain of bergs, so closely packed together that we could distinguish no opening through which the ships could pass, the waves breaking violently against them, dashing huge masses of pack ice against the precipitous faces of the bergs; now lifting them nearly to their summit, then forcing them again far beneath their waterline, and sometimes rending them into a multitude of brilliant fragments against their projecting points.*

"*Sublime and magnificent as such a scene must have appeared under different circumstances, to us it was awful, if not appalling. For eight hours we drifted slowly towards what to human eyes appeared inevitable destruction; the high waves and deep rolling of our ships rendered towing with the boats impossible, and our situation (was) the more painful and embarrassing from our inability to make any effort to avoid the dreadful calamity that seemed to await us . . . Soon we were within half a mile of the range of bergs. The roar of the surf, which extended each way as far as we could see, and the crashing of the ice, fell upon the ear with fearful distinctness, whilst the frequently averted eyes as immediately returned to contemplate the awful destruction that threatened in one short hour to close the world and all its hopes and joys and sorrows upon us for ever. In this our deep distress 'we called upon the Lord, and He heard our voices'. A gentle wind filled our sails. Hope was revived; and the greatest activity prevailed to make the best use of the feeble breeze. As it gradually freshened, our heavy ships began to feel its influence, slowly at first, but then more rapidly; and before dark we found ourselves far removed from danger.*"

If this was sailing "without difficulty" one shudders to think of the perils which must have beset Ross and Crozier on the more eventful stages of their voyage.

By mid-March the vessels had broken free from the pack; then, with a following wind, a full moon and brilliant coruscations from the Aurora Australis, they set course for Hobart, which they reached three weeks later after a pleasantly uneventful run in the westerlies.

On April 6th, 1841, Ross again dropped anchor in the Derwent after an absence in Antarctica of one hundred and forty-five days. In spite of the hazards he had passed through, his ships were in first-class condition, and every man of his crew was still with him and in perfect health. Rarely, if ever, had an explorer returned from uncharted seas with so great a wealth of discovery and so complete an absence of misfortune.

Ross spent two more seasons in the Antarctic. In his second and third voyages he suffered even greater perils—his ships being frozen solid in the pack, coming into violent collision and all but foundering in the lee of an iceberg whose walls literally scraped their rigging; but his discoveries on these occasions were less spectacular.

Not until September 1843 did the *Erebus* and *Terror* finally return to England, to be paid off at Woolwich after a commission of four years and five months—one of the longest and most eventful in naval history.

Ross, on his homecoming, was showered with every kind of honour, both scientific and popular; he was knighted and awarded the gold medal of a host of learned societies; and it might have been supposed that a brilliant future awaited him. But in fact, with the exception of one short voyage in 1848–9, he never put to sea again. He retired, married, went to live in Aylesbury (about as far from the sea as one can get in England!) and devoted the rest of his life to farming and the study of marine invertebrates. It would be no exaggeration to say that he had worn himself out, both physically and mentally, in the service of his three gods.

*   *   *

James Clark Ross is an explorer who is remembered to-day for what he did rather than for what he was.

What he did is soon told. In the last of the great voyages made wholly under sail, he discovered the last of the continents. This was a great achievement. And there is something fitting, I think, in Antarctica being discovered by a ship under sail. For five thousand years sailing vessels had brought grace and beauty to the oceans of the world; it was only just that they should penetrate to the last of the continents before giving way to steam.

What Ross *was* cannot be put so simply; for his personality does not come through to us to-day with the vividness, say, of Magellan's, Quiros's or Cook's. He remains something of an enigma: a God-fearing man who cared for his ship's company, a supremely competent seaman, a fearless ice-navigator and a man of courage and determination; but in character very much a product of his age and environment—a naval officer of the days of Jingoism and the *pax Britannica*, a defender of "my country right or wrong", a hero by Kipling out of Samuel Smiles. His virtues are unfashionable to-day; but he himself would have asked for a no more felicitous valediction than the opening words of his obituary notice: "(he) *was an officer of the Royal Navy who served his country with distinction.*"

THE LAST OCEAN

1. In the voyage of the Jeanette, *1879–81, George Washington De Long pioneers a
route through the heart of the Arctic*

BY the middle of the nineteenth century the face of every ocean but one
had been delineated. What lay under the oceans was still largely an
enigma, but with one exception their coastlines were known and their
winds and currents understood. The exception was the Arctic: an area bigger
than Australasia: five and a half million square miles of virgin sea whose
secrets were guarded by a seemingly impenetrable barrier of ice.

During the seventeenth and eighteenth centuries the English and Dutch
scratched at the edge of this barrier: the English feeling their way along the
coast of Greenland and among the islands of the Canadian north, the Dutch
exploring the shores of Spitzbergen and Novaya Zemlya. It was left to the
youngest of the great nations—America—to venture not merely along the
edge of the ice barrier but deep into its heart. This was a step in polar exploration as bold as it was novel. It ended in tragedy, and, according to the tenets
of the world, in failure. And yet as Mallory wrote on the face of Everest there
are times and places when failure and success mean nothing; and the so-called
failure of De Long and the crew of the *Jeanette* was in fact more glorious than
a multitude of triumphs.

*   *   *

George Washington De Long was born in New York on August 22nd, 1844.
He was an only child, a fact which was the dominating influence in the early
years of his life; for his mother guarded him from the perils of the world with
the care of a fanatic, forbidding him to take part in such "rough sports" as
swimming or sailing, and denying him the companionship of normal friends.
The result was the opposite of what she had hoped. Her son grew up with a
yearning for adventure all the greater for his being so sedulously denied it.
When the boy was twelve he begged his parents to allow him to join the
Navy; but the idea was not well received. Only two professions, Mrs. De
Long decided, were worthy of her son; he must be either a priest or a lawyer.
The yoke of parental discipline was not in those days set lightly aside, and the
summer of 1859 saw De Long duly ensconsed in the offices of the local
attorney. Here he might well have remained for the rest of his life had it not
been for the Civil War. When he suggested enlisting—he was now seventeen
—his parents were adamant in their refusal; but they did at last give grudging
assent to his applying to enter the Naval Academy. He was over-age, and (as
his parents knew) all the year's appointments to the Academy had already
been filled; but De Long now showed the refusal to admit defeat which was

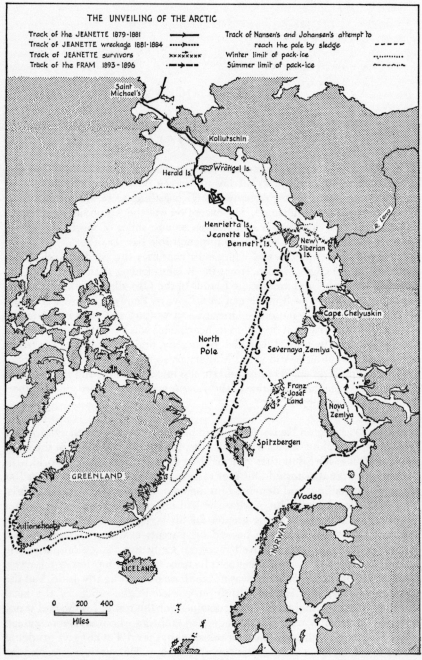

THE UNVEILING OF THE ARCTIC

Track of the JEANETTE 1879-1881
Track of JEANETTE wreckage 1881-1884
Track of JEANETTE survivors
Track of the FRAM 1893-1896
Track of Nansen's and Johansen's attempt to reach the pole by sledge
Winter limit of pack-ice
Summer limit of pack-ice

Saint Michael's
Koliutschin
Herald Is.
Wrangel Is.
Henrietta Is.
Jeanette Is.
Bennett Is.
New Siberian Is.
R. Lena
Cape Chelyuskin
North Pole
Severnaya Zemlya
Franz Josef Land
Nova Zemlya
Spitzbergen
GREENLAND
Vadso
Julianehaab
NORWAY
ICELAND

0   200   400
Miles

Fig. 37.

to take him, twenty years later, into the heart of the polar ice. His application was turned down again and again, but he never gave up and in the end he went to Washington and secured a personal interview with Gideon Welles, the Secretary of the Navy, who was so impressed with the boy's determination that he wrote to the Academy and ordered his immediate acceptance. "*This*," wrote De Long in his diary, "*is the happiest day of my life*."

He graduated in 1865 and in the late autumn was given his first sea-going appointment: midshipman in the U.S.S. *Canadaigua*. For the next eight years his career was unremarkable. Then came the incident which led, indirectly, to the voyage of the *Jeanette*.

In the summer of 1873 the U.S.S. *Juniata* was ordered north to search for the crew of a vessel which had got into difficulties in Melville Bay, and De Long volunteered to accompany her. The *Juniata* pushed as far north as Upernavik (on the 73rd parallel), but was then brought up short by the ice. It was decided to continue the search by cutter, and De Long was given command of the 32-foot sloop-rigged *Little Juniata*, with orders to search as much of Melville Bay as he could "*without jeopardising his ship or the lives of those aboard her*". In the search that followed De Long showed all the qualities which later characterized his leadership of the *Jeanette*: great personal courage, fine seamanship and a determination to gain his objective no matter what the cost; but he showed at the same time his inexperience and a streak of congenital recklessness—traits which the Arctic may forgive once but never twice. For the *Little Juniata* was caught embayed by a storm.

De Long has left a vivid account of what was nearly the end of his first command:

"*Friday, August 8th. By the afternoon the S.E. gale had caused a fearful sea, and working as we were on the edge of the ice pack, our situation became one of great danger. For the wind had started* (to drive) *the Melville Bay pack away from the land, making a bight in which we were fairly placed. The prospect at this time was a terrible one. Ice-bergs near us, one hundred feet in height, had the spray from the sea thrown over their tops; and on being driven towards the edge of the pack we could see a scene of great confusion. The bordering ice would be broken in large pieces, and hurled upon the more solid ice, only to be displaced by fresh pieces torn adrift by the gale, and rolled over and over upon the face of the pack. The fate of the boat appeared certain. We were half buried in the seas and shipping quantities of water. It rained in torrents . . . and the fog was thick, making it difficult to see the ice pack until we were fairly alongside of it, in which case we had to wear ship at once not knowing whether or not we would clear the grinding and crushing mass of ice.*

"*This state of affairs continued until ten o'clock on the morning of Saturday, at which time there came a lull. We had by then been in this heavy gale thirty hours and were in a very cold and exhausted state*".

They managed eventually to struggle back to their ship, after what has been described as "one of the most hazardous and venturesome undertakings in the history of small-boat sailing".

A lesser man might well have been daunted by such an initiation to the Arctic; but De Long saw in the far north a challenger with whom he was all too eager to join battle. His wife, in her biography *The Voyage of the Jeanette*, describes his reaction perfectly. "After the *Juniata* had returned to New York, Lieutenant De Long wrote to the Department tendering his services in event of another Arctic expedition. His indomitable energy, strong will, and passion for overcoming obstacles, all tended to develop in him that Arctic fever which so often fastens upon one who has once known the excitement, difficulty and peril of northern exploration."

But it was not, in fact, the Navy who enabled De Long to renew his battle with the Arctic. It was the *New York Herald*.

James Gordon Bennett, editor of the *Herald*, is chiefly remembered to-day as the man who financed Stanley in his expeditions to Africa; but he was equally interested in polar exploration. De Long was introduced to him early in 1874, and the idea of an expedition financed by the *Herald*, led by De Long and manned by personnel of the U.S. Navy was conceived at their first meeting. Their plans, however, suffered a temporary set-back because of the threat of war between America and Spain, and it was early in 1877 before De Long obtained leave of absence from the Navy Department to look for a suitable vessel.

After a long and frustrating search he found what he wanted in England: the yacht *Pandora*, owned by Sir Allen Young. The *Pandora* had a fine record of previous exploration in the Arctic; but De Long, in face of all the traditions and superstitions of the sea, insisted on renaming her. She was taken to Mare Island in San Francisco, refitted, and rechristened the *Jeanette*.

No expense was spared in her renovation, and the Navy gave De Long every co-operation in providing the best possible equipment and stores. The result was that in May 1879 the *Jeanette* came off the Mare Island slipway like a butterfly out of its chrysalis: a new ship, as near to perfection for work in the ice as the skill of designer and shipwright could make her. De Long was delighted with her—witness his letter to Bennett.

"*Let me tell you what had been done to the ship when I reached her on May 30th. The alterations were complete and the new boilers in place. The bow had been filled in solid and caulked for a distance of ten feet from the stem. A steam winch had been placed on deck forward of the smoke stack, capable of lifting the screw, unshipping the rudder and warping the ship ahead. Amidships was a very heavy system of kneed braces to guard against nips (the shape of the hull with its great dead-rise will also aid the ship in rising to pressure). The thickness of the vessel amidships had been increased to nineteen-and-a-half inches. The whole ship had been caulked and painted. The house for the crew to live in in winter had been built, fitted in place, and taken apart and piled up. A portable observatory had been made, and porches for the cabin doors. New sails throughout had been cut and fitted, as well as an entire new outfit of running rigging. Coal bunkers had been enlarged and new ones added, making her bunker capacity 132 tons instead of 98 tons as formerly. The machinery had been overhauled; new pumps added; new propellor blades cast, and an entire outfit of tools and stores placed aboard. Everything that the navy had on hand was placed at our disposal . . . And finally the ship was turned over to me. I am perfectly satisfied with her. She is everything I want for the expedition. Our outfit is perfect. We have a good crew, good food, and a good ship, and I think we have the right kind of stuff to dare all that men can do.*"

The objectives of the expedition, meanwhile, had been decided.

There are three possible ways of approaching the Arctic Ocean: *via* Spitzbergen, *via* Baffin Bay and *via* the Bering Strait. The first two approaches had been tried and were known to be blocked by ice; the third was largely unknown and was for this reason favoured by both Bennett and De Long. Indeed the more carefully this third route was studied, the more promising it appeared. For the warm water Kuro Shio (the Black Current of Japan) was known to flow northwards through the Bering Strait, and whalers working the Siberian Sea were unanimous in the view that once inside the strait their vessels were invariably drifted north by west; it was therefore expected that the *Jeanette* would have a reasonably easy passage as far as the coast of Wrangel Land. This land—which in fact is an island no larger than Hawaii—was believed in the 1870s to be the start of a vast continental land-mass which spread for some two thousand miles across the Arctic and joined on to Greenland; it was therefore assumed that when De Long had reached Wrangel, he could follow its coastline north as far as was practicable by ship and then proceed overland by sledge to the pole and thence to Greenland. The expedition also had a secondary objective: to discover the whereabouts of the Finnish explorer Nordenskjöld, who had set out the previous summer aboard the *Vega* to attempt the North-East Passage; and doubtless Bennett in particular had hopes that the two explorers would come together on some distant ice-floe in a meeting as dramatic as that of Stanley and Livingstone.

By the end of June 1879 the crew had been chosen—thirty-two officers and men hand-picked from over three thousand volunteers—the equipment and stores were aboard, and in the late morning of July 8th the *Jeanette* stood west out of the Golden Gate.

"*Never,*" wrote her Chief Engineer Melville, "*was departure more auspicious. It was a gala day for the good people of 'Frisco; the harbor was alive with their pleasure craft, and right royal was the farewell they tendered our ship. Cheers rang out from the crowded wharves; the masts and decks of the myriad vessels on the bay teemed with jolly tars huzzaing and firing guns; and as we steamed abreast of the Presidio, a heavy salute boomed forth from the fortification: a solemn amen to the godspeeds of the people.*"

The *Jeanette* stood north for Unalaska. Being heavily laden she was low in the water and made no more than four-and-a-half knots; but as De Long wrote to his wife, "*she* (was) *very dry and comfortable, I might almost say cosy; while the crew* (were) *first class, happy and cheerful*". As they neared the Aleutians they experienced the usual dense fogs and violent tide-rips, but by and large this first part of their voyage was pleasant and uneventful. At Unalaska they coaled, took aboard a number of deer and seal skins, and then stood north for Saint Michael's, a Russian trading-post in Norton Sound.

They reached Saint Michael's on August 12th: none too early for taking advantage of the annual recession of the ice, and were then held up still further by the non-arrival of their collier and supply ship the *Fanny A. Hyde*. De Long waited for her impatiently, using his enforced leisure to exercise the dog-teams and search—unsuccessfully—for news of Nordenskjöld. The supply ship finally put in an appearance on August 18th, and three days later the

Jeanette, her bunkers and holds full to capacity, stood north for the Bering Strait. They were at the approaches now of the unknown.

In fine weather they stood slowly west along the Chukotskiy Khrebet shore, landing whenever they came to a fishing village to ask for news of Nordenskjöld. It was August 31st before they found irrefutable proof of his movements. On landing near Koliutschin Bay, the natives told them that a strange ship—obviously the *Vega*—had wintered in the bay safely and had then stood east, only a month ago, for the Bering Strait. As evidence of this, the natives produced a number of Swedish, Danish and Russian naval buttons which Nordenskjöld, anticipating there might be a search for him, had left behind.

That same evening De Long stood north, happy in the knowledge that Nordenskjöld was safe and that he could now, with a clear conscience, "*set course for Wrangel Land and the Pole*".

It needed less than a fortnight to turn his dreams to dust.

Looking back on the voyage of the *Jeanette* it is possible to see now that the ship and her crew were doomed from the moment they stood out of the Golden Gate: victims of inexperience, poor planning and the inability of their commander to admit defeat. It was inexperience which led them so gravely to under-estimate both the strength and danger of the polar pack-ice. It was bad planning which caused their divided objective and their failure to arrive in the East Siberian Sea until the brief exploring season was almost at an end. And it was De Long's magnificent but tragic obstinacy which kept them in the ice for the better part of two years until their ship sank literally under their feet and they were left with insufficient stores to struggle to safety.

The very first evening they stood out of Koliutschin Bay they had a fore-taste of what was in store; for as De Long noted in his diary they "*were much bothered by loose ice, which required constant conning; and at 10 p.m., the ice growing heavier,* (we) *were forced to tack to the north-east*". Already, on their first day of exploration proper, the ice was establishing its mastery over the ill-fated *Jeanette*.

On their second day out from Koliutschin they made good progress, but on the third they were brought up short by solid pack-ice. For a while they attempted, without success, to force a passage north-westwards towards Wrangel. Then De Long, losing patience, stood the *Jeanette* north-east towards Herald Island where the ice conditions appeared to be less formidable.

Within forty-eight hours they were caught fast as a fly in amber.

De Long's diary—which Markham has described as "perhaps the most interesting of all polar documents"—gives a vivid picture of how their predicament built up: first their somewhat naïve annoyance at finding they could not make good the course they wished; then their resignation at finding themselves trapped; and finally, as they realized they were being borne inexorably north-west, away from land, the first faint doubts as to their fate.

"*September 5th, Friday*," wrote De Long—"*A clear and pleasant day throughout, with light northerly breeze. At 4 a.m. spread all fires and got a full head of steam, and entered the pack through the best looking lead in the general direction of Herald Island.*

THE FARTHEST ENDS OF THE EARTH

For the first two hours we had but little trouble in making our way, but at 6 a.m. we commenced to meet young ice ranging from one to two inches in thickness in the leads, and seemingly growing tougher as we proceeded. We ground along, however, scratching and in places scoring and cutting and doubling, until 8.40 a.m., when we came to pack ice from ten to fifteen feet in thickness, which of course brought us up . . . At 1 p.m., seeing another chance to make a mile or two, we got up steam and worked ahead through thin, new ice, and between detached pieces of floe. At four we anchored and banked fires.

"September 6th, Saturday—This is a glorious country to learn patience in. I am hoping and praying to be able to get the ship to Herald Island to make winter quarters. But as far as the eye can range is ice, and not only does it look as though it had never been broken up, it also looks as though it never will. Yesterday I hoped that to-day would make an opening for us; to-day I hope that tomorrow will do it. I suppose a gale of wind would break the pack up, but then the pack might break us up! This morning shows some pools of thin ice and water, but as they are disconnected, and we can not jump the ship over obstructions, they are of no use to us. A light northerly wind with a steady barometer, and a temperature ranging between 23° and 32°. At 1 p.m. the fog lifted, and we saw a chance of making about a mile towards the island. Spread fires again and commenced forcing our way, ramming whenever we were opposed, and with good effect. Ramming a ship through ice from ten to fifteen feet thick is of course impossible, but wherever a crack or narrow opening showed between two floes we could by judicious ramming and backing and ramming again shove them apart enough to squeeze through. Our steam winch did good service, for we could easily snub the ship's head into a weak place when we did not have room to turn her with the helm. At 4.20, however, we had come to solid floes again, and the fog closing in we came-to with our ice anchor. Wishing to save coal, I let the fires die out. This evening three bears came down to within a mile of the ship. Served out snow-goggles to all hands.

"September 7th, Sunday—A day of complete rest in every respect. The day begins with snow, clears, becomes and ends foggy. Ice shifting a little, and the ship seemingly moving to the N.W. At 10 a.m. muster the crew and hold divine service. At 12 got soundings in forty fathoms. In the watch from eight to midnight, experienced a slight pressure on the starboard beam, shoving the ship up on a tongue of ice and listing her 5° to starboard.

"September 8th, Monday—At 1.30 this morning the ship righted again. Thermometer ranging between 22° and 28°. Forenoon foggy; afternoon clear. No sign of a lead in any direction. The northerly winds seem to have cemented the ice into one enormous pack. Soundings at noon in thirty-six fathoms—so we have evidently moved since yesterday. In the first watch the ship heeled suddenly to starboard about 9°, and jammed the rudder hard a-starboard . . .

"September 9th, Tuesday—A superb day; bright sunlight, and the thermometer ranging between 21° and 25°. But no sign of a lead in any direction . . . Ship still heeled 9° to starboard, and great pressure on the rudder casing. We tried all day to explode torpedoes under the stern but our slow-match was defective and would not burn and we could not get an electric current through our non-insulated copper wire . . .

"September 10th, Wednesday—Calm from midnight to noon, with fog, mist and snow the rest of the day. Lowest temperature 16°, highest 25°. In the hope of helping the ship to right herself, got two tackles up, one at the foremast head and one at the mainmast head, hooking them to ice-claws, and setting them well taut. Broke away the ice around the stern and attempted sawing with ice saws, but with no other effect than to bend the

saws. The soundings of the past few days have steadily decreased: forty, thirty-six, thirty-five, thirty-two-and-a-half fathoms. So the whole pack, with ourselves fast in it, is evidently drifting—possibly this shoaling indicates an approach to Herald Island, but we cannot prove this until we get observations again for a position. Not a sign of a lead in any direction.

"September 11th, Thursday—The ship has not yet righted . . . and I am reluctantly forced to the conclusion that we must unship the rudder. A more severe nip might break the gudgeons or bend the pintles, and we might not only lose our rudder but also the means of shipping the spare one. Accordingly the rudder is unshipped (with great difficulty, owing to the small water space) and triced up to its davits, across the stern. A thick mist prevented us from seeing the island all day. Soundings at noon in 29 fathoms: still shoaling. Leaving the lead on the bottom, we found we were being carried away from it towards the NORTH WEST.

"September 12th, Friday—The day opened and continued calm and misty with occasional flurries of snow. The only thing to break the monotony was the catching of a dog in one of the bear traps . . . This inaction is most disagreeable, and it is even more disagreeable to see no chance for a change. The only hope of the pack breaking up is the occurrence of a gale; and as the weather has been so uniformly calm since our being beset that the ice has become well solidified, it will require a heavy gale to make a change. Meanwhile, we are getting no nearer to Herald Island; indeed we are making no advance in any direction, unless we are really drifting, ice and all, to the N.W. It is unpleasant to realise that our exploration for a whole year should come to a stop on September 6th. My disappointment is great, how great no one else will probably ever know. I had hoped to accomplish something new in the first summer, but we have done nothing."

In the next couple of days De Long made two other disquieting discoveries. A sledge party which he sent to Herald Island, returned after twenty-four hours with the news that there was neither wood on the island nor the slightest semblance of a harbour. So even if it proved possible to force the *Jeanette* inshore, there was no hope of her wintering there. The second discovery concerned their water. They had hoped that melted floes would provide reasonable drinking water, but the ice hemming in the *Jeanette* was undeniably salt; it had to be distilled; and this used up fuel. De Long himself led a sledge party in search of ice that was tolerably salt-free, and they eventually located a large "snowball" which gave off no more than four grains of chlorine to the gallon; since this was the least saline of the samples so far taken, they hauled it back to the ship. But De Long, that evening, told the surgeon to experiment, as a matter of urgency, with new methods of distilling.

The next day, September 15th, dawned bright and clear, and they were at last able to take accurate observations. *"At noon," wrote De Long, "we were in latitude 71° 46' N, longtitude 175° 36' W; and comparing this with our position on September 9th we found we had moved 15 miles to the N.W., i.e. we were drifting at the rate of 2½ miles a day away from Herald Island. At this rate we may, if the drift continues, reach land before spring. This is faint consolation, but it seems our only one; for from the masthead we can see nothing but a field of ice. If there is indeed a continuous current we shall test it by our drift this winter, and may perhaps be carried to some new land. But as to making any progress with the ship by our own efforts, I see no chance;*

PACK ICE

PRESSURE RIDGES IN THE CONSOLIDATED PACK

for it looks as if it would take an earthquake to get us out of our besetment. However,
'the darkest hour is just before the dawn', and our dawn may be soon coming."

There were, however, to be no more rose-tinted dawns for the *Jeanette*: only a gradual recession of hope as the winter closed in and the drift carried them inexorably north by west, ever deeper into the friendless wastes of the Arctic.

During October the mists gave way to snow, and the temperature dropped —on the first day of the month it was plus 20°, on the last minus 11°. Their drifting became erratic: so many days to the north, so many days to the west, then back again to the east until Herald Island came once more into sight; and all the while the ice grew thicker and the pressure on the *Jeanette's* hull increasingly unbearable.

But in spite of their incarceration the crew remained cheerful. No commander ever did more for his men than De Long, who was for ever improvising improvements for their welfare: now drilling holes in the door panels to increase ventilation, now experimenting with better pipes for the heating, now supervising the more efficient purification of their drinking water. They had, as yet, plenty of fuel, and seemingly unlimited supplies of food. In fact, ironically, the crew ate better that winter than almost any other polar expedition before or since. Here is their menu for a typical day (Sunday, September 28th).

Breakfast		Dinner	
Beef	8 lb	Ox-Tail soup	12 lb
Oatmeal	7 lb	Roast bear	26 lb
Potatoes	15 lb	Pork	4 lb
Bread	10 lb	String Beans	12 lb
Sugar	$4\frac{1}{16}$ lb	Potatoes	10 lb
Coffee	$4\frac{1}{8}$ lb	Beets	$4\frac{1}{2}$ lb
Butter	1 lb	Jelly	$\frac{1}{2}$ lb
Milk	$\frac{1}{2}$ lb	Hard bread	1 lb
		Raisins	3 lb
		Flour (Duff)	16 lb
Total	$49\frac{11}{16}$ lb	*Total*	89 lb

Supper	
Mutton	8 lb
Potatoes	15 lb
Damsons	6 lb
Pears	2 lb
Flour	6 lb
Yeast-powder	$\frac{1}{4}$ lb
Ginger	$\frac{1}{4}$ lb
Bread	15 lb
Sugar	$4\frac{1}{16}$ lb
Tea	1 lb
Milk	$\frac{1}{2}$ lb
Butter	1 lb
Total	$59\frac{1}{16}$ lb

Number of crew: 33 Total weight of food: $197\frac{3}{4}$ lb Average per man: 6 lb

This high consumption of food is all the more surprising when one remembers that the crew were comparatively inactive. For apart from stoking the fires, collecting snow for their drinking water and keeping the decks clean and ice-free, there was little for them to do. Their observations took no more than a few minutes every day, their hunting was almost invariably carried out within sight of the ship, and their winter routine could hardly have been easier.

This routine on and after November 1st was as follows: "*6 a.m., Call executive officer: 7, Call ship's cook: 8.30, Call all hands: 9, Breakfast by watches: 10, Turn-to, clear fire hole of ice, fill barrels with snow, clean up decks: 11, Clear forecastle, all hands to exercise on the ice: 11.30, Inspection by executive officer: 12 m., Take soundings: 1 p.m., One watch below: 2, Fill barrels with snow, clear fire hole of ice: 3, Dinner by watches: 4, Galley fires out, carpenter and boatswain report departments to executive officer: 7.30, Supper by watches: 10, Pipe down, noise and smoking to cease in forecastle, all lights to be put out except one burner of bulkhead lantern, man on watch report to executive, during the night anchor-watch to examine fires and lights every half hour.*" Seldom if ever in the history of exploration can a ship's company have been condemned to do so little for so long.

November saw a temporary end to the snow and the onset of fine clear weather. It was bitterly cold now with the average daily temperature down to minus twenty while the ice appeared to be set completely solid—"*The ship,*" wrote De Long, "*rides firm and steady as if in dry dock.*" But the illusion of solidarity was soon to be shattered. For the ice in fact was constantly on the move, great floes hundreds of miles square being driven this way and that by the winds and currents, and now coming into violent and terrible collision, now piling up in shoal water into reefs of confusion. Here is De Long's account of the events of November 11th.

"*Tuesday—A day of great anxiety. At 6.10 a.m. I was awakened by the trembling and creaking of the ship, and the man on watch came to inform me that the ice was in motion. Hastily dressing I went on deck. The grinding and crushing flow of ice to the westward had commenced, and the jamming of large pieces splintering into our floe caused great breaks and upheavals to within 75 feet of the ship. The vessel groaned and creaked at every squeeze until I thought the next would break her apart. The pressure was tremendous, and the noise not calculated to calm one's mind. I know of no sound that can be compared to it: a rumble, a shriek, a groan and the crash of a falling house all combined might serve to convey it. Great masses, twenty five foot in height, are sliding along at various angles of elevation and jam, and between and among them are large and confused masses of débris, like a marble yard adrift. Occasionally a stoppage occurs—some piece has caught against or under our floe; then comes a groaning and cracking; our floe bends and humps up in domes. Crash! a dome splits, another piece of floe breaks off, the pressure is relieved, and on again goes the flowing mass of rumbles, shrieks and groans etc. The performance lasted for half an hour . . . Then at 4.20 p.m. the excitement began again, and this time we had it heavily for four hours . . . The pressure was greater than we had ever experienced it before. To the ice rushing and growling alongside us I did not pay much attention; but a break in the floe directly across our bow gave me serious concern, for I saw the piled up ice advancing towards us seemingly as fast as a man could walk. It bore down directly upon us. At each grind, it piled up floebergs in front of it, and the ship shook and trembled. From my post on top of the deck-house the view was magnificent though awful. I fully expected we should be swept away into the grinding stream, and as the approaching ice made a more startling advance than usual, I grasped the mainstay to keep my place when the final crash should come. All hands had been called and stood ready, although there was really nothing to be done. But at 6.25, when the advancing wall was only 25 feet from our stem, the pressure suddenly ceased, and all was quiet."*

Nor does this description over-emphasize the dangers which from now on continually hemmed in the *Jeanette*, almost in fact the contrary: witness this description of the same day given by Chief Engineer Melville.

"When off the most north-easterly point of Wrangel Land the ship found shoaling water at sixteen fathoms, and as the floe crowded by the island it was cast up in great ridges; cracks ran across it in all directions, and the grinding and crashing of the tortured masses sounded like the roar of distant artillery. On November 11th the ship became entirely surrounded by the towering telescoping hills of ice. Huge floe-bergs, large as churches, bobbed up and down like whales. The situation was most perilous; for even if the vessel could sustain the enormous pressure brought to bear on her, there was imminent danger of the hummocks and 'bits', weighing anything up to fifty tons, toppling over—as they were on all sides—and crushing or burying her. In view of the impending disaster, preparations were made to abandon ship—a hopeless task . . . Soon the poor Jeanette began to crash and groan under the immense strain. Her decks bulged upwards; the oakum and pitch were squeezed out of her seams; and a bucket of water standing on her quarter-deck was half emptied by the agitation. Yet the discipline of the ship's company was perfect; they sang and joked with apparent sang froid while they cleared the decks of ice and levered away the overhanging masses that were crushing in the bulwarks. And at last the floe gave way, and the ship once again was still and quiet."

Such scenes were to be repeated many times in the next twenty-one months, and it was not long before the *Jeanette* was leaking badly—for a year and a half her pumps were manned continuously, night and day. Yet De Long never lost hope. The greater the discomforts and dangers he had to face, the more vehemently he clung to his belief that "the darkest hour is just before the dawn". Again and again these words appear in his diary. They occur on September 15th, 1879, only a few days after his ship's initial besetment in the ice; they occur again on September 21st, 1881, only a few days before his death; and how many times in between! This was De Long's tragedy and his glory: that he never knew when he was beaten: that no matter how darkly the sun set to-day, he always imagined it would rise gold tomorrow.

And so the *Jeanette* drifted on, tugged this way and that by the currents of an ocean into whose heart no vessel had ever ventured before.

For the most part their companions were cold, monotony, and a danger all the more to be feared because they could do nothing to avoid it or fight it. But there were moments of compensation: the friendship and humour of men thrown unusually close together, and, on days and nights that were fine, the beauty of the Arctic.

A great deal of nonsense has been written about the beauty of "the great white north"—usually by people who have never set foot beyond the Arctic Circle. For beauty is very largely in the eye of the beholder, and the delights of 50° of frost are better appreciated from in front of a log fire than from the deck of a ship that is being squeezed to death by the ice. De Long's diary is proof of this. Its early pages are full of passages of lyrical beauty — *"Imagine a moon nearly full, a cloudless sky, brilliant stars, a pure white waste of snow-covered ice, and in the foreground the ship standing out in bold relief, her every rope and wire enlarged by glittering frost."* But before long the sense of beauty is tainted by disillusion — *"Sometimes I go out onto the ice on these beautiful evenings and try to find words to express my feelings, but a lot of dogs wrangling over an empty meat can surround me and drag me down to matter of fact; so I take my half frozen nose tenderly in my hand and lead myself back to the ship . . . Attempts to be poetical may be praiseworthy, but I shall give them up. My sensation of being in a critical situation is too keen to allow me to write in cold blood about the beauties of ice scenery; so I will simply say that the pack is no place for a ship, and however beautiful it may be, I wish with all my heart that we were out of it."*

But his wish was not to be granted. As the old year gave way to the new, a series of gales not only drove the *Jeanette* still deeper into the pack-ice but came close to giving her the *coup de grâce*. Here is Melville's description of January 19th.

"Each gale was followed by the jamming up of the floes; and it was observed that during the continuance of the wind the whole body of ice moved evenly before it, but when it subsided, the mass that had been put in motion crowded and tumbled on upon the floes at rest, piling them tumultuously upward in a manner terrible to behold.

"It was in one of these oppressive intervals succeeding a gale, when the roar and crash of the distant masses could be distinctly heard, that the floe in which the Jeanette was imbedded began splitting in all directions. The placid and almost level surface of the ice suddenly heaved and swelled into great hills. Giant blocks pitched and rolled as though controlled by invisible hands, and the compressed bodies shrieked a shrill and horrible song that curdled the blood. The frozen waves advanced nearer and nearer. Seams ran and rattled across them with a thundering boom, while silent and awestruck we could only watch their terrible approach. The ship lay sunk in an amphitheatre, about ⅝ mile in diameter, with the moving banks of ice, fifty feet high, gradually closing in on her from all sides. Preparations were made for her abandonment; but — what then? If the circle continued to decrease, escape was hopeless and death inevitable. For to think of scrambling up the slippery sides of the rolling masses would be of equal folly with an attempt to scale the falling waters of Niagara.

"The ice is approaching at the rate of one yard a minute. It is three hundred paces distant; so in three hundred minutes we shall pass over to the Great Beyond."

Thus one of the crew announced his computation. And it is certain that had the Jeanette been two hundred yards in any direction from the exact spot she occupied on the floe, she would have been overwhelmed and destroyed by the grinding masses, as surely as a crab on the beach is buried beneath the roll of the surf. But her time had not yet come. The terrible circle slowly contracted to within a couple of hundred feet — and then stopped. And all was quiet, save the roar of the under-running floes at the bottom of the ship."

The ice walls had barely ground to a halt when one of the crew came scrambling up from the hold, and a second later the cry rang round the ship:

"Man the pumps!"

Under the pressure of the churned-up floes the *Jeanette's* hull had been split, and water was pouring into her bilges. It poured in fast, so fast that there was barely time to light the fires to provide the steam-pump with pressure before it came swirling into the boiler-room. Waist-deep in freezing slush the crew strove frantically to stem the flood, plugging oakum into the splits, baling out with barrels, and working non-stop on the hand-pumps; and by 3 p.m. water was being discharged from the *Jeanette* at the rate of 2,500 gallons an hour. Yet so fierce was the inrush that the pumps could do little more than hold their own. For several days the issue hung in the balance; but at last, inch by hard-won inch, the water level was lowered; oakum, plaster-of-Paris, ashes and felt were rammed into the splits; and by January 25th the leaks had been brought under control. But they were never conquered. For the next eighteen months the pumps were obliged to labour non-stop, night and day, to keep the water level constant; and by the end of her voyage over twenty-five million gallons had been pumped out of the tortured vessel. The effect can be easily imagined. Everything aboard the *Jeanette* became impregnated with damp: witness De Long's diary—"*Pump, pump, pump: the same old story. As soon as we pump out, the water comes in . . . The ship is wretchedly wet and uncomfortable. The berth deck is kept moist from the endless travel along it; the galley room is wet from dripping from the auxiliary pump; the deck-house is wet from the Baxter, and the quarter-deck is covered with ice or sludge from the fire-hose discharge. But,*"—and here we have it again—"*as the darkest hour is just before the dawn, we will surely have a bright spot in our future.*"

But there were to be no "bright spots" in store for the *Jeanette*. And the events of the next eighteen months can be summed up in the single heartfelt cry from De Long's diary: "*August 12th, 1880—How long, O Lord, how long?*"

For the prospect of their imprisonment stretched on and on with no foreseeable end. When it was winter they longed for spring, and the return of the sun; when it was spring they longed for summer and the recession of the ice; but when summer came the ice melted only sufficiently to move the floes and increase their leaks and never enough to free them, and they longed for the more solid ice of autumn; autumn brought storms and the shifting of floes, so that they longed for the frozen stillness of mid-winter. And so the year moved full circle, and they were still a mere two hundred miles from where they had entered the ice, with such high hopes, in the autumn of 1879. "*People beset in the pack before,*" wrote De Long, "*have always been carried to some land; but we are drifting about like a modern Flying Dutchman, never getting anywhere, but always restless and on the move. Coals are burning-up, food is being consumed, and thirty-three people are wearing out their lives and souls like men doomed to imprisonment for life.*"

A less able commander would almost certainly have been faced with discontent and sickness; but De Long managed to keep his ship's company remarkably fit and cheerful. This was emphasized by the subsequent Court of Inquiry: "*In view of the long and dreary monotony of the cruise, the labors and privations encountered, the disappointments consequent upon a want of important results, and the uncertainty of their fate, the general conduct of the personnel of the expedition seems to have been a marvel of cheerfulness, good-fellowship and mutual forbearance.*"

As for sickness, the *Jeanette* had been in the ice for a year and a half before the outbreak of any serious illness: and then, surprisingly, their enemy was not the anticipated scurvy.

By their second spring in the pack-ice the crew were all decidedly pale — "*like vegetables bleached in the dark*"—and were all suffering from a certain degree of debility; this was to be expected; but in May 1881 about a dozen of them were attacked by something far more serious: colic, stomach cramp and violent nausea. After a series of tests the doctor diagnosed lead-poisoning. But where did the lead come from? Their drinking water was an immediate suspect, but this on analysis was found to be lead-free; and it needed a co-incidence one evening during a wardroom supper to see the mystery solved. The menu that night included roast guillemot and canned tomatoes, and in the body of one of the birds, which had been shot only the day before, an officer discovered two or three grains of shot; this turned their conversation to their cases of lead-poisoning—though all agreed that these could hardly have been brought about by a few pieces of shot. Then Melville discovered a pellet of solder embedded in his tomato.

"Hey," he exclaimed, "who shot the tomatoes!"

The doctor took the pellet eagerly and at once turned his investigation to their tins of fruit and vegetables. He discovered that certain brands were soldered at their junctions with equal parts of tin and lead, and that this solder had been eaten away by the fruit's acid and had formed a deposit of black oxide of lead, often in the form of little pellets, at the bottom of the tins. And this they had been absorbing regularly for months.

It was soon after curing themselves of this poisoning that they sighted land.

It was only a tiny island, little more than a lump of volcanic rock; but after eighteen months of drifting in a wilderness of ice it seemed desirable as the greenest oasis. And a few days later another island rose black above the horizon. De Long sent sledge parties to both, claiming them for the United States, and christening them Henrietta and Jeanette.

The ship meanwhile was being carried west with gathering purpose and momentum. In the first year of her drift she had zigzagged hither and thither, and had covered a great-circle distance of a mere 200 miles (an average of seventeen miles a month). But in the last three months—February to May 1881—she covered a great-circle distance of 400 miles (an average of over 120 miles a month). It was obvious that at long last they were in the grip of a powerful north-west-flowing current. But the *Jeanette*, ironically, was to gain little advantage from this current. For she was breaking up.

Early in June 1881 the floe in which she was wedged began to disintegrate. The ship had been in the ice now for twenty-one months; she had been battered, squeezed, listed, tugged this way and that, and subjected to a thousand unendurable pressures. Now, under the renewed assault of the ice, her old wounds opened and she began to list and to fill. The wonder was not that she died now but that she had lived so long.

She was abandoned in good time and in good order, almost everything of value being transferred to the ice some hours before she went to the bottom — for De Long had been preparing for this eventuality for the last eighteen months.

"*On June 11th,*" he wrote, "*Mr. Melville reported a break across the ship aft of the boilers, showing that so solidly were the stern and starboard quarters held by the ice that the ship was breaking in two from the upward pressure exerted on the port bow. It soon became evident that the starboard side of the ship was breaking in, because water was rising rapidly in the starboard coal bunkers. Orders were given to land one half of the pemmican from the deck-house, and all the bread from on deck; the sleds and dogs were likewise carried to safety. At 4.30 there was a lull in the pressure, and it was assumed that the ice had united under the ship—which was now heeled 22° to starboard —and that we would suffer no further injury for the moment . . . But at 5 p.m. the pressure was renewed, and continued with tremendous force, the ship cracking in every part. The spar-deck commenced to buckle, and the starboard side seemed on the point of caving in. Orders were now given to get out provisions, clothing, bedding, ship's books and papers, and to move the sick to safety. While engaged in this work another tremendous pressure was received, and at 6 p.m. it was found that the ship was beginning to fill. From that time forward every effort was devoted to getting provisions etc. on to the ice, and this was not desisted from until the water had risen to the spar deck, and the ship, heeled 30° to starboard, was settling fast. Our ensign had been hoist to the mizzen, and every preparation made for abandoning; and at 8 p.m. the ship's company was ordered to leave the ship. Assembling on the floe, we dragged our boats and provisions clear of bad cracks and prepared to camp for the night.*"

FIG 38. The sinking of *Jeanette*

The *Jeanette* did not, in fact, go down till the small hours of June 12th. Here is Melville's account of her last moments:

"*Towards four o'clock the man on watch cried: 'Turn out if you want to see the last of the Jeanette. There she goes!'*

"*We had barely time to rouse up, when, amid the rattling and banging of timber and ironwork, the ship righted and stood for a moment almost upright. The floes that had crushed her backed slowly away; and then she began to sink, with slightly accelerated velocity, her yard arms stripped and broken upwards parallel to the masts. So, like a great gaunt skeleton clapping its hands above its head, she plunged out of sight . . . We saw her go down with mingled sadness and relief. We were now utterly isolated, and beyond any rational hope of aid. Yet in a way we were satisfied, knowing that the ship's usefulness had long ago passed away, and that we could now start at once—the sooner the better—on our long march to the south."*

Few ships ever did more to explore the face of the oceans than the *Pandora-Jeanette*. She had sailed the Ivory and the Malabar coasts; she had pushed north into Peel, Smith and Lancaster Sounds; and now, albeit unwittingly, she was pioneering a route across the last of the oceans. For the sinking of the *Jeanette* was by no means her end. Her ghost walked the ice-fields of the Arctic, flying bright signal-flags for those who had the courage and vision to read.

And the man who read the signals most clearly was Fridtjof Nansen: the last of the great explorers, the man who, following De Long's footsteps, was twelve years later to prove his theories and realize his dreams.

With the loss of the *Jeanette* De Long was in trouble, stranded five hundred miles from Siberia on ice that was drifting steadily off-shore. Yet he seems to have been unaware of the seriousness of his predicament. For a week he remained close to the spot where his ship had gone down, sorting stores and preparing boats and sleds for the long haul south. His decision not to move off until *"all our preparations* (were) *well made"* was undoubtedly sound. But his observation of June 13th that *"we are living royally on good things, and not working very hard"* indicates an optimism which events were to prove tragically misplaced.

They moved off on June 18th taking with them:

2 Cutters	5 Sleds
1 Whaleboat	3 Boat sleds
6 tents	270 lb coffee
33 packed knapsacks	36 lb cocoa
33 sleeping-bags	100 lb tea
5 cooking-stoves	4,950 lb pemmican
2 medicine chests	1,120 lb bread
39 blankets etc.	500 lb sugar
131 items spare clothing	205 lb tobacco
2,000 rounds ammunition	150 lb cheese
5 gall. whisky	270 lb soup
2 gall. whisky in lime juice	260 gall. alcohol
1 gall. brandy	282 lb canned meats
7 bottles brandy	42 lb onions
½ barrel lime juice	18 lb pickles
75 bottles malt extract	120 lb chocolate

And De Long seems to have had no doubts but that these supplies would see him through to the mouth of the Lena. In fact, he was so certain of this that he left behind on the ice not only a number of dinghies and sleds but also "many provisions".

They set out on June 18th, and ran at once into the most appalling difficulties.

The ice was at its worst in June, thawed sufficiently to make sled-hauling a nightmare, and yet insufficiently for them to take to the boats. Their runners split, their dogs sank up to their necks in slush, their boots were cut to ribbons on hard under-water ice, and it took them six journeys to haul their supplies from one depot to the next. On some days, after toiling almost non-stop from 6 a.m. to 6 p.m. they progressed a mere three-quarters of a mile.

By the end of the first week they calculated that they had covered thirty miles, heading south. But when De Long took his weekly observations, they found that they were farther than ever from the mouth of the Lena. For the ice on which they were travelling had drifted fifty-two miles to the north-west.

"*Nil desperandum*," wrote the unquenchable De Long, "*I shall have to modify my course.*"

The events of the next four months are among the most harrowing in the history of exploration.

De Long fought for the lives of his ship's company with courage, skill and a patience that was almost saint-like. Realizing their first necessity was to escape from the north-west-drifting pack, he altered course towards the New Siberian Islands. Their path was over slippery and uneven ice, covered by two feet of water and slush, and criss-crossed by sea-lanes over which their sleds had to be floated, and by solid floes over which their boats had to be hauled. Visibility was cut by swirling banks of fog, and the ice tore their boots to ribbons — within ten days they were walking barefoot.

On July 29th they struggled ashore on to Bennett Island, the most northerly of the New Siberians. But there was neither food nor shelter here: only steeply shelving scree which glissaded on top of them wherever they pitched camp. On this desolate shore they were marooned for ten days by a blizzard. Their supplies were running low by now and their strength beginning to ebb:

"*August 4th, Thursday — I do not remember ever to have passed a more disagreeable and uncomfortable day. Outside the tents the wind blew in such fierce gusts that it was hard to keep one's footing on the small pieces of ice left to us, while the driving snow and hail made it impossible to remain exposed. Inside the tents it was wet and cold and dreary. Packed close as we were, moving around was out of the question, and our feet were seemingly freezing all the time. We could do nothing but sit and like it . . .*"

Next day they killed half their dogs — "*the amount of food they eat is not compensated for by the work they do*". But the following day, August 6th, the weather cleared, and in bright sun and occasional flurries of snow they began the last stage of their journey: the voyage to the mouth of the Lena.

They were clear of the solid pack-ice now, and were able to row or sail, with only the occasional portage over a floe too big to be rounded. Four hundred miles away at the mouth of the Lena their maps indicated a number of villages, and once they reached these De Long imagined that their troubles would be over. What he failed to realize was that his maps were pitiably inaccurate: that the villages were wrongly placed, and, what is more, were inhabited only during the summer, and that even now as he was struggling mile by painful mile towards them, the Russians were beginning to pull back from the coast towards the comparative shelter of the hinterland.

Among the islands the going was difficult. In the south a water-sky beckoned them on; but they had not yet fought clear of the last of the pack-ice, and broken floes, some of them several miles in length, were drifting across their line of advance. Some days they could only lie up, listening to the roar of the autumn storms and watching the snow as it slanted thick and fast out of a leaden sky; some days their boats were driven backwards by adverse currents and winds; often they had to cover many miles, winding in and out of the floes, in order to make a few yards of progress; often too the winds were so fierce they dare not hoist sail but were obliged to row, the water solidifying to ice as it slopped over the thwarts. But at times they made good progress. Twice they found piles of driftwood and lit themselves the sort of roaring fire that brought back hope and the will to live; once they shot a deer; and on September 1st—eighty-one days after the sinking of the *Jeanette*—they came to open sea. Here, on the tip of Semenovsky Island, they were delayed for yet another week by blizzards; and by the time they were able to leave they had supplies for less than a fortnight. But they were now separated from the mouth of the Lena by less than ninety miles of ice-free water, and De Long's hopes were high. The events of the next few days, however, were to decide his fate. On September 12th the three boats were caught in open sea by a gale. They were separated. One foundered, and her ship's company were never heard of again. Another, under the command of Chief Engineer Melville, was driven to the east of the Lena delta; here, providentially, they were washed ashore close to the one village that was still inhabited, and were saved. But the third boat, under the command of De Long, was not so fortunate; they were driven on to the north-west tip of the delta; there were no villages here, no food and no shelter; and between the first day of October and the last her ship's company perished one by one of starvation, cold and physical exhaustion.

In words that have no trace of self-pity or bitterness De Long's diary describes their hopeless struggle against the onset of the Siberian winter. *"Grounded about a mile and a half from land in a piled-up mass of thin ice and about eighteen inches of water. Decided to unload and wade ashore, but found we were so weak after our exposure in the boat that we could not raise our legs to break the ice but had to push feebly through it . . . The land is soaking wet all the time, and so of course are we. Snow, hail or sleet is pretty well continuous . . . During the night we wake up frequently, shivering with cold. All of us have lost all feeling in our toes, and some of us in our feet and half way up our legs . . . We now have only 3½ days' supply of pemmican and have finished the last of our canned meats . . . Ericksen lay down in the snow this morning, asking us to leave him . . ."* On September 21st, on rounding a bend in the river, they stumbled across a pair of deserted huts; and that evening they shot a deer. *"Well done!"* wrote De Long. *"The darkest hour is just before the dawn."* But the deer meat was all gone in a week. *"October 3rd, Monday—One hundred and thirteenth day. At midnight it was so unbearably cold and wretched that I served out tea, and on that we managed to struggle along until 5 a.m. Our remaining food now consists of four-fourteenths pounds pemmican each, and one half starved dog. May God incline unto our aid. How much farther we have to go before reaching a settlement He alone knows . . . October 5th, Wednesday—One hundred and fifteenth day. S.W. gale continues. Mortification has set in in Ericksen's leg and he is sinking. Nothing to eat until evening . . . October 12th, Wednesday—One hundred and twenty-second day. Breakfast: our last spoonful of glycerine and hot water. Everybody getting weaker and weaker. S.W. gale. We are in the hands of God, and unless He intervenes we are lost.*" Towards the middle of the month the entries in De Long's diary become briefer; by the end of the month they record only the date and the deaths, one by one, of his ship's company. The last entry reads: "*October 30th, Sunday —140th day. Boyd and Gortz died during night. Mr. Collins dying.*" And soon after this, probably on October 31st, De Long ended his two-and-a-half-year battle with the Siberian Arctic.

*   *   *

To outward appearances the voyage of the *Jeanette* had ended in tragedy and failure. Yet in two widely different ways the death of her ship's company was a consummation rather than a defeat.

For although the Arctic murdered De Long and his crew, it was never able to break their spirit. De Long's wife hammers this point home in the closing words of her biography: "*The Voyage of the Jeanette* is the record of men subjected to even severer pressure by the forces of nature than their ship. The ship gave way, but the men kept their courage and faith to the end . . . The scientific results of the expedition were far less than had been aimed at, and it has been said that too high a price was paid for the knowledge that was obtained. But not by such cold calculation is human endeavour measured . . ." Mrs. De Long, of course, was writing a panegyric. But her eulogy has a basis of truth. There have been many more competent explorers than De Long, but none more steadfast or more courageous; and the manner in which he met his death bears witness for all time to the unconquerable spirit of man.

And by one of the most ironic twists in all the history of exploration, De Long and his ship achieved in death the goal they had failed to realize in life. For the great polar current sweeps everything before it, ship or wreck, man or body, clothing or dog; and in the summer of 1884, almost exactly three years after their death, the remains of the *Jeanette* were washed up on a shore the opposite side of the world to where they had died.

For those who had eyes to see, the lesson was plain. The voyage of the *Jeanette* ended not with her sinking off the islands of Siberia, but with the grounding of her wreckage three years later on the south-western tip of Greenland.

2. In the drift of the Fram, *1893–6, Fridtjof Nansen crosses the last of the oceans by the route dreamed of by De Long*

It was the bird that first attracted their attention: the single raven, diving, soaring and diving again over an ice floe at the mouth of the fjord. The place

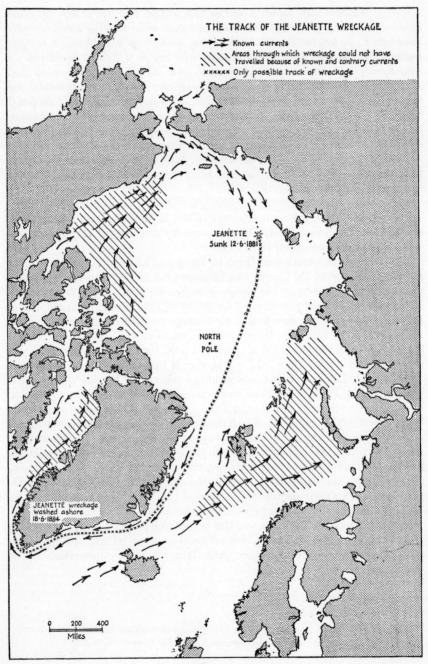

THE TRACK OF THE JEANETTE WRECKAGE

→→ Known currents

▨ Areas through which wreckage could not have
travelled because of known and contrary currents

××××× Only possible track of wreckage

JEANETTE
Sunk 12·6·1881

NORTH
•
POLE

JEANETTE wreckage
washed ashore
18·6·1884

0   200   400
Miles

FIG 39.

was Julianehaab, in south-west Greenland; the date June 18th, 1884; and the men a trio of Eskimo fishermen long-lining the fjord for bass and cod. The raven continued to swoop and soar as the Eskimos, intrigued, worked their kayaks towards the floe, and soon they could see the object of the bird's attention—the flotsam embedded half in and half out of the ice: a cotton sock, a pair of oilskin trousers, the remains of a tent, a seal- and dog-skin boot, splinters of wood and scraps of paper. They salvaged as many remnants as they could from the disintegrating floe, and took them to Carl Lytzen, the Danish *Kolonibestryrer* at Julianehaab.

Lytzen examined the flotsam with care. He noted that the oilskin trousers were marked with the name Louis Noros (one of the survivors of the *Jeanette*), and that a scrap of paper bore the signature George W. D. Long; and the significance of what the Eskimos had discovered struck suddenly home. He offered a reward to anyone producing further pieces of flotsam, and a few days later news reached him that fifty-eight pieces of clothing and wood had been washed ashore at Kassimiut, ten miles to the north.

When he had personally examined every fragment of wreckage, Lytzen sat down and wrote a remarkably clear-sighted article to *Geografisk Tidskrift* (the Danish counter-part of the *Geographical Journal*). First, he tabulated the more important articles to be washed ashore:

"*1. A list of provision signed by De Long. 2. A list of the* Jeanette's *boats. 3. A cap marked F. C. Lindermann or Nindermann (one of the* Jeanette's *crew). 4. A pair of trousers marked Louis Noros (one of the* Jeanette's *crew). 5. A number of buttons, including several of a type worn by officers of the United States Navy. 6. A number of pieces of paper, five of which were provision lists including items of American manufacture. 7. Part of a cheque book, containing American stamps. 8. Part of an American-type tent, together with guide-lines etc.*

If these articles," he wrote, "*had been unmarked, it would have been difficult indeed to establish from what ship they had come, since from time immemorial whaling and sealing vessels have been lost in northern waters. But several of the items recovered were clearly marked with the name of the* Jeanette *or with the name of one of her crew; and this is conclusive evidence that they must indeed have belonged to the American vessel which was lost more than three years ago off the Siberian coast.*" Lytzen goes on to comment on how far the wreckage must have drifted—"*a great circle distance of over 3,000 miles, or nearly as far as from North Cape to the Cape of Good Hope . . . and yet this need not surprise us too greatly, since it has long been known that the driftwood washed ashore each year on the coast of Greenland has its origins in the Siberian forests, and must therefore have been carried a similar distance.*" From this, Lytzen deduces the existence of a great west-flowing Polar current, which sweeps from the Bering Strait, *via* the Pole, to Spitzbergen and thence down the east coast of Greenland and into the Atlantic. And he ends his article with a prophecy. "*It will be seen therefore that although Polar explorers are bound to become embedded in the ice, yet this same ice will drift them across the Pole and will eventually bear them out and carry them to safety. It would therefore not be impossible for an Expedition to drift from Siberia, with the ice, right through to Southern Greenland, provided that such an Expedition was prepared to spend several years under-way.*"

It is remarkable how great a furore was to stem from this eminently sensible article.

In Scandinavia Lytzen's theories were given immediate publicity and were, in general, readily accepted. Professor Mohn enlarged on them with much erudition in the Autumn 1884 issue of *Morgenblad;* and Fridtjof Nansen, the moment he read Mohn's article, conceived the idea of his epic drift which eight years later was to unveil the secrets of the last of the oceans.

In England and America, however, the theory of a Polar Sea and a westerly current was regarded with scepticism, while Nansen's proposal to utilize this current to make a voluntary drift through the heart of the Arctic was dismissed as "impractical and verging on the lunatic". To-day, safe in the knowledge of hindsight, we can only marvel at the violence of the opposition that Nansen's proposal aroused. When, for example, in 1890 he outlined his plan for drifting over the Pole to the Royal Geographical Society in London, he met with the following comments from his eminent audience: "*The most adventurous programme ever brought to the notice of the Society*" (Admiral McClintock). "*All very well in theory, but extremely difficult in practice*" (George Nares). "*Extremely dangerous . . . the ice will go through a ship no matter how she is constructed*" (Sir Allen Young). "*I must speak discouragingly of this project. The* Jeanette *relics may well have drifted to Greenland* via *another route entirely: i.e.* via *Smith Sound*" (Admiral Richards). "*Nansen's project involves the greatest peril*" (Sir Joseph Hooker). It is perhaps only fair to add that the Society later atoned for its scepticism by donating the expedition the sum of £300.

But it was, surprisingly, in America that Nansen's plans met with the fiercest disapproval. His critics here were spearheaded by the veteran General Greely, a man of violent prejudices who wrote (in *The Forum*, 1891), "*It strikes me as incredible that the plan advanced by Dr. Nansen should receive encouragement or support. For it seems to me to be based on fallacious ideas and to foreshadow barren results. Dr. Nansen has had no Arctic service . . . and it is doubtful if any hydrographer would treat seriously his theory of polar currents, or if any Arctic traveller would endorse his scheme.*" It is possible to attribute this article to ignorance, and to forgive it. It is not so easy to forgive or forget the malicious attack which Greely launched on Nansen after his return, when he accused the Norwegian of "deliberately quitting his comrades on (an) ice-beset ship . . . thus deviating from the most sacred duty devolving on the commander of a naval expedition". And it was largely because of diatribes such as this that America offered Nansen little encouragement before his venture and less than his fair share of praise after it. And for this, history has taken an ironic revenge. Since the Americans chose to disassociate themselves from Nansen's expedition, the drift of the *Fram* is not connected in people's minds to-day with the voyage of the *Jeanette*. In every continent, now, the names of Nansen and his ship are respected and admired; but the names of their precursors, who died in pioneering the route they were later to follow, are forgotten. And this is a pity. For the two expeditions were in fact complementary, were aimed at the same goal and were conducted with the same determination and courage.

*   *   *

Fridtjof Nansen was born at Froen, not far from Oslo, on October 10th, 1861. His childhood was in happy contrast to De Long's; for his parents encouraged him to follow his first loves—seafaring and zoology—and before he was twenty-one he had already voyaged to Greenland and published a detailed treatise on the anatomy of the seal. The rest of his life has been described as "a succession of great plans and even greater achievements". He was one of those fortunate people on whom the gods seem to lavish every possible blessing. Six feet tall, fair-headed, blue-eyed and of magnificent physique, he combined kindness and gentleness with a keen scientific brain and a very considerable ability at organizing. He was several times a great man—explorer, scientist, artist, writer, politician, Nobel prizewinner and humanitarian—but perhaps the happiest years of his life were the decade 1887–97, when, in his physical prime, he led the two great expeditions which established his fame as an explorer: the first crossing of the Greenland ice-cap, and the first crossing of the Arctic Ocean.

In 1887 it was still widely believed that in the centre of Greenland there were verdant pastures, hemmed in between the tier after tier of mountain ranges which could be seen from the coast. Several large-scale expeditions, with sledges and dogs, had tried to penetrate the interior, but cold and the exceedingly difficult terrain had been too much for them, and none had managed to push inland for more than some seventy miles (about a tenth of the country's width). Nansen had a theory that the interior of Greenland would prove to be not alternating mountain and valley but a relatively flat ice-cap, and that it ought to be possible to cross it on skis. The experts laughed at him. But it was Nansen who had the last laugh. For he put his theory to the test, and proved by practical experiment that he was right.

Towards the end of May 1888 Nansen and five companions, all expert skiers, boarded the sealer *Jason* and set course for the coast of Greenland. For six weeks they pushed slowly north up a littoral guarded by pack-ice and desolate as any on earth. Several times the *Jason* tried to stand inshore, but the ice was too dangerous; and at last the explorers decided to take to their kayaks and try to paddle the two or three miles to land. They had a hair-raising passage, being blown out to sea by a sudden gale, capsizing, and finally having to haul their boats over more than a mile of solid ice; but at last they managed to scramble ashore, and on August 16th were ready to start their assault on the ice-cap.

The initial ascent was hard. By day the snow was soft, so they travelled by night, with the temperature down to −40°F, hauling their sledges and skis up and everlastingly up over terrain criss-crossed by crevasse and serac. But when, at last, they topped 8,000 feet, they came, as Nansen had predicted, *"to a huge flat plain, with no more than an imperceptible rise to the west. For weeks* (we) *toiled across this interminable desert of snow. Flatness and whiteness were its features. And we looked like a diminutive black line traced feebly on to an infinite expanse of white."* But at least the going was faster now. By September 2nd they had discarded their snow-shoes in favour of skis, and a few days later they lashed their sledges together and rigged up a sail. *"With the wind behind us, our 'ship' flew over the snow with a speed that quite took away the breath. We were swept over drift and hollow, often jumping from the crest of one snow wave to the next.*" It took them little more than a fortnight to cover the five hundred miles of the central plateau, and on September 20th they began their descent of the mountains lining the west coast. A fortnight later they were safe in Godthaab. Nansen's theories had been completely vindicated, and on his return to Norway he was given an ecstatic welcome.

In view of the fact that he had been proved right once, one might have thought that when Nansen advanced his next polar theory he would have been listened to universally. But this was not the case. He was listened to only in Scandinavia.

Soon after his return from Godthaab, Nansen began making plans for drifting a vessel in the ice from Siberia to Greenland *via* the Pole. In almost every country in the world his scheme was received with scepticism and active disapproval. The Norwegian government alone were sufficiently courageous and far-sighted to give him their backing; they granted him £15,000 (which was subsequently increased); funds were also raised privately, and by the summer of 1890 it was clear that Nansen's scheme had sufficient backing to be put into practice.

It was a scheme dependent on two imponderables. Was there indeed a great polar current that drifted the apparently static ice the width of the Arctic Ocean from east to west? And was it possible to design a vessel that could withstand the pressure of being frozen into these moving ice floes for several years?

If the answer to either question was "no", then Nansen would lose his reputation and his crew their lives.

There was more at stake, therefore, in captaining the drift of the *Fram* than in leading a team of skiers across the Greenland ice-cap, and Nansen assembled his evidence and laid his plans with the most meticulous care.

He compiled so much evidence to support his theory of a polar current, that it is hard to-day to see how anyone of intelligence could have failed to be convinced. To geographical societies all over the world he pointed out that the *Jeanette* had sunk off the coast of Siberia; that three years later her wreckage had been washed up on the west coast of Greenland, and that the only possible route by which her wreckage could have drifted to Julianehaab was *via* the Pole. (The map on page 252 indicates why the *Jeanette* relics could not have reached Greenland from any other direction.) He pointed out that each year the coast of Greenland was strewn with aspen, fir and larch which the botanists agreed could have had their origin only in the forests of Siberia. He pointed out that a "throwing-stick" washed up at Godthaab was found to be inlaid with Chinese beads, and could have come only from the vicinity of the Bering Strait. He pointed out that the German botanist Griseback had conducted experiments which proved that Greenland's *flora* included a number of strains which were of Siberian origin. He quoted the evidence of mud analysis, and of the inflow and outflow of polar currents. Yet still the pundits were unconvinced—"*It is doubtful,*" wrote Greely in the autumn of 1891, "*if any hydrographer would treat seriously* (this) *theory of polar currents.*" But though he failed to convince others, Nansen, as his evidence accumulated, became more convinced than ever that he was championing the cause of truth; this led him to the opinion that the success or failure of his expedition would depend on the design of his ship.

The idea of building a special ship for working in the ice was in itself an innovation—previous explorers such as Parry, Nordenskjöld and De Long had always used vessels which were adapted to meet their needs rather than specially constructed—and Nansen was fortunate in having sufficient funds to build exactly the ship he wanted. He was fortunate too in finding a man able to transform his ideas on ship design into reality: Colin Archer.

Colin Archer was the son of a Scottish boat-builder who had settled in Norway in the early years of the nineteenth century. Throughout the '70s and '80s he turned out, from his yard in Laurvik, a succession of sealers, whalers and grain-ships whose strength and beauty of line became a by-word among the seamen of five oceans. And in the summer of 1890 Nansen commissioned him to design the *Fram*.

Archer made plan after plan and model after model, abandoning each as fresh improvements and innovations made his earlier designs obsolete. It took him six months to finalize the drawings, and twenty-six months to finish the building—an unprecedented time by the standards of the nineteenth century. But what a magnificent vessel he created!

"*When one bears in mind,*" wrote Archer, "*the fundamental idea behind Dr. Nansen's plan, it will be readily seen that his ship must differ radically from all previous vessels. Two points must be especially borne in mind: (1) that the shape of the hull should offer as small a target as possible to the attack of the ice; and (2) that the whole should be built so solidly that it can withstand the greatest pressure from without, from whatsoever direction . . . Thus more attention must be paid to making the ship a safe and warm stronghold during her drift than to endowing her with good sailing qualities.*" With these essentials in mind the *Fram* was given a smooth U-shaped hull, "*so that she could slip like an eel out of the embraces of the ice*"; while her sides were encased in layer after layer of oak frames, sandwiched with pitch and saw-dust, and buttressed from within by a veritable spider's web of supports. Here are extracts from Nansen's description of her:

"*She was considerably larger than I had anticipated: length of keel 102 feet, length of deck 128 feet, beam 36 feet, draught (with full cargo) 14 feet, and displacement (fully loaded) 800 tons. Her hull was pointed fore and aft, both ends being made especially strong. The stem consists of three beams, one inside the other, forming a thickness of 4 feet of solid oak, strengthened with breast-hooks of iron and protected by an iron stem. The stern, which is so often the Achilles' heel of polar vessels, is of special construction. On either side of the rudder-posts is fitted a stout oak counter-frame, forming a double stern, with a well for rudder and screw in between; thus no ice could touch the rudder, and indeed in spite of the violent pressure to which we were later subjected our rudder received no trace of injury during our years in the pack ice. Everything possible was done to strengthen the sides. The frame timbers were of choice Italian oak which had lain under cover for thirty years. The frames were built in two tiers, with the interstices filled with pitch and sawdust. The outer planking consists of three layers. The inner layer of 3″ of oak carefully caulked, the centre layer of 4″ of oak also caulked, and the outer layer of 6″ of green-heart. Inside the frames is a lining of 4″ to 8″ of pine. The total thickness of the ship's side is therefore from 24 to 28 inches of solid water-tight wood. It will readily be understood that such a breastwork with its rounded form, would of itself offer a very good resistance to the ice; but to make it stronger still the inside (of the vessel) was shored up in every possible way, so that the hold looks like a cobweb of baulks, stanchions and braces, the diagonal stays being placed as nearly as possible at right angles to the ship's sides so as to distribute the force of external pressure.*

"As regards rigging, it had to be simple, strong and easily worked from the deck. For this reason the Fram *was rigged as a three-masted fore-and-aft schooner—a design at which many Arctic whalers shook their heads, but which we found extremely serviceable. Her masts were high and massive, the crow's nest being 102 feet above the water; (it was important to have this as high as possible so as to ensure a good view for picking our way through the ice). The sail area is about 6,000 square yards.*

"Our quarters lay under the half-deck, and were arranged so that the saloon, which formed our dining and drawing room, was in the middle, surrounded on all sides by the sleeping quarters. These consisted of four cabins with one bunk, and two cabins with four bunks. The object of this arrangement was to protect the saloon from external cold, which was also achieved by having the ceilings, walls and floor covered with many layers of non-conducting material, thus preventing the warm damp air penetrating from one side of a wall to the other and depositing moisture which would soon turn to ice. The sides of the ship were lined with tarred felt, cork padding, deal panelling, a thick layer of felt, air-tight linoleum and finally an inner panelling. The ceilings had even more layers—air space, felt, deal panelling, reindeer hair and deal panelling, which, with the 4-inch deck-plates gave a total thickness of over fifteen inches. The flooring comprised cork padding 7 inches thick laid on top of the deck-plates, and covered with thick wood and linoleum; the skylight was protected by three panes of glass. The companionways were fitted with four doors consisting of wood and felt, each of which had to be opened on entering or leaving the saloon . . . One of the greatest difficulties of previous expeditions was always the moisture which collected on the cold outside walls and either froze or ran down in streams on to the bunks and deck, it being not unusual to find the mattresses turned into solid masses of ice. By our arrangements, however, we completely avoided this unpleasant state of affairs, and even when a fire was lit in the saloon there was not a trace of moisture on the walls or in the cabins."

Nansen goes on to describe the pumps, watertight compartments, dynamos and windmills, etc., which were specially designed in case of emergency in the ice; and he ends his account of the *Fram* with a tribute to her designer —*"we must recognise with gratitude that the success of our expedition was due in no small measure to Colin Archer."* And this is no empty encomium. For never before in the history of exploration had a ship been designed with so much care, ingenuity and attention to detail as was lavished on the *Fram*.

Their food and equipment were of the same high standard as their ship. They carried supplies for five years, and to quote Nansen: *"Every single item of food that we took with us had been chemically analysed before being adopted, while the greatest care was taken that it should be properly packed—even such items as bread and dried vegetables, etc., being soldered down in tins as a protection against damp."* Their scientific instruments (many of them lent by research institutes) were of the latest type and covered a vast range of uses—thermometers, barometers, aneroids, psychrometers, hygrometers, anemometers, theodolites, spectroscopes, electroscopes and photographometers, etc. The all-Norwegian crew of twelve had been carefully hand-picked from a multitude of volunteers.

And on June 24th, 1893, after nine years of mental and three years of physical preparation, Nansen and the *Fram* stood north out of Christiania.

Their original scheme had been to approach the Arctic *via* the Bering Strait, following the track of the *Jeanette;* but after a careful analysis of ice conditions Nansen decided that he would be better advised to approach the new Siberian Islands from the west: i.e. *via* Novaya Zemlya, the Kara Sea and the Taymyr Strait. The *Fram* therefore stood north that summer up the Norwegian coast. Three days out from Christiania she ran into a heavy swell. She was no sea-boat. Fat, cumbersome, top-weight and oddly-keeled, she was soon rolling gunwale-under; her deck timber and her drums of paraffin were torn adrift, the sea burst into her chart-house and Nansen had visions of his ship turning turtle before the expedition was fairly under way. But by hugging the inshore fjords they managed to avoid the worst of the swell, and on July 17th they came to Vadso, the last outpost of civilization. Here they were given a royal farewell: *"a sumptuous banquet, with speeches and champagne flowing in streams. And here too in the local sauna,"* wrote Nansen, *"our bodies enjoyed one last rite of purification before embarking on a life of primitive savagery. We lay on shelves in the bath-house and were parboiled with hot steam while young girls flogged us with birch twigs . . . I wonder if old father Mahomet has a bath like this in his paradise!"*

Next morning they weighed anchor at 3 a.m. *"The town,"* wrote Nansen, *"lay wrapped in sleep, and our last impression of Norway was just the right one to carry away with us. Such peace and calm; the masts in the harbour, the roofs and chimneys, standing out against the cool morning sky, and on the deck of the revenue cutter outside the harbour a single man fishing in the pale half-light. Then the sun broke through the mist and smiled down on the shore—rugged, bare and weatherworn in the hazy morning, but still lovely—dotted here and there with tiny houses and boats, and all Norway lying behind it . . . While the* Fram *was quietly working her way seaward towards our distant goal, I stood and watched our land fade gradually into the horizon. I wonder what will happen to her and to us before we once again see Norway rising out of the sea?"*

Their passage to the New Siberian Islands was far from easy. Only a few days out from Vadso they ran into fog—*"Ugh! that endless, stubborn fog of the Arctic Sea! When it lowers its curtain, and shuts out the blue above and the blue below, and everything becomes a damp grey mist, day in and day out, then all one's vigour and elasticity is needed to save one from being stifled in its clammy embrace. Fog, and nothing but fog, wherever we turn our eyes. It condenses on the rigging, and drips down on to every tiniest spot on deck. It lodges on your clothes, and finally wets you through and through. It settles on the mind and spirit, and everything becomes drab and uniform and grey."* And as soon as the fog lifted they met with another setback: ice— unexpectedly far south at the approaches to Novaya Zemlya. But this early encounter with the pack at least gave them confidence in the strength of the *Fram. "It is a royal pleasure,"* wrote Nansen, *"to work her ahead through difficult ice. She twists and turns like a ball on a platter, and no channel between the floes is too difficult for her to get through. But it is hard work for the helmsman. 'Hard a-starboard! Hard a-port! Steady! Hard a-starboard again!' goes on incessantly without the slightest breathing space. As he rattles round the wheel, the sweat pours off him, and the ship swings this way and that; if there is a passage wide enough for her to slip through, she wriggles eel-like along it; if there is no passage she drives full tilt at the ice, runs her bow up it, treads it under her and bursts the floe asunder. And how strong she is! Even when she charges a floe at full speed there is not a crack nor a sound of complaint from her timbers . . ."*

So they stood east through the Barents Sea, until on August 1st they came to Khabarova, a Russo-Norwegian trading post at the mouth of the Yugor Strait. Here they took aboard their dogs, listened to the not very encouraging reports of ice conditions in the Sea of Kara, and admired the flowers of the tundra—the saxifrage, mountain poppies, forget-me-nots and bluebells which, for a few brief weeks, metamorphose the barren wastes of the Arctic into a mosaic of jewels. Then on August 3rd, with their launch taking soundings ahead, the *Fram* edged carefully through the shallow waters of the Yugor Strait. By August 4th they were into the Sea of Kara. Only one more obstacle, now, had to be cleared before they could set course for the New Siberian Islands; this was Cape Chelyuskin, the northernmost extremity of the Old World. But the rounding of Cape Chelyuskin was to take them over a month. For ice conditions in the Sea of Kara were bad.

Time and again, that autumn, the *Fram* was blocked by solid pack-ice; she was forced inshore, was bedevilled by head winds and wreathed in alternate eddies of fog and snow. Fifteen years earlier Nordenskjöld had passed through the Sea of Kara in August with "little or no hindrance from the ice"; but the *Fram* in 1893 was so sorely beset that by early September Nansen had resigned himself to spending their first winter several hundred miles short of their starting-point. On September 10th, however, after a series of heavy gales, the ice broke away from the shore, leaving a narrow but clear passage through the shallows. "*Never before*," wrote Nansen, "*had the Fram gone so fast; it was as if she realised how much depended on her getting a move on*"; and after a splendid two days' sail they passed Chelyuskin, to the accompaniment of music, fresh fruit, cigars, rum punch and toasts to their continued progress.

In the next weeks they covered more than three hundred miles, heading north by west, through a sea that was miraculously free of ice. "*Tuesday, September 19th*," reads Nansen's diary, "*I have never had such a splendid sail, on and on towards unknown lands through a sea no ship has ever sailed before. We are heading north with a good wind, as fast as steam and sail can take us, and with always the same dark sky ahead to beckon us on. 'Nothing but clear water', is the hourly shout from the crow's next, and even at dusk there is not the slightest trace of an ice blink. I can hardly believe our luck! I have to ask myself if it isn't all some wonderful dream!*"

The dream ended on September 20th.

"*As I was sitting in my cabin, looking at the map and thinking that my cup would soon be full—for we had almost reached 78°N—there was a sudden luff, and I rushed on deck. Ahead of us lay the edge of the ice: long, compact and shining through the fog.*"

The *Fram* was face to face now with the adversary she was to do battle with for the next three years.

They were still some hundred miles short of the New Siberian Islands; but Nansen saw little hope, at this late stage in the season, of making further progress to the east; also he was anxious to avoid any possibility of becoming blocked by land. He therefore decided to let the *Fram* become frozen in. *"Previous explorers in the Arctic,"* he wrote, *"have always tried to keep close to land. But this is just what I want to avoid. It is the open, drifting ice that I want to get into. It therefore seemed to me that we might do a great deal worse than give ourselves up to the ice right away. So we made fast to a floe and prepared to clean the boilers and shift coal. We are lying in open water at the moment, with only a few large blocks of ice here and there; but I have a presentiment that this is our winter harbour."*

A couple of days later his diary reads: *"The ice is thickening around us . . . We are freezing in faster and faster. Beautiful still weather; 13 degrees of frost last night. Winter is coming . . ."*

The longest—and one of the greatest—voyages in the history of exploration had begun.

At first they had plenty to do: coaling, setting up their various instruments, and transforming the *Fram* from a sailing ship into an immobile fortress . . . *"As the ice thickened, we gradually converted our ship into comfortable winter quarters. The rudder was hauled up, to prevent it being damaged by the pressure of the ice. The engine was dismantled, and each part was carefully oiled and put away for the winter. We cleared out the hold to make room for a joiner's workshop; the smithy was set up first on deck and later transferred to the ice; our mechanical workshop we had in the engine room; tinsmith's work was done in the charthouse; shoemaker's and sailmaker's and odd jobs in the saloon. And soon there was nothing, from wooden shoes to the most delicate instruments, that could not be made aboard the* Fram *. . . We began putting up the windmill which was to drive our dynamo and so give us electric light . . . There was always something to occupy us."*

They had no difficulty, that first winter, in keeping boredom at bay. They printed their own newspaper, the *Framsjaa;* they hunted the polar bears whose curiosity was so strong that it led them sometimes to try to clamber aboard; and no birthday, saint's day or national holiday passed without celebration. But it was the recording of scientific observations which was the most effective cure for ennui.

Nansen had always held that the object of their voyage should be, *"not so much to reach the exact Pole, as to explore and bring back information about the unknown polar regions."* And this is what he did.

It is a surprising thought that less than a hundred years ago the Arctic was believed to consist of shallow seas interspersed with large tracts of land (*vide* Sir Allen Young in 1890: *"Dr. Nansen assumes the blank space around the axis of the earth to be a pool of water or ice; but all previous navigators have reported mountains farther and farther north, and I think that near the Pole he will find land in every direction".*)

The observations taken by Nansen during his three-year drift completely demolished this widely-held theory, and established beyond any possible doubt the true configuration of the Arctic: a deep, steep-sided ocean, free of islands, bisected by a west-flowing current and crossed by a well-defined pattern of winds. The fruits of Nansen's observations are published in six massive volumes, which together form one of the most important contributions ever made to meteorology and oceanography; and as Nansen's biographers have pointed out, "although much Arctic exploration has been done since the voyage of the *Fram*, very little has been added to our knowledge of the Arctic basin". The recording of this vast mass of scientific data took up a great deal of time and also gave the crew something in which they could take pride and interest during the long Arctic winter.

Throughout October and November the *Fram* pursued the same wayward course as the *Jeanette*, now making steady progress towards the north and west, now drifting back again to the south and east. Their wanderings became a barometer of the ship's company's morale—high when they were borne forward in the west-flowing current on whose existence they were gambling their lives, low when the counter-currents and gales dragged them back to the Siberian coast. But at least their ship seemed able to hold her own against the assaults of the pack.

They had their first real joust with the ice on October 9th.

"All at once," wrote Nansen, *"as we were sitting idly in the saloon, there began a deafening noise, and the whole ship started to shake. This was our first taste of ice pressure, and everyone rushed on deck to see what was happening. The* Fram *behaved beautifully. On came the ice, advancing in a ridge; but we rode over the top of it, being lifted slowly, then falling again as the ice broke under our weight. This 'squeezing' continued on and off for most of the afternoon, and was at times so strong that the* Fram *was often lifted several feet."* A few days later they suffered an even sterner test, being caught in the middle of the sort of pile-up of floes which had battered the life out of the *Jeanette*.

"Such an ice conflict," wrote Nansen in his diary, *"is a stupendous spectacle. First you hear a sound like the thundering rumble of an earthquake far away on the great waste; then you hear it in several places together, coming always nearer and nearer. The silent world re-echoes with thunder; nature's giants are awakening to battle. The ice cracks on every side of you, and begins to pile up; and all of a sudden you find yourself in the midst of the struggle. There are howlings and thunderings around you; you can feel the ice trembling, and hear it rumbling under your feet; there is no peace anywhere. In the semi-darkness you can see the ice tossing about and piling up into great ridges that creep nearer and nearer—floes, 10, 12 or 15 feet high, broken and flung on top of each other as if they were feathers. They are close to the ship now. You jump back to save yourself. But the ice splits in front of you, a black gulf opens, and up streams the water. You turn in another direction, and there through the darkness you can just make out a new ridge moving towards you. You turn in another direction, and there is the ridge again . . ."*

Many times, in the next three years, the *Fram* was tested as no ship had ever been tested before. Yet so magnificently had she been designed and built, that she sprung not the slightest leak, and after the first few months her crew never doubted her ability to withstand the worst that the ice could do to her.

Their ship—the first of the two imponderables—was coming up to expectation. But the second imponderable—the polar current—was proving unexpectedly wayward.

Throughout the autumn of 1893 the *Fram*, like the *Jeanette* fourteen years before her, drifted uncertainly hither and thither, the sport of wind shifts and backwater eddies. Nansen's spirits were like a pendulum. As the *Fram*, for several days at a stretch, drifted steadily west-north-west, he felt certain that the great polar current had caught them at last in its grip; but then came a storm or a counter-current, and they were pushed back to the south and east, almost to the fringe of the New Siberian Islands. But as the weeks passed, slowly and almost imperceptibly their drifts to the north and west became longer and faster, and their retrogressions to the south and east shorter and slower; and by Christmas 1893 it was clear that the *Fram* was moving slowly towards the heart of an unknown ocean.

Early in the New Year Nansen made his first great discovery. Towards the end of December the *Fram* was carried over the edge of the continental shelf, and it soon became clear from their soundings that the supposedly shallow polar sea was in fact of tremendous depth: at one point over 17,000 feet. When he realized the great depth of the ocean he was being carried into, Nansen had temporary qualms about his current (for currents, generally speaking, run fastest and steadiest in waters that are comparatively shallow). But he reassured himself with the thought that the *Jeanette* relics and the Siberian driftwood could not lie, and "the way they went we must go too".

So the first winter passed pleasantly, uneventfully and with the crew enjoying the novelty of their incarceration. Only Nansen had moments of doubt. He was happy, of course, that the current was drifting his ship towards the Pole; but he could not help realizing that the farther they went, the more surely they were burning their bridges behind them. Already they were past the point of no return. For them there could now be

No retreat, no retreat: they must conquer or die, who have no retreat.

So the *Fram* drifted on in the wake of the *Jeanette*, locked in ice and silence, as cut off from the rest of the world as if she had been impaled on the face of the moon.

But there was one big difference between Nansen's drift and De Long's. Nansen in the *Fram*, being comfortable and relatively safe, was able to look on the polar ice as his friend; and, viewing it with a more favourable eye, he was better able to appreciate its beauty. In all the literature of exploration there is no more lyrical evocation of the glory of nature than Nansen's description of the polar night.

"Late that evening I wandered on to the pack ice . . . There is nothing more beautiful than the Arctic night. It is dreamland, painted in the imagination's most delicate tints; it is colour etherealised. One shade melts into the next, so that you cannot tell where one ends and the other begins, and yet every colour of the spectrum is there. Nothing has a definite shape, all the patterns are faint and dreamy, like a far away melody played on muted strings. The sky is like an enormous cupola, blue at the zenith, shading down into green, and finally, at the edges to lilac. The ice fields are patterned with cold blue shadows, and with pink tints here and there as a ridge catches the last reflection of the vanishing day. Up in the cupola shine our unchanging friends, the stars; while in the south hangs a great red moon, encircled by an aura of gold. Presently, over the whole vault of heaven the aurora borealis shakes its veil of glittering silver, which changes now to yellow, now to green and now to red. It spreads, contracts, and spreads again in ever restless change, now forming wavering bands of silver, now shooting out a series of brilliant violet rays. The glory fades, melting away in the moonlight like a departing sigh; and all that is left are a few wavering streamers, vague as a foreboding—the dust

flung from the aurora's glittering cloak. But now the brilliance is growing again, shooting up great shafts of light, and the endless game has begun anew. And all the while the utter stillness, and the peace that passes all understanding."

When one page of Nansen's diary is enriched by descriptions such as this, and the next page paints a glowing picture of sumptuous feasts and happy and carefree comradeship, one almost gets the impression that life in the *Fram* was one long round of pleasure.

But the coin had another side to it: the cold, the danger and, above all, the monotony—the feeling of being suspended in the ice, as if in a vacuum, week after week, month after month, year after year, while life passed them by. Nansen describes this feeling exactly. "*How tired I am of the cold beauty of the Arctic! I long to return to life. Let me come home again: as conqueror or beggar, what does it matter? But let me get home to begin life anew. The years are passing here, and what do they bring? Nothing but dust, dry dust, which the first wind blows away; new dust comes in its place, and the next wind takes it too. Truth? Why should we make so much of truth? Life is more than truth, and we live but once.*"

It was, most probably, on a day when such thoughts were oppressing him, that Nansen decided to make his dash for the Pole.

By their second Christmas in the pack-ice it was clear that the *Fram* was drifting west rather than north, and that they were going to pass not over the Pole but considerably to the south of it. Nansen therefore decided to leave his ship in charge of the experienced and highly competent Sverdrup, and with one companion make a dash by sledge to the north. It was a risky venture; for with the *Fram* drifting unpredictably there was no hope of the two explorers returning to her; they would have to make their way back to either Franz Josef Land or Novaya Zemlya, a round journey of over a thousand miles. They planned to take with them twenty-eight dogs, three sledges, two kayaks, one tent and provisions for one hundred days — which was travelling, by any standards, fantastically light. Seldom if ever in the history of exploration has so hazardous a journey been undertaken with such slender resources; and a comparison between what Nansen was leaving and what he was going to is the best rebuttal of Greely's jibe that he deserted his ship.

For Nansen stayed with the *Fram* until his theory of a polar current had been proved, and his ship had demonstrated her ability to survive in the ice. By the time he left her the *Fram* had already drifted the better part of a thousand miles towards her goal (the exit between Spitzbergen and Greenland); she had survived two winters in the ice; she still had provision for three years, and her crew were in first-class health and morale. She was in neither danger nor the expectation of danger. Nansen and his companion, on the other hand, were facing the perils of a solitary journey by sledge over a thousand miles of unmapped and uninhabited ice.

They set out on March 14th, 1895. And their journey is an epic of physical endurance unsurpassed in the annals of exploration.

At first the going was good: "*We found large expanses of flat ice and covered the ground quickly, pushing ever away from our companions and into the great unknown.*" But after a week they were brought up short by a series of pressure ridges: hummocky, unstable ice which capsized their sledges, tore holes in the skin of their kayaks, and slowed their progress to under a mile a day. And the farther they went the worse the ice became. Day after day they hauled their sledges through a series of miniature glaciers; the harder they laboured the more they sweated, and soon *"body moisture condensed in* (their) *outer garments which became frozen solid into complete suits of ice armour, so stiff that the arms of* (their) *coats rubbed sores on* (their) *wrists."* Early in April, to add to their troubles, they found themselves in the grip of a contrary current which drifted them south, away from the Pole, as fast as they tried to struggle towards it. On April 8th, in position 86°13′ N, 98°47′ E, they came to a halt. The temperature was minus 30°, ice conditions were appalling, and they had already killed several of their dogs for food. *"I went a little way ahead on snow shoes,"* wrote Nansen, *"and climbed the highest hummock I could find. But ahead, only the same kind of ice was to be seen: a veritable chaos of ice-blocks, stretching as far as the horizon. There was no sense in keeping on; we were wasting valuable time and accomplishing nothing. And indeed if there is much more ice like this between here and Franz Josef Land, we shall need all the time we have."* They cooked themselves a ceremonial banquet—lobscause (a stew of meat, vegetables and ship's biscuit), whortleberries and hot whey—and then on April 9th reversed course and headed for land. They had penetrated farther north than man had ever penetrated before; and a few days later, unbeknown of course to them, their ship also achieved a rare distinction—when the *Fram* approached the 86th parallel she set up a record for farthest north which was to stand for over sixty years; no ship approached the Pole so closely until 1958, when Anderson took the *Nautilus* on her epic voyage under the Arctic ice.

The trek home for which they had allowed two months was to take them over a year.

The going was unpredictable at first; some days they covered twelve or fifteen miles, some days less than one. Towards the end of April they ran into a series of blizzards, and were held up by sea-lanes choked with brash. By the end of May they were running short of food. Uncertain of their position, they floundered on through slush and melting snow, heading for the mythical Petermann Land which explorers had reported to the north of the Franz Josef Islands. But no land rose to welcome them over the horizon, only a water sky, ever tempting them on. *"June 12th,"* wrote Nansen, *"The situation is getting worse and worse. Yesterday we advanced less than a mile. Wretched snow, uneven ice, treacherous sea lanes and villainous weather."* But on June 22nd they shot a seal—which provided them with food for several weeks—and a month later, as they struggled across an enormous pressure-ridge, they sighted land. Their joy was past comprehension: *"At last the marvel has come to pass—land, after we had almost given up our belief in it. After nearly two years we can once again see something solid rising above the cold white line of the horizon . . . How long has it haunted our dreams, this land; and now it rises in front of us like the vision out of a fairy-tale."* Their troubles, however, were far from over. For between pressure-ridge and land lay a mosaic of sea-lanes, brash and floes, which it took them several weeks to cross. Through rain, mist and grinding ice they struggled towards the land, jumping their loaded sledges from floe to floe, several times slithering into the icy water and frequently sinking up to their thighs in slush. And no sooner had they hauled themselves, exhausted, ashore, than Johansen was almost killed by a bear. The great creature slunk up to them unobserved while they were transferring supplies from sledge to kayak, and the first Nansen knew of its presence was a whisper from Johansen—"Get your gun." Looking up, he saw his companion flat on his back, with the bear standing over him, paws drawn back for the kill. He made a grab for his rifle, but the sledge it was lying on slithered away and he had to go scrambling after it. "You'd better look sharp!" said Johansen coolly. Nansen did not have time to get to his feet. He fired sitting down: a shot through the brain; and the bear fell dead over Johansen's feet. A few days later, on August 6th, they shot the last of their dogs, lashed their kayaks together and set sail along the

FIG 40. Kayaks of the type used by Nansen and Johansen

north coast of the Hvidtenland Islands. "*It is a real pleasure to see the kayaks dancing over the water and to hear the waves splashing against their sides . . . we rigged up a sail and made good progress. What a change after having to force our way forward inch by inch over the ice.*" They were aiming now for the south-west coast of Franz Josef Land, and for several weeks the going was good. But towards the end of August, when they were still some 150 miles short of their goal, they ran into bad weather which forced them ashore. On August 28th, Nansen decided it would be too risky to push on, for the autumn storms were likely to hit them at any moment; they would have to winter.

Never before had men faced the onset of an Arctic winter with such pitiably slender resources. They had the clothes they stood up in, their sledges and kayaks, food for five weeks, and nothing more. Yet it never occurred to Nansen to doubt their ability to survive. They dug a rectangular hole in the ground—their spade the shoulder-bone of a walrus lashed to a ski-stick; round the hole they piled up stones, filling the crevasses with moss and earth; on top of the stones they laid driftwood and walrus hide; and this was the hovel, ten feet by six feet by six feet high, in which they spent the next nine months. Walrus blubber provided them with heat and light—

"*With the aid of lamps we managed to keep the temperature at round about freezing-point in the centre of the room; at the walls, of course, it was much colder.*" Game, throughout the winter, was plentiful and right on their doorstep—in fact, the polar bears came sometimes too close for their peace of mind. They celebrated Christmas by turning their shirts inside out and bathing in a quarter of a cup of hot water. Most of the time they slept—"*We carried the art of sleeping to a high degree of perfection, and could sometimes sleep twenty hours out of twenty-four.*" It was the filth which troubled them most: the smoke of the oil lamps and the grease and stench of the blubber. "*If it was difficult to get our bodies clean, it was sheer impossibility as regards our clothes. We tried in all possible ways. We boiled our shirts in the pot, we wrung them out; but all to no avail. I never realised before how wonderful an invention is common-or-garden soap . . . In the meantime our hair and beards grew entirely wild. It is true that we could have cut them; but as our supply of clothes was by no means lavish, we thought it best to retain our hair, which soon began to flow over our shoulders.*" They had little to do that winter, and only a few pages from a nautical almanac to read. For nine months they endured cold, hunger, filth and the sort of monotony that would have driven lesser men to the brink of madness. Yet in all Nansen's diary there is never a hint of complaint and never a cross word. While the world outside lay cold and sere in the grip of the long Arctic night, Nansen and Johansen, in their pitiable hut, bore living witness to the qualities of courage, inquisitiveness and adaptability. They survived. And in April 1896 they prepared to continue their trek.

But the Arctic spring came late that year, and it was May 19th before they finally left their hut and struck out along the shore, hauling their sledges and kayaks over the uneven ice. After covering about sixty miles they came to open water and were able, once again, to take to their boats. They were on the final stage of their journey now, and perhaps it was the knowledge of this that made them careless. For on June 12th they all but lost their kayaks—and their lives. "*In the evening,*" wrote Nansen, "*we put in to the edge of the ice* (partly to stretch their legs and partly to look for game; for once again they were short of food). "*As we clambered ashore the question arose of how we should moor the kayaks. 'It doesn't need much to hold these light vessels', I said, and secured them with a halyard . . . And we climbed to the crest of a hummock. As we stood there Johansen suddenly shouted: 'The kayaks! They're adrift!' We rushed down as fast as we could; but the two boats were already clear of the ice and drifting rapidly away. The halyard had broken. 'Here, take my watch', I cried to Johansen; and tearing off some of my clothes so as to be able to swim more easily—I dared not take everything off in case I got cramp—I sprang into the water, and made after the kayaks. But the wind was off the ice, and the light kayaks with their high rigging were drifting fast. The water was ice cold; it was hard work swimming with clothes on; and often the boats drifted faster than I could swim. It seemed impossible for me to make it. But all our hope was drifting there; all we possessed was on board—we hadn't even a knife with us; and whether I got cramp and sank here and now, or turned back without the kayaks, it would come to pretty much the same thing; so I exerted myself to the utmost. When I tired, I turned over and swam on my back and then I could see Johansen pacing the ice. Poor fellow! He thought it dreadful not to be able to do anything . . . he told me afterwards it was the worst moment he had ever lived through . . . But when I turned over again the kayaks seemed to be a little nearer, and my courage rose. I redoubled my efforts. Soon, however, my limbs began to stiffen and to lose all feeling. I knew then that in a few minutes I should not be able to move at all. My strokes became feebler and feebler. But I told myself I must hold out somehow, and the distance became gradually shorter. At last I was able to grasp hold of a snow shoe which lay across the stern of the kayaks. And we were saved . . . But as I tried to pull myself up, my whole body was so stiff with cold that I could not manage it; and I thought for a moment that, after all, it was too late—that having got this far I would not be able to get in. After a little, however, I managed to swing one leg over the sledge which lay across the decks, and in this way managed to tumble in. There I sat, but so stiff with cold that I could hardly paddle . . . I shivered, my teeth chattered and I was numb all over.*" But in spite of his ordeal, Nansen was sufficiently collected, as he paddled back, to take his gun and shoot a pair of auks which had alighted close to the kayaks—"*For we were short of food, and the thought of auk for supper was too tempting to be missed.*" Back on the ice Johansen stripped him and wrapped him, exhausted and trembling, in his sleeping-bag. It took him several hours to thaw out. But by supper time he was sitting up, apparently none the worse for his ordeal. "*Auk and hot soup soon effaced the last traces of my swim. During the night my clothes were hung out; next day they were almost dry again, and so we pushed on.*"

As if the Arctic recognized at last that Nansen was unconquerable, it vouchsafed his journey a sudden and fortuitous end. "*On June 17th we were encamped in a land which I believed to be unseen by human eye and untrodden by human foot, when a sound reached my ear like the barking of a dog. I strained my ears, but heard no more, only the same bubbling noise of thousands of birds. I thought I must have been mistaken . . . But then the barking came again, and there was no longer room for doubt.*" Nansen went scrambling and halloing up the hummocks of ice. His shouts were answered. And a moment later he was face to face with Frederick Jackson, leader of the British Expedition to Franz Josef Land. It was a coming together as dramatic—and a good deal more unexpected—as that of Stanley and Livingstone. "*A more remarkable meeting than ours,*" wrote Jackson, "*was never heard of. Nansen did not know that I was in Franz Josef Land, since I did not leave England until a year after the* Fram *had started; while I had not the slightest idea that he was within hundreds of miles of me . . . Had he missed meeting us, it is doubtful if he could ever have left Franz Josef Land; for 160 miles of open sea lies between these islands and the nearest known land: a sea which cannot be crossed in leaky canvas canoes.*"

By a happy coincidence Jackson's relief ship, the *Windward*, was due to arrive in a few weeks. Nansen and Johansen waited for her—"*clean, comfortable, relaxed and surrounded by friends, we were filled with a great sense of peace.*" The *Windward* arrived in late July, and having unloaded her fuel and supplies, she gave the explorers a passage home. By midsummer—after a voyage of almost exactly three years—they were back in Norway.

A week later Nansen was handed a telegram which filled his cup of happiness to the brim: "*FRAM* ARRIVED IN GOOD CONDITION. ALL WELL ON BOARD. SHALL START AT ONCE FOR TROMSO. WELCOME HOME. OTTO SVERDRUP."

The three-year experiment had come to an end; Nansen's theories had been completely vindicated; and the veil had been torn aside from the last and most obdurate of the oceans.

*   *   *

The drift of the *Fram* was the last of the great voyages of exploration which unveiled the shape of the world. There have been great voyages since of course —those of Bombard, Anderson and Thor Heyerdahl to mention only a few— but these have been motivated by something other than a desire to unroll the map. It was the *Fram* which fitted the final piece of jigsaw into the map of continents and oceans. And there is something heartening, I think, about the spirit in which this last great voyage was made.

Men, down through the ages, have taken to exploration for different motives. As long ago as the tenth century these motives were tabulated in the *King's Mirror:* "If you wish to know why men journey to far places, often at great danger to their lives, it is the threefold nature of man that draws him thither. One part of him is emulation and the desire of fame; another part is the desire of knowledge, and the third part is the desire of wealth." It was the second, and noblest, of these motives which inspired Nansen—and has, in a minor key, inspired the majority of explorers ever since.

"The desire of knowledge." This is the link which binds Pytheas to Gil Eannes, Gil Eannes to Cook, and Cook to Nansen. This is the touchstone common to the brightest stars in the galaxy of great explorers: the men who had a theory, *and* the faith to leap into the unknown to prove it right: the men who had the imagination to dream, *and* the courage to bring their dreams to reality. And it is, I think, fitting to end our long saga of exploration with the words of the last of the great explorers, Fridtjof Nansen (writing not long before his death): "The ice and the long moon-lit polar nights, with all their yearning, seem now like a far-off dream from another world—a dream that has come and passed away. But what would life be worth without its dreams?"

APPENDIX A

THE LOCATION OF VINELAND

1. *Sailing directions in the sagas.* Both Bjarne and Leif tell us that Vineland lay south-west of Greenland at a distance of between 1,500 and 2,000 miles. (This distance is computed as follows: five days' ordinary sailing=600 miles; four days' sailing close-reefed before a storm=600 miles; allowances for the distances offshore from which the various lands were sighted=150 miles; allowance for coasting=400 miles; total, 1,750 miles.) This narrows our search to the American seaboard south of Nova Scotia and north of Chesapeake Bay.

2. *Evidence of the wild grapes.* Wild grape vines do not grow "in abundance" north of Nova Scotia; and this confirms the possible northerly limit of Vineland.

3. *Evidence of the salmon.* Salmon are not found in large numbers south of Connecticut and Rhode Island; and this raises the southerly limit of Vineland to the 41st parallel, well north of the foot of Chesapeake Bay.

4. *Evidence of the mild winter.* The statements that "there was little frost" and that "the grass hardly withered" indicate a location south of Cape Anne; for north of this cape, on the Maine and New Hampshire littoral winters tend to be fairly severe.

5. *Evidence that there was still light at Eyktenstad (3 p.m.) and at Dagmalastad (9 a.m.) even on the shortest day.* This confirms a probable location of between the 41st and 43rd parallels.

6. *Evidence of local physiography.* Within the limits set out above, there is only one stretch of coast which includes "capes, islands, sound, shallows and an island to the north of the land." This is Nantucket Sound. And the descriptions of the sagas fit this area with a precision too exact to be due to coincidence. Here, therefore, was the Vineland-the-good discovered by Leif Eriksson in the autumn of A.D. 1003.

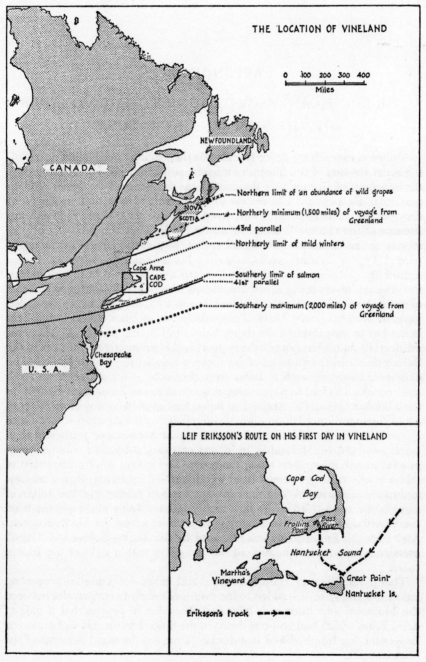

THE LOCATION OF VINELAND

0   100 200 300 400
Miles

NEWFOUNDLAND

CANADA

......Northern limit of an abundance of wild grapes

.......Northerly minimum (1,500 miles) of voyage from
        Greenland

NOVA
SCOTIA ......43rd parallel

.......Northerly limit of mild winters

Cape Anne
CAPE
COD ......Southerly limit of salmon
........41st parallel

.......Southerly maximum (2,000 miles) of voyage from
        Greenland

Chesapeake
Bay

U.S.A.

LEIF ERIKSSON'S ROUTE ON HIS FIRST DAY IN VINELAND

Cape Cod
Bay

Frollins   Bass
Pond   River

Nantucket Sound

Martha's
Vineyard   Great Point
                                Nantucket Is.

Eriksson's track ━ ➤ ━ ➤

FIG 41.

APPENDIX B

THE ECONOMIC BACKGROUND TO THE VOYAGES
OF THE SIXTEENTH CENTURY

Ambition to reach the Spice Islands was the driving force behind nearly all the great voyages of the fifteenth and sixteenth centuries. For in those days the economy of Europe was dominated by the demand for spices, and in particular for pepper. The reason for this demand was that in Northern Europe vast numbers of cattle and sheep had to be slaughtered each autumn because of the chronic shortage of winter fodder, and the only way of preserving the carcasses (and of disguising their putrefaction!) was by the use of pepper. Pepper, in other words, was not a luxury but a necessity.

Initially this pepper was gathered, sorted and first sold in the Moluccas, the original buyers being Malay merchants who paid only for the trivial cost of native labour in picking and baling. It was then shipped, by square-sailed junk, to Malacca or the Malay Peninsula, a fair number of vessels and lives being lost *en route* through the depredations of Chinese pirates. At Malacca, visiting Hindu traders bought the pepper, and after paying a heavy tax to the Sultan then ran the gauntlet of yet more pirates in the Bay of Bengal. The cargoes that got through to India were then sold at a good profit to Arab traders, who also had to pay a substantial tariff to the Zamorin of Calicut on the Malabar Coast. The Arabs then sailed for Egypt in convoy in an effort to avoid the marauding Hindu dhows which plagued the Arabian coasts. Once in the Red Sea the spices were landed at either Massawa or Jidda and then taken overland to Alexandria by desert caravan, successive tributes being paid at almost every oasis along the route. The caravans were composed of relays of fifty camels, fastened head to tail and led by an ass; they were slow and easily ambushed. When the caravans reached Alexandria, the Sultan of Egypt collected a third of the now highly inflated value of the pepper from the Venetians who came to convoy their treasure across the Mediterranean. And even this final convoy was menaced by the Turks, Sallees and Tripoli corsairs, who not infrequently cut out stragglers within sight of the Italian coast.

The pyramiding of transport costs and taxes—of cumshaw, squeeze, baksheesh and gabelle—added to the profits of nearly twenty resales between the Moluccas and Europe so increased the value of pepper that a bale of dried beans which had cost one ducat in the Spice Islands sold in London or Bruges for one hundred and five ducats—over ten thousand per cent of the original price.

Small wonder that importers, bankers and governments alike longed to find an alternative route to the fabulous Spice Islands.

BIBLIOGRAPHY

CHAPTER ONE
The Early Explorers, Isabel Barclay.
Sailing Ships and Their Story, E. K. Chatterton.
Lost Land of Ophir, Cdr. C. Craufurd (*Journal of the Central Asian Society*, Vol. 14).
Conquest by Man, Paul Herrmann.
The Gold of Ophir, A. H. Keane.
The Indian Ocean, Alan Villiers.
Sons of Sinbad, Alan Villiers.

CHAPTER TWO
The Story of Maps, Lloyd A. Brown.
The Ancient Explorers, M. Cary and E. H. Warmington.
Nechao et le Circumnavigation d'Afrique, H. Gaubert (*Geographia*, Paris, 1955).
Conquest by Man, Paul Herrmann.
Die Umseglung Afrikas, W. Muller.
The Geographical System of Herodotus, Major R. Rennell.
The Geography of Herodotus, J. Wheeler.

CHAPTER THREE
Pythéas le Massaliote, G. E. Brocke.
A History of Ancient Geography, E. H. Bunbury.
The Ancient Explorers, M. Cary and E. H. Warmington.
The First Polar Expedition, Rev. Eital (Royal Geographical Society of Australia, 1903).
Pytheas, Discoverer of Britain, C. R. Markham (*Geographical Journal*, 1893).
In Northern Mists, Fridtjof Nansen.
Great Adventures and Explorations, Vilhjalmum Stefansson.
Ultima Thule, Vilhjalmum Stefansson.

CHAPTER FOUR
Directory for the Navigation of the Indian Ocean, A. G. Findlay.
Arab Seafaring, G. F. Hourdani.
The Commerce and Navigation of the Erythraean Sea, J. W. McCrindle.
Intercourse Between India and the Western World, H. G. Rawlinson.
The Periplus of the Erythraean Sea, W. H. Schoff.
The Commerce and Navigation of the Ancients in the Indian Ocean, W. Vincent.

CHAPTER FIVE
Vita Brendani, (MS).
Land to the West, Geoffrey Ashe.
Early Norse Visits to America, W. H. Babcock.
Saint Brendan's Explorations and Island, W. H. Babcock (*Geographical Review*, New York, 1919).
Brendaniana, Rev. Denis O'Donoghue.
British Coracles and Irish Curraghs, James Hornell.
Brendan the Navigator, George A. Little.
Lives of the Saints of Ireland, Charles Plummer.
Atlantic Crossings before Columbus, Frederick J. Pohl.

CHAPTER SIX
The Flatey Book (MS).
Hauk's Book (MS).
Leif Eriksson, Discoverer of America, E. F. Gray.
The Norse Discoverers of America, G. M. Gathorne-Hardy.
America: 1355–1365, Hjalmar R. Holand.
Westward from Vinland, Hjalmar R. Holand.
The Ship, Björn Landstrom.
Nine Against the Unknown, J. L. Mitchell and L. Gibson.
In Northern Mists, Fridtjof Nansen.

CHAPTER SEVEN
Boletim Cultural da Guiné Portuguesa (selected articles).
Boletim da Sociedade de Geographia da Lisbon (selected articles).
Discovery and Conquest of Guinea, Vols. I and II, Gomes de Azurara.
Southward the Caravels, Ernle Bradford.
Esmeraldo de Situ Orbis, Duarte Pacheco Pereira.
The Portuguese Pioneers, Edgar Prestage.
The Caravels of Christ, Gilbert Renault.

CHAPTER EIGHT
The Voyages of the Cabots and the Corte-Reals, H. P. Biggar.
The Pre-Columbian Discovery of America, J. Cortesão (*Geographical Journal*, 1937).
The Alleged Pre-Columbian Discovery of America, G. R. Crone (*Geographical Journal*, 1937).
The Discovery of America, A. Davies.
The Truth about Columbus, Charles Duff.
Les Corte-Reals et leur Voyages, Henry Harrisse.
O Descobrimentada da América, Manuel Heleno.
The Discovery of North America, Sofus Larsen.
Portuguese Voyages to America, Samuel Eliot Morison.

CHAPTER NINE
The World Unveiled, Paul Herrmann.

Early Spanish Voyages to the Straits of Magellan, Sir Clements Markham.
So Noble a Captain, Charles McKew Parr.
The Caravels of Christ, Gilbert Renault.
Magellan's Voyage Round the World, James A. Robertson.
The First Voyage Round the World, Stanley of Alderley.
Conqueror of the Seas, Stefan Zweig.

CHAPTER TEN
The Barents Relics, J. K. J. De Jonge.
The Lands of Silence, Sir Clements Markham.
Northern Conquest, Jeanette Mirsky.
Barents's Three Voyages to the Arctic (Hakluyt Soc:), Gerrit de Veer.

CHAPTER ELEVEN
The Exploration of the Pacific, J. C. Beaglehole.
An Account of the Discoveries made in the South Pacific Previous to 1764, Alexander Dalrymple.
Early Voyages to Terra Australis, R. H. Major.
The Voyages of Pedro Fernandez de Quiros (Hakluyt Soc), Sir Clements Markham.
The First Discovery of Australia, T. D. Mutch.
Explorers' Maps, R. A. Skelton.

CHAPTER TWELVE
The Journals of Captain Cook, Vol. I, *The Voyage of the Endeavour*, 1768–1771 (Hakluyt Soc:).
Philosophical Transactions of the Royal Society.
The Exploration of the Pacific, J. C. Beaglehole.
Captain Cook, Gordon Campbell.
Life of Captain Cook, Hugh Carrington.
The World Unveiled, Paul Herrmann.
The Kon-Tiki Expedition, Thor Heyerdahl.
Captain Cook, John R. Muir.

CHAPTER THIRTEEN
The Parry papers in the Scott Polar Research Institute.
A Journal of a Voyage of Discovery to the Arctic Regions, A. Fisher.
Journal of a Voyage for the Discovery of a North-West Passage, W. E. Parry.
A Voyage of Discovery for the Purpose of Exploring Baffin's Bay, John Ross.
The Search for the North-West Passage, Nellie M. Crouse.
The White Road, L. P. Kirwan.
In Quest of the North-West Passage, L. H. Neatby.
Parry of the Arctic, Ann Parry.

CHAPTER FOURTEEN
Flora Antarctica, J. D. Hooker.
Siege of the South Pole, H. R. Mill.

Voyages of Discovery in the Antarctic and Arctic Seas, R. McCormick.

A Voyage of Discovery and Research in the Antarctic Regions, Vols. I and II, James Clark Ross.

Sir James Clark Ross, Ann Savour (*Geographical Journal*, 1962).

CHAPTER FIFTEEN

1. Loss of the *Jeanette*: Court of Inquiry.

The Voyage of the Jeanette, Vols. I and II, Emma de Long.

The Lands of Silence, Sir Clements Markham.

In the Lena Delta, G. W. Melville.

Northern Conquest, Jeanette Mirsky.

2. *A New Route to the North Pole*, A. W. Greely.

A Thousand Days in the Arctic, Frederick Jackson.

Relics from the Jeanette *Expedition*, Carl Lytzen (*Geografisk Tidskrift*: Copenhagen 1885–6).

The Great Polar Current, H. M. Prentiss.

Northern Conquest, Jeanette Mirsky.

Farthest North, Vols. I and II, Fridtjof Nansen.

Towards the North Pole, Fridtjof Nansen (*Longman's Magazine*, 1890).

Index

Index